LANGUAGE AND POWER

Routledge English Language Introductions cover core areas of language study and are one-stop resources for students.

Assuming no prior knowledge, books in the series offer an accessible overview of the subject, with activities, study questions, sample analyses, commentaries and key readings – all in the same volume. The innovative and flexible 'two-dimensional' structure is built around four sections – introduction, development, exploration and extension – which offer self-contained stages for study. Each topic can also be read across these sections, enabling the reader to build gradually on the knowledge gained.

Language and Power, Second Edition has been completely revised and updated and includes:

- ❑ a comprehensive survey of the ways in which language intersects and connects with the social, cultural and political aspects of power;
- ❑ an introduction to the history of the field, covering all the major approaches, theoretical concepts and methods of analysis in this important and developing area of academic study;
- ❑ coverage of all the 'traditional' topics, such as race, gender and institutional power, but also newer topics such as the discourse of post-truth, and the power of social media;
- ❑ readings from works by seminal figures in the field, such as Robin Lakoff, Deborah Cameron and Teun van Dijk;
- ❑ real texts and examples throughout, including advertisements from cosmetics companies; newspaper articles and headlines; websites and internet media; and spoken dialogues such as political and presidential speeches;
- ❑ a supporting companion website that aims to challenge students at a more advanced level and which features extra reading, exercises, follow-up activities, and suggestions for further work.

Language and Power will be essential reading for students studying English language or linguistics.

Paul Simpson is Professor of English Language and Head of English at the University of Liverpool, UK, where he teaches and researches in stylistics, pragmatics, critical linguistics and related fields of study.

Andrea Mayr is Lecturer in Modern English Language and Linguistics at Queen's University Belfast, UK, where she teaches and researches in media discourse and in multimodal critical discourse analysis.

Simon Statham is Lecturer in English Language and Linguistics at Queen's University Belfast, UK, where he teaches and researches in stylistics, critical linguistics and language and the law.

ROUTLEDGE ENGLISH LANGUAGE INTRODUCTIONS

SERIES CONSULTANT: PETER STOCKWELL

Peter Stockwell is Professor of Literary Linguistics in the School of English at the University of Nottingham, UK, where his interests include sociolinguistics, stylistics and cognitive poetics. His recent publications include *The Cambridge Handbook of Stylistics* (2014), *Cognitive Grammar in Literature* (2014) and *The Language and Literature Reader* (2008).

SERIES CONSULTANT: RONALD CARTER

Ronald Carter is Research Professor of Modern English Language in the School of English at the University of Nottingham, UK. He is the co-series editor of the Routledge Applied Linguistics, Routledge Introductions to Applied Linguistics and Routledge Applied Corpus Linguistics series.

TITLES IN THE SERIES:

Grammar and Vocabulary
Howard Jackson

Psycholinguistics
John Field

Language in Theory
Mark Robson and Peter Stockwell

Child Language
Jean Stilwell Peccei

Sociolinguistics
Peter Stockwell

History of English
Dan McIntyre

Language and Media
Alan Durant and Marina Lambrou

Researching English Language
Alison Sealey

Practical Phonetics and Phonology, Third Edition
Beverley Collins and Inger M. Mees

Stylistics, Second Edition
Paul Simpson

Global Englishes, Third Edition
(previously published as *World Englishes*)
Jennifer Jenkins

Pragmatics, Third Edition
(previously published as *Pragmatics and Discourse*)
Joan Cutting

Introducing English Language, Second Edition
Louise Mullany and Peter Stockwell

Language and Law
Alan Durant and Janny HC Leung

English Grammar, Second Edition
Roger Berry

Language and Power, Second Edition
Paul Simpson, Andrea Mayr and Simon Statham

Discourse Analysis, Second Edition
Rodney Jones

For more information on any of these titles, or to order, please go to www.routledge.com/series/RELI -

LANGUAGE AND POWER

A B C D

A resource book for students

Second edition

**PAUL SIMPSON, ANDREA MAYR AND
SIMON STATHAM**

Routledge
Taylor & Francis Group

LONDON AND NEW YORK

This edition published 2019
by Routledge
2 Park Square, Milton Park, Abingdon, Oxon, OX14 4RN

and by Routledge
711 Third Avenue, New York, NY 10017

Routledge is an imprint of the Taylor & Francis Group, an informa business

First edition published by Routledge (2009)

British Library Cataloguing-in-Publication Data
A catalogue record for this book is available from the British Library

Library of Congress Cataloging-in-Publication Data
Names: Simpson, Paul, 1959– author. | Mayr, Andrea, 1972– author. | Statham, Simon, author.
Title: Language and power : a resource book for students / Paul Simpson, Andrea Mayr and
   Simon Statham.
Description: Second edition. | Milton Park, Abingdon, Oxon ; New York,
   NY : Routledge, 2018. | Series: Routledge English Language
IntroductionsIdentifiers: LCCN 2018006830 |
Subjects: LCSH: Sociolinguistics. | Power (Social sciences) | Language and languages–Political aspects. |
   Discourse analysis.
Classification: LCC P40. S462 2018 | DDC 306.44–dc23
LC record available at https://lccn.loc.gov/2018006830

ISBN: 978-1-138-56927-0 (hbk)
ISBN: 978-1-138-56923-2 (pbk)
ISBN: 978-0-429-46889-6 (ebk)

Typeset in Minion Pro
by Apex CoVantage, LLC

Visit the companion website: www.routledge.com/cw/simpson

HOW TO USE THIS BOOK

The Routledge English Language Introductions are 'flexi-texts' that you can use to suit your own style of study. The books are divided into four sections:

A Introduction – sets out the key concepts for the area of study. The *units* of this section take you step-by-step through the foundational terms and ideas, carefully providing you with an initial toolkit for your own study. By the end of the section, you will have a good overview of the whole field.

B Development – adds to your knowledge and builds on the key ideas already introduced. Units in this section might also draw together several areas of interest. By the end of this section, you will already have a good and fairly detailed grasp of the field, and will be ready to undertake your own exploration and thinking.

C Exploration – provides examples of language data and guides you through your own investigation of the field. The units in this section will be more open-ended and exploratory, and you will be encouraged to try out your ideas and think for yourself, using your newly acquired knowledge.

D Extension – offers you the chance to compare your expertise with key readings in the area. These are taken from the work of important writers, and are provided with guidance and questions for your further thought.

You can read this book like a traditional textbook, 'vertically' straight through from beginning to end. This will take you comprehensively through the broad field of study. However, the Routledge English Language Introductions have been carefully designed so that you can read them in another dimension, 'horizontally' across the numbered units. For example, unit A1 corresponds with unit B1, and with units C1 and D1. Reading A5, B5, C5, D5 sequentially, for example, will therefore take you rapidly from the key concepts of a specific area, to a level of expertise in that precise area, all with a very close focus. You can match your way of reading with the best way that you work.

The glossarial index at the end, together with the suggestions for Further Reading, will help to keep you orientated. Each textbook has a supporting website with exercises, extra reading, follow-up activities, and suggestions for further work.

Language and Power

This book is organized on the basis of 12 key themes in the study of language and power. The numbered units of Section A are designed to be compact and relatively self-contained, so reading progressively through this introductory section will help you develop a broad picture of the ways in which language intersects with the social and political reflexes of power. Then, or alternatively, you can use the numbered units of Section A to follow a particular *Strand* horizontally across the book. The units that make up Section B develop the themes and issues raised by their equivalents in Section A by providing illustrated surveys of the major research developments in the relevant area along with the key analytic models that have informed this research. Further across the Strand, into the corresponding C Section, the topic is explored through clearly framed suggestions for practical work. These practical activities, which are designed to give you the confidence and skill to explore language and texts in different contexts, are often carried over into the important web resources that accompany the book. Finally, Section D rounds off the Strand with each unit comprising an original reading by a world-renowned scholar. Our introductions to these readings place them in context, while our follow-up commentaries provide suggestions for yet further work based around the theme of the individual reading. In all, through this unit-based system, student readers will be able to learn about the major issues in the study of language and power, to understand the significance and implications of these issues, to develop organized and principled skills for study and analysis, and to gain access to original, seminal research by professional academics working in this important field of study.

We refer above to the importance of the web resources that accompany this textbook. The website companion for *Language and Power* aims to challenge students at a more advanced level and it features extra reading, exercises, discussion points, follow-up activities, and suggestions for further work. It also includes additional worked examples that build in a more detailed way on several of the analyses we carry out in Strand C of the book.

CONTENTS

How to use this book   v
Contents cross-referenced   x
List of illustrations   xii
Transcription conventions   xiii
Acknowledgements   xiv

A INTRODUCTION: KEY TOPICS IN THE STUDY OF LANGUAGE AND POWER   1

1   Language and power   2
2   The discourse of institutions and organizations   7
3   Power and talk   11
4   Language and gender   16
5   Language and race   21
6   Humour, language and power   26
7   Language and the law   31
8   Language and advertising   35
9   Language in the new capitalism   39
10   Language and politics   43
11   The discourse of social media   49
12   The discourse of 'post-truth'   53

B DEVELOPMENT: APPROACHES TO THE STUDY OF LANGUAGE AND POWER   57

1   Critical Linguistics and Critical Discourse Analysis   58
2   Registers of discourse   65
3   Studying spoken discourse   69
4   Gender and power: using the transitivity model   73
5   The representation of social actors   80
6   The discourse of humour and irony   84

7   Developments in forensic discourse analysis   88

8   Advertising discourse: methods for analysis   95

9   Language and new capitalism: developments   105

10   Studying political discourse: developments   111

11   The language of a social media campaign   115

12   Post-truth and Critical Linguistics   120

C EXPLORATION: ANALYSING LANGUAGE AND POWER   125

1   Beginning analysis   126

2   Exploring register and ideology   134

3   Power and resistance in spoken discourse   135

4   Analysing gender   140

5   A workshop on the representation of social actors   145

6   Analysing humour and power   149

7   Exploring forensic texts   151

8   Analysing advertisements   155

9   Analysing the language of new capitalism   157

10   Analysing political discourse   160

11   Tweeting politics   163

12   'Truth' and mediated reactions   165

D EXTENSION: READINGS IN LANGUAGE AND POWER   169

1   Critical Linguistics (Roger Fowler and Gunther Kress)   170

2   Bureaucracy and social control (Srikant Sarangi and
     Stefaan Slembrouck)   175

3   Power and resistance in police interviews (Kate Haworth)   181

4   Masculinity and men's magazines (Bethan Benwell)   189

5   Discourse and the denial of racism (Teun van Dijk)   196

6   Humour and hatred (Michael Billig)   202

7   Forensic Linguistics (Malcolm Coulthard)   210

8   Language, style and lifestyle (David Machin and Theo
    van Leeuwen)   217

9   Language in the global service economy (Deborah Cameron) 223

10 Critical Metaphor Analysis (Jonathan Charteris-Black)   229

11 Social media online campaigns (Innocent Chiluwa and
    Presley Ifukor)   236

12 Populism and post-truth politics (Robin Tolmach Lakoff)   242

Further reading   249
References   257
Name index   279
Subject index   285

A **INTRODUCTION**

B **DEVELOPMENT**

1

Language and power

2

Critical Linguistics and Critical Discourse Analysis

58

2

The discourse of institutions and organizations

7

Registers of discourse

65

3

Power and talk

11

Studying spoken discourse

69

4

Language and gender

16

Gender and power: using the transitivity model

73

5

Language and race

21

The representation of social actors

80

6

Humour, language and power

26

The discourse of humour and irony

84

7

Language and the law

31

Developments in forensic discourse analysis

88

8

Language and advertising

35

Advertising discourse: methods for analysis

95

9

Language in the new capitalism

39

Language and new capitalism: developments

105

10

Language and politics

43

Studying political discourse: developments

111

11

The discourse of social media

49

The language of a social media campaign

115

12

The discourse of 'post-truth'

53

Post-truth and Critical Linguistics

120

Further reading

References

Author index

Glossarial index

Supporting material

Web section 1: Further discussions: Studying Language and Power

Web section 2: Additional development materials

EXPLORATION	**EXTENSION**	

C	**D**	
Beginning analysis 126	**Critical Linguistics (Roger Fowler and Gunther Kress)** 170	1
Exploring register and ideology 134	**Bureaucracy and social control (Srikant Sarangi and Stefaan Slembrouck)** 175	2
Power and resistance in spoken discourse 135	**Power and resistance in police interviews (Kate Haworth)** 181	3
Analysing gender 140	**Masculinity and men's magazines (Bethan Benwell)** 189	4
A workshop on the representation of social actors 145	**Discourse and the denial of racism (Teun van Dijk)** 196	5
Analysing humour and power 149	**Humour and hatred (Michael Billig)** 202	6
Exploring forensic texts 151	**Forensic Linguistics (Malcolm Coulthard)** 210	7
Analysing advertisements 155	**Language, style and lifestyle (David Machin and Theo van Leeuwen)** 217	8
Analysing the language of new capitalism 157	**Language in the global service economy (Deborah Cameron)** 223	9
Analysing political discourse 160	**Critical Metaphor Analysis (Jonathan Charteris-Black)** 229	10
Tweeting politics 163	**Social media online campaigns (Innocent Chiluwa and Presley Ifukor)** 236	11
'Truth' and mediated reactions 165	**Populism and post-truth politics (RobinLakoff)** 242	12

Further reading

References

Author index

Glossarial index

Supporting material

Web section 3: Additional practice exercises	**Web section 4**: Strengthening Critical Discourse Analysis: *The Baby Book* revisited (Kate McFarland)

ILLUSTRATIONS

Figures

B1.1   A three-dimensional model of discourse
        (adapted from Fairclough 1992: 73)   62
B5.1   *Jurnalul National*, 9 August 2012   83
B6.1   Extract from *Private Eye*, issue 987, 1999, p. 36   86
B8.1   Front page, *Daily Mirror*, 7 September 2017   96
B8.2   Aurore advertisement   98
B11.1   *Voz da Comunidade* (courtesy of Fernando Barcellos)   117
B11.2   *Extra* online page, 24 April 2014 (courtesy of Editor
        Fabio Gusmão)   118
C5.1   *Daily Mail*, 11 August 2015   146
C5.2   *Daily Mail*, 11 August 2015   146
C5.3   Belfast City Council, 'Kicking racism out of football', 2006 147
C9.1   Secondary school website, Northern Ireland   158
D4.1   Ultratone™ advert in *Loaded* magazine   193

Tables

B7.1   Checklist of presupposition triggers in English   90
B12.1   The Model of Universal Pragmatics (adapted from
        Habermas 1979: 68)   123

TRANSCRIPTION CONVENTIONS

In different parts of this book, passages of spoken interaction are transcribed in such a way as to capture varying aspects of real speech. The following is a key used to understand the transcription symbols used in these passages.

[	Interruption and overlap (two speakers talking at the same time)
[ ]	turn is completely contained within another speaker's turn
(?), [?]	unintelligible words
(unsure)	words in round brackets are unsure transcriptions
{non-verbal}	description of non-verbal behaviour (e.g. changes in posture)
=	no hearable gap between adjacent utterances, the second being latched immediately to the first (without overlapping it)
CAPS	emphatic stress in capitals
(.)	short pause
(-), (—)	longer pause
[5 secs]	indicates inter-turn pause length
:	indicates that the preceding sound is elongated
eh, er, ermh, um,	hesitation
.hh	audible inbreath
hh.	audible outbreath
ar-	cut-off syllable or word

Shorthand conventions for capturing non-standard pronunciation

wudnae = wouldn't
wud = would
tae = to
daein = doing
oan = on
Ah'm = I am

ACKNOWLEDGEMENTS

The authors and publishers wish to thank the following for permission to use copyright material. Whilst every effort has been made to trace and contact the copyright holders, this has unfortunately not been possible in every case. Any omissions brought to our attention will be remedied in future editions.

B.9 'University of Leicester "Enterprise Strategy" 2015', with kind permission of the university.

C.9 'University of Nottingham Strategy 2020'. The University of Nottingham Ningbo China. All rights reserved.

D.1 Reprinted from Fowler, R., Hodge, R., Kress, G. and Trew. T. *Language and Control*. London: Routledge & Kegan Paul, 1979, pp. 26–45. With permission of the publisher.

D.2 'Chapter 6'. *Language, Bureaucracy and Social Control*, by Stefan Slembrouck and Srikant Sarangi, London: Routledge, 2015, pp. 123–132. With permission of the publisher.

D.3 'The dynamics of power and resistance in police interview discourse', by Kate Haworth, from *Discourse & Society, volume 17, issue 6*, pp. 739–759. Copyright © 2006 SAGE Publications, Ltd. Reprinted by permission of SAGE Publications, Ltd.

D.4 'Is there anything "new" about these lads? The textual and visual construction of masculinity in men's magazines', in *Gender Identity and Discourse Analysis*, Litosseliti, L. and Sunderland, J. (eds) (2002). Published by John Benjamins Publishing Company – Amsterdam/Philadelphia.

D.5 'Discourse and the denial of racism', by Teun van Dijk, from *Discourse and Society, volume 3, issue 1*. Copyright © 1992 SAGE Publications, Ltd. Reprinted by permission of SAGE Publications, Ltd.

D.6 'Humour and hatred: The racist jokes of the Ku Klux Klan', by Michael Billig, from *Discourse and Society, volume 12, issue 3*, pp. 267–289. Copyright © 2001 SAGE Publications, Ltd. Reprinted by permission of SAGE Publications, Ltd.

D.7 Coulthard, M., 'Whose voice is it? Invented and concealed dialogue in written records of verbal evidence produced by the police', in *Language in the Legal Process*, Cotterill, J. (ed.), published 2002 [Palgrave Macmillan]. Reproduced with permission of SCSC.

D.8 'Language style and lifestyle: the case of a global magazine', by David Machin and Theo van Leeuwen, from *Media, Culture and Society, volume 27, issue 4*, pp. 577–600. Copyright © 2005 SAGE Publications, Ltd. Reprinted by permission of SAGE Publications, Ltd.

D.9 'Styling the worker: gender and commodification of language in the globalized service economy', by Deborah Cameron, from *Journal of Sociolinguistics, volume 4, issue 3*, pp. 323–347. Copyright © 2002 Blackwell Publishers Ltd. Reprinted by permission of John Wiley and Sons.

D.10 Charteris-Black, J., 'Metaphor in British party political manifestos', in *Corpus Approaches to Critical Metaphor Analysis*, Charteris-Black, J. (ed.), published 2004 [Palgrave Macmillan] Reproduced with permission of SCSC.

D.11 '"War against our children": Stance and evaluation in #*BringBackOurGirls* campaign discourse on Twitter and Facebook', by Innocent Chiluwa and Presley Ifukor, from *Discourse and Society, volume 26, issue 3*, pp. 267–296. Copyright © 2015 SAGE Publications, Ltd. Reprinted by permission of SAGE Publications, Ltd.

D.12 'The hollow man. Donald Trump, populism, and post-truth politics', by Robin Lakoff, *Journal of Language and Politics, volume 16, issue 4* (2017), pp. 595–606. Published by John Benjamins Publishing Company – Amsterdam/Philadelphia.

Figure B5.1 PHILIPPE DESMAZES/AFP/Getty Images.

Figure B8.1 *Daily Mirror*/Mirrorpix. Reproduced with permission.

Figures C5.1 and C5.2 REUTERS/Rick Wilking.

Section A

INTRODUCTION:
KEY TOPICS IN THE STUDY OF LANGUAGE AND POWER

A1 LANGUAGE AND POWER

This book is about the ways in which language intersects with the social and political reflexes of *power*. Over the last 40 years, scholars working in Linguistics, English Language and related fields of study have become ever more interested in how powerful groups can influence the way language is used and in how these groups can exercise control over access to language. Similarly, scholars have been interested in the obverse or reflex of this situation; that is, in how the exercise of power meets with resistance and how 'ordinary' people can and do contest discursive power through a variety of language strategies. This book sets out a comprehensive programme of study for this significant and expanding area of language and linguistics. Across its four sections, the book provides a history of the field and its associated methods of analysis. It covers the major approaches, the core technical terms and the main theoretical concepts. Additionally, it presents a series of seminal readings by some of the major academic figures in the field. Our aim is for students using the book to be able to identify the ways in which power is disseminated through language, whether that be through print, broadcast or social media, through legal or advertising discourse, or through political and other forms of institutional rhetoric.

What is power?

In short, power comes from the privileged access to social resources such as education, knowledge and wealth. Access to these resources provides authority, status and influence, which is an enabling mechanism for the domination, coercion and control of subordinate groups. However, power can also be something more than simply dominance from above; in many situations, for example, power is 'jointly produced' because people are led to believe that dominance is legitimate in some way or other. This second, more consensual, understanding of power suggests a two-way distinction: power through dominance and power by consent. As both concepts of power feature prominently across this book, it is worth saying a little more about their respective senses here.

Research on power often falls into one of two traditions, the 'mainstream' and the 'second-stream' (see Scott 2001). The mainstream tradition, the origins of which are located in Weber's study ([1914] 1978) of authority in modern and premodern states, tends to focus on the corrective power of the state and its institutions. This tradition, essentially the view of power as dominance, focuses on the varying abilities of actors, such as judicial and penal institutions, to secure the compliance of others, even in the face of resistance or insurgence. Importantly, power in this sense does not only reside within the state, but also in other sovereign organizations, such as businesses and the church. In democratic societies, power needs to be seen as legitimate by the people in order to be accepted and this process of legitimation is generally expressed by means of language and other communicative systems. When institutions legitimate themselves with regard to citizens, it is through language that the official action of an institution or the institution itself is justified. Of course, the process of legitimation also presupposes that opposing groups will simultaneously be 'delegitimated'.

The second-stream tradition of research on power has been mainly concerned with the significance of its persuasive influence, and a central figure in the development of this tradition is Gramsci (1971). Gramsci's concept of *hegemony* describes the mechanisms through which dominant groups in society succeed in persuading subordinate groups to accept the former's own moral, political and cultural values and institutions. Power is therefore not exercised coercively, but routinely. Within this framework, discourse constructs hegemonic attitudes, opinions and beliefs and, as we shall see throughout this book, does so in such a way as to make these beliefs appear 'natural' and 'common sense'. Developing further the idea of hegemony, Gramsci argues that it is through the cultural formations of individuals (which he calls 'subjects') by the institutions of civil society, such as the family, the educational system, churches, courts of law and the media, that dominant groups in society can gain a more stable position for themselves than through the more obviously constraining powers of the state. An important factor in this process is 'consent': subordinate groups are said to consent to the existing social order because it is effectively presented by the state and its institutions as being universally beneficial and commonsensical. The reason why the concept of hegemony as power is especially important is that it operates largely through language: people consent to particular formations of power because the dominant cultural groups generating the language, as we have noted above, tend to represent them as natural or common sense.

Gramsci (1971) also points out that dominant groups have to work at staying dominant. They attempt to secure domination firstly by constructing a ruling group through building and maintaining political alliances; secondly, by generating consent – *legitimacy* – among the population; and, thirdly, by building a capacity for coercion through institutions such as the police, the courts and the legal system, prisons and the military in order to create authority. The more legitimacy dominant groups have, the less coercion they need to apply. Again, each of these three hegemonic functions relies on language and communication, which in Louw's words involves the dissemination of 'representations which inculcate identities, beliefs and behaviours confirming the practices and discourses of the ruling group' (2005: 98).

Situated closer to the second stream of research than to the first is Foucault's theoretical model for the analysis of power in discourse (1977, 1980). Rather than seeing power merely as a repressive phenomenon, Foucault sees the concept of power as *productive*, as a complex and continuously evolving web of social and discursive relations. For example, instead of assuming that a powerful person in an institutional setting is in fact all powerful, Foucault argues that power is more a form of action or relation between people that is negotiated and contested in interaction and is never fixed or stable. So Foucault does not regard power as an already given entity that is maintained through the ideological operations of society. We shall return to Foucault's understanding of power in later Strands.

Throughout the book, we will locate instances of power in a range of texts and text types, and the distinctions drawn here will be progressively elaborated and refined as we evaluate different manifestations of power in both public and private contexts. For the moment, we need to introduce another concept which is integrally allied to the idea of power.

Ideology

Intertwined with our understanding of power, *ideology* refers to the ways in which a person's beliefs, opinions and value-systems intersect with the broader social and political structures of the society in which they live. It is an important assumption of the present book that language is influenced by ideology and moreover, that all texts, whether spoken or written, and even visual language, are inexorably shaped and determined by a web of political beliefs and socio-cultural practices. The position we take is diametrically opposed therefore to a 'liberal' view of language where texts are seen simply as natural outcomes of the free communicative interplay between individuals in society, uninhibited by political or ideological influence. By contrast, our view is first that texts are anything but neutral or disinterested, and, second, that close linguistic analysis can help us understand how ideology is embedded in language and consequently help us become aware of how the reflexes of 'dominant' or 'mainstream' ideologies are sustained through textual practices. In short, ideology, and its expression in the textual practices that shape our everyday lives, is not something that exists in isolation as a product of free-will, but is instead partial and contingent.

Although coined in the early 1800s by the French philosopher Destutt de Tracy, the term *ideology* is normally associated with Karl Marx, and particularly with his treatise on 'The German Ideology', a project developed in 1845–46, but published, in various languages and instalments, from the 1930s onwards (see Marx [1933] 1965). Over the intervening years, the concept has been adopted more widely (and without any necessary adherence to Marxist doctrine) to refer to the belief systems which are held either individually or collectively by social groups. However, in Marx's original conception, ideology captures means by which dominant forces in society, such as royalty, the aristocracy or the bourgeoisie can exercise power over subordinated or subjugated groups, such as the industrial and rural proletariat. This position is captured in one of Marx's best known axioms: 'the ideas of the ruling class are in every epoch the ruling ideas' (1965: 61).

Althusser (1971) was one of the first to describe power as a discursive phenomenon, arguing that ideas are inserted into the hierarchical arrangement of socially and politically determined practices and rituals. Althusser highlights the significant roles of ideologies in reproducing or changing political relations through so-called *ideological state apparatuses*, such as the church, the legal system, the family, the media and the educational system. One contemporary example of an ideological state apparatus (ISA) at work is in the construction of citizens as 'consumers' in the language of public health materials in late modernity. The ISA constructs readers as consumers who should take personal responsibility for their health through proper lifestyle choices. By accepting the role of subjects with personal choices in a consumer culture, people are reproducing the ideology of consumerism and the construction of health problems as individual rather than public or structural problems that need collective solution.

We shall explore further the notions of both ideology and power over in B1 and in A2 below.

Language as *discourse*

Throughout this unit, we have been using the terms *language* and *discourse* rather loosely, but it is important to make clear that there exists an important distinction between the two. *Discourse* is what happens when language 'gets done'. Whereas *language* refers to the more abstract set of patterns and rules that operate simultaneously at different levels in the system (the grammatical, semantic and phonological levels, for example), *discourse* refers to the instantiation of these patterns in *real* contexts of use. In other words, discourse works above the level of grammar and semantics to capture what happens when these language forms are played out in different social, political and cultural arenas. Admittedly wide as the concept of discourse is, there is general agreement that the term usefully captures both the meaning and effects of language usage as well the interactive strategies used by different individuals and groups in the production and interpretation of actual texts.

Against this conception of language as discourse, scholars researching the interconnections between language and ideology build from the premise that patterns of discourse are framed in a web of beliefs, opinions and interests. A text's linguistic structure functions, as discourse, to privilege certain ideological positions while downplaying others – such that the linguistic choices encoded in this or that text can be shown to correlate with the ideological orientation of the text. Even the minutiae of a text's linguistic make-up can reveal ideological standpoint, and fruitful comparisons can be drawn between the ways in which a particular linguistic feature is deployed across different texts. For instance, the following three illustrative examples differ only in terms of the main verb used:

> The Minister explained the cut-backs were necessary.
> The Minister claimed the cut-backs were necessary.
> The Minister imagined the cut-backs were necessary.

Whereas the first example suggests that while the cut-backs were unavoidable, the Minister's actions are helpfully explanatory. The more tenuous 'claimed' of the second example renders the Minister's attempt to justify an unpopular measure less convincing. The third example is arguably more negative again, with the 'non-factive' verb 'imagined' suggesting that the obverse condition applies in the embedded clause; namely, that the Minister is mistaken in his or her belief that the cut-backs were necessary. A fuller and more nuanced exposition of such 'verbs of speaking' is provided by Caldas-Coulthard (1994: 306).

The point is that when language becomes embodied as discourse it often throws into relief the totality of other possible ways of representing. Ideological standpoint in language can therefore be productively explored through comparisons between different texts, especially when the texts cover the same topic. Here are two short texts that illustrate this comparative aspect to critical linguistic analysis.

(a) PRIME Minister Theresa May explained that Britain would start the formal process for leaving the European Union by the end of March 2017.

(b) Unelected Prime Minister Theresa May has claimed that Brexit gives her the right to re-shape Britain in her own image.

In the aftermath of the vote in June 2016 for a British exit ('Brexit') from the European Union, the popular press was predictably divided. These fragments, from a right-wing and left-wing tabloid respectively, hardly need any linguistic analysis to unveil how the two ideological stances are reflected in patterns of language. Text (a) underscores Theresa May's formal status through a technique known as *functionalization* (see further unit B.5), but in contrast, with its up-front 'Unelected', text (b) attempts to delegitimize May's standing by referencing her accession as Prime Minister (without a general election) after the resignation of her predecessor David Cameron. Moreover, the texts feature two of the verbs described in the illustrative examples above: the material 'explained' by May in (a) is presupposed as objectively true, but the use of 'claimed' in (b) contains no such appeal to external validity and instead intimates that May's intentions for Brexit are only narcissistically driven.

A rather more stark illustration of the variability of discourse representation is provided by the passages below which are taken from two different press accounts of an event of civil disorder in May 2004 in the Gaza Strip:

(c) **Israeli attack kills 10 Palestinians in Gaza**
Israeli forces have killed at least ten Palestinians, most of them children, after firing on a crowd of demonstrators in the Gaza Strip today.

(d) **Rafah Incident**
Today's incident in Rafah is a very grave incident and the Israeli Foreign Office expresses deep sorrow over the loss of civilian lives.

Without introducing any specific linguistic model at this stage, it is nonetheless worth looking at how certain language structures are deployed across these texts. For example, of the texts, only (c) has a main verb in its headline while (d) consists of nouns only. Moreover, the verb in the (c) headline is transitive: it takes a Direct Object such that the action performed by the grammatical Subject of the sentence ('Israeli attack') is clearly enacted upon this object. The transitive pattern is further played out through verbs in the opening text ('killed' and 'firing on'), while the agents involved and affected entities are both named, counted and described ('most of them children'). By contrast, the main action in (d) is expressed through a single noun 'incident' – the action has been 'nominalized', in other words. Nominalization offers a less specific representation of an action, largely because it 'stands for' a process while simultaneously eliding those involved in the process. Notice how 'incident' is repeated twice in the opening text while another nominalization, 'loss' – which stands for the process 'somebody lost some thing' – is used. The main 'action' of (d) is located in an altogether different area: the representation of a mental state ('expresses deep sorrow') is offered rather than any account of physical activity (or violence).

Although informally presented here, what we are trying to demonstrate is that linguistic analysis offers a useful analytic tool for probing an ideological standpoint across different portrayals in the media of the same event or experience. It is not a question of searching for a version of events that is definitive or truthful, but more a matter of understanding that discourse offers a constellation of different narrative possibilities. Texts (c) and (d) are just two representations from perhaps many possibilities; in this case, from an Israeli Defence Force press release and from British newspaper the *Guardian* (and you can probably guess which is which). These narrative possibilities privilege certain standpoints over others – often reflecting and reinforcing certain ideological positions while suppressing others.

THE DISCOURSE OF INSTITUTIONS AND ORGANIZATIONS A2

This unit is about language and power in institutional contexts. It is concerned with the ways in which language is used to create and shape institutions and how institutions in turn have the capacity to create, shape and impose discourses. Institutions have considerable control over the organizing of our routine experiences of the world and the way we classify that world. They therefore have the power to foster particular kinds of identities to suit their own purposes because they are primary sites for 'reality construction' (Mayr 2008: 1). The questions we might ask ourselves then are how does this discourse materialize in organizations and institutions? How is it internalized in social practices? And how does it define the identities of people? Across this Strand, we look at the ways power works in the linguistic practices people use in these settings and we examine language and power across a variety of institutional contexts.

Institutions

Institutions (and how they work) have been the object of many investigations in the fields of sociology, media, and cultural and organizational studies. More recently, there has been a 'linguistic' turn in the study of organizations and institutions with many language-focused explorations of how power and discourse may function in specific institutional settings. Linguistic and discourse analytical approaches to institutional research generally regard linguistic exchange as an important aspect of interaction (Fairclough and Wodak 1997) where language is understood as constitutive of organizations and institutions. From this perspective, language is the principal means by which institutions create their own social reality. Mumby and Clair elaborate this point thus:

> Organizations exist only in so far as their members create them through discourse. This is not to claim that organizations are 'nothing but discourse', but rather that discourse is the principal means by which organizational members create a coherent social reality that frames their sense of who they are.
>
> (1997: 181)

As Mumby and Clair suggest, the view of discourse as constitutive of social reality does not mean that discourse is all there is. Although discourses play an important role in creating the patterns of understanding that people apply to social interactions, people are not completely constrained by them. On the contrary, people can and do resist and subvert dominant institutional discourses and practices by drawing on oppositional knowledge or tailoring dominant understandings to their personal circumstances. Resistance in discourse is more likely to take active forms in institutional settings where the domination of one group over others is partial and contested (such as management and shop floor), than in more coercive settings (such as government agencies, mental institutions or prisons), although people still can and do resist in discursive behaviour even if that occurs 'offstage' and outside the direct surveillance of those in power (see Scott 1990). Imposed identities can and are constantly (discursively) negotiated, contested and resisted and this will be an important focus for discussion in some of the other Strands of this book. Units A3 and A4, for example, include descriptions of how the process of contestation takes place in the institutional context of a prison. Humour is another form of resistance to dominant (institutional) practices and will be explored in Strand 6, while in part of the following Strand, the discussion of the concept of 'anti-language' (C3) focuses on how alienated social groups can resist through special, often secret vocabularies. In short, 'resistance' is articulated in many ways and is just as complex a concept as 'power' such that the two should be explored alongside one another.

We have noted how an institution's power and politics are frequently exercised through the discourses of their members. One only has to think of the news media in this respect: we might assume that the fourth estate has an obligation to provide impartial and balanced coverage of important political and social events, but the media is also a large organization that needs to maintain itself and its position. What this means in practice is that to some extent it is the institutional procedures and practices that define what becomes news more so than the events themselves. Additionally, these organizations are owned by ever larger corporations who have their own agendas, not least to produce revenue for their shareholders. And as they push for more profits this puts new constraints on what kinds of events can become news and creates new opportunities for those organizations that are best able to respond to such changes. So, in order to understand news texts we need to understand them as the result of these institutional processes. It is because of these institutional, practical and financial concerns that news media offer only a partial view of the world that fits with the interests of the socially and economically powerful (e.g. war reporting that excludes acts of violence perpetrated against civilians) and so we should be cautious about the public pronouncements of news bosses that their perspective is a disinterested report of objective truth. Fowler (1991: 1–2) provides a good example of this in the statements of Andrew Neil, a former editor of the British quality broadsheet the *Sunday Times*. During the British miners' strike of 1984–85, *The Sunday Times* consistently voiced a line that supported Margaret Thatcher's right-wing government and that opposed the actions of the miners and their supporters. Neil, as editor, pointed out that his paper had a duty to defeat the strike for the 'sake of liberal democracy'. He claimed that his reporters could help break the strike by giving the paper's readers 'an impartial and well-informed picture of what was really happening'. Whether Neil was being disingenuous is hard to say, but his comments show us how 'naturalization' works, where rank political bias masquerades as a 'common-sense' position. Strand 11 of this book will address the contemporary context of social media, and consider whether or not this provides citizens with a platform of counter-power to push back against partisan positions taken by mainstream media outlets such as the *Sunday Times* (and see further unit B1).

Institutions therefore attempt to legitimize their own interests and existence through discourse through which they seek to transform ('recontextualize') social practices. Weber ([1914] 1978) observes that in democratic systems, the power of institutions needs to be legitimized and justified in order to be accepted by people. For example, the invasion of Iraq by Allied Forces was justified by some Western governments and their military through what Chomsky (1999) has referred to as the 'rhetoric of military humanism': discourse that rationalizes military intervention by proclaiming human-itarian goals, such as 'liberating' a country from dictatorial rule or defending liberal Western values.

Discourse, institutions and power

Mumby and Clair (1997) have identified various strands of research in the study of the relationship between discourse, institutions and power. One strand explores how members of oppressed groups can discursively penetrate the institutionalized form of their oppression; another how subordinate individuals discursively frame their own subordination thereby perpetuating it. A third strand, and especially important for the concerns of this unit, is concerned with the analysis of how dominant groups discursively construct and reproduce their own positions of institutional dominance (Mumby and Clair 1997: 195; see also van Dijk 1993a). However, the concept of *institution* itself is curiously hard to define. Institutions are commonly associated with physical buildings or settings, such as schools, hospitals, media organizations, prisons or courts of law. Popular definitions of an 'institution' see it as an established organi-zation or foundation, especially one dedicated to education, public service or culture, or the building or buildings housing such an organization. Clearly, there appears to be a certain overlap in the sense of the terms 'institution' and 'organization'. These terms are often used interchangeably, although 'organization' seems to be used more for commercial corporations, whereas 'institution' is more associated with the public organs of the state.

Institutions are also seen as inextricably linked to power and, as we have seen, serv-ing the interests of certain powerful groups. Agar defines an institution as 'a socially legitimated expertise together with those persons authorized to implement it' (1985: 164), which suggests that institutions are not restricted to physical settings and can refer to any powerful group, such as the government or the media. Agar's definition also includes the conception of institutions as involving asymmetrical roles between institutional representatives or 'experts' and 'non-experts' or 'clients', who must com-ply with institutional norms and objectives. Working from these broad definitions, we will now consider some conceptualizations of 'institutional discourse' and pres-ent our own working definition of the term. We will also explore the relationship between institutional discourse practices, power and resistance, because power and dominance are usually organized and institutionalized to enhance their effectiveness.

In what ways can institutional discourse be differentiated from 'non-institutional' discourse or interaction? The term 'institutional talk' was coined by Drew and Heri-tage (1992: 21), although they stress that there is not necessarily a hard and fast dis-tinction to be made between it and 'non-institutional talk' in all instances of interac-tional events, nor even at all points in a single interactional event. They define talk in institutional settings as involving

> role structured, institutionalized, and omnirelevant asymmetries between par-ticipants in terms of such matters as differential distribution of knowledge, rights to knowledge, access to conversational resources, and to participation in the interaction.
>
> (Drew and Heritage 1992: 48)

This contrasts with ordinary conversation between speakers of roughly the same status. Institutional settings include the courtroom, business meetings, service encounters, doctor–patient consultations or classroom interaction, and in such settings, there is at least one participant who may restrict the contributions of the other participant. Drew and Heritage sum up the features of institutional talk as follows:

1   Institutional interaction involves an orientation by at least one of the participants to some core goal, task or activity (or set of them) conventionally associated with the institution in question. In short, institutional talk is normally informed by *goal orientations* of a relatively restricted conventional form.
2   Institutional interaction may often involve *special and particular* constraints on what one or both of the participants will treat as allowable contributions to the business at hand.
3   Institutional talk may be associated with *inferential frameworks* and procedures that are particular to specific institutional contexts.

(after Drew and Heritage 1992: 22)

This means that in practice interactions in institutional settings have a very specific goal and are often asymmetrical in their distribution of speaking rights and obligations. Courtroom interaction is a particularly marked form of institutional discourse (as we shall see in Strand 7) and many of Drew and Heritage's criteria are borne out in an influential study by Harris on the linguistic structure of interactions in a magistrate's court (1984; see also Cameron 2001). For feature 1 of institutional talk, *goal orientation*, Harris observed how the goal was eliciting answers from the defendants through a series of questions about non-payment of fines, as in:

M: How much do you earn a week?
D: I don't earn any determinate amount.

(Harris 1984: 18)

As for feature 2, one particular *constraint* Harris observed was that defendants were not allowed to ask questions. If they did ask questions, they were reprimanded by the magistrate for the inappropriateness of their conduct, as in:

M: I'm putting it to you again – are you going to *make* an offer – uh – uh to discharge this debt?
D: Would you in my position?
M: I – I'm not here to answer questions – you answer *my* question.

(Harris 1984: 5)

The third characteristic of institutional talk, associated with certain *inferential frameworks*, suggests that people who are engaged in institutional interactions may interpret utterances in a way they might not in other circumstances. In Harris's study, questions are not asked as straightforward requests for information; rather they become accusations in the courtroom context. In this exchange

M: How much money have you got on you?
D: I haven't got any on me your worships
M: How'd you get here?
D: I uh got a lift – part way here

the Magistrate's two questions carry with them accusations which are, respectively, that the defendant has been lying about not having any money and that the defendant must have money because he paid to travel to court. Commenting on Harris's study, Cameron (2001) points out that the powerless position of defendants is not simply reflected in the courtroom exchanges, but it is also established and maintained through this asymmetry in speaking rights.

These three dimensions – goal orientation, interactional inferences and restrictions on the kind of contributions that can be made – are the main features that underpin the study of institutional interaction. Studying institutional talk is of interest to analysts of discourse not only because of these characteristics but because it is also a way of studying the workings of institutions themselves.

POWER AND TALK   A3

In this unit, we will look further at institutional talk. We will explore how the power relations between speakers in such contexts can be analysed through the language they use. We will also show how speakers draw on linguistic resources in different ways, depending on their different and unequal institutional status. In many institutional contexts, such as that of the police or news interview, the person asking the questions is deemed to be in a more powerful interactional position. By contrast, the person who has to answer these questions is in a weaker position because their opportunities for contribution are limited. However, as we shall see across this Strand, the role of the institutionally powerful can be 'diluted' through linguistic strategies of resistance on the part of the institutionally weaker person.

Institutional talk as asymmetrical talk

Every time people interact they enact, reproduce and sometimes resist (institutional) power relationships through language. Studying these power relationships has been central to the analysis of institutional discourse, and particularly to the analysis of the asymmetrical distribution of speaker rights and obligations. Even casual conversation, which according to Kress (1985: 27) is the genre with the least or no power differential because people speak 'on their own behalf', power is still not always equally distributed. Instead, power in conversation is "constantly under contestation" (Eggins and Slade 1997: 43) and is only concealed by the apparent equality of the casual context.

The notion of people being able to contribute equally in talk has been expressed in Sacks *et al.*'s turn-taking model (1974) and in Grice's 'co-operative principle' (1975) – the latter a model that states that conversations can only happen when people tacitly agree to co-operate in talk and contribute to the interaction on an equal basis. But what if people cannot contribute on an equal basis, because they do not have equal status? Having equal status means having the same discoursal rights and obligations, such as the same right to ask questions and make requests and the same obligation to comply with these, and also the same obligation to avoid interruption or silence.

However, in conversations among unequals, so-called 'unequal encounters' (Thomas 1988: 33), the rules for conversational interaction can be very different from the ones obtaining for ordinary or informal conversation. For example, in a traditional class-room setting, students take turns usually only when the teacher directs a question to the class or an individual. What they can say in the turns they take is also constrained: essentially students are limited to giving 'relevant' answers to the teachers. What is relevant or irrelevant depends on the context of course. But the teacher, or any person who has more power in an interaction such as a judge or police officer, can, as we have noted in A2, define the context and decide what is discoursally relevant.

Institutional discourse is therefore characterized by asymmetrical speaking rights and obligations that differentiate it from ordinary conversation. In Critical Discourse Analysis (CDA), these asymmetries are regarded as pre-inscribed features of the con-text. Thus, institutional interactions can be defined, following Thomas (1988: 33), as those taking place within social institutions such as schools, the police or the law courts which have a clearly defined hierarchical structure. In such hierarchical struc-tures, the power to discipline or punish those of lower rank is invested in holders of high rank, respectively head teachers, inspectors or judges, for example.

Power in spoken discourse according to CDA is therefore expressed by the more pow-erful person in an institutional setting constraining the contributions of the less power-ful participant(s). Fairclough (1989: 135–137) lists four devices that are used to do this:

- ❑ interruption
- ❑ enforcing explicitness
- ❑ controlling topic
- ❑ formulation

An analysis of these features can provide insights into power asymmetries in institu-tional interactions. We will discuss each in turn, providing textual examples along the way.

Interruption

Interruption is one common device through which dominant speakers can dismiss or ignore contributions that they consider irrelevant. An example of the more powerful participant interrupting a subordinate person occurs in the following extract from an exchange between a doctor (D) and a medical student (S) that takes place in a neo-natal unit (transcript adapted from Fairclough 1989: 44):

```
 1  S:  well here's a young baby boy (.) who we've decided is.
 2        thirty (.) seven weeks old now (.) was born (.) two weeks
 3        ago (.) um is fairly active (.) his eyes are open (.) he's
 4        got hair on (.) his head [(.) his eyes are [open
 5  D:                              [yes           [yes you've
 6        told me that
 7  S:  um he's crying or  [making
 8  D:                     [yeah we we we we've heard
 9        that now what other examination are you going to make
10        I mean [—]
```

11 S: erm we'll see if he'll respond to
12 D: now look did we not
13   look at a baby with a head problem yesterday.
14 S: right

In line with the asymmetrical relationship between the doctor and the medical student, the doctor as the more powerful speaker directs the medical student through interruptions and questions, whereas the student as the institutionally weaker person is restricted to merely responding. In other words, it is the institutionally determined social roles that determine the discoursal rights and obligations of the speakers (Fairclough 1989, 1995a).

Interruptions have been defined as displays of dominance or sometimes as male 'violation' of female speaking rights (e.g. Zimmerman and West 1975). Other research, however, has suggested that there are occasions when interruptions can evidence co-operation rather than dominance and are not perceived by the person interrupting nor the person interrupted as a sign of violating the latter's speaking rights. So, interruptions can have positive functions and can be conceived as 'a restoration of order (turn-sharing) rather than conversational deviance' (Murray 1987: 104). For example, when speakers feel that a turn has been used up, they may consider it their right to interrupt. This shows that all speech devices are *plurifunctional*. Thus, in some instances and contexts, interruption may be egalitarian, indicating solidarity or heightened involvement in a discussion. Consider, for example, the following extract which is from a classroom interaction in a Scottish prison between two prisoners and a prison officer (the teacher). The officer attempts to convince the prisoners that a news reporter not only has the right to divulge to the police the name of a source (a drug addict) who has told him about a drugs ring, but also that 'they' (i.e. the police) might be able to help the source overcome his drug addiction. Two inmates vigorously contest this:

1 OFFICER: In a way they are daein him a favour wouldn't they?
2 JIM: Ah wudnae fuckin speak tae [them!
3 TAM: [naw they wudnae they wud get him
            tae jail

                                                        (Mayr 2004: 117)

Although Tam overlaps with Jim's utterance, this is hardly an attempt to dominate. Rather, Tam supports Jim with his argument, indicating solidarity with his view. Their argument is based on one tenet of the inmate code, which is never to act as an informer to the police.

Enforcing explicitness

In institutional interactions, a less powerful speaker may use ambiguous or vague utterances to deal with the more powerful person, but the latter may demand 'discoursal disambiguation' (Thomas 1988: 2) by asking the speaker to make their statements less ambivalent. A common way to do this is by asking questions such as 'Are you saying that …?' or 'What is your opinion exactly?' Part of the reason why dominant speakers demand explicitness is to do with the fact that discourse is essentially ambivalent and, as we have indicated, displays multiple functions. Often, the subordinate speaker is asked to show co-operation with the dominant speaker's discoursal and social goals. In the following prison classroom situation, the officer asks the class if knowledge of a drugs ring is not reported to the police, is it acceptable to let drug dealers get away with their criminal activities?

1 OFFICER:	So ye're saying then it's quite awright for these people tae get away wi' (.) threatening tactics [intimidation
2 JOHN:	[But they have been daein it [for
3 OFFICER:	[Ah'm no askin if they have been daein it for years, Ah'm askin is it right for them tae get away with it [pause 6 secs]
4 JOHN:	eh=
5 OFFICER:	=Go oan!
6 JOHN:	No no really but

(Mayr 2004: 104–105)

In this exchange, the officer attempts to enforce explicitness through 'So ye're saying …'. The inmate, however, is evasive and comes up with a proposition of his own ('But they have been daein it for …'), which the officer interrupts ('Ah'm no askin if …'). A long pause follows, showing that the inmate has been put on the spot. Only when the officer asks him to 'Go oan!' does he continue, but he still resists the officer's attempt to give a more explicit answer ('No no really but'). This shows that subordinate speakers can and do resist the dominant speaker's attempts to control them.

Topic control

In informal conversation, the way topics develop is often unpredictable. In many forms of institutional interactions, however, topics are introduced and changed mainly by the dominant person according to a pre-set agenda. Very often questions are used as a means of controlling the topic which are designed to steer the participant(s) in a certain direction or incorporating what has been said and indicating by further questions that more information is wanted. In the following extract from a TV interview with former British conservative politician John Stanley (JS), the interviewer (Nick Ross) challenges Stanley for being evasive:

1 NR:	[Ok let me put my question
2 JS:	[so the Soviets have come to the conclusion
3 NR:	[my question to you again because in truth you know
4 JS:	[the Soviets-
5 NR:	= you're not [tackling my question
6 JS:	[the Soviets have made it quite clear

(adapted from Thornborrow 2002: 96)

The way Stanley pursues his own topic leads Ross to accuse him of not 'tackling my question'. Although questions are a prerogative of the dominant speakers, this does not mean that they always manage to achieve their interactional goals, depending on the institutional context. As we have just seen, in interviews, politicians often do not provide the desired answer (see also unit B3). This is because in this institutional context both parties have roughly the same power and status. In a court of law, however, non-compliance of defendants with their discoursal obligations may, as we noted above in A2, have serious consequences for the onwards progression of the interaction.

Formulation

Formulation is the practice of 'summarizing, glossing or developing the gist' of a speaker's previous statements (Heritage 1985: 100). Formulations are common in institutionalized settings such as police or news interviews, courtrooms and classrooms. They are the conversational privilege of people with institutional power. As such, formulations serve to check understanding of what has transpired from an interaction, but they are also control devices, a way of making participants accept one's own version, thereby constraining their options for further contributions.

In news interviews, formulations are addressed not only to the interviewee, but also to the overhearing audience. Interviewer formulations serve to make the interviewee's meaning more explicit, but they can also be what Heritage (1985) terms an 'elaborative probe' to produce a more detailed response from the interviewee. In both cases, they can result in confirmation or disconfirmation from the interviewee (Thornborrow 2002). Formulation has also been described as a weapon in the news interviewer's armoury (Heritage 1985: 114) enabling him or her to control the interaction while at the same time clarifying matters for the audience, which of course is institutionally legitimate.

In the following extract interviewer Nick Ross uses formulation to challenge a prior point by interviewee Denzil Davies:

```
1   NR:   now this is fascinating (.) you're saying
2         that you're trying to allay groundless
3         fears (.) all this taxpayer's money (.)
4         which we could spend on other things (.)
5         you're going to put into conventional
6         armaments (.) to allay groundless fears
7   DD:   no (.) it's not the case of the fears
6         being groundless (.) the fears are [still there
8   NR:                                       [I'm sorry but
9         that was your phrase
```

(adapted from Thornborrow 2002: 100)

Here the interviewer uses formulation to challenge a statement given by Davies in a previous turn, which the latter then goes on to disconfirm.

So far we have been talking about the linguistic strategies that institutionally dominant people have at their disposal to control an interaction. However, as we will see across this Strand, institutionally less powerful people also have ways and means to contest the agenda set by the more powerful interactant.

A4   LANGUAGE AND GENDER

Over the last 50 years there has been intense interest in the relationship between language, gender and power, as both an academic and a popular subject. The questions academics have been concerned with have been whether men and women use language differently, whether sexism is expressed and transmitted through language, whether changing sexist language will change attitudes and, lastly, how representations of men and women in the media affect or 'construct' the understanding we have of both sexes.

Sex and gender

Although the terms 'sex' and 'gender' are often used as synonyms, it is important to point out that linguists and gender theorists make an important distinction between the two: whereas 'sex' is a biological and physiological category, referring to the anatomical differences between men and women, 'gender' is a social category and a social construct. This means that 'gender' refers to the traits that men and women are assigned and how these can vary within different classes, cultures and societies. Importantly for gender theorists, these traits are not immutable but assigned by a culture, socially determined and learned, and therefore not beyond change (Wodak 1997). As the French feminist philosopher Simone de Beauvoir once said, 'One is not born a woman, one becomes one' and indeed, the same axiom can be extended to the social determination of men. Moreover, how men and women behave can vary from one class or community to another and even from one situation to the next, while assumptions about what is appropriate in discourse for both men and women often become naturalized into taken-for-granted beliefs about linguistic usage. These beliefs translate as *androcentrism* which, as many feminist linguists have observed, equates male with what is normal, and female as a deviation from that norm.

The distinction between sex and gender has important political implications, in that traditionally and historically, socially constructed differences between men and women have been given biological explanations, thereby justifying practices that discriminate against the sexes, particularly women. As observed, these distinctions can be said to be ideological and have often been used to justify male privilege. For instance, women's inherently 'natural' roles as 'mothers', 'nurturers' and 'carers' and men's supposedly natural function as 'providers' and 'breadwinners' have been used to reassert and cement stereotypical family and gender roles. Other examples of 'gender ideologies' are the postulations that women by nature are more suitable for the lower status and less well-paid 'caring' professions, such as nursing or social work, whereas men by nature are better qualified for the more prestigious technical professions, such as medicine, engineering or aviation. Early pre-feminist linguistic research on men's and women's language, rather infamously represented by Jespersen (1922), has argued that linguistic differences are due to the biological differences between the sexes. This 'biological determinism' has been severely criticized by gender theorists and feminist linguists for perpetuating gender stereotypes about men's and women's behaviour, including their linguistic behaviour. In sum, feminist linguists take the view that differences are down to socially prescribed gender roles rather than any biological difference between the sexes.

Sexist language

The term *sexism* can be defined as 'discrimination within a social system on the basis of sexual membership' (Wodak 1997: 7) and denotes a historically hierarchical system of inequality, just like inequality based on class or race, where women (and sometimes men) are discriminated against, exploited and constrained in some way or other on the basis of their sex. Throughout this book we take the view that language is a powerful resource for reflecting but also, to some extent, shaping the way we see the world. This is also true of 'sexist' language, although what constitutes sexist language is open to debate and has been the object of many studies that have looked at gender bias in the language. Litosseliti (2006: 14–15) provides a useful checklist of areas where this gender bias in the language becomes apparent:

- ❏ sex specification
- ❏ gratuitous modifiers
- ❏ lexical gaps and under-lexicalization
- ❏ semantic derogation
- ❏ asymmetrically gendered language items
- ❏ connotations of language items

Sex specification can be found in gendered terms such as 'actress', or in the use of 'she' to refer to countries, ships and cars, while gratuitous modifiers draw attention to sex as difference, as in constructions such as 'lady driver', 'woman doctor', 'male nurse' or 'male prostitute'. Lexical gaps and under-lexicalization can be found in inequalities between complementary sets of gendered terms, such as in having more, often derogatory, terms for sexually active women than for men; or, by contrast, in lexical gaps where there are no female equivalents, in, for example, 'henpecked', 'pussywhipped' or 'rent boy'. Semantic derogation is where certain terms describing women have changed over time from neutral to negative in connotation. These terms often include a sexual slur, as in 'mistress', 'madam', 'queen' or 'harlot' – the last of these originally meaning 'a fellow of unkempt appearance'! Compare also 'bachelor' as opposed to 'spinster', or 'slag/slapper' as opposed to 'stud'. In short, the number of terms that denote the sexual behaviour of women, mainly in negative terms, is far higher than that for men. Asymmetrically gendered language items include the use of 'Mrs' to describe married women, thereby divulging their marital status, whereas the same does not apply to 'Mr'. The same principle applies to so-called 'agent' nouns such as 'fireman', 'policeman' or 'chairman', although admittedly these terms nowadays do have the equivalents of 'firefighter', 'policewoman', 'chairwoman'/'chairperson'/'chair'. The connotations of language items are exploited in references such as 'girl' to describe grown-up women, where expressions such as 'weathergirl' arguably trivialize the referent and indicate a lack of maturity in the subject. More recently, 'boys' is sometimes used alongside 'girls', particularly on 'lifestyle' and make-over television programmes. Another 'connotative' example is the use of 'lady' as a euphemism in contrast to 'woman', while the term 'single mother' often has negative connotations and 'working mother', while not as downbeat as 'single mother', can also have negative associations.

So far we have seen that many words in the English language contain certain pre-suppositions about gender and taken-for-granted attitudes about men and women. Newspapers, particularly the popular press, are full of examples of wordings that portray women and men in stereotypical ways. In general, women are defined more in terms of their social roles ('granny', 'mother of two') and are judged more harshly ('divorcee', 'career woman'). Women in particular tend to be represented on the basis of their appearance far more than men, even when described in their professional settings. Thus, in the context of sport, the tabloids will still refer to tennis player Maria Sharapova as 'a Russian babe' (*Sun*, 1/06/05). In politics, former British Home Secretary Jacqui Smith causes 'a stir' with her 'low cut top' ('Home secretary admits she may be showing too much cleavage', *Mail* online, 11/10/07), whereas former Conservative leader David Cameron is applauded for sporting a new hairstyle ('David Cameron unveils his new look – a centre parting', *Mail* online, 4/6/08).

Linguistic studies on gender: deficit, dominance and difference

The early gender and language studies in the 1970s and 1980s were characterized by the emergence of three schools of thought: 'deficit', 'dominance' and 'difference'. Put simply, the issues were (i) whether women's language was 'weak', lacking and deficient, (ii) whether differences in speech styles between men and women were a result of gender inequality and male dominance over women, or (iii) whether these differences were due to men and women being socialized into different gender roles, with mis-communication between the two arising from this. We offer here a theoretical over-view of these issues.

Arguably the most influential (and most criticized) example of the 'deficit' view of women's language, Robin Lakoff's book *Language and Women's Place* (1975) argued that women's 'weak' language reflected and perpetuated their subordinate status in society. Based largely on anecdotal evidence, Lakoff claimed that women's language was characterized by the following features:

❑ *lexical disparity*, as in the use of certain female-specific colour adjectives like 'beige', 'mauve' or 'crimson'
❑ *empty adjectives*, as in 'divine', 'gorgeous' or 'sweet'
❑ *hedges*, such as 'well', 'y'know' or 'sort of'
❑ *intensifiers*, like 'so' or 'very'
❑ *overly polite forms*, in 'milder' swearing expressions such as 'oh dear' and 'sugar'.

As well as claiming that women have a tendency not to tell jokes, Lakoff also makes the claim that women's language is peppered with tag questions such as 'isn't it?' or 'don't I?' and, related, that women, in a general sign of their insecurity and uncer-tainty, use certain intonation patterns to seek their interlocutor's approval. Subsequent research by Cameron *et al.* (1988), Coates (1996) and Toolan (1996) has disproved this claim, arguing that meaning is context-dependent and that tags and other so-called 'weak' forms have multiple functions. Rather than indexing insecurity, tags and other hedges can have a facilitative function; that is, they can keep the conversation flowing, although the question still remains as to who is doing the facilitating. Cameron *et al.* suggest that much of the facilitating is left to the subordinate speaker in a conversation, who may or may not be female, in, for example, 'unequal encounters' such as in the workplace, in doctor–patient interactions or in job interviews. In some institutional contexts, such as courtroom questioning and 'disciplinary interviews', tags, rather than being facilitating, can be used to humiliate the addressee. They can therefore also be an interactional resource of the *powerful* rather than the *powerless*. Consider the following excerpt from a disciplinary interview between a male prison governor and a female prisoner (taken from the documentary *Jailbirds*, BBC2, 1999) which exemplifies this use of tag questions:

1	GOVERNOR:	You will have to get sorted out at some point ye know … *aren't you?* Instead of that you're getting more aggressive each time you come. Whether you are doing it or not, you shouldn't be doing it you know that=
2	PRISONER:	=Yes Sir
3	GOVERNOR:	And that's what we are dealing with here *isn't it?* Is there anything you'd like to say in mitigation?
4	PRISONER:	Nothing
5	GOVERNOR:	Nothing. Nothing at all [Prisoner: Nothing]. Not even I'm sorry?

The Governor's first tag could be interpreted as a request for confirmation or explanation from the prisoner, who meekly agrees with his proposition ('Yes Sir'). But by his third turn it becomes clear that the prisoner is not so much being asked to clarify anything, but more to verbalize her guilt and submission. She, however, resists the offer to explain her behaviour by saying 'Nothing' twice. The important point here is that the use of any linguistic form depends on many factors apart from gender, such as the speakers' status and relative (institutional) power, their objectives, the type of interaction and the overall context.

The other two main theoretical positions in the gendered language debate were the 'dominance' and 'difference' approaches, one seeking to expose the supposed dominance of men over women through their linguistic behaviour (e.g. West and Zimmerman 1983), the other one relating differences in conversational behaviour mainly to the sexes growing up in different subcultures (e.g. Tannen 1990; Holmes 1995). Dominance theorists were concerned with exposing gender bias in the English language, particularly in grammatical forms that rendered women invisible. Echoing many of the features of Litosseliti's checklist above, these forms included 'generic' *he*, *man* and *chairman*; lexical items that represented women in a stereotypical way, as in *blonde*, *redhead*, *manageress*, *woman doctor*; and openly derogatory terms for women, as in *bitch* or *slapper*. Dale Spender's *Man Made Language* (1980) was a pioneering work in this tradition. A provocative polemic, its theoretical position was that because we live in a patriarchal system, meaning has been defined by men, and men's language has been seen as the norm: 'it has been the dominant group – in this case males – who have created the world, invented the categories, constructed sexism and its justification and developed a language trap which is in their interest' (Spender 1980: 142). Spender therefore argued that men have named the world in certain ways, and have invested *their* meanings in terms such as 'motherhood', 'frigidity' or 'emasculate'; women by contrast have fought back through terms such as 'sexual harassment' or 'chauvinism'. Spender, *contra* Lakoff, pointed out that it was not women who were deficient but the social order. Spender's work has been subsequently criticized as being overly deterministic in the sense that it positions language alone as the key determinant of our social reality. According to Cameron, Spender ignores 'the contextuality and indeterminacy of meaning', instead producing 'an account of Orwellian thought-control via malespeak which is patently false' (2006b: 16). Moreover, Spender's highly idealistic programme had little to offer in the way of challenging and changing sexist language (Simpson 1993: 159–178).

Whereas studies in the 'dominance' tradition have attributed differences in male and female language to male privilege, the 'difference' approaches that became prominent in the 1980s took the view that these differences were largely due to girls and boys growing up in different subcultures and being socialized from an early age into different gender roles. According to this paradigm, men's and women's speech is essentially different but equal. For example, one view generally held in the 1980s and 1990s was that women are more co-operative speakers and more sensitive to the 'face wants' of others (Tannen 1990; Holmes 1995; Coates 1996). This difference has been used to explain the use of certain language features by women (such as hedging, indirectness and supportive simultaneous speech as a tactic to display interest) to engage the interlocutor or to mitigate face-threats. For Coates, who referred to women's and men's 'styles' rather than 'women's speech', these came about because of the pressures of socialization that encouraged girls to be 'nice' but boys to be 'competitive'. Difference theorists such as Holmes and Coates also undertook a positive re-evaluation of women's language by focusing far more on women in their speech communities and in all-female groups. A number of studies emphasized the positive functions of everyday women's talk and 'gossip', which far from being 'trivial', actually was found to have important social functions in that it helps women to construct, negotiate and maintain their identities (Coates 1996).

The difference approach also gained wide currency in the USA, particularly with Deborah Tannen's bestselling 'pop-linguistic' book *You Just Don't Understand* (1990) and John Gray's book *Men are from Mars, Women are from Venus* (1992). Tannen argued that miscommunication between men and women was due to different conversational expectations placed on women. Women, it is suggested, tend to use emphatic 'rapport talk' as opposed to men's information-laden 'report talk', while both books urge their male and female readers to understand each other more and blame each other less. Both publications, while very popular in lay circles, have come under sustained criticism from linguists, particularly Cameron (1998), for their neglect of power relations between the sexes. Tannen has since addressed these criticisms in rather more scholarly work (1993, 1994).

The claims of both books have seeped steadily into popular consciousness, confirming and enhancing long held folk-linguistic beliefs about the differences in men's and women's speech patterns. These are widely drawn upon in gender awareness programmes, have been re-appropriated to teach staff in organizations about so-called male and female leadership styles, and have become a staple of the advice sections in women's and men's lifestyle magazines.

Beyond dominance and difference

The dominance and difference frameworks were felt to be compromised because they offered too simplistic a model of gender differences in language. In consequence, the scholarly emphasis has shifted more recently to how women and men are *constructed* through language and discourse. This development has been referred to variously as 'Third Wave' or 'poststructuralist' feminism because it has challenged the view taken by Second Wave feminists that gender is simply a binary opposition. Third Wave feminism, influenced by Foucault's understanding of power, is interested in the multiplicity of gendered identities and associated linguistic behaviours (e.g. Baxter 2003). From this perspective, gender is seen as a process of negotiation and not something that is given. Particularly influential here is Judith Butler's notion of 'performativity' (1999). Gender, according to Butler, is what men and women *perform*: men and women constantly negotiate their gender roles and are therefore able to challenge them. Masculinity and femininity is a construct, an identity that 'has constantly to be reaffirmed and publicly displayed by repeatedly performing acts in accordance with the social norm' (Cameron 1997: 49). One example of gender performativity, given by Hall (1995), would be the telephone sex worker adopting a 'feminine' and seemingly 'powerless' speech style to construct a version of femininity that she thinks her male customers expect.

The idea of gender as performance has been taken up by many gender theorists, particularly in work on masculinity (e.g. Johnson and Meinhof 1997). One such example is Cameron's (1997) analysis of young male American college students' talk and their use of 'gossip' and other features normally associated with female talk, such as cooperation and solidarity features, when talking about women and gay people. In their attempt to distance themselves as a group from homosexuality, the students thereby 'perform' heterosexual masculinity using gossip as a tool. Another important site of gender performativity is women's and men's lifestyle magazines, a theme that will be developed in the remaining units of this Strand. There are many contemporary studies examining the genre of women's magazines and representations of femininity (e.g. Caldas-Coulthard 1996; Machin and van Leeuwen 2003; Machin and Thornborrow 2006), and these studies are supplemented by research on textual and visual representations of men in popular culture, such as those in men's magazines (Benwell 2001, 2002, 2003).

LANGUAGE AND RACE   A5

Following van Dijk *et al.* (1997: 146) we use the terms 'race' and 'racial' in inverted commas to emphasize that races do not exist biologically, but are merely 'social constructions based on the common-sense perceptions of superficial differences of appearance (mostly of skin colour)'. 'Race' along with other comparable concepts such as gender and class are constructed in a society shaped by social stratification and inequality. Employing 'race' as real, whether in the news media, in government politics or in entertainment is to contribute to racialization and to reproduce race thinking (Hartmann and Husband 1974; van Dijk 1993a). Racialization involves the construction of a specific image based on a set of assumptions or stereotypes according to a certain race. It not only refers to a process of differentiation according to race, but is an imposition of racial character on a person or action. Racism, on the other hand, which is predicated on these imagined biological differences, is real and can be defined as a 'social system of "ethnic" or "racial" inequality, just like sexism, or inequality based on class' (van Dijk 2000: 35).

According to van Dijk, racism has both a social and a cognitive dimension. Racist discourse, like any other discourse, is a social practice and it therefore consists of everyday and institutional discriminatory action. But social practices also have a cognitive dimension, which is the set of beliefs and attitudes people have and the ideologies they subscribe to. In the case of racism, racist stereotypes and ideologies explain why people engage in discriminatory practices in the first place. This might be because they think that outsiders are inferior, less competent, less modern or culturally different, such that discourse as a social practice is the main source for people's racialized thinking.

Although racism is often directed against immigrants and other minorities, it is important to note that racism and racist discourses are not necessarily about skin colour and nor are they confined to minorities. For example, essentialist racialized ideas and discourses of (negative) national character and ethnic differences are often mobilized by states and the media in times of conflict and war in order to gain popular support for wars. Sport is another area where sweeping generalizations about foreign outsiders, using ideas of 'race', have been prevalent. One only has to think of media representations of football in the British popular press. English football in particular is often represented as a form of war against other nations, particularly the ones with which England has had a military past. Headlines from the popular press demonstrate that an ethnic and militaristic discourse backgrounds other modes of representations in favour of an absolute and simplistic opposition between 'them' and 'us':

Achtung! Surrender! For You Fritz, ze Euro 96 Championship is over!
(*Daily Mirror*, June 1996)

Our Dad's army get stuck in to send the Germans packing
(*The People*, June 2000)

Give them Edam a good thrashing!
(*Daily Mirror*, June 1996 against Holland)

8pm Tonight: PAY BACK TIME: At last! England's Chance to Avenge the Hand of God
(*Daily Mirror*, June 1996 against Argentina)

The discursive (re)production of race

Why has 'difference' been such a preoccupation in the representation of people who are racially and ethnically different from the majority population? In recent decades, globalization and the restructuring of national and international boundaries and economics have certainly been a strong contributing factor in this, with the flow of economic migrants (so-called 'new immigrants') and asylum seekers further adding to ethnic diversity but also conflict in countries on every continent. However, it seems that people cannot do without 'difference' or without differentiating themselves from others at all.

The cultural theorist Stuart Hall (1997: 234–238) describes the recognizing of ethnic difference as 'othering'. He offers four theoretical perspectives as to why othering is such a compelling theme in representation, and we shall summarize all four here.

The first perspective is associated with the French structural linguist Saussure. Saussure ([1916] 1960) argued that difference is important because it is essential to meaning; without difference, meaning would not exist. People know what 'black' is because they can compare it to 'white'. Hall argues that this principle is also valid for broader concepts such as 'Britishness', because it enables people to mark their difference from the 'non-British'. Binary opposites such as 'white/black', 'British/alien' or 'men/women' tend to oversimplify distinctions with their rigid two-part structure, but we do not seem to be able to do without them.

The second perspective goes back to the Russian linguist and critic Mikhail Bakhtin ([1935] 1981) who argued that we need difference because meaning can only be constructed through a dialogue with the 'Other'. Meaning, according to Bakhtin, is established in a dialogue between two or more speakers and arises through the 'difference' between the participants in dialogue. This implies that meaning can never be fixed and is always open to interpretation and contestation. So what it means to be 'British', 'Romanian' or 'Asian' is always negotiated between these national cultures and their 'Others'. The downside to this is that a group can never be in charge of the meaning it wants to make for itself. What is more, ideas and definitions of 'race', racism and ethnicity have been subjected to heated debate in the media, in politics and among ordinary people and will continue to do so, informing the 'politics' of language choice and use.

According to the third, anthropological, explanation, 'difference' is the basis of the symbolic order of what people call 'culture'. Social groups impose meanings on their worlds by ordering and organizing things into systems of classification, erecting symbolic boundaries (Douglas 1966). These are central to all stable cultures and keep categories clear and unambiguous. Things or people that do not fit into these categories because they are 'different' make people 'close ranks' symbolically and marginalize or expel what is alien, abnormal or 'impure' to them. The same process of 'purification' is happening when countries close their borders to foreigners.

The fourth, psychoanalytical, explanation argues that the 'Other' is fundamental to the constitution of the self. For Freud, people can only develop a sense of self and subjectivity through the symbolic and subconscious relations they form with an 'Other' that is outside and different from them. This means that the self is never unified, but always lacking in something the 'Other' has or is believed to have. The self is therefore split, and it is split into 'good' and 'bad' parts. According to one psychoanalytic explanation of racism, things that are undesirable about the self, such as desires one does not want to admit to or one feels guilty about, are projected on to the 'Other' (Fanon [1952] 1986). Racism in this sense is essentially a defence mechanism.

These four accounts about the importance of marking 'racial difference' and the 'Other' complement each other. Hall concludes that 'difference' is ambivalent. On the one hand, it is necessary for establishing meaning, language and culture, social identities and a sense of self; on the other hand, it is a site of negativity, aggression and hostility towards the 'Other'. Typical in the representation of racial difference is the practice of what Hall calls 'naturalizing difference'. This concept echoes the idea of naturalization developed in this book, where 'phenomena which are the product of social and cultural processes come to appear as just there by force of nature, innate ability or circumstances beyond human control' (Gabriel 2000: 68). In Hall's interpretation, naturalization works as a 'representational strategy designed to fix "difference", and thus secure it for ever' (1997: 245). For example, in the eighteenth and nineteenth centuries slavery was part of the 'natural' order of things and representations of slavery involving ownership and servitude of black people were regarded as completely 'natural' as well.

Linguistically, othering is achieved through the use of utterances that establish particular 'we' and 'they' groups and that invite identification with the 'we' group and at the same time distancing from the 'they' group. Research has shown that the use of pronouns is an effective means of interpersonally representing in- and out-group status (Fowler and Kress 1979; Reisigl and Wodak 2001; Bishop and Jaworski 2003). By the use of pronouns – we and they, in particular, but also you and I in some contexts – speakers or writers can construct identities, draw or erase borders between groups, and stress social distance or resentment against the other groups (cf. van Dijk *et al.* 1997). On top of this, lexical choice, such as the use of words like 'scroungers', 'illegals' or 'benefit cheats', is obviously another important way of creating linguistic othering.

Two key mechanisms in the construction of 'whiteness' in the media are exnomination and universalization (Gabriel 2000: 68). Exnomination refers to whiteness being taken for granted and not being mentioned or named. For instance, 'ethnic' is widely equated with minority culture, as if the white dominant culture does not have ethnicity. Universalization means that values that are essentially white European or American are simply assumed to be held by all. Universalization has, for instance, been invoked by sectors of the Western media and politicians in the 'war on terror' where a common enemy (a minority group of Muslim terrorists) has to be defeated in defence of freedom for all.

Changing representations of 'race'

In Western societies where there has been an awareness of 'race issues' for some time, blatant expressions of racism and racist language and images ('old racism') have become relatively rare. Contemporary forms of racism are often characterized as cultural racism or new racism (Barker 1981, 1984), where the superiority of one's own culture and nation is no longer emphasized either openly or straightforwardly. Racist practices are now legitimized on the basis of so-called principal otherness. Presumed biological-genetic differences in the post-war period, argues Barker, have been replaced by differences between cultures, nations or religions represented as homogeneous entities. Barker characterizes the new racism as 'pseudo-biological culturalism'. In this vision, the building blocks of the nation are not the economy or politics, but human nature:

> It is part of our biology and our instincts to defend our way of life, traditions and customs against outsiders – not because these outsiders are inferior, but because they belong to other cultures.
>
> (Barker 1981: 78)

Van Dijk (1993a, 1993b) has commented on the special role of 'elites' in the production of this 'new' or 'symbolic' racism, in which immigrants and ethnic minorities already living in Western countries are often addressed as cultural outsiders. Van Dijk introduces the idea of 'elites' as those groups in the socio-political power structure that develop fundamental policies, make the most influential decisions and control the overall modes of their execution. Elite groups, such as the government, parliament, directors of state agencies and the media, produce and reproduce racial thinking and racial discourses. This elite racism is therefore 'typically enacted in many forms of subtle and indirect discrimination (in action and discourse) in everyday situations controlled by these groups' (van Dijk 1993b: 5). Van Dijk does not dispute the existence of 'popular racism', which is routinely attributed to lower-class whites or the extreme Right by elites, but argues that elite racism is far more potent as elites have the power to 'linguistically institutionalize' their dominance over minority groups. So elite or new racism is covert and subtle, but nonetheless pervasive.

This process can be seen in the way the media and other elites have moved to reporting tactics that amount to a 'denial of racism' (van Dijk 1992). This is evident, for example, in the discourse strategies of negative other-presentation, such as reporting on ethnic minorities exploiting 'our' welfare system, and positive self-presentation, as embodied in sentiments like 'we have nothing against foreigners but' (see further unit D5). A particularly shocking example of this denial of racism was the news coverage of the murder of Stephen Lawrence, a black youth who was stabbed to death at a London bus shelter by a group of five young white men in 1993. Initially, the mainstream media barely recognized the occurrence of another racist murder in Britain. In fact, it was only in 1997, when an inquest jury finally returned the verdict that Lawrence was the victim of an unprovoked racial attack perpetrated by five white men that media apathy turned into media frenzy. The *Daily Mail* newspaper started a media campaign, running a story with the headline 'Murderers: The Mail accuses these men of killing. If we are wrong, let them sue us' (February 1997). Under the heading, the paper named all five suspects, called them 'murderers', showed their pictures and challenged them to sue the newspaper for libel (which they never did). Singling out the young men's vicious attack and labelling them 'thugs' and 'murderers' effectively 'othered' them, thus sidelining concern about more endemic racism in British society. Allegations of racist treatment by the police made by the Lawrence family and their legal team was downplayed by most of the media. Instead, it focused on the inability of the legal system to deliver justice to a wronged family, turning the whole case into a personal tragedy and preventing political considerations of widespread institutional racism and racial inequality and its broader societal, political and cultural implications. Institutional racism (also called 'structural' or 'systemic' racism) is a form of racism that occurs specifically in corporations, educational and other public institutions such as the police, or organizations with the power to influence the lives of many people. A form of elite racism, it can be detected in processes, attitudes and behaviour that amount to discrimination through unwitting prejudice, ignorance or racist stereotyping of minority ethnic people.

The inquiry following the murder of Stephen Lawrence ('The Macpherson report') in 1999 found the investigating police force to be 'institutionally racist'. The report made a total of 70 recommendations for reform, covering both policing and criminal law. These proposals included criminalizing racist statements made in private and abolishing the double jeopardy rule (the law that nobody can be tried twice for the same crime in a British Court of Law). Lord Macpherson also called for reform in the British Civil Service, local governments, the National Health Service, schools and the judicial system, to address issues of institutional racism (Holdaway and O'Neill 2006).

It took more than 18 years before two of Lawrence's killers, Gary Dobson and David Norris, were finally brought to justice after initially being acquitted in 1996. They were jailed for life in January 2012 for their role in the attack. Their convictions did not depend on evidence they had stabbed Lawrence, but on forensic and DNA evidence that convinced the jury they were part of the group engaged in murdering him. It was precisely the change in the double jeopardy law in 2005 (recommended by Lord Macpherson in 1999) that made this possible. Three other suspects, however, have remained free. The Metropolitan police have vowed to continue to pursue the others involved.

In 2013 the case again regained prominence when allegations about corrupt police conduct during the original case handling resurfaced and a former undercover police officer stated that he had been pressured to find ways to discredit the victim's family and to deter public campaigning for better police responses to the case. Although further inquiries in 2012 by both Scotland Yard and the Independent Police Complaints Commission had ruled that there was no basis for further investigation, the then Home Secretary Theresa May ordered another independent inquiry into undercover policing and corruption by a prominent QC. The outcome was described as 'devastating' when published in 2014. A further inquiry into whether members of the police force shielded the alleged killers was set up in 2015.

A6 **HUMOUR, LANGUAGE AND POWER**

In January of 2015, two heavily armed terrorists entered the offices of the French satirical weekly newspaper *Charlie Hebdo*. They killed 12 people and injured 11 others. The 'justification' for the attack was made on the grounds of *Charlie Hebdo*'s type of comedy and, in particular, its satirical cartoons, some of which mocked religious leaders. However, the killings mobilized supporters of freedom of speech, and in an expression of solidarity, the sentence 'Je suis Charlie' was adopted by millions of people worldwide to signal empathy with those who were killed at the Hebdo offices.

With only a few exceptions (see further B6), the analysis of humorous language has *not* been a feature of Critical Linguistics (CL) or Critical Discourse Analysis (CDA). However, in the context of the observations above, humour – or at least, the perception of what is appropriate in humour – is clearly very much embedded in relationships of power. In this instance, the power was exercised through extreme violence, but 'citizen' power followed in its wake and so universal was this statement of solidarity that it, for instance, became one of the most popular news hashtags in Twitter history (and see further unit A11 on the role of the hashtag in Twitter).

The position we wish to adopt across this Strand is that humour, in its myriad linguistic forms and genres, is endemic to all human society and culture, and so cannot be ignored in any serious study of the way language interacts with power. However, we want to go further and argue that it has been a marked failing of CDA that it has not recognized the importance of humour as a form of linguistic, social and cultural praxis. Many popular forms of humour, such as parody, irony and satire, have, for centuries, been oriented towards the structuring and restructuring, at both the micro- and macro-level, of personal, political and social relationships. It is strange that a discipline such as CDA, whose principal remit is after all to highlight and to challenge the discourse practices of powerful and interested groups, has not noticed how humour can be used as (i) a tool of repression and ridicule by the powerful, as (ii) a form of resistance by the less powerful (see C3), or as (iii) an instrument to help galvanize social bonds among disenfranchised groups.

As the *Hebdo* incident demonstrates, we do not need to look very far to see how humour ties in with the sorts of issues we have been addressing in other parts of this book. We offer here some additional illustrations of this intersection between language, humour and power, although we anticipate that readers will have no trouble finding similar case histories in other times and places. Our first incident concerns events in Burma (Myanmar), where after nearly two decades of military rule, the Burmese people (including their Buddhist monks) took to the streets in 1990 in a major pro-democracy uprising. The ruling junta's crack-down on the street protestors was vicious, but this action was not its first response to the uprising. Rather, its response to the first signs of civil unrest was to round up and imprison the country's leading comedians. Most famous among these was Par Par Lay (1947–2013), former leader of the 'Mustache [sic] Brothers' troupe whose vaudeville-style routine, known as *a-nyeint pwe*, included jokes, drag artistry and satirical sketches. Here is an example of one of Par Par Lay's humorous jibes at the regime, which, it must be said, does not seem especially scatological in its satirical intent:

> Par Par Lay goes to India to seek relief for a toothache. The Indian dentist wonders why the Burmese man has come all that way to see him.
> 'Don't you have dentists in Myanmar?' he asks.
> 'Oh, yes, we do, doctor,' says Par Par Lay. 'But in Myanmar, we are not allowed to open our mouths.'

The dictatorship had already signalled its uneasiness about *a-nyeint pwe* in 1990 when it imprisoned Par Par Lay for six months for jokes like the one above. In the intervening years, Par Par Lay was arrested two more times for his political humour, most recently in 2007, only six years before his death.

Our second illustration concerns the case of the lawyer Halima Aziz. An Asian Muslim working in Bradford for the British Crown Prosecution Service (CPS), Aziz was dismissed from her job by her employers on the grounds of certain inflammatory remarks she was alleged to have made at Bradford Crown Court. One remark (which she strenuously denied) claimed that Jews were responsible for the attacks of 9/11, a comment that allegedly incited a race riot among white and Asian youths within the court building. After a seven-year legal battle, the Employment Tribunal found that Ms Aziz had been suspended without, in the words of the judgement, 'a shred of evidence' and that the CPS had discriminated against her in suspending her without first taking any action to establish whether there was any evidence that she had made such remarks.

However, during an interview on a news channel on the day the story broke, Aziz herself did admit to making the following remark, which also featured in the CPS's case against her:

> as I was going through the security entrance [to Bradford Court] the security guard said to me 'You're a security risk'. And all I did was, I said to him 'Yeah, I'm a friend of Bin Laden'. [I] just turned round to him, just took it as a joke, rather than taking it offensively.
>
> (Channel Four News, 5 September 2008)

It is surely apparent to anyone reading this that there is a mismatch between the literal content of Aziz's reply to the security guard and the non-serious meaning intended in the discourse context. Ms Aziz was, in short, being ironic. We shall explore the linguistic strategies of irony more fully in B6, but it is worth noting for the moment how the speaker herself monitors the intended humour in her reply ('just took it as a joke') which she develops perhaps as an antidote to a potentially hostile remark or, as with much humour, to defuse the tension in the situation. (It is also worth speculating on whether the security guard's remarks were also intended ironically, something that is not clear from Aziz's account and which was not investigated). Whatever the micro-dynamics of this exchange as humour, the CPS pursued Aziz relentlessly, dismissing her from her job and prompting seven years of litigation. The absurdity of a major institution like the CPS persecuting someone over a piece of manifestly ironic discourse quite rightly provoked outrage among all of the media outlets that covered the story. Here for example is the lead from the same report that carried the interview with Ms Aziz:

> Six hundred thousand pounds compensation, another half a million pounds of taxpayers money in legal costs – and all for failing to apologise for racial discrimination against a Muslim lawyer who made a throwaway remark about Osama bin Laden.
>
> (Channel Four News, 5 September 2008)

As the report suggests, Aziz won a record pay-out against her employers of approximately £600,000, to cover aggravated damages, injury to feelings, and past and future loss of pension and earnings. The Tribunal also found that the CPS was culpable in many ways, including discriminating against Aziz on the grounds of race. More alarmingly again, three figures at the top of the organization – 'persons of a senior level in the CPS' in the words of the judicial ruling – were found to be deceitful and to have withheld crucial material evidence from the court. Ms Aziz subsequently indicated her intention to build an orphanage in Pakistan with her pay-out, while the three disgraced senior officials in the CPS escaped disciplinary proceedings, with two of them subsequently promoted.

Further illustrations of the widespread intersections between language, power and humour are easy to find. It is worth noting that the election of Donald J. Trump as President of the United States in November 2016 was accompanied by a subsequent rise in political satire. Various humour-related websites appeared, some offering 'Trump-spoofing apps' with another supplying assorted clips of Trump's pronouncements so that users could assemble their own do-it-yourself spoof footage (*Variety.com* 2017). Press coverage of the Emmy Awards of 2017 drew attention to the strong showing of satirical shows ('Political Satire Wins the Night'), while the NBC's long-running 'Saturday Night Live' programme had its best ratings for over 20 years, due in large part to actor Alec Baldwin's excoriating caricature of President Trump. There is no doubt that satirical discourse operates in a responsive and reactive way in modern societies and cultures, and for many it works as a form of resistance to egregious or disreputable behaviour by the elite and the powerful (Simpson 2003: 85).

Finally, a thought-provoking episode involving humour and power, which in this instance led to one party acquiring a criminal record, is the now infamous 'Twitter Joke Trial'. In 2010, Twitter-user Paul Chambers expressed his irritation at weather-induced travel delays at Doncaster Sheffield Airport (formerly Robin Hood Airport) in Yorkshire, UK. He posted the following message:

> Crap! Robin Hood Airport is closed. You've got a week and a bit to get your shit together otherwise I'm blowing the airport sky high!!

Anti-terror police subsequently arrested Chambers at work, his home was searched, and he later lost his job as an accountant. He was convicted for sending a public message of a 'menacing character' that contravened the Communications Act of 2003. Some of the questions this case raises are addressed in detail in an article by Kelsey and Bennett (2014) who discuss, among other things, the interpretation of texts in cyberspace where there is no access to face-to-face interaction. Suffice it to say, public reception of the case was divided, with media pundits and politicians on the political right (the incident drew much airtime) arguing that the conviction was warranted because if he (Chambers) said it, then he must have meant it. The alternative view was taken by the numerous high-profile celebrities and comedians who publicly supported Chambers, such that, after two failed attempts, his conviction was eventually overturned by the High Court.

As in the Halima Aziz case, the use of irony is at the core of this uneasy relationship between the authorities and the language of humour. There is for instance a growing number of airports that now place explicit embargoes on the use of humour, as in this signage from Chicago's O'Hare airport:

> *All comments regarding guns and bombs are taken seriously. Please no jokes.*

The warning to travellers is clear: any attempt at playful language, even if manifestly designed to defuse (so to speak) a perhaps tense situation, risks some very serious consequences.

Incongruity as a humour mechanism

In terms of humour's rhetorical and linguistic design, most researchers in 'humorology' agree that for a piece of language or text to be funny, it must exhibit (at least) some sort of incongruity. The incongruity may operate at any level of language, which means that it can be found in the narrower features of vocabulary and grammar, or, in the wider context, in the broader units of discourse organization and social interaction. Puns and related forms of verbal play are good illustrations of the type of incongruity that operates in the narrower linguistic context. By contrast, pragmatic devices such as irony and other types of figurative language, as we shall see in B6, situate the humour mechanism in an incongruity at the level of discourse. In this latter broader context, and echoing some of the humour examples touched upon in our illustrations above, the verbal play inheres in a mismatch between the conventional meanings of speech acts and the suggested meaning that those utterances have in a particular context.

In spite of the unifying criterion that an incongruity lies at the heart of its production, humour comes in many forms and guises; we are all familiar with puns, witticisms, jokes, anecdotes, slapstick, parody and satire. Whatever the genre of humour, the essential point is that its use introduces levity and non-seriousness into a discourse situation, inducing what we might call a 'humour footing'. Consider, for instance, the way puns and related forms of wordplay are used in the tabloid media. A pun is a linguistic structure that simultaneously combines two unrelated meanings. The central incongruity in the formation of a pun is that a chance connection between two elements of language is identified, and this allows a controlled 'double meaning' to be created in the text. Take the following example from a tabloid newspaper from 2017, where the headline introduces a story about the perceived political and moral weakness of the British opposition leader, Jeremy Corbyn.

DON'T CHUCK BRITAIN IN THE COR-BIN

(*The Sun Online*, 7/6/2017)

This play on words works through a happenstance connection in sound and grammar. Unravelling puns in tabloid headlines always runs the risk of stating the obvious, but for the record, the text here advances its humorous message by aligning an everyday compound noun phrase 'dust-bin' with the two segments of Corbyn's surname. While the second segment of the surname is unconnected semantically and etymologically, it is linked coincidentally by phonetic similarity to the informal clipped nominal 'bin'. The informality in register is sustained further in the headline's use of the lexical item 'chuck'. This type of text is known as a 'phonological sequencing pun' but the relevant point here is that verbal play like this brings a levity and sense of dismissiveness to the story. Creating an association with the image of rubbish, the message is that the politician's credo is disposable, dispensable and of no particular consequence (see further C6).

Incongruity, as we have argued, can work at different levels of language. A common form of it, which employs different varieties of discourse as its raw material, is the echoing or mixing of different styles and registers. In fact, the idea of register-mixing is implicit in the exercise in unit C2, on news reportage covering the first Gulf War, where a non-congruent style was used to relate a serious episode in the conflict. This, however, underscores the point we made at the start of this unit, concerning the lack of awareness in CDA of how the humour function works in certain texts under analysis. The mixing of styles for comic and other effects, for instance, has been around for hundreds of years and was documented as long ago as the sixteenth century in the burlesques of the Comedia dell'Arte in Italy. The concept of burlesque is essentially the merger of two distinct forms of discourse where low burlesque (or travesty) uses an undignified style in addressing lofty or serious subject matter, while high burlesque uses an elevated or portentous style to deal with an inconsequential or trivial topic. It is not difficult then to see how journalists, by introducing a stylistic tone that seems at odds with the subject matter it embraces, can deflate, ridicule or ironize certain elements of their news stories.

We hope that the observations drawn in this unit will highlight how humour can intersect with relationships of power in both the private and public domains. Humour is, as it were, a serious business, and the consequences can be grave for those who use it injudiciously or who are caught out by the strictures of regimes intolerant of criticism. We have also observed how the broad concept of irony is often a key to understanding how certain types of humorous discourse work (or fail), and in B6 we develop some methods for the assessment of this important pragmatic feature.

LANGUAGE AND THE LAW   **A7**

There is little doubt that the most powerful institution in any society that adheres to a 'rule of law' is its justice system. The power of the legal system approximates very closely to our first sense of the concept of power – namely, the idea of power as domination, coercion and social control. In this context, where the enactment of law constitutes dominance of a very palpable kind, it is no surprise that linguists have become increasingly interested in the role language plays in the legal process and in the discourse of judicial and penal institutions. This relatively recent academic focus, on the interconnections between language and the law in all its forms, has come to be known as *Forensic Linguistics* or *Forensic Discourse Analysis*.

Forensic linguistics

The last two decades have witnessed a marked growth in work in forensic linguistics, evidenced by the formation of international academic associations, the publication of a dedicated academic journal along with numerous book-length publications, and the provision of higher degree courses in Forensic Linguistics in many universities around the world. A number of key international practitioners have emerged in this research field, and useful glosses and summaries of their publications may be found in the now plentiful introductions to forensic linguistics (see Olsson and Luchjenbroers 2014; Coulthard *et al.* 2016; and in the same series to which the present book belongs, Durant and Leung 2016). One of the most persuasive aspects of published work in forensic linguistics is that it often details the 'hands on' experience of the professional linguist who is working in the legal context. It also frequently presents the research as a narrative of lived experience, positioning the experiences and outcomes of real people against the more formal outworking of the legal process. It is for this reason that forensic linguistic research makes for insightful, compelling and often disturbing reading.

The remit of Forensic Linguistics is wide, with linguists being tasked to report on all areas where language intersects with the legal process. The activities listed below reflect a consensus across the published literature in the field and therefore signal the main duties a forensic linguist can expect to perform:

- ❏ performing expert analysis and commentary on the language of legal documents, courts and prisons
- ❏ improving translation services in the court system
- ❏ helping alleviate (linguistic) disadvantage produced by the legal process
- ❏ providing forensic evidence that is based on professional academic knowledge of language and discourse
- ❏ offering advice in legal drafting and interpreting, often with an emphasis on the use of 'plain language'.

As the techniques of analysis in linguistics and discourse analysis have developed, so has the variety of the roles that linguists have played in the legal process. Many linguists are now recruited for court appearances as *expert witnesses*. The expert witness, until recently the domain largely of the medic or psychologist, is someone who, because of their subject knowledge and their professional standing, is able to offer opinion that can count as evidence – the only type of witness who has such privilege in a court. This is an important legal endorsement because it accords a linguistic profile the same legal status as a medical or psychological profile, and not surprisingly, linguists through this provision have been able to make genuine interventions in the outcome of trials. This is especially true of cases where authorship is contested – cases involving, say, an alleged forged will or fabricated statement – because the full panoply of linguistic methods can be brought to bear on the contested text (see Coulthard *et al.* 2016; and see further B7). But nowhere has the intercession of linguist-as-expert-witness come more to the fore than in cases involving contested police evidence. This is largely because the toolkit of modern linguistic analysis has enabled linguists to probe contentious or suspect transcripts that (might) contain incriminating material. That said, the strictures of the legal system can often prevent the submission of linguistic evidence, such that the work of the forensic linguist is stalled by legal procedure itself. Baldwin and French (1990: 105–108) document a particularly frustrating case involving an accused who was alleged to have made threatening telephone calls demanding money. Despite compelling phonetic evidence linking the voice of the caller to that of the accused, the telephone evidence was ruled inadmissible because its content (the accused makes reference to his own criminal misdemeanours) would prejudice the outcome of the case. In other words, the very admission of guilt was itself inadmissible because it, well, amounted to an admission of guilt. This is one of a number of tortuous legal paradoxes that present challenges for the forensic discourse analyst, and other similar legal anomalies that fly in the face of logic, common sense or even natural justice are discussed elsewhere in this Strand.

Before looking in more detail at some of the problems for forensic linguists, it is worth firming up some key definitions and distinctions attendant to the legal process. First, not all legal systems are the same, with different parts of the world subject to different kinds of 'rule of law'. For example, Shari'ah Law exists in many parts of Africa and Asia, often running in tandem with traditional tribal systems or with other more secular systems. Roman Law is the lineal descendent of the legal system of the Roman Empire and is practised in most of continental Europe and in parts of the world such as South America and Southeast Asia where the European countries have had colonial influence. Common Law is the system embraced in England, Ireland, North America and Australasia, and in many other English-speaking countries where there has been British colonial influence. In contrast to the inquisitorial system embraced by Roman Law, Common Law is an *adversarial* system because it involves a prosecution and a defence, and in higher courts, the use of juries.

The law as institution

As we suggested in unit A2 above, legal language is *the* institutional discourse *sine qua non*, and its highly specialist nature makes for a problematic relationship with the ordinary lay people whose everyday language practices are far removed from the judicial system. While 'Legal English' can be thought of as a specialist register, or perhaps as a mosaic of interconnected specialist registers, it is, crucially, a form of discourse with which non-specialist members of the public are nonetheless expected to negotiate. Moreover, legal language, in the way of specialist registers (B2), offers 'insider-ness' and galvanizes the group bond among its practitioners. Tiersma is unequivocal about the all-pervasive influence of the law and about the way its language affects the daily lives of virtually everyone in our society. He also notes that in using legal language lawyers create and solidify group cohesion within the profession, subtly communicating to each other that they are members of the same club or fraternity (Tiersma 1999: 3).

There are many reasons for the level of linguistic specialism and detail found in legal registers. Undoubtedly, the proliferation of specialist language in oral and written legal documents has in part been prompted by the judiciary's struggle for exactitude, precision and consistency, although a far-reaching conservatism has also played a significant part in its retention of language forms that are at once archaic and arcane. One of the most significant contributory factors in the development of modern-day legal language has been the preservation of words and expressions (sometimes with their original meanings) from different periods of linguistic history, a feature, incidentally, that is common to the legal discourses of many nations (Gibbons 2003: 41). The inception of English legal language came through the early codification of Anglo-Saxon laws in the seventh century, and the written documents produced then have ensured the survival to this day of many Old English words, such as *bequeath*, *swear*, *guilt* and *theft* (although curiously the word *law* itself is from Old Norse not Anglo Saxon). The influence of Christian missionaries in sixth-century England resulted in Old English legal vocabulary becoming overlain with many scholarly Latin words, while the Norman invasion of 1066 introduced an entirely new set of legal terms (many of which had Latin roots also). When one bears in mind that this complex admixture of linguistic sources was well in place before the end of the eleventh century, there is little wonder that the history of legal language is both venerable and complex. Thereafter, Latin continued as the language of the educated elite into the 1700s, while French was still used in seventeenth-century court proceedings centuries after it had ceased to be an everyday spoken language.

There are a number of features of this complex admixture of source languages that are embodied in present-day legal discourse and are worth commenting on here. One is that, as noted, certain terms retain special senses that have disappeared in everyday usage: the word *witness*, from Anglo-Saxon 'witan' (*to know*) preserves the older sense of 'wit' as knowledge. Similarly, in grammatical structure, early modern English non-empathic *do* has long been obsolete in everyday speech but was still a feature of barristers' speech well into the twentieth century, as in 'I put it to you that you *did* leave the building and that you *did* run from the police …'. Similarly, vestiges of Norman French syntax, where the order of adjective and noun is reversed, can still be found in legal phrases: *court martial*, *attorney general* or *malice aforethought*. Additionally, there exist specialist terms and senses that are exclusive to the legal context, such as *committal*, *intestate* or *plaintiff*, while legal language employs a whole range of connecting words that are rarely found outside it: *forthwith*, *heretofore*, *theretofore*, *herein*, *thenceforth* or *aforesaid*. Untranslated Latin borrowings still survive to the present day, in *decree nisi*, *affidavit*, *in camera*, *habeas corpus* or *subpoena*, along with numerous French terms: *tort*, *judge*, *quash*, *void* or *voir dire*. Occasionally the original meaning of the term has shifted in everyday parlance while the legal use retains the older sense: the word *petty* (in 'Petty Sessions') retains the original sense of 'small' (*petit*) but without its derogatory sense in non-legal discourse.

Legal discourse also employs sets of paired, often synonymous words known as *binomials*. In many cases, the paired words are derived from different languages, as in an expression such as *last will and testament* where the first term is Old English in origin. The second term is Latin, deriving from the practice of Roman soldiers gripping their testes (considered their most valuable possession) while swearing an oath. Following Tiersma (1999), here are some more binomials with the source language indicated beside each term in the expression:

> *assault* (L) *and battery* (F)
> *breaking* (OE) *and entering* (F)
> *fit* (OE) *and proper* (F)
> *goods* (OE) *and chattels* (F)
> *save* (F) *and except* (L)

Binomials may even occur in the form of triplets, as in:

give (OE), *devise* (F) *and bequeath* (OE)

Tiersma (1999: 14) makes the intriguing point that many binomials have a rhetorical structure that echoes their origins in the alliterative techniques of Anglo Saxon writing. Here are some examples:

aid and abet
to have and to hold
clear and convincing

While they may seem strained and oddly repetitive by the standards of contemporary language, binomials are evidence of at least some attempt at legal continuity across different linguistic influences. The older terms from written legal documents of the Anglo Saxon period were retained and often simply conjoined with the later Latin and French terms. This was done, on the one hand, to avoid losing the sense of legal precedent and, on the other, to provide a kind of linguistic 'overkill' in covering as many languages as possible so that the language backgrounds of all parties involved might be accommodated. In spite of this seeming accommodation to the 'lay' audience, there is still good reason to be concerned about the power of legal discourse in its interaction with ordinary members of society.

Unit B7 develops these issues by examining some specific cases where the intersection of power and legal discourse has come to the fore.

LANGUAGE AND ADVERTISING

Advertising is simply the promotion of goods and services through various media. That said, advertising comes in several different forms, draws on a vast range of linguistic strategies and is targeted at a host of (very carefully researched) potential consumer groups. In his seminal book on advertising discourse, Cook suggests some useful contrasts that, in the context of this diversity of advertising practices, will help organize and focus our subsequent analysis and discussion:

❑ product vs. non-product ads
❑ hard sell vs. soft sell ads
❑ reason vs. tickle ads
❑ slow drip vs. sudden burst ads
❑ short copy vs. long copy ads

(after Cook 2001)

The first distinction captures the difference between those advertisements that draw attention to a specific product – a car, say, or a bottle of perfume – and those that more generally represent the image of a company or organization. The latter category, non-product advertising, is frequently designed to 'encourage warmth' which is why the strategy is often employed by political parties in their election broadcasts. Multinational conglomerates such as oil companies or IT giants habitually use non-product advertising because the presentation of a positive image is a crucial first step for their expansion into new global markets. For instance, IBM ran a series of ads in post-communist Bulgaria that comprised, minimally, the IBM logo and a simple message 'Good Luck Bulgaria!' Mindful of the precarious economic situation of 1980s Bulgaria, IBM clearly felt that specific product advertising was pointless; better then to 'plant' the image of the multinational as a caring and loyal friend.

The 'hard sell–soft sell' distinction centres on the degree of explicit persuasion embodied by an ad. Hard sell ads employ direct and unambiguous appeal: they exhort potential consumers to 'buy now' and they make use of overt statements that play up their product's merits and qualities. Indeed, in the early days of television advertising, when the hard sell strategy tended to dominate, many American television programmes would be held up live on air while the show's (invariably male) host urged viewers to buy the product that he was holding up to camera. Soft sell, by contrast, is less immediate, less urgent and less explicitly persuasive, and is often multimodally constructed through the additional use of music and pictures (see further B8). Research on trends in advertising discourse suggests that outside the margins of dedicated satellite shopping channels, the hard sell gambit has pro-gressively given way to the use of soft sell techniques in many media contexts. For instance, in a study of television advertising in the People's Republic of China, Short and Hu (1997) report that hard sell advertising, characterized by the foreground-ing and repetition of brand names, has come to be replaced by increasingly more sophisticated texts. These newer forms are typified by the use of indirect speech acts and the frequent blending of linguistic with non-linguistic information; they also invite from viewers a broader range of more complex (and less obvious) inferences about the product.

The 'reason' and 'tickle' distinction overlaps with the hard sell–soft sell contrast because of its concern with the degree of explicitness and persuasiveness embodied by advertisements. Reason ads are those that suggest a motive or reason for purchase while tickle ads tend to appeal to humour, emotion and mood (see further B8).

Slow drip advertisements are those that are fed out gradually through various media over a period of time, and are often 'soft sell' or 'tickle' in their general design. By con-trast, sudden burst ads, as the metaphorical label suggests, tend to explode abruptly onto our TV and computer screens or onto the pages of our newspapers or electronic media. Sudden burst ads often signal new products, such as the release of a film or the launch of a new model of car, and saturation coverage ensures that the commodity is quickly established in public consciousness. Sudden burst ads can also announce com-modities where duration is limited, such as the 'January Sales' in Western countries. Televised sudden burst commercials are often synchronized simultaneously in adver-tising slots across several networks – as any 'channel hopper' who has tried to escape the ad knows all too well.

Short copy ads, as their name suggests, are low on textual matter, particularly with respect to the amount of written detail they contain. This is either to create a 'mini-malist' message where onus is put on the addressee to resolve the ad's 'meaning' or it is done in contexts, such as on advertising hoardings, where space is at a premium.

Long copy ads are those that appear as features in print media such as weekend news-paper supplements and lifestyle magazines, sometimes in the guise of 'advertorials'. Advertorials combine article and advertisement in a style that shows how advertising has spread from actual advertisements into other genres of discourse (van Leeuwen 2005: 149). Long copy ads also offer potential customers the time to read articles that detail the specification of, for example, a new car, although common sense dictates that publicity for the same car be much pared down if it appears on an advertising billboard beside a busy road.

We might even add a further distinction to the contrasts drawn thus far, that between 'space-based' and 'time-based' advertising (Brierley 1995). Space-based advertising appears in print media, in the ads appearing on the pages of newspapers or magazines, or on billboards and related publicly accessible poster sites. Ads appearing in print media typically supplement the reproduction of the brand name and stills of the product with a sequence of written text which normally constitutes the key 'reason to buy' component of the ad (see below). Broadcast media advertising, where the ads appear on television or in cinemas, is 'time-based'. This medium allows the chrono-logical development of an ad as a visual and aural spectacle. In this way, multiple cam-era shots, cuts and extensive editing enable the creation of ads that function as often very sophisticated narrative texts.

The anatomy of advertisements

Advertisements employ a range of formal properties, many of which have become the established patterns for copywriters (that is, the people who design the ads in market-ing campaigns). In the developmental stages of an advertising campaign, professional copywriters attempt to attribute to a product a 'Unique Selling Proposition' (Brierley 1995: 140) and this often translates into a set of relatively fixed patterns that comprise the structure of a finished advertisement. Print ads generally exhibit five types of for-mal design, though of course not all ads have all five of these features:

- ❏ headline
- ❏ body copy
- ❏ signature
- ❏ slogan
- ❏ testimonial

(after Delin 2000; Brierley 1995)

The headline is designed to catch the reader's or viewer's attention. Like the headline of a news story, it often interacts with the visual image of the ad and works as an attention-getting device. Headlines often outline a problem or a need, using questions and commands in direct address to the consumer: 'Have you thought about your car insurance?' 'Stop paying over the odds for your internet provider' (and see further B8). The body copy, by contrast, is designed to do informative and persuasive work. It often offers the 'solution' to the problem posed in the headline and, frequently using first person reference, gives reasons for buying the product: 'We can help sort your financial problems', 'This is why we have created ...' and so on. The signature is a small picture of the product itself or a graphic bearing the trade name of the product and/or company. The slogan often accompanies the signature and normally constitutes a memorable phrase or line that may in time become the touchstone for the product: 'Because you're worth it' (L'Oreal), 'Every little helps' (Tesco) or 'The World's Local Bank' (HSBC).

Occasionally, ads are supported by a testimonial. This is an endorsement of the product by a well-known actor, media personality or figure of authority. In certain contexts, such as in the marketing of more humble, domestic goods, it is more appropriate that an 'ordinary' member of the public attest to the value or worthiness of the product on show (Brierley 1995: 145). A testimonial from a high-profile member of the business community offers the chance for a cross-fertilization of products and images. This type of business 'synergy' is borne out, for instance, in an advertisement for Samsonite suitcases that featured entrepreneur millionaire Richard Branson testifying to the excellence of the Samsonite brand while pictured beside one of his own aircraft.

It is important to emphasize the creative element that permeates all aspects of advertising. Linguistic innovation and striking verbal play work as mnemonic aids in helping to make products and brands more memorable. And although a particular characteristic of slogans, advertising 'jingles' can feature in all of the formal components of an advertisement. Grammatically cryptic forms are popular because they require some reader effort in their deciphering: an ad for an apple juice drink allegedly free of additives is accompanied by the enigmatic slogan 'the More, the Less'. The body copy for a domestic boiler runs thus:

'We don't expect you to buy it until you haven't seen it first'

where the unexpected negative in the second clause plays up the boiler's compactness and unobtrusiveness. Semantic word play in the form of puns (see A6 and C6) is of course popular: a London hair salon bills itself as 'British Hairways', its high street awning decked out in the familiar livery of the airline in question. Other verbal play works through the transformation of familiar idioms. For example, an ad for Cif kitchen cleaner shows two cleaning products, one a run-of-the-mill all-purpose cleaner on the left of the picture and on the right, the Cif cleaner. Running over both images, with one clause placed sequentially above each product, is the slogan 'Jack of all Trades, Master of One'. (The inference invited through the transformation of the everyday idiom is that Cif should be the preferred specialist cleaner because it is designed specifically for the task in hand.) The stylistic creativity of advertising, through its use of a host of linguistically creative techniques, is a fascinating area for linguistic analysis, as shown in several studies by Cook (2001), Myers (1994), Ringrow (2016) and Toolan (1988) among others.

LANGUAGE IN THE NEW CAPITALISM

The expression *new capitalism* is applied to contemporary transformations of capitalism that are characterized by a 'restructuring' of the relations between the economic, the political and the social (Jessop 2000). This restructuring produces dramatic shifts in relations between different domains of social life – most significantly, between the economic field and other domains such as politics, education and culture. There is the sense that there has been a colonization of the other domains by the economic field. This colonization has resulted in the reconstruction, along business lines, of a wide range of traditionally 'non-business' institutions, including schools, universities and hospitals. One example of this trend is the current 'marketization' of universities and the construction of students as 'consumers'. It is assumed that this development was initially encouraged and promoted by Britain's New Labour government of 1997–2010, part of whose ethos was to promulgate pro-managerial educational discourses and policies, and to advocate an entrepreneurial culture and educational system; subsequent Tory-led governments have solidified the process (see B9 and C9).

Governments have reacted differently to these changes but many have adopted or at least made concessions to neo-liberalism, the dominant political project to effect the restructuring of social relations in the new capitalism (Jessop 2000). Neo-liberalism can be understood as an endeavour to remove obstacles that do not fit the demands of new capitalism and is characterized by anti-unionism, free market economics and the dismantling of the welfare system. The neo-liberalist world order has also been imposed on China, Vietnam and the countries of the former Eastern bloc, so there now seems to be no escape from free market capitalism. Neo-liberalism and its discourses present the economic changes as a challenging but inevitable development. This is, for example, what former British Prime Minister Tony Blair, in a speech to the Confederation of British Industry (CBI), once said about the inevitability of 'change':

> We all know this is a world of dramatic change. In technology; in trade; in media and communication; in the new global economy refashioning our industries and capital markets. In society; in family structure; in communities; in life styles.
>
> (Blair 1998; quoted in Fairclough 2000: 28)

What is remarkable about this extract is its underscoring of the pervasiveness of these (supposedly inevitable) changes, which not only affect the economy and politics but also people's personal lives. As Fairclough points out, one of the characteristics of neo-liberalism is to claim '*universal* status' for this particular representation and vision of economic change (2003: 45; our emphasis). Other representations of this economic order might focus on the injustices and inequalities created in the emergent global world order. However, as Bourdieu and Wacquant (2001) point out, words such as 'class', 'exploitation', 'domination' and 'inequality' are largely absent from what they call the 'new planetary vulgate', a kind of neo-liberal version of George Orwell's Newspeak (see further unit A10). For example, in the language of New Labour introduced above, the discourse of 'poverty' has been displaced by the discourse of 'social exclusion' (Fairclough 2000). The language of new capitalism is replete with empty and ideologically contested buzzwords, such as 'flexibility', 'knowledge-driven economy', 'learning economy', 'lifelong learning', 'enterprise culture' and so on. Because change is always round the corner and uncertainty a way of life, people continually have to adapt and learn new skills. Therefore, new ways of working have brought with them demands for people to change not only their work practices but also their linguistic capabilities and performance to fit the demands of the new capitalism. Jeffries and Walker (2017) have used corpus linguistic tools alongside critical linguistics to study the neo-liberal political buzzwords that marked the New Labour years, demonstrating how lexical items such as 'terror', 'choice' and 'reform' gained new prominence and significance under the 'Sultans of Spin' who crafted the discourse of Tony Blair's Downing Street.

Discourses in the new capitalism: the 'knowledge-driven' economy

We have just referred to the importance of language in bringing about the restructuring of contemporary capitalism. These changes have been ushered in by the 'knowledge-driven' economy, an economy in which new knowledges and hence new discourses are continuously produced, circulated and applied. These discourses are intended to shape how people act in the world, both in the workplace and, increasingly, in their private lives. The adoption of new managerial approaches in an arena of intensified global competition has increased awareness of language as a valuable commodity that needs to be 'managed'. Even worker's verbal behaviour is now treated as a commodity and is part of what employers are selling to their customers, an element of their 'branding' and corporate image (Cameron 2000, 2006a; and see D9) and this explains the increasing tendency for employers to regulate the speech patterns of their workers, particularly in the service industries. This knowledge-driven economy can also be said to have produced a 'new work order' (Gee *et al.* 1996) with two categories of workers: a knowledge-producing elite and a less privileged group serving and servicing the needs of others (Reich 1994; see also Sennet 2006). Old style authoritarian hierarchy may be largely a thing of the past, but in new capitalist businesses the 'top' is sometimes the boss/coach, sometimes the consumer and/or market and sometimes both. In many present-day service contexts customers have become 'a second boss', as employers often use customer evaluations to reward or punish service workers (Tracy 2000: 120). The importance now given to student evaluations in neo-liberal universities which increasingly view students as customers instead of scholars is another prime example of this process.

One typical discourse in the new work order is the discourse of 'teamwork' (Fairclough 2005). Epitomized by buzz words such as 'participation', 'collaboration' and 'empowerment', this form of discourse suggests a *partnership* between management and workers and a commitment to democratic values in the workplace. In the new capitalist work order, workers are 'empowered' to think and work on their own as well as in teams. 'Teamwork' is meant to constitute a move away from hierarchical to supposedly more egalitarian workplace cultures, in which employees all work together for the good of the company to achieve particular institutional goals ('team objectives'). In order to be able to work in teams and deal successfully with the consumers, employees are often deemed to be in need of training in the more 'co-operative' ways of communicating, such as negotiation (see B9).

The discourse of 'flexibility' is another fetish of new capitalism (Harvey 1990; Fairclough 2005). A 'flexible' and 'adaptable' workforce is preferred, which in times of economic downturn can be reduced and taken on again when demand arises. If workers can be persuaded that 'flexibility' is an inevitable fact of contemporary capitalist systems, they may be more likely to accept that they have to acquire an ever-widening set of skills (including communication skills) so they can perform a broader range of tasks with varying responsibilities. As Gee *et al.* point out, in the fast changing environment of the new capitalism, 'workers must be "eager to stay" but also "ready to leave"' (1996: 19). The moral and social implications of these business practices, such as increasing job insecurity for employees, are omitted from a discourse that is based on pragmatism and instrumentalism. As Cameron puts it, 'the capitalist's flexibility is the worker's insecurity' (2000: 12).

As an ideology, the discourse of flexibility is promoted in politics (A10), the mass media, in popular management and even in the 'self-help' books that can be found at airports and railways stations. What is more, economic and organizational thinking of this kind is believed to be applicable to manufacturing industries and public service organizations not only in the Western world but in the rest of the globe as well. In spite of new capitalism's promise of organizational democracy and empowerment, the research reported in this Strand suggests a very different picture: new capitalist language can be said to embody 'new, perhaps more hegemonic, techniques of control' which now masquerade in the name of 'democratic organizational reform across the globe' (Gee *et al.* 1996: 19). It is to these linguistic techniques of control that we now turn.

Technologization of discourse

In the new capitalism, new knowledges are constantly produced, circulated and consumed as discourses (economic, organizational, managerial, political or educational) and disseminated through 'discourse technologies'. Fairclough describes these technologies as follows:

> Examples of discourse technologies are interviewing, teaching, counselling and advertising ... [I]n modern society they have taken on, and are taking on, the character of transcontextual techniques, which are seen as resources and toolkits that can be used to pursue a wide variety of strategies in many diverse contexts. Discourse technologies ... are coming to have their own specialist technologists: researchers who look into their efficiency, designers who work out refinements in the light of research and changing institutional requirements, and trainers who pass on their techniques.
>
> (1992: 215)

In this respect it is important to bear in mind that knowledge and information are now organized into what Giddens has termed 'expert systems' (1991: 18): these are 'modes of technical knowledge' that have validity independent of the practitioners and clients who make use of them. This means that discourse practices are relatively context-free and as such can be applied to a variety of settings. For example, knowledge about what language to use for conducting successful (job) interviews or negotiations is produced and taught by management consultants not only in commercial companies but also in schools and universities. The teaching of 'communication skills' can also be said to qualify as a 'transcontextual technique' with the skills seen as useful and often indispensable for a variety of purposes, situations and institutions.

Contemporary societies are knowledge- and discourse-based not only in their economies but also, and increasingly so, in their expectations about how people should lead their private lives and conduct their personal relationships. Expert knowledges and discourses that have the capacity to shape people's lives are disseminated through texts of different sorts and are transmitted through the media and modern information technologies. The print media, and lifestyle magazines in particular, are top-heavy with expert advice on how people should conduct almost every aspect of their lives (see, for example, Machin and van Leeuwen 2003, 2005a).

Globalization and the commercialization of the media

Over the past two decades, deregulation in the media industry has led to a commercialization of news production and a shift from addressing citizens to addressing consumers. In this respect it has been noted that 'visual discourses' (i.e. images) have become more central and more salient in the new capitalism than in earlier forms of capitalism. Communication increasingly happens on a multimodal level; that is, ideas are expressed through both language and the visual mode (Kress and van Leeuwen 2001; and see B8). This can be observed in new capitalism's dependence upon new communication technologies, the ever-increasing importance of 'brands' and the 'branding' of products, and the concomitant importance of representations and images in the media. As part of the increasing commercialization of the press, many papers have been 'rebranded'. 'Branding' is a process whereby products are given certain associations – from advertising we know that cars or clothes can be made to connote freedom and 'coolness', perfumes can connote passion and certain foods can connote a healthy lifestyle. Newspapers have also begun to think much more systematically about visual communication in their attempt to attract readers/consumers. As Machin and Niblock state, news no longer has, first and foremost, the role of documenting reality. Instead, what readers find in terms of content and address often connotes values such as 'creativity' and 'forward thinking', which is not articulated as any concrete political strategy but is 'a concept tied to the mood of neocapitalism' (Machin and Niblock 2008: 257). In this neo-capitalist mood, 'social awareness' does not mean awareness about poverty but about 'market-defined trends and lifestyle issues'. The visual style of newspapers, according to Machin and Niblock, connotes

> values that belong to the same discourses of 'regeneration' involving expensive property investment, chic restaurants, etc. It is essentially the same business language that is now also used in university mission statements and local councils that are 'forward thinking' and 'creative'.
>
> (2008: 257; see also B9)

In this vein the structure of newspapers' physical and online presence has also been consistently updated to reflect reader/customer lifestyle focuses. *The Times* moved to a tabloid-size edition as early as 2004, whilst the *Guardian* announced in June 2017 that from 2018 onwards the paper would no longer be printed in a broadsheet edition. The *Guardian* website was updated in 2015 to better reflect the prominence of advertisements; the websites of most mainstream newspapers are now unrecognizable from their early news-focussed formats.

LANGUAGE AND POLITICS

Given the coverage of this book, it is perhaps somewhat of a truism to say that language and politics are closely connected. The study of this connection has been a key concern since antiquity – it was after all Aristotle who said that people are by nature 'political animals'. Our interest here is in the ways and the extent to which these two aspects, language and politics, are linked. Scholars working in sometimes very different academic traditions have investigated the details and particulars of the use of language in those situations which we, often informally and intuitively, call 'political'. In this unit we will look at ways in which language can be used to achieve political ends, focusing on some of the rhetorical strategies often used by politicians and other public figures to create an impact on the public. However, it is not just professional politicians who are involved in political activity and processes. Ordinary people also engage in politics, as voters, demonstrators and consumers, and as unit A11 below will show, the rise of social media in the last decade may enable citizens to challenge established politicians and their practices.

Throughout this book, we have presented linguistic approaches that can be called 'political'. Both Critical Linguistics (CL) and Critical Discourse Analysis (CDA) have changed the view of language as an essentially transparent and neutral medium by concentrating on topics that are thought to be of particular socio-political relevance: political rhetoric, media discourse, racism, nationalism, sexism, education and many other topics of critical interest. Furthermore, contemporary approaches to CDA deal specifically with the reproduction of '*political* power, power abuse or domination through *political* discourse, including the various forms of resistance or counter-power against such forms of discursive dominance' (van Dijk 1997: 11; our emphasis). Political discourse analysis can therefore be subsumed under a broader critical approach to discourse. However, what constitutes 'political discourse' is a matter of interpretation. Here we offer some definitions.

What is political discourse?

An easy, but incomplete, answer to this question is that political discourse is discourse produced by politicians. To be sure, a great many studies of political discourse deal with the language of professional politicians and political institutions, some of which are discourse-analytical (e.g. Harris 1991; Fairclough 2000; Chilton 2004; Charteris-Black 2014; Cameron and Shaw 2016). However, what is 'political' depends very much on the viewpoint of the speaker. Language as we have seen so far in this book is capable of having many functions, not all of which are political and/or manipulative. Still, even the most everyday decisions people make can be called 'political'. For example, people may decide to boycott certain products coming from countries with oppressive regimes; they may decide to buy fair trade and 'cruelty-free' products; or they may use public transport instead of their cars to get to work in order to protect the environment. People talk of 'sexual politics', 'environmental politics' or even 'office politics'. So although crucial in the analysis of political discourse, politicians are not the only actors in the political process. We must therefore also acknowledge the various *recipients* in political communicative events, such as 'the public, the people, citizens, the "masses" and other groups and categories' (van Dijk 1997: 13).

People, however, are not just passive recipients of politics. They are actively and increasingly engaged in what has been described as 'subpolitics' (Beck 1999); that is, grassroots social movements, such as protests against nuclear submarines, globalization or the destruction of the environment, to name just a few. Many people seem to have developed a general feeling of distrust in the ability of political institutions and the state to deal effectively with public problems, particularly in the current late modern climate. Some of the characteristics of late modern life are the social fragmentation and breakdown of civic institutions (parties, unions, churches) and the weakening of social and political identifications. Concomitantly, there has been a resulting increase in people adopting their own authorities (see A11 and D11) and making more personal choices about health, science, moral values and public problems. In this climate of multiple uncertainties new forms of political expression have arisen, often concerned with lifestyles and consumer choices and variously described as 'life politics' (Giddens 1991), 'lifestyle politics' (Bennett 2003), or 'political consumerism' (Bennett 2003).

The organization of public life around lifestyle-oriented service and consumer activities has also shaped conceptions of political representation. It may therefore not come as a surprise that politicians themselves have adopted a more personalized rhetoric of choice and lifestyle values to communicate their political messages to citizens. As Bennett points out, many politicians in Western countries have abandoned 'the old rhetorics of sacrifice and collective political projects in favour of promises of greater personal choice in basic policy areas such as health and education' (2003: 140). This has happened against the neo-liberal ideological backdrop and the development of a public issue discourse that advocates personal choice and responsibility.

Of course, distrust in politicians and political institutions is not new (see further A12). It was the view of ancient rhetoricians such as Plato, Cicero and Aristotle that politicians use persuasive and manipulative rhetoric to deceive the public. And in the twentieth century it was George Orwell who painted a nightmarish scenario of a totalitarian political system sustained by total linguistic manipulation ('Newspeak') in his novel *Nineteen Eighty-Four*. Orwell's critique of political discourse was taken up by critical linguists, such as Fowler, Kress and Hodge (see B2) who sought to apply his insights in some of their linguistic studies. Noam Chomsky, another linguist to have taken an interest in Orwell's views, is well known for his radical critique of American state politics, particularly the 'propaganda' of its foreign policy and the role of the mass media in 'manufacturing consent' (Herman and Chomsky 1988). Chomsky can by no means be called a critical linguist, as his 'transformational-generative' theory of language simply does not view language as part of the socio-political process. However when he refers to the 'manufacture of consent' through political rhetoric he does refer essentially to discourse processes.

One of the goals of politicians is to persuade their audience of the validity of their claims. Let us now look at some of the ways this can be achieved in political discourse.

Presupposition and implicature

These linguistic strategies, introduced in units B7 and B8, are ways of delivering information implicitly and leaving it to the hearer to deduce meaning and make assumptions. By implying rather than asserting an idea, speakers and writers can to a certain extent evade responsibility for what they say (see units B7 and B10). Presupposition and implicature are of course not just used in political discourse; they are also common in everyday conversations. And as shown in Strand 8, they are particularly prevalent in advertising because both strategies can make it more difficult for the audience to reject certain views communicated in this way. They are also widely used by journalists in political interviews to put politicians 'on the spot' (see, for example, the interview involving Jeremy Paxman and George Galloway in B3). Unlike presuppositions, implicatures operate over more than one sentence or phrase and are far more dependent (i) on shared background knowledge between the speaker and hearer and (ii) on the surrounding context of discourse.

Metaphor

Metaphor has long been recognized as an important feature of political rhetoric and as an important means of conceptualizing political issues and constructing world views (Charteris-Black 2004: 48). A metaphor is basically the means by which we understand one concept in terms of another, through a process that involves a transference or mapping between the two concepts. The different concepts in a metaphorical construction are known as the *target domain* and the *source domain*. The target domain is the topic or concept that you want to describe through the metaphor while the source domain refers to the concept that you draw upon in order to create the metaphorical construction. Common conceptual metaphors in English are LIFE IS A JOURNEY, as embodied in expressions such as 'He has no direction in life', 'We are at a crossroads', 'She'll certainly go places', 'Don't let anyone stand in your way' and so on; or IDEAS ARE FOOD, as in 'I can't digest the entire book', 'Those ideas are half-baked', 'That's food for thought', 'Let me stew over that one' and so on. In these two metaphors, the target domains (i.e. the entities being talked about) are, respectively, 'life' and 'ideas' while the source domains (the concepts used for the transmission of the metaphors) are, respectively, 'journey' and 'food'. In common with many metaphors, these two display a pattern of 'concretization' where the more abstract concepts and experiences of the target domain are captured in the source domain by means of more familiar, physical or tangible concepts in human understanding. For Fairclough, metaphors are one way of using language to conceal underlying power relations (2000: 33). Charteris-Black (2014) analyses metaphors in the rhetoric of prominent British and American politicians, examining speeches given by Tony Blair and David Cameron, and John F. Kennedy and Barack Obama.

Pronouns

Just as in advertising discourse, pronoun use by political speakers has an important persuasive function when it comes to referring to themselves, their party or the nation as a whole. Like passives and nominalizations, pronouns can be used to obscure responsibility and agency. Pronouns, particularly 'we', as we show in unit C1, can be either 'inclusive' or 'exclusive'. In political discourse it is inclusive 'we' that often predominates as it helps to share the responsibility for actions that are controversial. Inclusive 'we' is also effective if a government wants to persuade the nation to go to war or accept an unpopular policy. The following short text, in which we have highlighted the relevant pronouns, concerns the 'credit crunch' of 2008. It details the proposals by the UK's then Prime Minister to deal with the problem:

> **Let's roll up *our* sleeves and sort out the mess, Gordon Brown tells Britons**
> Mr Brown said that the country would get through the crisis. 'This is the time to roll up *our* sleeves,' he said. '*I* have a great deal of confidence in the energy and initiative in the British people. *I*'m confident about the future of Britain. *We* have done what is necessary. *We* will continue to take decisive action. Nobody should be in any doubt that *we* will do whatever it takes.'
> (*The Times* online version, 1 October 2008; our emphasis)

In this example it is not clear who the 'we' refers to. Does it refer to the Government (exclusive 'we') or to Britain and its people as a whole (inclusive 'we')? Whatever the intended (ideological) meaning, Brown's tactics misfired seriously with some readers, as the following online comments show. Notice particularly how these two respondents introduce the second person 'you' to distance themselves from both Brown and his policies (emphasis added):

> Brown mismanaged the economy for years as chancellor and now wants *us* to sort it out. Sorry but *you* created the problems, *you* sold *our* gold reserves, *you* helped inflate house prices and stood by as *our* industries were sold off abroad. He is *our* biggest single economic mistake for decades.

> Dear Mr Brown … please roll up *your* sleeves, open the door of number ten and leave so that *we* can have a general election and boot *you* and *your* incompetent government out. *You* want to claim credit for the good times and blame everyone else when it goes pearshaped!

This analysis is not to suggest that this pattern in pronoun-use is restricted to this particular politician. A year later, another UK Prime Minister, while in opposition, claimed in a conference speech that, as far as austerity was concerned, 'We're all in this together'. David Cameron's telling phrase resurfaced in the media when he refused, four years later, to interfere with the extravagant bonus system of failing taxpayer-owned banks. It was obvious that 'we' were not all in this together. In analysing the language of the opposing sides in the 2016 referendum campaign which resulted in Britain's decision to secede from the European Union, Buckledee (2018) demonstrates, among several strategies in an emotionally charged campaign, how the inclusive 'we' pronoun was used to create the 'illusion of a classless alliance' which erroneously suggested that the 'common man' had as much to gain from Brexit as economic and conservative elites.

Euphemism

A euphemism is a figure of speech that uses mild, inoffensive or vague words as a means of making something seem 'more positive than it might otherwise appear' (Thomas *et al.* 2004: 48). Euphemisms are commonly used in political discourse for controversial subjects such as war, old age, poverty and unemployment. Thus, politicians might talk about 'senior citizens' (old-age pensioners) or 'regime change' which is the removal of a foreign government by force (and see further B2). The expressions 'disinvestment', 'downsizing' and 'right-sizing' are three of many terms referring to the 'laying-off' of workers (itself a euphemism for 'sacking'!). The metaphorically informed expression 'credit squeeze' is a rather gentle way of capturing the reality of debt and poverty. A now infamous political euphemism is the expression 'being economical with the truth' which, although first recorded in the eighteenth century, achieved notoriety when a UK Cabinet secretary used the phrase during the Australian 'Spycatcher' trial in 1986. A euphemism for lying, the expression resurfaced, with some embellishment, during the Matrix Churchill scandal in 1992 when British Tory MP Alan Clark claimed that he was 'being economical with the actualité'.

Parallelism

A device we have already seen at work in advertising discourse, parallelism is the expression of several ideas through a series of similar grammatical structures and it is often used by politicians when they want to make parts of their message stand out. This is an example from US President John F. Kennedy's inaugural address:

> Let every nation know, whether it wishes us well or ill, that *we shall pay any price, bear any burden, meet any hardship, support any friend, oppose any foe* to assure the survival and the success of liberty.

Here we see the repetition of parallel structures using the quantifier 'any' along with a verb phrase construction introduced by 'shall': *we shall pay any price, bear any burden, meet any hardship, support any friend, oppose any foe*. Often, politicians use three-part parallel statements, as in former UK Prime Minister Tony Blair's slogan 'Education, education, education' (1996). And in a perhaps inadvertent echo of JFK, another former UK leader, Gordon Brown, offered the following widely reported remarks on the British banking crisis:

'I'm confident that reason will prevail, reason must prevail and I think reason will prevail.'

The strategic functions of political discourse

Chilton and Schäffner (1997: 212–213) and Chilton (2004: 45–46) propose certain 'strategic functions' that political discourse may have. A number of these functions

have been implicit in the discussions in various units of this book, so in the short syn-
thesis that follows, we make cross-reference to these units where relevant.

Coercion

Coercion largely depends on the speaker's resources and power (see A1) and is not
always linguistic. In dictatorial regimes, people are often controlled by the use of force,
and even democracies still use force legally, as in the dispersal of a crowd of demonstrators. Examples of linguistic coercion are discourses backed up by legal and/or
physical sanctions, such as laws, commands, rules and regulations (see A7). Those
with institutional power often resort to linguistic coercion in setting agendas and topics for conversation (see B3 and C3) or exercise various kinds of censorship.

Resistance, opposition and protest

Many of the discursive strategies employed by people in positions of power may be
resisted by institutionally weaker persons or the relatively powerless. We point out in
a number of places the various resistance strategies people have at their disposal, such
as the creation of 'reverse discourse' (B3), forms of slang or secret languages (C3) or
humorous discourses that employ techniques of satire or irony (Strand 6). Depending
on institutional circumstances, some of these discourses of resistance may be more
overt than others.

Legitimation and delegitimation

Political actors, at least in liberal Western societies, cannot act by physical force alone;
their power usually has to be legitimated so that the public believes in their right to be
obeyed. For example, international organizations such as the United Nations lack the
power to coerce, bribe or buy compliance with international laws. Their only source of
power is their capacity to mobilize support on the basis of legitimacy. As we saw in A1,
the process of legitimating is generally expressed through overt or implied linguistic
strategies and other communicative systems. These include self-justification, where
the organization uses positive self-presentation and claims to be a source of authority. Legitimation always involves delegitimizing of the 'other', whether an individual
or a group; this can manifest itself in negative other-presentation, acts of blaming,
excluding, marginalizing, attacking the moral character, sanity and even humanness
of the other (see Strand 5). Legitimation and delegitimizing are also part and parcel
of election campaigns, and are at the fore in broadcasted debates between political
opponents. In examining how political language constructs legitimization, Cap (2017)
considers how political and organizational leaders construct imminent outside threats
in order to claim that constraining preventive policies are necessary and justifiable.

Representation and misrepresentation

According to Chilton, political control involves the control of information. Some
amount of information may be given, but perhaps less than enough to satisfy the needs
and interests of the hearers. Misrepresentation in its extreme form may be lying, but it
also includes denial and evasive tactics. Euphemisms of course are another good example

of misrepresentation – see our comments above on the British political euphemism 'being economical with the truth' (see further Strand 12).

In practice, all of these strategies are usually interconnected and they can be found in other forms of discourse as well, not just in political discourse. However, the ways in which these political strategies are enacted through choice in language can be explored through close linguistic analysis.

THE DISCOURSE OF SOCIAL MEDIA   **A11**

This Strand will address the recent and seemingly ever-growing discourse arena of the internet. Most of the news outlets, print media as well as broadcast media channels that have been discussed in previous Strands and units now have a significant online presence, maintaining huge website operations that accommodate access to discourse that is largely unchecked by time or location. Alongside these websites, the rise of social media in the last decade in particular has led to 'an explosion in online interactivity and user participation' (Seargeant and Tagg 2014: 2). Social media platforms such as Facebook, Twitter and Instagram, as well as blogs and websites marked for 'participant content' as opposed to previously dominant 'one-to-many mass media' represented by newspaper websites for example (Page *et al.* 2014: 7), have contributed significantly to online interaction between internet users. Mandiberg (2012: 1) states that this activity has led to 'uprooting the established relationship between media producer and media consumer', resulting in these traditional relationships becoming 'blurred' and 'partially fragmented'.

This unit will evaluate the potential of social media discourse communities who engage in 'computer-mediated communication' (CMC) to play an active role in shaping social and political events. The unit also offers a range of perspectives and representative examples that may point to an emerging ability of citizens to transcend traditional and long-established boundaries between those who produce institutional discourses and those for whom the common-sense realities they construct are naturalized and legitimized.

The proliferation of online content and the rise of social media, often referred to in terms of the emergence of Web 2.0 (O'Reilly 2005), the programming model which enables these participatory websites, has led inevitably to increased scholarly interest in the language of the internet. Linguists have investigated social media language through a focus not just on traditional textual analysis but by analysing across the entire 'multimodal ensemble' (Page *et al.* 2014:16) of social media platforms. Zappavigna (2012) for example carries out a thorough analysis of the language of Twitter, whilst later work (Zappavigna 2015) investigates the linguistic functions of the convention for which this particular social network is most famous, the popularization of the hashtag (#). Employing Halliday's Systemic Functional Linguistics (see in particular unit B4) the hashtag is shown to possess more than just an experiential function that classifies what a post is about, #election2016 for example. On Twitter the hashtag also operates interpersonally, accommodating an evaluative comment on a post that 'resonates across an entire post to construe an evaluative comment' (Zappavigna 2015: 279), #soawesome or #hilarious for example (see unit B11 for an introduction to evaluation in a social media context). Hashtags also act textually in a post, operating almost like punctuation in carrying out an organizational function, in a post such as 'Donald Trump is the new #POTUS wow!' the hashtag indicates and specializes the topic within the rest of the post. Whilst Machin (2016) notes that many initial studies into social media networks are focussed more on theoretical underpinnings and the methodologies of sharing texts online rather than on the ideological meanings carried by these texts, there is certainly an emerging nucleus of contemporary linguistic work into social media that is more akin to the concerns of critical language studies. As well as Twitter, other analysts have focussed on the discourse of networks such as Facebook (Georgalou 2017) and Instagram (Veum and Undrum 2017). Social media, like all discourse communities, accommodates a range of possibilities for making meaning, such as the hashtag on Twitter. On the Instagram network much of this meaning-making potential is realized visually, as users share photographs and images, often captioned and edited in a further augmenting of the 'meaning' of these pictures. Veum and Undrum analyse a corpus of 'selfies' from Instagram, focussing on the embedded ideological meaning in this communication. Their analysis contends that 'typical selfie makers' – young females who comprise 78 percent of the images in their data corpus – represent themselves online in ways 'surprisingly similar to visual representations in advertisements and image banks' (Veum and Undrum 2017:87). Self-documentation on social media would seem therefore to be influenced by the discourses of commercialism that have also colonized the language of institutions such as universities, as noted throughout Strand 10. Selfies are shown to be edited to decontextualize the background of the images in a manner akin to many examples of advertising discourses addressed in Strand 8. It is also interesting to note with the Language and Gender concerns of Strand 4 in mind that very few of these selfies depict any narrative activity, and any that contained an ongoing act – such as performing sports – were posted by male users.

Alongside recognizing the ideological meanings contained within much of this computer-mediated communication itself, it is important to consider the potentiality possessed by social media discourse to accommodate the participation of users in the wider social world. Clearly there are overlaps in that, for example, the text and discourse practices of advertising language being present in online selfies has tangible social practice consequences in the strengthening of consumerism and capitalism. Many theorists have adopted a somewhat more emancipatory perspective on the role of social media as influencing social relations in a more direct way. Rosen (2012: 13) refers to a 'shift in power that goes with the platform shift' represented by the growth of participatory social media networks, offering a range of characteristics that define 'the people formerly known as the audience'. He says this audience refers to those 'who were on the receiving end of a media system that ran one way … who today are not in a situation like that *at all*'. Theorists such as Rosen view online discourse communities constructed through blogs and podcasts as extending the freedom of the press by opening up the potential to report to more actors. From this perspective a 'highly centralized media system that connected people "up" to big social media agencies and centres of power' now operates as a 'horizontal flow' that connects citizens to one another and that is 'as real and consequential as the vertical flow' (Rosen 2012: 14).

It is particularly important from the perspective of critical linguistics to consider the potential influence of these apparent consequences as they indicate the social outcomes of text and discourse practice. Such consequences are often manifested in the contemporary perception that through platforms such as social media wider audiences are not only made aware of socio-political issues but also become involved in certain campaigns through engaging in discourse interaction, which in turn might infuse and inspire other practices, such as public meetings or demonstrations surrounding societal issues. Bouvier (2017) analyses the case of a Twitter campaign known as @TwoWomenTravel, which centred around two Irish women who documented through Twitter their journey to Britain to secure the legal termination of a pregnancy in August 2016. Abortion was made illegal in Ireland in 1983, when the Eighth Amendment to the Irish Constitution was adopted. @TwoWomenTravel generated 40,000 tweets using the hashtag #twowomentravel over two days, which generally focussed on discourses of bravery, love, solidarity and choice (Bouvier 2017: 7–8). The Twitter feed was presented as a voice within the growing 'Repeal the 8th' movement in Ireland, which focussed on restoring a woman's legal right to choose through a referendum on the issue, and as such is a representative example of a connection between social media discourses and an engagement with socio-political realities. The @TwoWomenTravel campaign also tagged Enda Kenny (@EndaKennyTD), Ireland's Taoiseach (Prime Minister) in 2016, as a direct appeal to the country's power base to address the ongoing and controversial issue of abortion in Ireland. On 25 May 2018 Ireland voted by a majority of 66% to repeal the Eighth Amendment, and the Irish parliament is now set to legislate for abortion in Irish Law. This study also acknowledges the emerging role of social media as a source of information for mainstream news. Social issues that 'trend' on social media networks, such as Twitter, meet many of the values of newsworthiness that drive the content of major news outlets (Galtung and Ruge 1973; Harcup and O'Neill 2010).

It is not, however, always the case that what is popular on social media will automatically affect what is reported through mainstream news, and certainly the discourse of these organizations remains infinitely ideological, often putting a rather different spin on a story than might be present in the sometimes more emancipatory realm of participatory social media. Sanz Sabido and Price (2016) report on the so-called Ladders Revolution in Spain in 2015, a national strike against telephone giant Telefónica-Movistar after workers were forced to become 'self-employed' and safety procedures were downgraded. Technicians occupied the famous Telefónica building in Barcelona to protest against low wages and the lack of basic entitlements. Regardless of the fact that 150,000 employees of a major company had initiated an open-ended strike based on working conditions, the mainstream media framed the event in terms of its disruptive effect upon the company's customers. In this case the demonstrators utilized social media to attempt to countermand negative press coverage, disseminating information through blogs and online articles. Sanz Sabido and Price point out that whenever any news media outlet covered the strike or the occupation, the article would 'be posted on the blog, alongside a commentary that addressed its reliability and attempted to clarify any misunderstandings or misinformation contained in the original source' (Sanz Sabido and Price 2016: 257).

The Ladders Revolution demonstrates that a somewhat complex power relationship can exist between social media and traditional or mainstream media; in this case the tools and the platform of the former were used to critique the reliability of the latter. Of course mainstream news outlets have now colonized social media platforms themselves. Each of the major newspapers and broadcast news conglomerates have Facebook and Twitter presences, and so the earlier notion that social media might provide a context untarnished by the consent through which ascendant groups exert control may have been somewhat transcended. Certainly, the situation has been complicated by the fact that these groups boast 'likes' and 'retweet' rates that often far exceed smaller or independent 'citizen reporters'.

One particularly marked feature in the context of social media as a tool for mobilizing greater interest or involvement in political processes has been the role of social media in political campaigns. During his successful 2008 presidential campaign, former US President Barack Obama utilized social media platforms in a manner previously unseen in American elections. As well as making policies available online and communicating with donors and supporters through email and text message, the Obama campaign launched its own social networking site: my.barackobama.com became known in the campaign as MyBO. The strategy was credited with mobilizing mass support for Obama's run to the White House, and is a clear example of utilizing online language to drive social action. Online communication is credited with raising $200 million for the 2008 Obama campaign, and social media is now an established tool on all serious political campaigns. Obama's successor to the US Presidency, Donald Trump has a prolific and controversial presence on Twitter which has drawn significant criticism from his detractors, often accusing the President of being 'unpresidential' and even inarticulate (see units A12 and C11). In a somewhat telling tweet in the context of this unit Trump responded in July 2017, saying 'My use of social media is not Presidential – it's MODERN DAY PRESIDENTIAL', signing off with his somewhat ironic and presupposition-rich slogan 'Make America Great Again!'

Whilst the participatory nature of social media platforms – this horizontal rather than vertical view of information – has certainly changed the nature of news reporting, enabling any citizen with an internet connection and a digital recording device to essentially partake in the process of the news, it is not necessarily the case that power relations have shifted enormously. Certainly, social media platforms can be a force for good, and can potentially make more level a traditionally elevated playing field. They accommodate massively increased capacity to comment and debate upon socio-political events, raise awareness of campaigns and occurrences ideologically constructed along institutional lines by powerful groups on other more mainstream platforms (see A12 for more examples of this). They also provide more direct access to power than has ever before been possible, although one assumes that Donald Trump does not read all his Facebook messages himself. However, powerful groups have themselves adapted, and now utilize social media much like they do traditional sites of power.

Fuchs (2014: 77) reminds us that the massive resources possessed by these groups give them the edge in terms of control online just as they do in offline contexts, stating that political counter-power on the internet faces a massive asymmetry that is due to the fact that 'the ruling powers control more resources, such as money, decision-making powers, capacities for attention generation, etc'. Political counter-power movements on the internet should 'only be assessed as potential' (Fuchs 2014: 77). Occasionally this potential is realized (see unit B11), but the internet is not immune to the power relations that serve certain groups and systems in the same way that the institutional discourses addressed throughout this book frequently do. Often proponents who view social media and online discourse communities as having irrevocably shaken the foundations of power relations can flirt with technological determinism, echoing theorists such as Castells (2012) who view social media as 'decisive tools' in driving political events such as the Egyptian Revolution in 2011 or the Occupy movement. However, it is more accurate to recognize that the internet is embedded in the antagonisms of society; it can certainly be used to mobilize counter-power movements but it is not an instigator of them.

Unit B11 offers an account of an occasion where the counter-power potential of social media was partly realized to present an alternative voice to the mainstream news coverage of a controversial event.

THE DISCOURSE OF 'POST-TRUTH'

A12

In this final Strand, we offer an overview and analysis of a phenomenon that, in the early decades of the twenty-first century, has come to the fore in popular consciousness. This phenomenon is the concept of 'post-truth' and it is important because of the ways in which it characterizes much contemporary media and political discourse. In fact, the advent of post-truth is inextricably intertwined with epoch-defining major political events, such as the election in 2016 of Donald J. Trump as forty-fifth President of the USA or the 'Brexit' vote in the UK (see A1). It has been suggested that the outcomes of these events have been influenced by, and to some extent *determined* by, lies and deceitfulness in the media. Commentators have suggested that people have now come to realize that the media are *not* independent agencies who hold the system to account but are, rather, an 'elite-directed component of that system' (Harrison 2016: 7). Referring to the political strategies that are fed through such media, D'Ancona argues that post-truth politics at its purest is the triumph of 'the visceral over the rational, the deceptively simple over the honestly complex' (2017: 20). It is not that 'honesty' is dead, he continues, but that honesty is only one priority among many and nor is it the highest priority at that (34).

A core axiom of this textbook has been that everyone should maintain both an inquiring attitude towards, and a healthy scepticism of, the discourse of politics and media. However, the public, it seems, has never been more sceptical about both politicians and mainstream media. Two intersecting issues therefore need to be addressed here: the defining characteristics of the idea of post-truth and the extent to which it has (if at all) become embedded unalterably into the discourse of late modernity.

Defining 'post-truth'

Is post-truth new? There is unfortunately no straightforward answer to this question. For sure, there is nothing novel about 'fakery' in the media. The history of the popular press is suffused with instances of 'fake news' and even outright hoaxes. The writer Mark Twain once worked as a journalist for the *Enterprise*, Nevada's leading newspaper. In October 1862, under the name of Samuel L. Clemens, he wrote a story about the discovery of a petrified human body that had been preserved in an unusual position, seemingly thumbing its nose in a pose of mockery. Twain described his spoof as a 'string of roaring absurdities', admitting later that he had conceived the piece as 'a delicate satire' (see B6) on what he perceived as a contemporary media obsession with stories about petrifications (Fedler 1989: 44). However, in a case of 'going viral' nineteenth-century style, the story was reprinted nationally in numerous other papers and in consequence many Americans read about and believed the story of the 'petrified man'. Over 70 years later, film director Orson Welles presented a one-hour radio dramatization of H.G. Wells's *The War of the Worlds*. The broadcast was supplemented by cleverly simulated live reports from the military and from fake on-the-ground correspondents. Although stories of ensuing mass panic seem exaggerated, many citizens did take the broadcast seriously, with one group opening fire on a water tower believing it to be a 'giant Martian war machine' (Chilton 2016). Media hoaxes have continued into the present century. Indeed, the British red top tabloid *The Daily Sport* (and its Sunday variant), which ceased publication in 2011, was notorious for the preposterousness of its news reportage. Among its more egregious front page headlines were reports of a statue of Elvis Presley on Mars, a Second World War bomber on the moon and a man turned into a fish finger by extra-terrestrials. All of this was common fare for the paper's readership, who consumed this fake news without even the slightest expectation of journalistic integrity.

So, what, if anything, is special about our contemporary understanding of the concept of 'post-truth'? Part of the answer to this can be found in our discussion of social media in the previous Strand. Modern forms of media are constituted in such a way as to facilitate the rapid creation of 'news'; it is easy for anyone with access to the requisite technology to spread stories that are untrue to a very wide audience. By contrast, the clarification or rectification of these false accounts takes much longer, and often happens only after the initial impact of the story has faded. A contributing factor to the rise in what Small (2017: *passim*) calls 'bullshit' is the inversely proportional decline in the circulation of mainstream media. Small argues that the business model of 'serious' news outlets is under sustained pressure as both circulation revenue and advertising revenue become starved (2017: 10). As people pay less, these outlets reach ever smaller audiences, with revenue for some print media platforms dropping by as much as 15% year-on-year. Small concludes:

> Less money means fewer reporters, each doing more work than ever with lower budgets, making regurgitating what politicians say a much more cost-effective proposition than digging into *what* they're saying.
>
> (Small 2017: 10; our emphasis)

A corollary of this situation is that there has been a marked decline, from 2015 onwards, in the public's trust in what would ordinarily have been authoritative, respected or even revered hard-news sources. *The Daily Sport*'s absurdities were of a nature that no reader needed to interrogate seriously the accuracy of this fakery – it was just part of the entertainment. However, the decline in trust of venerable institutions such as the BBC in the UK or the *Washington Post* in the USA (see further below) is altogether a more serious matter. The communications agency Edelman, in January of 2017, published a global report that declared that trust was 'in crisis' around the world (Edelman 2017). Apart from India and Indonesia, the 26 other nations surveyed in the report all showed that their public's trust in business, government, non-governmental organizations and, particularly, the media was at an all-time low. The sharpest declines were in France, the USA and the UK. Furthermore, the Edelman report argues that distrust turns into *fear*, and it is fear that has fuelled the rise of populist movements in Western democracies. Among the phenomena people say they fear most are corruption, globalization and immigration. Edelman bases these conclusions on its analysis of fear among voters in both the US presidential election of 2016 and the UK's Brexit referendum of the same year. While 45% of those who voted for Democrat Hillary Clinton said they were fearful and that the system was failing, this rises to 67% on the same questions among voters for Republican Donald Trump. In the Brexit vote, 27% of those who voted to remain in the UK (so-called 'Remainers') expressed fear, but twice as many of the 'Leavers' (54%) said they were fearful. There is strong evidence then that the outcomes of both events were determined by fear and distrust, brought about in an environment of post-truth.

Another reflex of post-truth is its capacity to suffuse both media and political discourse in a seeming circle of mistrust. During his election campaign and afterwards, Donald Trump was challenged repeatedly over the accuracy of his claims. Notorious among these claims was his rather petulant assertion that more people had turned up to his inauguration ceremony than to that of his predecessor Barack Obama in 2009 (See Small 2017; D'Ancona 2017; see also unit D12). Presidential aide Sean Spicer claimed that it has been the largest crowd ever to attend an inauguration. When the photographic evidence patently told a different story, Kellyanne Conway, senior presidential aide, said that Spicer's statement was simply a case of offering 'alternative facts'. In other words, it appears perfectly legitimate to choose one's own reality, even if that reality flies in the face of rational evaluation and incontrovertible statistical evidence. Moreover, in a move known as 'mirroring' (D'Ancona 2017: 56), Trump began to accuse his critics in the media of peddling 'fake news' themselves. This is embodied in Tweets such as the following, which attracted 94,936 'likes':

> The Fake News Media has never been so wrong or so dirty. Purposely incorrect. Stories and phony sources to meet their agenda of hate. Sad!
>
> (3:35am – 13 Jun 2017)

Here, mainstream media stands accused of breaking with journalistic principles, in a manner that casts the authoritative news sources themselves as the progenitors of post-truth. For the president, this offers a relatively simple method for challenging anything unfavourable. Criticism can be dismissed as unfounded attack, from a politicized and partisan media. This dismissal itself then becomes a new way of manufacturing and distributing 'alternative facts'. That said, there is a sting in the tail, which to some extent flies in the face of our observations above around dwindling print media circulation. According to Harrison (2016: 8), the *Washington Post* reports that every time Trump and others accuse the paper of peddling fake news, there is actually a rise in subscriptions!

In the context of the foregoing observations, it is no surprise that the notion of post-truth has come under scrutiny in research in critical discourse analysis. Of particular concern to critical linguists are the complex intersections between post-truth and distrust, and following from this, the role that fear has played in the rise of populist movements in western democracies. Wodak and Krzyżanowski (2017) note that the unpredicted successes of right-wing populist parties, notably in Europe and in the USA, have transformed anxieties into legitimate apprehension and fear. They call for linguists to address these shifts in right-wing media and popular discourses and to explore the manner by which such 'discursive shifts' have become (following our definition of the concept in units A1 and B1) *naturalized* into everyday communication. The reading that completes this Strand, by Robin Lakoff, revisits in a more systematic way the issues raised in this unit. In the remaining two units of the Strand, B12 and C12, we survey key research developments in this area and suggest some methods and tools of analysis that can be used to explore further the idea of post-truth and its reverberations in discourse.

Section B

DEVELOPMENT: APPROACHES TO THE STUDY OF LANGUAGE AND POWER

CRITICAL LINGUISTICS AND CRITICAL DISCOURSE ANALYSIS

The units in Section B provide some context for the concepts and issues broached in the equivalent Section A unit. In this unit, we therefore outline the history of linguistic investigations into power, identify some of the main developments and pinpoint some of the key players. The unit also offers an opportunity to firm up some of the ideas touched upon in A1, notably the issue of how the beliefs and attitudes of the powerful can be represented as 'natural' or 'common sense'.

The approaches that will be described in this section are 'critical' because they focus on the social and ideological functions of language in producing, reproducing or changing social structures, relations and identities. This approach to discourse has its roots in the movement known as 'Critical Linguistics' (henceforth CL) and is now mainly associated with what has become known as Critical Discourse Analysis (henceforth CDA). Both traditions are pre-eminently concerned with the linguistic realizations of power. Before you explore some of the methods for a critical analysis of discourse in C1 the following overview should give you an idea of some of the main theoretical mainstays of the 'critical' view of discourse, power and ideology.

Critical Linguistics

The term 'critical linguistics' was coined in the late 1970s by Roger Fowler and his colleagues at the University of East Anglia in the UK, and the spirit of what was then a new and challenging approach to the study of language is captured in their seminal publication *Language and Control* (see Fowler *et al.* 1979; and see D1). Generally seen as the precursor of Critical Discourse Analysis, CL set out to demonstrate that grammatical and semantic forms can be used as ideological instruments to make meaning in texts and to categorize and classify things, people and events. An early example of work in this area was Trew's study of print media (in Fowler *et al.* 1979) where he compared headlines from different British newspapers that covered the same event of civil disorder in pre-Independence Rhodesia. Trew attempted to show that the choice of certain linguistic devices in accounts of a particular action (e.g. choosing the passive rather than the active voice) could affect the meaning and force of the text as a whole. Therefore, and in the manner suggested by the examples at the end of unit A1, linguistic analysis could expose the potential ideological significance of using agentless passives rather than opting for other constructions in which agents are explicitly stated. For example, Trew discusses in detail (1979: 94) the implications of one of the newspaper headlines: *Rioting Blacks Shot Dead by Police as ANC Leaders Meet*. Here, 'Blacks' are classified as rioters and put in sentence-initial position, while the actions of the police, who are in fact responsible for the killing, are de-emphasized by the passive construction such that the apportioning of blame is affected. By contrast, the structure of the headline in another paper, *Police Shoot 11 Dead in Salisbury Riot*, effectively does the reverse: that is, the police become sentence-initial and acquire a focal prominence absent in the other paper, while the phrase 'rioting blacks' is transformed into a numeral which is expanded in subsequent text to 'Eleven African Demonstrators'. In sum, Trew suggests that linguistic structure has an important effect on the slant given to the story, a slant which it is argued can be aligned with the ideological orientation of the two papers.

One possible limitation of CL, expressed by Fairclough (1992), is that the interconnectedness of language, power and ideology has been too narrowly conceived. Clearly, while the features of grammar, semantics and vocabulary that fall within the normal purview of CL may have ideological significance, other larger structures, such as the whole argumentative and narrative fabric of a text, are significant as well. The early critical linguists have also been criticized for their tendency to see texts as products and for their giving only scant attention to the processes of producing and interpreting texts, or to the possibility that texts can have different meanings to different groups of readers. Nonetheless, CL's development of a theory of language as a social practice, where 'the rules and norms that govern linguistic behaviour have a social function, origin and meaning' (Hodge and Kress 1993: 204) has had a profound influence on much subsequent research, and particularly on scholars working within CDA (see below). The reading for this Strand (D1) is, appropriately, an example of writing from the formative years of CL.

Critical Discourse Analysis (CDA)

Probably the most comprehensive attempt to develop a theory of the interconnectedness of discourse, power, ideology and social structure can be found in the large and loosely grouped body of work collectively referred to as Critical Discourse Analysis. CDA criticizes mainstream linguistic approaches 'for taking conventions and practices at face value, as objects to be described in a way which obscures their political and ideological investment' (Fairclough 1992: 7). CDA also incorporates social-theoretical insights into discourse analysis and its practitioners are often outspoken about their social commitment and interventionist intentions.

Although often associated with the work of Norman Fairclough, Ruth Wodak and Teun van Dijk, there is no single, homogeneous version of CDA (as critical discourse analysts themselves often point out) but a whole range of critical approaches that can be classified as CDA (e.g. Gee 1990, 2001; Scollon 1998; Rogers 2004; Richardson 2007). Common to all these approaches, and echoing the position adopted in unit A1, is the view of language as a means of social construction: language both *shapes* and *is shaped by* society.

But why *Critical* Discourse Analysis?

The word 'critical' signals a departure from the more descriptive goals of discourse analysis where the focus has been more on describing and detailing linguistic features than about *why* and *how* these features are produced. A critical approach to discourse typically analyses news texts, advertisements, political interviews and speeches, doctor–patient interactions, counselling sessions, job interviews or other so-called 'unequal encounters'. These encounters often employ linguistic strategies that appear normal or neutral on the surface; strategies that are *naturalized* but that may in fact be ideologically invested (see further below). The term 'critical' therefore principally means unravelling or 'denaturalizing' ideologies expressed in discourse and revealing how power structures are constructed in and through discourse.

Fairclough sums up the idea of 'critical' language study as follows:

> Critical is used in the special sense of aiming to show connections which may be hidden from people – such as the connections between language, power and ideology … Critical language study analyses social interactions in a way which focuses upon their linguistic elements, and which sets out to show up their generally hidden determinants in the system of social relationships, as well as hidden effects they may have upon that system.
>
> (Fairclough 1989: 5)

Indeed, it is our contention that the term 'critical' is itself open to critique, and as this book develops we suggest ways in which we might interrogate, in a more self-reflexive way, our own position in relation to the discourses we analyse.

CDA's main principles

In a seminal paper, Fairclough and Wodak (1997) outline eight key theoretical and methodological principles of CDA. Below, we summarize these principles as a series of bullet points and, where useful, offer a short gloss expanding the general gist of each.

❑ *CDA addresses social problems* CDA is cast here not as a dispassionate and objective social science, but as engaged and committed; it is also seen as a form of intervention in social practice and social relationships (Fairclough and Wodak 1997: 258). Fairclough and Wodak go further, arguing that many analysts are politically active against racism, or as feminists, or within the peace movement and that what is distinctive about CDA is that it intervenes on the side of dominated and oppressed groups and against dominating groups, and that it openly declares the emancipatory interests that motivate it.

❑ *Power relations are discursive* This means that the primary focus is on how power relations are exercised and negotiated in discourse (Fairclough and Wodak 1997: 258).

❑ *Discourse constitutes society and culture* This is the commonly adopted position that language both reflects and (re)produces social relations in a two-way relationship: 'every instance of language use makes its own contribution to reproducing and/or transforming society and culture, including power relations' (Fairclough and Wodak 1997: 273).

❑ *Discourse does ideological work* This principle is expanded to mean that ideologies are particular ways of representing and constructing society that reproduce 'unequal relations of power, relations of domination and exploitation' (Fairclough and Wodak 1997: 273). When critical discourse analysts (particularly Fairclough) argue that texts are ideologically shaped by power relations they use the term ideology in the sense of *hegemony*, which, as we saw in A1, refers to control through the active *consent* of people rather than through domination.

❑ *Discourse is intertextual/historical* This is the claim that discourse must always be analysed *in context* in order to be understood. Context includes socio-cultural knowledge as well as *intertextuality*. The concept of intertextuality refers to the way discourses are 'always connected to other discourses which were produced earlier as well as those which are produced synchronically or subsequently' (Fairclough and Wodak 1997: 276). Examples of intertextuality would be direct and indirect quotes in, for example, newspaper articles or political speeches that may relate to other speeches or may be turned into a news story. Intertextuality also applies to texts that contain allusions to previous texts, such as the use of proverbs, biblical or literary references, idioms and so on, and where the understanding of which depends on certain intertextual knowledge on the part of the listener or reader.

❑ **The link between text and society is indirect or 'mediated'** CDA attempts to show the connection between properties of text on the one hand, and social and cultural structures and processes on the other. The link between text and society is generally understood as mediated through *orders of discourse* which is Foucault's all-encompassing term covering a range of institutional discourse practices. For instance, the order of discourse that organizes, say, a university will be characterized by a host of interrelated textual practices such as the discourses of essays, meetings, lectures, seminars, administrative texts and so on.

❑ **Discourse analysis is interpretative and explanatory** CDA typically distinguishes three stages of critical analysis: description, interpretation and explanation (see further below).

❑ **Discourse is a form of social action or social practice** CDA in this mode is intended to be 'a socially committed scientific paradigm' (Fairclough and Wodak 1997: 280). One application of this principle has been the production, following linguistic research, of guidelines for certain communication and behaviour patterns, such as the use of non-sexist or non-racist language. The intended outcome of CDA is therefore a change in discourse and power patterns in certain institutions. For example, van Dijk's discovery of potentially racist language in Dutch schoolbooks led directly to the production of new teaching materials (van Dijk 1993a). As these eight key principles show, CDA has a clear concern about the exercise of power in social relations, including gender and race.

In the years since its inception and establishment CDA has developed to account for ideologies that are transmitted through a range of discourse media. *Multimodal CDA* addresses visual and celluloid texts, offering methodologies to analyse the whole range of discourses that are prominent in contemporary society, such as visual journalism (Machin and Polzer 2015) and so-called factual television (Machin and Mayr 2013).

CDA has drawn some criticism, with detractors (Widdowson 2004; Poole 2010) having expressed doubt about the depth of CDA analysis and reservations about the selectivity and partiality of the data chosen for analysis. In response, CDA scholars have sought to place the discipline on firmer ground by embracing corpus linguistic techniques to ensure the representativeness of data. Statham (2016), for example, establishes that newspaper articles critically analysed for their ideological construction of certain crimes are representative of the media in general. Statham prefaces qualitative CDA investigations with a quantitative corpus exercise employing the newspaper resource Nexis UK.

Fairclough's three-dimensional model of discourse

An important approach in CDA is Fairclough's three-tiered model for the analysis of discourse (1992, 1995a) which is designed as an important first step towards the analysis of language and power in different types of text. The model conceives discourse as *text*, written or spoken, as *discourse practice* and as *social practice*. In other words, Fairclough's framework explores not only the text itself but also its production and interpretation within a larger social context. Therefore, any discursive 'event' (i.e. any instance of discourse) is simultaneously a three-dimensional phenomenon: it is a piece of spoken or written text, an instance of discourse practice and an instance of social practice. The interconnections between the elements in Fairclough's framework are summarized in Figure B1.1.

The 'text' dimension involves the analysis of the language of the texts, and includes such features as:

- ❏ choices and patterns in vocabulary (e.g. wording and metaphor)
- ❏ grammar (e.g. the use of passive verbs as opposed to active structures in news reports; the use of modal verbs)
- ❏ cohesion (e.g. conjunctions; the use of synonyms and antonyms) and text structure (e.g. turn-taking in spoken interaction).

The 'discourse practice' dimension specifies the nature of text production, distribution and consumption in society. Looking at discourse in terms of discourse practice means that in analysing vocabulary, grammar and text structure, attention should be paid to intertextuality (see above) because this is an aspect of discourse that links a text to

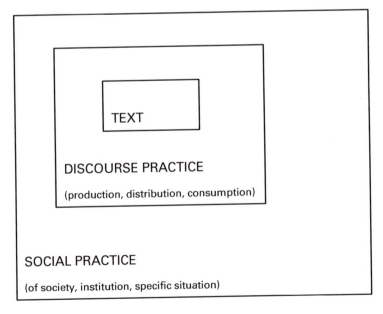

Figure B1.1 A three-dimensional model of discourse (adapted from Fairclough 1992: 73)

its context. Fairclough distinguishes further between types of intertextuality. *Manifest intertextuality* is overtly drawing upon other texts, such as quoting other people or organizations; *interdiscursivity*, by contrast, is when texts are made up of heterogeneous elements or various discourse types, such as a mix of formal and informal language in a newspaper article.

Finally, the 'social practice' dimension of the model deals with issues important for social analysis, such as the power relations and ideological struggles that discourses (re)produce, challenge or transform in some way. Fairclough borrows Gramsci's concept of *hegemony* (1971) (see A1), which is not simply about dominating subordinate groups but rather about integrating them through their consent to the moral, political and cultural values of the dominant groups.

Fairclough's model of discourse is built on his view of ideological processes in society, for discourse is seen in terms of processes of and changes in hegemony. He has identified a number of hegemonic processes, which he sees as indicative of wider changes in discourse practices or in orders of discourse (see above) in society. In general, these developments characterize ways in which discourse genres from one sphere of life have come to influence others. Two such processes are especially important: the *conversationalization* and the *commodification* of discourse. With respect to the first of these, the language of advertising, for example, has become increasingly conversational in its attempt to establish a personal relationship with customers:

'Have YOU tried the only razor with a precision trimmer?'

Here the reader is addressed personally as if on an individual basis. Similarly, the conversationalization or apparent 'democratization' of discourse is apparent in a great many institutions. It involves the reduction of overt power asymmetries between people of unequal institutional power (such as that between teachers and students, employers and workers, doctors and patients, counsellors and 'clients') and the transformation of these asymmetries into more covert forms. Another example would be recent political speeches and interviews, which are now often characterized by a casual manner, colloquial speech forms, and informal forms of address (see, for example, Fairclough and Mauranen 2003; see also B3 below).

With respect to the second type of process, the 'commodification' or 'marketization' of discourse has particularly affected, for example, British universities and other higher education institutions as a result of externally exposed market conditions. The design of university prospectuses can be said to reflect these pressures on universities to 'sell' their courses, using discourse techniques borrowed from advertising, so that the boundaries between information ('The University was founded in 1900 and currently has 15,000 students') and persuasion ('The University is set in a *beautiful* 200 acre parkland campus'; 'Graduates of the University are *greatly in demand by employers*') are blurred. This inevitably results in a more 'consumer-oriented' relationship between students and universities (see further Strand 9, particularly the exercise in C9).

The text cannot be satisfactorily analysed without analysing the other two dimensions, discourse practice and social practice. Every text is thus an instance of discourse and social practice, such that a method of analysis will include:

- a linguistic description of the text
- an interpretation of the relationship between the discourse processes and the text
- an explanation of the relationship between the discourse processes and the social processes.

Naturalization and 'common sense'

A common theme running through much work on language and power is the understanding that the linguistic structure of a text often works 'silently' or 'invisibly' to reproduce relationships of power and dominance. In consequence, the processor of a text – such as the reader of a tabloid newspaper, for example – is encouraged to see the world in particular ways, and in ways that are often aligned with the dominant or mainstream ideology espoused by the paper. Crucially, these ideological assumptions are transmitted surreptitiously, and are mediated through forms of language that present as 'natural' or 'common sense' certain beliefs and values that may prove to be highly contestable or dubious in their own terms.

Consider the following discourse event that unfolded over a few months some years ago in the British tabloid newspaper the *Sun*. This popular daily voiced vehement opposition to the British government's plans to celebrate the advent of the millennium by the construction, at taxpayers' expense, of a festival dome (now the O2 Arena) in Greenwich, London. Notice how in these extracts the paper sometimes uses italicization to enforce the common-sense status of its position on the 'Millennium Experience':

> The *Sun* Speaks Its Mind: DUMP THE DOME, TONY! (17/6/97)
> MPS, businessmen and charities yesterday backed our *see-sense campaign* to axe the £800 million Millennium Exhibition planned for Greenwich. (18/6/97)
> That damned Dome has disaster written all over it. The creative director accuses the Dome secretary … of acting like a dictator who is too easily swayed by public opinion. If only he was. Maybe then this waste of public money would be axed. *For that's what public opinion wants.* (12/1/98)
>
> (original emphasis)

An appeal to 'common-sense values' of the sort displayed here allows the paper to present its objection to the dome as a position with which any sensible member of society could concur. (Notice how the paper foregrounds these values through italicization.) The paper's tactic is a good example of *naturalization* in the sense we intend in this book because it captures the process whereby an ideological position is presented as if it were simply part of the natural order of things. Naturalization encourages us to align ourselves with mainstream or dominant thinking, even when that thinking is itself partisan, self-serving and driven by economic and political interests. Indeed, to demur from the *Sun*'s position would be to place oneself outside the community of notional sensible subjects who share the same set of normative values as the paper. Yet if proof were needed of the partisan and capricious nature of such naturalized ideological positions in discourse, consider the following breath-taking 'U-turn' which appeared in the very same tabloid newspaper shortly after the publication of the diatribes above:

> The plans for the Millennium Experience are dazzling. If it all comes off, the Prime Minister's prediction will be correct: *the Dome will be a great advert for Britain.*

(24/2/98)

It may have been entirely coincidental that this sudden change in direction occurred on the same day that the paper's owner Rupert Murdoch pledged £12 million worth of sponsorship to the Millennium Dome.

Unit C1 comprises a systematic application of Fairclough's tripartite model to a newspaper article from another British tabloid.

REGISTERS OF DISCOURSE

B2

This unit introduces the important concept of *register*. It is a feature of many institutions and organizations that their presentation in the public domain is achieved discursively through fixed patterns of language and the purpose of this unit is to explore and to some extent challenge the ways in which institutions and organizations mediate power through these specialist registers. In C2, the theme is developed further with suggestions for practical work, while the Strand is rounded off with a reading by Sarangi and Slembrouck which explores the idea of bureaucracy and social control.

Registers

A *register* of discourse is a regular, fixed pattern of vocabulary and grammar. It is defined according to the *use* to which language is being put. In this respect, it can be distinguished from a *dialect*, the definition of which involves some account of the social and geographical characteristics of the language user. A register shows what a speaker or writer is doing with language at a given moment. Most of our current understanding of the concept of register comes through the tradition of *systemic-functional* linguistics inspired by Halliday and his co-researchers (see, for example, Halliday 1978, 1994; Eggins 2004; Thompson 1996; Martin *et al.* 1996). Because of its emphasis on language as a 'social semiotic', the Hallidayan model – as we signal throughout the B section of the book – has found much favour as a method of inquiry in both Critical Linguistics (CL) and Critical Discourse Analysis (CDA). Halliday conceives language in terms of the two axes of *system* and *function*. When moulded together, these concepts form his systemic-functional axiom; namely, that the *system* of language is shaped by the *function* it serves.

The language system is organized into and by three key functions, the core characteristics of which we present here briefly but which are expanded in later units as indicated. The *experiential* function is relayed through transitivity. It expresses the meaning of the clause as representation and encodes our patterns of experience into texts, whether spoken or written (see B4 below). The *interpersonal* function is relayed principally through polarity and modality. It shows how a clause is organized as an interactive event and how the meaning of the clause as exchange is mediated through the dynamic interplay of speech roles (see C1 and B8). The *textual* function is relayed principally through cohesion and discourse semantics. It accommodates the information-building and text-building properties of language, both inside and across sentence boundaries (see further B8).

The three contextual variables in register analysis are known as *field*, *tenor* and *mode*. Here are the three features summarized:

> *Field*: the topic, setting and purpose of the interaction
> *Tenor*: the relationship between the participants in interaction
> *Mode*: the medium of communication (that is, whether it is spoken, written or relayed visually)

Each of the three functions informs an associated register variable. Thus, the experiential function determines field of discourse, the interpersonal function determines tenor of discourse and the textual function determines mode of discourse.

Registers come in many forms and are embodied in many day-to-day routines and activities. For instance, we are confronted with a register every time we read a cookery recipe, read the terms and conditions for a new piece of software or write an essay on English Language. All of these situations involve some exposure to and use of a specialized variety of language.

In the systemic-functional model there is a yet higher unit, known as *genre*, which subsumes register in the hierarchy of discourse. The distinction between a register and a genre is not always clear-cut but basically a register is adapted to the context of situation while a genre is oriented towards context of culture. Genres are derived out of registers to accomplish culturally determined goals, to 'get things done' in Martin's terms (1985: 250). Thus, whereas the 'university essay' is a genre of discourse in the sense that it realizes a culturally determined linguistic activity, a *particular* university essay in, say, English Language, instantiates a register because its framework of reference is activated by a specific field of discourse within a given context of situation.

The concept of register therefore usefully links patterns in language to variations in situation, but what, in the context of our definitions above, does register variation have to do with the linguistic politics of power? A particular concern in research in CL and CDA is with the way powerful individuals and institutions have come to use, even to appropriate, particular registers of language. This is not to say for a moment that all registers are inherently sinister or ideologically insidious in some way. It would be unthinkable for a specialist activity *not* to involve a register – just imagine a surgeon performing a complex operation while wilfully refusing to use any specialist medical terms! Instead, what concerns us here is the way in which the language used by powerful individuals and institutions can be used to mask or to deceive. A register indicates a specialism or expertise of sorts, and perhaps, in cases like legal language, even prestige (see A7). And as our own day-to-day routines of language are largely unreflective, so the implicit agenda of many apparently innocuous registers can be absorbed without suspicion.

Let us focus on a particular example where unpalatable information has been distributed in the reassuring guise of a specialist register. In times of war and conflict, new registers of language are quietly disseminated through the print and broadcast media. The widespread deployment of nuclear weapons in the 1970s and 1980s, and its linguistic representation in the print and broadcast media, became the focus of an influential collection of essays edited by Paul Chilton (1985). Chilton's collection adapted the term 'Nukespeak', in a conscious nod towards Orwell's 'Newspeak', to refer to a (mis)use of register that masked what for the general public were unpleasant or problematic issues. Two contributors to the collection describe Nukespeak thus:

> In sociolinguistic terms, Nukespeak is a REGISTER: a specialized variety of usage with its own range of meanings and of contexts for use. It is a salient mode of discourse, for one of its principal functions is to adorn its users with the badge of expertise.
>
> (Fowler and Marshall 1985: 4; original emphasis)

Although very much of its time, the Nukespeak project was nonetheless a good example of an attempt by linguists to make an intervention, in this case an intervention against the backdrop of an alarming proliferation of weapons of mass destruction by Britain and the USA. What was of particular concern to the linguists was the way in which the various media institutions rallied unquestioningly behind the British and US governments. Voices objecting to the nuclear deployment were silenced, censored or vilified (Chilton 1985).

The use of register was of particular interest in the linguistic analysis of Nukespeak. Chilton sets the agenda thus:

> One method by which governments legitimise themselves and their policies is to create, through language and also through other semiotic means, a compatibility between policies and relatively stable stereotypes [that are] already present in traditional and popular culture.
>
> (Chilton 1985: xvii)

Thus, weapons of mass destruction were cast in popular lay terms, appealing to myth, stereotype and nationalism in the popular consciousness. Moss (1985: 52–53) notes, for instance, how justification for laser-guided bombs played to popular film culture: 'LASER – MAY THE FORCE BE WITH YOU' where *Star Wars* is the cultural vehicle used to make the connection. The naming of missile systems is also interesting. The *Pershing* missile takes its name from John Pershing, the famous American general who led the American Expeditionary Force during the First World War. (As Pershing died in 1948, we will never know whether he would have approved of the association.) The seaborne missile *Trident* owes its origins to mythology, as Poseidon's three-pronged spear, comfortably removed from any contemporary reality, while *Tomahawk* plays on America's frontier past where, as Moss (1985: 55) points out, lone strength and resilience were critical attributes. What is at issue here is simply that the powerful institutions that disseminate these terms in the reassuring guise of a specialist register encourage us to see the world in particular ways, and in the ways *they* want.

It is salutary to note that since its publication, the findings of the 'Nukespeak' contributors still reverberate in today's discourses of war. For instance, the phrase 'human assets' often replaces the more human(e?) term 'soldiers', while the 'reification of frontiers' refers to an invasion of someone else's country and 'collateral damage' helps get round the thorny problem of dead civilians. In his statement to the House of Commons calling for UK air strikes in Syria in November 2015, Prime Minister David Cameron spoke explicitly about the Brimstone missile system as enabling 'us to strike accurately with minimal collateral damage' and of Reaper drones having 'low collateral, high precision missile systems'. In its echo of a lurid medical condition, 'incontinent ordnance' covers the problem of missiles that are somewhat less precise, while 'human remains transportation pods' – 'body bags' in short – is the rather more sanitized label for something the very sight of which makes many of us wince. So-called 'friendly fire' is a tortuous contradiction in terms, while, almost laughably, the phrase 'advanced marine biological systems' refers to trained missile-carrying dolphins, whose role was reassuringly downgraded to defence duties during the Allies' invasion of Iraq in 2003. With the new context of the so-called 'Global War on Terror' comes new items of nukespeak, 'extraordinary rendition' refers to the kidnapping and transporting of people to 'black sites' – countries with less stringent human rights legislation – where they are exposed to methods of 'enhanced interrogation', better known as torture.

Let us conclude this unit with a longer text that pre-dates anything considered thus far in terms of the way register and power interlock. Withholding for the moment its original context, here is part of a seemingly rather innocuous report on vehicle maintenance:

Modifications to Vehicles in Service:
In the light of observations, the following technical changes are needed:
1 The normal load is nine per square metre. In Saurer vehicles, which are very spacious, loading to full capacity would affect the vehicle's stability. A reduction in capacity seems necessary, rather than, as hitherto, reducing the number of items loaded.
2 Bulbs must be caged to prevent them being damaged. It has been observed that when the doors are closed, the merchandise presses hard against them. Light would therefore be useful both before and during the first few minutes of operation.
3 For easy cleaning of the vehicle, there must be a covered drain in the middle of the floor. The diameter should be between 200mm and 300mm. It should be a drain for liquids to escape during the operation.

Beneath this ostensibly bland and unassuming technical register is an agenda so appalling that it makes this the most disturbing piece of text imaginable. On the face of it, the text bears all the trappings of the formal technical register. It abounds in technical and technically related vocabulary ('diameter', '200mm', 'a reduction in capacity' and so on). Many of its sentences ('It has been observed …', 'Bulbs must be caged …' and so on) are cast in the passive voice (see unit B4, and elsewhere) one function of which is, as is the norm in technical registers, to render the text 'anonymous' by removing personalized reference to the writer. Related to this is the use of nominalization (A1) where processes are converted to nouns, as in 'loading', 'reduction' or 'cleaning'. Again, this type of grammatical operation removes from the process the individual responsible for engendering that process.

However, only when its full context is revealed does the true horror of this piece of writing become apparent. This text is part of a communiqué sent by Saurer Vehicles (Berlin) to SS-Obersturmbannführer Walter Rauff on 5 June 1942 (see Lanzmann 1985). In the early days of 'the final solution', this text reports a test run in genocide, where a prototype van has been specially designed to pump poisonous exhaust fumes into the rear of the vehicle. With that context, the unassuming, even turgid style is clearly designed to disguise its grotesque, ghoulish portent. By now, readers will, we assume, have worked out the true referent of the generalized nouns such as 'load', 'items' and 'merchandise', just as the significance of the processes described will have become transparent. It is worth adding that prior to the particular section cited here, the text's invisible author carefully notes that '97,000 units' had been processed 'with no major incident'. With no major incident.

What we have tried to underscore in this unit is that because socially powerful forces are able to shape and influence language practices, critical linguists will continue to explore the widespread interconnections between register and power. Some years ago, an official report into English language teaching in Britain observed that 'the working of a democracy depends on the discriminating use of language on the part of all its people' (DES 1988). In this respect, exploring the way registers are used is empowering because to see through language is, as it were, to see language for what it is. We reiterate again that registers of language are not of themselves insidious, sinister or malevolent; but in the hands of powerful interested groups the linguistic patterns encoded in a text encourage us to see the world in particular ways, and in ways that do not necessarily accord with our perspectives in and on society.

STUDYING SPOKEN DISCOURSE   B3

In this unit, we offer an overview of Conversation Analysis (CA), another major paradigm for analysing talk-in-interaction. Unlike Critical Discourse Analysis (CDA), CA argues that interaction is best studied at the micro-level, that is, by analysing the smallest details of talk without paying too much attention to the institutional context in which the interaction takes place. CA emerged in the 1960s and 1970s in the work of American sociologists Sacks, Schegloff and Jefferson (1974). Inspired by Goffman's suggestion (1959) that sociology should pay more attention to the logic of mundane social interaction than to grand 'rules' that govern social behaviour, these sociologists approached everyday talk as an important instrument for the organization of social life. CA has been used for the qualitative analysis of both informal and institutional conversation rather than written text. It is also 'data-centred' in the sense that it does not look for evidence that is not in the talk itself. CA therefore does not begin with theoretical assumptions or frameworks, but proceeds as an attempt to understand inter-action as it makes sense to those involved. This makes CA a rather different approach from CDA, where verbal behaviour is related to the setting in which it occurs and who the speakers are. CA in its 'pure' version adheres to the principle that analysts should not use information that has not been made relevant by the speakers themselves. This is because CA has its roots in *ethnomethodology* which means literally 'the study of people's methods'. This is a sociological method of enquiry that, unlike other schools of thought in sociology, such as structural functionalism or Marxism, avoids making claims about the character of social life and investigates instead how social phenomena are achieved in local environments of action. According to ethnomethodology, social order is not created by abstract structures, but by people in their everyday lives. The social context of talk, such as the gender of the participant for example, is only relevant to the understanding of the interaction if the participants make it relevant; that is, if they talk as if they are gendered in particular ways.

News interviews

CA research has focused on how routine institutionalized speaking practices enable and constrain programme participants in their tasks and objectives. CA studies of broadcast talk focus on 'the locally produced orderliness' (Greatbach 1998: 164) of news interviews, but also on departures from this conformity to interview conventions.

Greatbach (1998: 167) describes the differences between media interviews and ordi-nary conversation, where the expected role of the interviewer in the UK is not to take sides or give opinions but to take a 'neutralistic stance'. 'Neutralistic' means that the interviewer's conduct should be beyond formal charges of bias. This does not mean that s/he can never be accused of bias, even though s/he does not express a personal opinion. Aggressive and hostile questioning in particular may be taken as bias on the part of the interviewer.

Media interviewers gain their power to ask questions as representatives of the news organization, not as individuals. If they produce statements they must distance them-selves from them by attributing them to others. Greatbach (1998: 167) also observes that interviewers do not affiliate or disaffiliate with interviewees. They avoid 'acknowl-edgment tokens' such as 'mmh', 'uh uh' or 'really', which in ordinary conversation fill pauses and offer 'backchannels'. Interviewers fill pauses with new questions, which in ordinary conversation would be strange, suggesting the other person is not paying close attention. All these strategies serve to maintain a neutralistic stance. Importantly, the ability of the interviewer to occupy this position depends in part on the co-opera-tion of the interviewee, who may of course challenge it.

The linguistic style of interviewers over the years has changed from the deferential to the critical. There are examples where interviewers have asked the same question over and over again to get an answer and occasions when interviewees have walked off in protest. Clayman and Heritage point out that both 'conversationalization' and what Tannen (1998) has termed 'argument culture' are in part responsible for 'a mas-sive reduction in the social distance between politicians and journalists and, through them, the public' (2002: 339) (see further Strand 10). This means that politicians have become far more accountable than they used to be. At the same time, interviewees, particularly politicians, have developed strategies to resist the interviewer's agenda.

One of the most infamous examples of this is the 1997 interview by Jeremy Paxman of the then U.K. Home Secretary Michael Howard on BBC's *Newsnight* programme. In this interview, Paxman, who was known for his abrasive interviewing style, challenged the account Howard had given to Parliament of a dispute between him and the head of the prison service. Paxman, overstepping his powers to some extent, asked Howard 13 times whether he had threatened to overrule the head of the prison service, to which Howard gave only evasive replies. The interview received much media coverage and arguably dented the political ambitions of Michael Howard, who lost his bid for the leadership of the Conservative party. Although he did ascend to this position later, his party lost the General Election of 1997, paving the way for the rise of New Labour under Tony Blair.

Here we will focus on another BBC *Newsnight* interview involving the same presenter, Jeremy Paxman. This is a video-linked interchange with George Galloway just after his election victory in May 2005 over Labour's Oona King in the London borough of Bethnal Green and Bow. The exchange offers an excellent example of interviewee resistance, with the interviewee avoiding and changing the topic, using evasive tactics and finally walking off the set.

Extract 1

JP:	1	We're joined now er from his count in er Bethnal Green and Bow by George Galloway. Mr Galloway, are you proud of having got rid of one of the very few black women in Parliament?
GG:	2	What a preposterous question. I know it's very late in the night, but wouldn't you be better by c- starting by congratulating me for one of the most sensational election results in modern history?
JP:	3	Are you proud of having got rid of one of the very few black women [in Parliament?]
GG:	4	[I'm not] – Jeremy – move on to your next question.
JP:	5	You're not answering that one.
GG:	6	No because I don't believe that people get elected because of the colour of their skin. I believe people get elected because of their record and because of their policies. So move on to your next question.

Paxman starts off with a customarily abrasive line of questioning, in which he implicitly accuses Galloway of underhand tactics, if not racism. Galloway is in a double bind: he cannot say 'yes' because that would confirm the presupposition that his was unacceptable behaviour yet he cannot reply with 'no', because that would still imply that he has got rid of a black woman in Parliament (see B7 on presupposition). So Galloway rejects the question with a negatively evaluative comment ('What a preposterous question') and follows it up with a suggestion, a negatively worded question in fact, that Paxman should rather congratulate him on his election victory ('… wouldn't you be better by c- starting by congratulating me …'). Negative formulations of questions like this are usually a resource for hostile questioning of the interviewer because they are 'so severely framed in favour of a particular kind of answer that they are frequently treated as an opinion statement' (Clayman and Heritage 2002: 217–218). Here though it is Galloway who uses this tactic.

Paxman in turn ignores the negative formulation and pursues his original question which Galloway sidesteps, again replying 'I'm not', meaning 'I'm not going to reply to your question' and then tells Paxman to move on to the next question. This use of the imperative is significant because Galloway clearly sees himself as the conversational (and institutional) equal of Paxman. This then leads to an accusation by Paxman ('You're not answering that one'), which looks like a statement, but is more a question. Galloway just confirms with a 'no' that he is not answering the question but then provides a 'justificatory account' (Clayman and Heritage 2002: 264) of why he refuses to answer the question: '… because I don't believe that people get elected because of the colour of their skin …'. Clayman and Heritage note that of all forms of interviewee resistance, 'blanket refusals to answer constitute perhaps the strongest "breach of contract" in an interview'. So far in the exchange the two speakers have only given what in CA are called 'dispreferred responses' to each other. These responses can be broadly divided into supporting and confronting. A supporting response would be answering a question or acknowledging what another speaker has said, thereby implying consensus; replying to a question with a counter-question or as in the interview above, with a reply that disclaims the authority of the question ('What a preposterous question!') is a confronting response, indicating resistance.

The 'interview' continues thus:

Extract 2

JP:	**7**	Are you [proud] –
GG:	**8**	[Because] I've got a lot of people who want to speak to me.
JP:	**9**	I-phew- [You] –
GG:	**10**	[If] you ask that question again, I'm going, I warn you now {*points finger at Paxman*}
JP:	**11**	Don't try and threaten me Mr Galloway [please].
GG:	**12**	[You're the one you're the one who's trying to badger me =
JP:	**13**	= I'm not trying to badger you, I'm merely [GG: ?] trying to ask if you're proud at having driven out of Parliament one of the very few black women there, a woman you accused of having on her conscience the deaths of 100,000 people.
GG:	**14**	Oh well there's no doubt about that one. There's absolutely no doubt that all those New Labour MPs who voted for Mr Blair and Mr Bush's war have on their hands the blood of 100,000 people in Iraq, many of them British soldiers, many of them American soldiers, most of them Iraqis and that's a more important issue [JP: absolutely] than the colour of her skin.
JP:	**15**	Absolutely, because you then went on to say including a lot of women who had blacker faces than her
GG:	**16**	Absolutely, absolutely
[…]		
JP:	**29**	Right, Tony Banks was sitting here five minutes ago, and he said that you were behaving inexcusably you had deliberately [GG: well] chosen to go to that part of London and to exploit the latent racial tensions there.
GG:	**30**	Wh -You are actually conducting one of the mo- - even by your standards one of the most absurd interviews I have ever participated in. I have just won an election. Can you find it within yourself to

recognize that fact? To recognize the fact that the people of Bethnal Green and Bow chose me this evening.

Paxman attempts to keep his superficially neutralistic stance throughout, a journalistic tactic described by Chilton (2004) as token adherence to a notional institutional code of neutrality. Paxman achieves this by distancing himself from evaluative judgements about Galloway by attributing them to others ('Right, Tony Banks … said that you were behaving inexcusably you had deliberately chosen to go to that part of London and to exploit the latent racial tensions there', turn 29). Galloway for his part not only successfully manages to avoid Paxman's central question ('Are you proud of …') by telling Paxman twice to move on to the next question (turns 4 and 6), but also to use the interview to his ends. He does so by embarking on a tirade against the Labour government for its involvement in the Iraq war in turn 14. He also successfully sidesteps all accusations made by Paxman about exploiting racial tension and making comments about Oona King that could be construed as racist ('a lot of women who had blacker faces than her', turn 15). Overall, Paxman does not manage topic control because that would mean getting his questions answered. On the contrary, Galloway hijacks the topic by deflecting the discussion away to suit his own agenda. In turn 30, in another evasive technique, Galloway makes a strong attack on Paxman's interviewing style by calling it 'absurd' and perhaps indirectly on Paxman's judgement and character. He thereby implies that Paxman is 'offering contentious statements of opinion rather than relevant "background information"' (Clayman and Heritage 2002: 140). Finally, the amount of overlaps and interruptions occurring in the interview also increases the confrontational nature of the exchange.

In TV and radio interviews, conflicts between interviewer and interviewee are usually ended by the interviewer, sometimes without reaching a consensus or resolution (Clayman and Heritage 2002). There certainly is no resolution in the interview above, and there is a battle for supremacy until the very end when Galloway is seen taking off the microphone to end the interview. Paxman retaliates by turning away from Galloway while he is still talking (although the audience can't hear him anymore) and addresses another person in the studio, with 'Alright David tell me what you think of Mr Galloway'.

So far we have seen that within the institutional context of the studio, interviewers have the power to set the agenda. Interviewees, on the other hand, derive most of their power from their social status as politicians and as other public figures and therefore can refuse to answer questions or use the interview to their own ends. In the Paxman–Galloway interview both sides had different but fairly well-balanced sources of power, which shows that politicians can easily dispute the agenda of the interviewer.

GENDER AND POWER: USING THE TRANSITIVITY MODEL   B4

In this unit we will introduce a particular linguistic model that has had an important bearing on the way gender issues in texts, especially in media discourse, have been explored and understood in critical linguistics. That said, we want to stress that many of the models introduced in these Section B units have a wider application beyond the specific theme of the Strand in which they appear. The model introduced here, *transitivity*, is a case in point and readers are asked to bear in mind its potential application across a range of themes to do with language and power.

Transitivity

Transitivity is concerned with the semantic structure of clauses and refers, broadly, to who does what to whom, and how. An analysis of transitivity therefore probes a clause to find out who are the actors, the acted upon and what processes are involved in that action. Deriving from the seminal work of M.A.K. Halliday (1994), transitivity in this sense transcends traditional grammatical approaches which distinguish between verbs that take objects ('John broke the vase') and verbs that do not ('Mary slept'). For Halliday, the grammar of a language is a system of 'options' from which speakers and writers choose according to social circumstances, with transitivity playing a key role in 'meaning making' in language. This means that the choice of certain linguistic forms always has significance, the roots of which are arguably often ideological. In media accounts of important political events, such as acts of civil disorder, the responsibility of authorities and police may be systematically backgrounded or omitted; simultaneously, as we saw in our brief discussion of the 'Rafah Incident' in A1, agency and responsibility for actions may be left implicit. News is simply not a reflection of reality, but a product shaped by political, economic and cultural forces. This makes transitivity analysis a powerful basis not only for analysing what is *in* texts, but also for analysing what is *absent* from them. A question Critical Discourse Analysis (CDA) often asks is why some information is omitted from a text, information that logically should have been there. In this respect, it is not surprising in the context of our observations in unit A4 that particularly productive applications of the transitivity model have been made to issues of gender in discourse.

When analysing agency (who does what to whom) and action (what gets done) we are interested in describing three aspects of meaning:

- ❑ participants (this includes both the 'doers' of the process as well as the 'done-tos' who are at the receiving end of action; participants may be people, things or abstract concepts)
- ❑ processes (represented by verbs and verbal groups)
- ❑ circumstances (adverbial groups or prepositional phrases, detailing where, when and how something has happened).

(after Halliday 1994)

For example, in the sentence

Soldiers killed three insurgents yesterday

the Actor element is the 'soldiers' who carry out the process of killing. The Goal is the 'three insurgents' who have been killed and the Circumstances are 'yesterday' which anchors the process in a temporal context. So in a Transitivity analysis we have first to identify the participants in a clause and then the process types used. Halliday distinguishes six process types: *material, mental, behavioural, verbal, relational* and *existential*. Let us now take a closer look at each of these in turn.

Material processes

Material processes describe processes of *doing*. Usually, these are concrete actions that have a material result or consequence, such as 'The soldiers <u>killed</u> three insurgents', although they may also represent abstract processes such as 'Prices <u>fell</u>' or metaphorical processes such as 'She <u>demolished</u> his theory'. The two key participants in material processes are the *Actor* and the *Goal*. The Actor is the part that performs the action and the Goal is the participant at whom the process is directed (the direct object in traditional grammar). Some material processes have one participant only, the Actor, as in '<u>The boys</u> ran away' or '<u>The temperature</u> rose'.

Mental processes

Mental processes are processes of *sensing* and can be divided into three classes: 'cognition' (verbs of thinking, knowing or understanding), 'affection' (verbs of liking, disliking or fearing) and 'perception' (verbs of seeing, hearing or perceiving). Examples of the three classes of cognition, affection and perception are, respectively: 'I <u>understood</u> the story', 'Peter <u>liked</u> the film a lot' and 'The soldier <u>saw</u> them'. The participant who thinks, feels or perceives in a mental process is called the *Senser*, and so is usually, but not always, a human being. Unlike material processes, mental processes always have two participants. So in addition to the Senser there is a *Phenomenon* which is the entity being sensed. The Phenomenon can be a conscious being, an object or an abstraction, although occasionally it represents a more complex process of its own, as in 'I like <u>eating my dinner early</u>' or 'He liked <u>the fact that they apologized</u>'.

Behavioural processes

Behavioural processes denote psychological or physical behaviour and are embodied in activities such as *watch, taste, stare, dream, breathe, cough, smile* and *laugh*. They are semantically 'in between' material and mental processes. For example, 'look at' and 'listen to' are behavioural processes, but 'see' and 'hear' are mental processes. Behavioural processes are also in part about action, but, unlike material processes, the action has to be experienced by a single conscious being, which is the participant known as the *Behaver*.

Verbal processes

Verbal processes are expounded by the verb of 'saying' and its many synonyms. A verbal process typically consists of three participants: *Sayer, Receiver* and *Verbiage*. The Sayer can be a human or human-like speaker, as in 'The teacher <u>explained</u> it again', but it can also be an inanimate item, as in 'The paper <u>says</u> it will rain'. The Receiver is the one at whom the verbal process is directed: 'They told <u>me</u> to leave at once', while the Verbiage is a nominalized statement of the verbal process: 'They gave me a <u>detailed account</u>' or 'I said <u>that this wasn't true</u>'.

Relational processes

These are processes that encode meanings about states of being, where things are stated to exist in relation to other things. A rather complex category, relational processes come in three main types: *intensive, possessive* and *circumstantial*. With an intensive relational process, there is a relationship of equivalence, 'x = y', as in 'The house is beautiful'. A possessive relational process expresses an 'x has y' relationship, as in 'Patricia has a Fiat coupé' or 'The bicycle is Andrea's'. Circumstantial relations are of an 'x is at/on/in/with y' type. Here, a feature that would normally be part of the circumstances becomes upgraded to that of a full participant in the process, as in 'The conference is <u>on all week</u>' or 'We were <u>in the house</u>'.

These relational processes construe the concept of 'being' in two different ways – through *attribution* and *identification*. Cutting across the three-way distinction drawn above, there is therefore a further two-way distinction in relational processes, with different participant roles relevant to each:

1   Attributive processes with the participant roles of *Carrier* and *Attribute*
2   Identifying processes with the participant roles of *Identified/Token* and *Identifier/ Value*

In type (1), the Carrier is always a noun or noun phrase while the Attribute expresses a quality, classification or a descriptive epithet. Here is an example from a newspaper story that we shall discuss in more detail later:

'The mother of abducted Shannon	is	Workshy' [Attributive]
Carrier	Pr: int.	Attribute

The essential characteristic of the Attributive intensive process is that it is *not* reversible, which means that the sequence of elements in the clause cannot be switched around. We could not therefore derive the following alternative from the above: 'Workshy is the mother of abducted Shannon'.

Identifying intensive processes contrast with the Attributive ones both semantically and grammatically. Semantically, an identifying clause is not about ascribing or classifying, but defining in such a way that *x serves to identify the meaning of y*. Grammatically, defining involves two participants, an *Identified/Token* (that which stands for what is being defined) and an *Identifier/Value* (that which defines). The most frequent identifying verb is *to be*, but synonyms such as *mean, define, symbolize, represent, stand for, refer to* and *exemplify* are also classed as relational processes. For example:

'Shannon Matthew's mum	is	one of many on benefits' [identifying]
Identified/Token	Pr: int.	Identifier/Value

In the clause above, *Shannon Matthew's mum* is identified as the 'holder' or 'occupant' of the identity or category. In Identifying clauses the Identified/Token and Identifier/ Value elements are realized by noun phrases and because these phrases represent two relatively autonomous participants, all identifying clauses are reversible: 'One of many on benefits is Shannon Matthew's mum'.

Existential processes

Existential processes represent something that exists or happens, as in 'There was silence' or 'Has there been a phone call for me?' The word *there* has no representational function in this sense but is simply needed grammatically to supply the Subject element of the clause. It is different therefore from 'there' used as a circumstantial element: 'Where is my book? *There* on the table'. Existential processes typically use the verb 'to be' or synonyms such as 'exist', 'arise' or 'occur' and they only have one participant, the *Existent*, as in 'There was a party'. This participant, which is usually preceded by *there is/there are*, may be any kind of phenomenon. It often expounds an event in the form of a nominalized action: 'There was an assault'.

Of course, the processes and participant types outlined above have no particular ideological function out of context. However, things are very different when transitivity is embodied as discourse. For example, the relationship between Actor and Goal can be ideologically significant if agency is backgrounded through the use of the passive voice. In passives the position of these elements is reversed ('Three insurgents were killed by soldiers') and it even allows the Actor to be omitted completely ('Three insurgents were killed'). An even more 'remote' realization again is through the use of a one-participant process such as 'Three insurgents died' where the action appears to be self-engendered (see Simpson 1993: 92–95 for a fuller account of this special type of process).

As we have attempted to demonstrate, transitivity patterns, especially in the manipulation of agency at the grammatical level, can be significant in terms of the intersection between language and power. Another important transitivity feature is the use of nominalization, a feature touched upon in earlier units, where verbal processes are converted into nouns thus removing any explicit indicator of agency. Thus, in 'The *introduction* of variable tuition fees marked a new era in Higher Education provision', the Actor responsible (the government) is only implied. Elsewhere, relational processes ('be', 'have', 'represent', 'mark' and so on) are often used in discourse to present information as 'facts' as they suggest an unqualified sense of certainty. They are also very clear in apportioning blame and expressing explicit opinion, and as Conboy observes, can be 'a strong indicator of the position of a news institution' (2007: 52). We can see this in a headline from British tabloid *News of the World*, from a story in which a mother was alleged to have been complicit in her own daughter's kidnapping:

'Shannon Matthew's mum is a violent, foul-mouthed, chain-smoking, boozy slob'
(13 April 2008)

Here the Attributive relational process, where Ms Matthews is the Carrier and the remaining noun phrase the Attribute, passes harsh judgement on a woman who the paper deems has violated the consensus of the 'caring' mother. This is symptomatic of a broader political agenda in the popular press, which obsessively foregrounds women who do not conform to traditional notions of femininity or 'motherhood' (Jewkes 2011). In the following section, we will focus on precisely this issue by looking at the often stereotypical coverage of women (and to some extent men) in the popular press and we hope to illustrate how transitivity can play a part in the cultural patterning of such representations.

Transitivity and gender representation in the media

Feminist and critical linguists have been interested in the construction and proliferation of certain gendered discourses and ideologies in the media. It is probably fair to say that the press significantly contributes to gendered discourses. Most media organizations are still owned by men, journalists are overwhelmingly male and media discourse is still dominated by 'masculinist' concepts and practices (Page 2003). This clearly impacts on how men and women are represented in the media, in particular through features such as naming or labelling. In a key article in the British popular press, Clark (1992) examines both naming practices and transitivity patterns. She claims that naming is a powerful ideological tool because different names for an object represent different ways of perceiving it. By naming men and women in certain ways, powerful gender stereotypes are perpetuated. But alongside the powerful connotations these lexical items may have, transitivity also plays an important part in gendered representations. Clark investigated transitivity patterns in news coverage in the *Sun* of violent and sex crimes perpetrated against women. Focusing on press coverage from November 1986 to January 1987, she found that the paper often used linguistic patterns that suggested that women, even when they were victims of violent assaults, were partly to blame for what happened to them. Blame or lack of responsibility, emphasis or absence of a participant can all be encoded through choice of transitivity. Here is an example from the *Sun* given by Clark (1992: 213), where agency actually is made explicit:

Fiend rapes woman in a Big Mac bar (*Sun*, 27 November 1986)

This headline shows how language can be used to make it clear who is to blame for an act. The 'fiend' is shown as Actor acting upon the 'woman' who is the Goal. The way the participants are named ('fiend' versus 'woman') also leaves no doubt as to who is to blame for the crime.

However, according to Clark, more often than not the *Sun* employs several strategies to make blame less explicit, for example by making an attacker invisible and by blaming somebody else. Clark provides the following example from the *Sun* where this is the case:

Girl, 7, murdered while Mum drank at the pub
Little Nicola Spencer was strangled in her bedsit home – while her Mum was out drinking and playing pool in local pubs.

(*Sun*, 20 December 1986)

Both the headline and the sentence below it have two clauses, one describing the murder, the other stating what the mother was doing at the time of the daughter's killing, implying that she is not blameless in the girl's death. At the same time, the murderer is completely omitted (compare 'Girl, 7, murdered' against 'Man murdered girl, 7'). The only Actor here is the mother for whom the paper uses active material processes ('drank' and 'was out drinking' and 'playing pool'). The *Sun* therefore passes judgement on the mother's 'irresponsible' behaviour rather than on the murderer.

Clark also suggests that the *Sun* distinguishes 'fiend' attackers from 'non-fiends', as well as between 'genuine' victims and 'non-genuine' ones. For example, when a violent crime is committed against a 'respectable' or sexually unavailable victim, the perpetrators are usually labelled as 'fiends' or with words from the same lexical set such as 'beast' or 'monster'. This naming practice does not, however, obtain when the crime is committed against a victim named or deemed 'unrespectable'.

Let us consider two additional examples from the *Sun* that help underscore Clark's claims. The first is the headline and introductory text covering the 'House of Horrors' case in Austria in 2008, where a man imprisoned his teenage daughter for 24 years in the cellar of his house, fathering seven children by her.

Dungeon beast: My Story
'I lusted after my mother.'
Dungeon incest monster Josef Fritzl wanted to have sex with his own mother, it emerged yesterday.
Fritzl, 73, made a sickening confession to his lawyer as he tried to explain away his appalling crimes against his children.

(*Sun*, 9 May 2008)

This is a good example of Clark's concept of 'fiend naming' (1992: 224) where the criminal is referred to as a 'dungeon beast' and a 'dungeon incest monster'. We should not, however, be fooled by such seemingly strong censure because disapprobation through 'fiend naming', while apparently blaming attackers, also suggests that the attacker is so evil and so alien that he is utterly outside humankind and society. By positioning 'fiends' in this way, a discussion of why society produces men who commit violent acts against women and children becomes impossible. This demonizing of the attacker has, according to Cameron and Frazer (1987: 19), become a cultural stereotype, where male perpetrators of sexual violence are presented as fiends, monsters and maniacs – as anything but 'men'. A consequence of this dehumanizing strategy is that it shrouds those very aspects of the patriarchal system that need to be challenged. No 'real' man, it is implied, would be capable of such an act. The discourse constructions, such as those exposed by Clark, reverberate within society's conventional perception of sexual assault as so-called 'stranger rape', so established are the disconnected representations of rape peddled in media language. A British government report found in 2013 that there were around 85,000 victims of rape each year in the UK. Ninety percent of these victims knew their attackers (Statham 2016: 205).

A second example is drawn from an article about the British 'Suffolk Ripper' case, where a man killed five women within a short period of time in 2006. The women murdered worked as prostitutes and the following extract describes the situation of one of the five victims:

Tragic Mother
Anneli Alderton met her violent death after being sucked into a life of prostitution. The Ipswich-born 24-year-old's cravings were so bad that other hookers described her as 'crackhead Annie'. Tragic Annie, whose naked body was found dumped near Nacton, Suffolk, only began walking the streets of Ipswich in recent weeks.

(*Sun*, 13 December 2006)

As we can see, the victim is identified and named through a number of personal details: her name, age, appearance (the article shows a picture of her face and she is also described as a 'blonde'), and we also learn that she is a mother. According to Clark, personal details, instead of individualizing and personalizing victims, often just label them, and in doing so often create 'a voyeuristic rather than sympathetic reading of events' (1992: 222). Some of the labels used here appear to be sympathetic to the victim ('tragic mother' and 'tragic Annie'), but others focus on the fact that she was a drug addict ('crackhead Annie') and a prostitute, although she is not labelled in this way by the paper which only quotes 'other hookers' calling her a 'crackhead'. Looking at transitivity, she is cast as a victim ('… after *being sucked* into a life of prostitution') but the text also underscores her active role in it ('… *met* her violent death', '… *began walking* the streets') as if she was not completely blameless in her death.

Clark's original conclusion, which has resonance for this more contemporary case, was that 'under its veneer of moral indignation against fiends … the *Sun* helps to maintain the status quo' and also manipulates and shifts blame subtly on to the victims of violent sex crimes depending on how 'respectable' they are. Essentially extra-societal 'fiends' rape 'respectable' women and 'unrespectable' women are complicit in the attacks upon them. This ideological, discourse-constructed distinction continues to abound in contemporary media.

What our discussion of transitivity and naming patterns also hints at is that much media discourse is constructed around an 'essentialist' notion of women (Jewkes 2011). This is the notion that women are biologically predisposed to caring and nurturing and not to violence. Women who fail to conform to the cultural stereotypes of the maternal, caring and monogamous woman often face particularly vitriolic treatment by the popular press.

THE REPRESENTATION OF SOCIAL ACTORS

B5

As we pointed out in A5, research in media and critical discourse studies has reported on the often negative representations of ethnic minorities in the British national press, where these have been mainly represented in connection with crime, violence, social welfare and problematic immigration (Hartmann and Husband 1974; Murdock 1984; Gabrielatos and Baker 2008). And while this kind of open anti-immigration stance has also given way to more positive representations of multiculturalism and ethnic minorities (see, for example, Cottle 2000; Machin and Mayr 2007), a substantial body of research in CDA has demonstrated that media representation of ethnic minorities continues to delegitimize them by focusing on negative characteristics (e.g. Richardson 2014). A number of studies have identified a shift of racial discourses to so-called 'new' racism, which is predicated upon an assumed socio-cultural incompatibility rather than racial inferiority (see A5). The analysis of racism has also taken a visual turn, focusing on how language and image combine to make meaning (Richardson 2008). Before we discuss this research in more detail, we introduce the categories of a model for analysis that has proven especially useful in the study of discourses of racism. This model is known as *social actor analysis* (van Leeuwen, 1996, 2008).

Categories for social actor analysis

Van Leeuwen suggests two basic ways in which people can be categorized: *functional-ization* and *identification*. When 'functionalized', social actors are categorized in terms of their occupation or social activity, such as 'immigrant', 'asylum seeker' or 'community leader'. Here verbs that denote activities, 'immigrate', 'seek' and 'lead', have become fixed categories by being turned into nouns. It is also useful to ask which kinds of participants are individualized and which are collectivized in texts, as this can reveal which group is humanized. By contrast, 'identification' means that social actors are defined 'in terms of what they, more or less permanently, or unavoidably, are' (van Leeuwen 1996: 54).

Identification can be divided further into *classification*, *relational identification* and *physical identification*. When social actors are classified, their identity is defined through how a given society or institution normally differentiates between classes of people. They can be classified in terms of age, gender, provenance, class, race or religion (e.g. 'the 28-year-old Romanian'). Relational identification represents social actors in terms of their personal or kinship relations, as in 'aunt', 'brother', 'a mother of four' and so on. Finally, physical identification represents social actors in terms of their physical characteristics, providing them with a unique identity (e.g. 'dark-skinned'). *Aggregation* is another important social actor category. It means that participants are quantified and treated as statistics, such as in '200 Roma', which makes them look like a homogeneous group and also has a distancing effect. Social actors can also be represented through *nomination*, which is typically expressed through proper nouns. These can be formal (a surname with or without honorific title, 'Mr Smyth'), semi-formal (a surname and first name, 'Steve Smyth') or informal (with first name only, 'Steve').

As well as being *included*, social actors may also be *excluded* from texts; that is, they may not be named or mentioned at all, newspapers can include or exclude social actors to suit their interests and purposes in relation to the readers for whom they are intended. What is absent in a text is just as important as what is present.

Applying social actor analysis

We shall now examine these issues in more detail by summarizing some research that applies the social actor model. In an example of a *multimodal* CDA approach, Breazu and Machin (2018) analyse how Romanian newspapers cover the camp evictions and repatriation of Roma migrants from France. These evictions began in 2010 and continue to the time of writing. Breazu and Machin adopt the categories outlined above alongside other linguistic observations in order to distinguish how social actors are represented in text. Below we provide a general summary of their linguistic findings on the Romanian news article '"I cried with joy": The reaction of a French woman after a Roma camp was demolished' (*Jurnalul National* 09 August 2012), which should be read alongside the website materials that address the *Leicester Mercury*. The present section is particularly interested in the visual application of social actor analysis, which demonstrates that representational strategies are also used in images that accompany media texts. In C5 you have the opportunity to carry out a similar analysis of media images from another racially charged event.

Breazu and Machin (2018) report that the French government, in 2010, began a systematic process of camp dismantling and forced repatriation of Roma migrants to Romania and Bulgaria, practices that are ongoing (European Roma Rights Centre [ERRC] 2017). According to reports from the ERRC and Amnesty International, these evictions, which number between 10,000 and 20,000, have a negative effect on families and children, forcing them into constant re-location. There is extensive research pointing to how the Roma have been represented in various European media as a homogeneous and deviant group who do not conform to the values and practices of society at large (Erjaevec 2001; Richardson 2014). They are consistently attached to representations of illiteracy, crime, violence and corruption; representations which Richardson and O'Neill (2012) argue have been detrimental to social inclusion and integration. Breazu and Machin's study shows how representations of the Roma in the Romanian press serve quite specific ends, one of which is to justify the Romanian government's failure to gain access to what is known as the 'Schengen zone'. This zone was formed through a treaty signed by selected EU member states to guarantee free movement of people within the relevant area. Access is regulated such that applicant countries undergo an evaluation to assess whether they meet all conditions for joining the zone.

Breazu and Machin focus on textual components which are deleted, added or substituted. Their analysis demonstrates that events become recontextualized in the service of certain ideologies regarding the eviction and repatriation of Romanian migrants. The article 'I cried with joy' is framed in terms of the reactions of a French woman to the evictions of the Roma; the focus on reactions like this plays an important role in the overall evaluation of social actors as the reader is given access to the thoughts and emotions of chosen individuals. It is significant that the reader is not informed of the reactions and feelings of the Roma who are being evicted. Indeed 'tears of joy' might appear somewhat callous were equal salience given in the article to the role that Amnesty International (2012a, 2012b) say bulldozers and attack dogs play in these evictions. The Roma have neither Mental nor Verbal agency in this article, rather the discourse focuses on Material processes such as 'stealing' and 'making smoke', and Verbal processes such as 'threatening' or 'cursing'. These assigned processes seek to demonstrate how the Roma violate the norms and values of civilization and modernity. By contrast the Verbal processes assigned to the inhabitants and tenants collectively appear to be measured and civilized: they 'complained', 'set up an association', 'started a blog'. Through the use of these representational strategies, the locals become victims. For example, one resident was informally nominated as 'Melanie' and identified as 'a young lady' and a 'neighbour', and relationally identified as a 'mother-to-be'; the Roma on the other hand are impersonalized through categorization and collectivization: 'the Roma', '200 Roma', 'camp of Roma'. This collectivization and aggregation of the Roma operates to distance them from the reader.

We would now like to turn to multimodal social actor analysis of an image that accompanied this article, because visual application of this model can provide important clues about the representation of people and their actions in images. The picture is reproduced in Figure B5.1.

In this image neither the woman who cried for joy nor the locals are represented. This is an example of an archive image, ideologically selected by the newspaper sub-

Figure B5.1 *Jurnalul National*, 9 August 2012

editor to support the strategic constructions that are reinforced in the text. Breazu and Machin note that this particular image has been used and reused many times in the Romanian press, and that in fact it depicts Roma moving across the border from Hungary into Austria and Germany. Given that photographs are thought to represent reality and to bear witness to events however, readers may often mistakenly assume that they document incidents addressed in the articles that they accompany (Ledin & Machin 2017).

This photograph shows a group of four adults being moved along a road by a single police officer. The social actors are depicted in fairly typical tabloid representation of the Roma, who are dressed in colourful and mismatched attire. The lone police officer is anonymized, his back is turned on the viewer and we do not see his face. In terms of actions, there is absolutely no representation of the force and violence that human rights organizations claim are typical of these evictions. Instead, the image shows a policeman simply pointing the way. In this 'offer' image the Roma appear in a long shot and they do not make eye-contact with the viewer, dual strategies to distance social actors from the viewers to whom they are portrayed. Whilst the police officer is individualized and functionalized in this image, the Roma are collectivized and physically identified. In many media representations of immigration these visual social actor categories are used to support textual constructions that portray immigration as a 'problem of numbers', a photograph like this might be used to reinforce ideologies that are present in metaphorical constructions like 'waves of immigrants', 'tides of foreign workers' or 'invading groups of migrants'. A visual social actor analysis of this image contends that the newspaper is seeking to align the reader with French locals, who are represented in the accompanying text as victims of circumstances created by out-of-control numbers of Roma migrants. Newspaper texts like the one referred to here can play a considerable part in communicating discourses about a Roma 'problem' which clashes with the values of modern European societies. These representations might also serve to background solutions to the situation, such as exploring social policy which would help to integrate rather than problematize immigrant communities.

In C5 we present two photographs from a newspaper article that addresses race relations in the United States. Application of a multimodal social actor analysis can be used to reach a number of conclusions about the ideologies of this discourse.

B6 THE DISCOURSE OF HUMOUR AND IRONY

In this unit we intend to look more closely at the interconnections between humour and power, and explore some of the terms, categories and distinctions set up in unit A6. In particular, we want to develop some criteria for the analysis of irony in discourse, because this important pragmatic device has a profound influence on the way texts are both understood and intended to be understood. A text's potential to be read as ironic should, we believe, be a serious consideration in CL and CDA work, and we illustrate this by examining a short text in which irony is used to attack certain practices in the news media.

Irony in discourse

Irony is most commonly and straightforwardly defined as a form of language that means the opposite of what is asserted. This type of 'oppositional' irony is at the core of utterances like 'You're a fine friend!' when said to someone who has just let you down. This conception of irony is certainly a useful start, but it falls short in a number of respects given the broad range of strategies available for communicating irony in discourse. Consider the following three hypothetical utterances, spoken by someone during a thunderstorm:

(a) 'Nice day!'
(b) 'It seems to be raining'
(c) 'I just love good weather'

All three of these utterances are ironic in some sense, yet it is only in (a) that the speaker clearly means the opposite of what they say. The second example does not relay the opposite sense to what is uttered; it is just *less* than what the speaker thinks pertains to the context. Example (c) poses another problem for the traditional belief that irony is saying the opposite of what you believe. Here the speaker is saying something that they *do* believe to be true, so the irony resides more in a conceptual paradox between the speech act and its interaction with the physical conditions of the immediate interactive context.

The conception of irony is problematized further by another type of strategy that falls outside the pattern seen in examples (a)–(c). Consider this exchange:

(d)
A: I've had enough of this critical linguistics stuff.
B: *You've had enough!* How do you think I feel!

Here the proposition uttered by the first speaker is explicitly mentioned in the response by the second. The 'mention' version indicates that the previous utterance has been heard and understood, and that the hearer is expressing their immediate reaction to it. However, the status of the 'mentioned' proposition is not the same as when the proposition is used in a sincere way by speaker A. Speaker B's utterance is therefore an 'echoic mention' which is a type of irony in which the utterance echoes other utterances and forms of discourse (see Sperber and Wilson 1981: 303).

Unfortunately, the distinctions in irony drawn thus far still do not represent the full picture, and there are yet more forms in common usage that could be identified. However, to attempt such identification risks us becoming side-tracked into a comprehensive survey of ironic discourse, so we propose to keep matters simple here with the following set of definitions (after Simpson 2011: 36–40). These, more flexible, definitions subsume both types of ironic device addressed thus far, getting around the 'oppositeness' problems in (a)–(c) also, and we hope they constitute a relatively adaptable model of analysis.

Core definition:	*Irony is the perception of a conceptual paradox, planned or un-planned, between two dimensions of the same discursive event.*
Sub-definitions:	*Irony is a perceived conceptual space between what is asserted and what is meant.*
	Irony is a perceived mismatch between aspects of encyclopaedic knowledge and situational context (with respect to a particular discursive event).

We prefer the idea of a paradox in the definitions, rather than oppositeness, in order to accommodate all the examples (a)–(c). Similarly, the idea of a 'conceptual space' helps to reign in the 'echoic' form of irony as well – where the echoed form creates a space in meaning between it and the 'bona fide' use it echoes. We also emphasize the 'perception' of irony throughout the definitions: irony cannot work without some perception of it, and while much irony undoubtedly passes us by in everyday interaction, we also perceive irony that was not planned or intended (and see further below). This also signals that irony is to some extent *negotiable*, because we can claim an ironic intention even if a hearer does not identify one, or alternatively, we can rescind an ironic intention if we decide it doesn't suit or doesn't work.

In a study that draws in part on the 'echoic mention' idea of irony, Gavins and Simpson (2015) explore an allegedly racist insult that was directed by high-profile English professional footballer John Terry towards another player, Anton Ferdinand, during a televised match in October 2011. The substance of Terry's utterance, which included the noun phrase 'fucking black cunt', was found by a Chief Magistrate 'not to be racist', although the fact that these actual words were used was not in dispute. In defence of his position, the magistrate argued that Terry was merely repeating an allegation made to him, and dismissing it. Couched in linguistic terms, Terry was therefore *echoing* ironically an earlier accusation by Ferdinand; namely, that Terry had previously called him a black cunt. Terry therefore 'mentions' Ferdinand's purported accusation only to communicate his distance from it. The possibility that what Terry said 'was not intended as an insult, but rather as a challenge to what he believed had been said to him' (Gavins and Simpson 2015: 717–718) was enough to have him acquitted by the court of a racially aggravated public order offence. He was, however, later found guilty by the regulatory commission of the English Football Association of racially abusing Ferdinand and was banned for four matches and fined £220,000.

It should be pointed out that irony, and especially the principle of echoic mention, is central to the idea of parody. This genre works as a 'discourse of allusion' (Nash 1985: 100) because it plays off previous texts or more general characteristics of other genres of discourse. Once echoed, the stimulus text becomes part of a new discourse context so it no longer has the status it once had in its original context, and that is what often engenders parody's ironic humour. Register mixing or the embedding of different styles as burlesque (A6) are often the mainstay of political satire and other forms of social commentary that target institutions, discourse practices and figures of authority. Consider, for example, this short piece of satirical discourse, from British satirical magazine *Private Eye* (Figure B6.1). This piece of satirical writing appeared shortly after a time of catastrophic floods on the Indian subcontinent during the late summer of 1999, leading to the loss of thousands of lives in both Bangladesh and India. The text requires close scrutiny.

Although analysed in some detail by Simpson (2003: 97–108), it is worth indicating briefly how this text operates through both irony and incongruity, and what marks it out as a piece of satirical discourse. First of all, it is entirely fictional, and although it does play off certain genuine aspects of Indian culture (respectively the (then) new coalition government, hockey and Bollywood) it is not the case that there was, in that period, a train crash in London which killed forty people. However, what sets it apart from other types of fictional writing is its hybridity. It echoes, with its quasi-Gothic type font, the *Daily Telegraph* – that stalwart of the quality broadsheet tradition of British journalism. This is consolidated by the insertion of 'Delhi' for 'Daily' in the made-up masthead, a punning strategy (A6) which disjunctively allows the text to point simultaneously in different semantic directions.

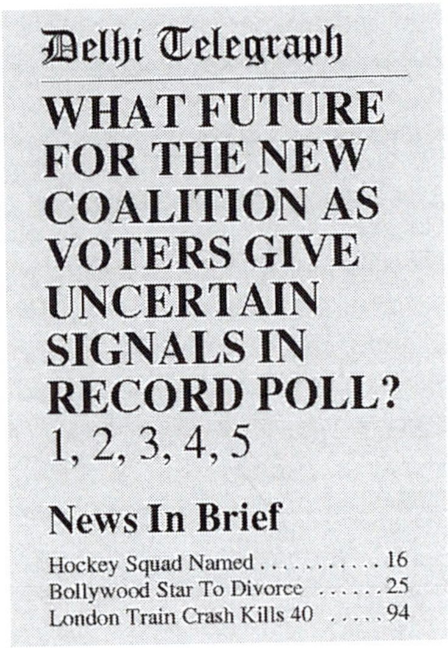

Delhi Telegraph

WHAT FUTURE FOR THE NEW COALITION AS VOTERS GIVE UNCERTAIN SIGNALS IN RECORD POLL?
1, 2, 3, 4, 5

News In Brief

Hockey Squad Named 16
Bollywood Star To Divorce 25
London Train Crash Kills 40 94

Figure B6.1 Extract from *Private Eye*, issue 987, 1999, p. 36

The seemingly throwaway content of the third of the 'news in brief' items, the fake report of the London train crash, is what creates a significant ironic mismatch. It does so because it holds a mirror up to the ways Western societies gather news stories, projecting how a hypothetically equivalent Indian print media might conduct a parallel news gathering exercise. Galtung and Ruge (1973) argue that what we choose as a news 'event' is strongly culturally determined. Most significant is the constraint that news communication is *elite-centred* in that the more a particular event concerns either an elite nation or an elite individual, the more likely it is to become a news item. In the *Private Eye* text, the hybridity that comes from the mixing of the 'Indian' strand with the British news tradition serves to turn the elite/non-elite distinction thoroughly on its head. Echoing the preoccupation with elitism, two of the 'news in brief' items lead with reports of events surrounding individual elites, promising stories about the national hockey squad and a Bollywood star. It is only once this context is established that the third item is delivered, with its (spurious) report of many deaths in the British capital, and even then it is purportedly shunted off to a distant page 94, well away from those concerning the individual elites. It is this seemingly sundry item of news about a calamity in a major world economy, portraying the British people in starkly non-elitist terms, that delivers the ironic jolt necessary to reappraise the status of the entire text as satire. The satirical 'point' of the text is to show a perceived iniquity in the way the Western media, with its tendency to upgrade trivia about elite individuals at the expense of the suffering of non-elite peoples, chooses what makes an important news story.

Private Eye (issue 1385, 2013) famously took a similar approach in its coverage of the birth in the UK of Prince George of Cambridge in July 2013. Whilst the mainstream British press reacted in a predictable clamour to the arrival of a new royal baby, the plain, picture-less front cover of *Private Eye* reported in mundane block capitals '**WOMAN HAS BABY**'. And to further satirize the fascination of non-elite readers with elite 'celebrities' in contemporary society, this headline was followed up in the next issue (1386, 2013) with the echoic headline 'Another Woman to Have a Baby' to report the announcement that American socialite Lauren Silverman was pregnant to well-known music mogul Simon Cowell. The similarity of the headlines comments not only upon a contemporary obsession with celebrities, but also that their elite 'newsworthiness' is not constrained by aspects of class or selectivity.

Irony, and sexist and racist humour

In unit A6, we remarked that issues to do with humour and irony have been largely ignored in CDA and this was a failing because it ignores a key aspect of a text's status as discourse. A penetrative analysis, which tackles irony head on, is Benwell's study of men's lifestyle magazines (2004 and see A4). Echoing implicitly our observations above on the negotiable status of irony, Benwell (2004: 7) talks of the value of irony as 'a strategic disclaimer' that can soften the contentious or less palatable views expressed in such publications. Furthermore, the discourse of 'new lad' masculinity is ambivalent and inscrutable, Benwell suggests, because the ironic framework through which it is mediated allows a deferral of both authority and attribution.

Whereas most studies of humorous discourse accentuate its positive aspects, Billig (2005) takes an altogether more sceptical position. The main thrust of his study is towards forms of humour, such as racist or sexist humour, where particularly vulnerable groups are the target of jokes delivered among dominant or socially more powerful groups. Billig also touches on issues to do with irony. He cites as an 'unamusing' anecdote an episode from the European Parliament in 2003 involving the right-wing billionaire and former Italian premier Silvio Berlusconi (Billig 2005: 173ff). In the course of a speech that was not being well received, Berlusconi likened a German MEP to the commandant of a Nazi concentration camp. In response to the predictable booing that followed, Berlusconi claimed that he was being 'ironic'. In terms of our model, this disclaimer is an attempt to re-orientate the discourse situation in such a way as to claim that there was some paradox inherent in the initial utterance. When asked to apologize, Berlusconi refused – to do so would of course have acknowledged that the original words spoken were both non-ironic and sincere. Instead, Berlusconi 'regretted' that the 'ironic joke' hadn't been taken up, which, in other words, lays the blame on his listeners for lacking the sufficient humour resource to get the joke. Billig (2005: 174) argues that self-proclaimed irony and insulting humour (like Berlusconi's) should not be ignored because it is just as important an area of study as so-called 'successful' humour. And as if to confirm Billig's contentions, readers might refer to the defence offered by Donald Trump when he claimed in July 2016 that Russia should use espionage to retrieve emails of his former rival for president Hillary Clinton (and to be sure there is irony here), and in August 2016 that Barack Obama is the 'founder of ISIS'. In both cases Trump claimed he was being 'sarcastic'.

B7 DEVELOPMENTS IN FORENSIC DISCOURSE ANALYSIS

In this unit we want to highlight some of the important issues that have come to the fore in forensic discourse analysis and to introduce some of the techniques and methods that have been employed by linguists in their capacity as 'expert witnesses' (see A7). Some of the issues we raise have been touched upon implicitly in certain units outside this Strand – in our survey of power and talk, for instance, reference was made to unequal rights in courtroom interaction (A2) while the concept of *register*, of which legal discourse is a pre-eminent example, was introduced in B2.

Presupposition and the 'leading question'

The issue of the 'leading question' is a good illustration of the sometime lack of fit between the perspectives of lawyers and the perspectives of language analysts, showing how legal understanding and interpretation is often at odds with linguistic categories and analysis. Whereas legal definitions of the concept of a 'leading question' are inconsistent, linguists for their part have no trouble identifying it: a leading question contains a presupposition that is embedded in a sentence in such a way as to make it undeniable or non-negotiable. We can unpack this definition through some illustrations. In the following example, there are two main propositions, one an 'entailment' and the other a 'presupposition':

'Have you stopped beating up your partner?'

The entailment here is concerned with whether some process (in this case, the process of 'beating up') has come to a halt at some time, and the question seeks clarification through a polarity (yes/no) response. However, the rather more insidious proposition that lurks beneath the surface of the question is the understanding that the addressee, whatever their answer in polarity terms, has been beating up their partner. In other words, *both* a 'yes' *and* a 'no' answer are incriminating replies. This of course would not be an issue in an interactive context untrammelled by strong power constraints – we could simply refuse to answer the question. But if 'directed' by a judge to provide a yes/no answer, there is no escape from endorsing the embedded presupposition – whether it is true or not. In terms of formal explanation, this type of presupposition is activated by the 'change of state' verb *stop*.

Presupposition strategies are common at various levels in courtroom exchanges. For instance, at the 2014 trial of Oscar Pistorius for the murder of Reeva Steenkamp, Pistorius was asked a range of questions with presupposed elements. Here are some examples from a single day during Pistorius' Cross Examination by prosecutor Gerrie Nel:

> You know that it's impossible for her to have eaten after you went to bed that night?
> Do you have any idea why the only thing outside that overnight bag is her jeans?
> When you armed yourself and you spoke to Reeva, what did you say?
> Why would she stand right up at the door, looking at you, at the danger?
>
> (Pistorius Cross Examination 14 April 2014)

In answering either *yes* or *no* to these questions, the following propositions remain intact:

> It was impossible that Reeva could have eaten after bed.
> The only thing outside the overnight bag was a pair of jeans.
> Pistorius armed himself and spoke to Reeva.
> Reeva stood at the door, and looked at Pistorius.

There are a number of other presupposition 'triggers' in English, and Table B7.1 provides a checklist setting out some of the major types, along with glosses that identify the semantic impasse that might face a defendant in a hypothetical court-room setting.

The information carried by a presupposition can also be progressively 'buried' as the grammatical structure that houses it becomes more complex. In other words, the more embedded clauses there are in a particular structure, the more difficult it is to pick out and challenge the informational 'nub' of its central presupposition. It is also much harder to deny or rescind a presupposition when it is framed as a negative, as in 'Do you not remember hiding the stash?' or 'Didn't you regret returning to the crime scene?' Here is an interesting exchange which shows both of these features, grammatical embedding and negative framing, at work. It is from a session of British Parliament's

Table B7.1 Checklist of presupposition triggers in English

Type of trigger	Example	Gloss
Iteratives	'Did you visit the crime scene again?'	The particle *again* presupposes previous presence at the scene. A yes/no response does not countermand this presupposition.
Change of state verbs	'Did you continue to threaten my client?'	Like 'stop', *continue* (and other verbs like *start, finish, cease* or *carry* on) presupposes the truth of the action expressed in its embedded clause.
Factives	'Do you *regret* entering the house that night?	Verbs like *regret* (and *be aware, realize* and so on) presuppose as 'fact' the proposition in their embedded clause. Again, a yes/no response does not countermand the presupposition.
Alternative questions	'Were you inside or outside the building on the night in question?'	This structure only allows two possibilities, both of which presuppose a proximity to the building.
Cleft structures	'It was you who prompted this sick attack'	The cleft structure re-shapes the information focus of the sentence; here, the defendant can deny involvement but not the presupposition that a sick attack was prompted.
Comparators	'The co-accused seems to be as short-tempered as you.'	While this entails that the co-accused is short-tempered, the *presupposition* also establishes the second person addressee as short-tempered. Notice how both denial 'No he isn't' and affirmation 'Yes he is' still leaves the presupposition intact.
'Wh-type' questions	'Where exactly did you put the stash?'	Questions framed with *what, where*, or *how* seek to establish the circumstances in which a transitivity process took place (see A4). However, they also serve to embed the remaining parts of the sentence as presupposition (i.e. that the stash was put somewhere by the defendant).
Genitive constructions	'Where exactly did you put your stash?'	In addition to the 'Wh-type' question, genitive structures like 'your' strongly presuppose as true the addressee's ownership or possession of the entity described.
Definite referring expressions	'Where exactly was the stash?'	In addition to the 'Wh-type' question, the definite reference 'the', like the genitive particle above, is a strong presupposition-carry-ing device. In this case, the existence of a stash is presupposed.

'Question Time' where a question from a member of the opposition is put to the then Prime Minister Tony Blair:

Q: Does the Prime Minister not regret making this blatant U-turn over
          tobacco advertising?
Blair: The right honourable member will recall what I said in my speech in
          Maastricht …

Ordinarily, and if directed to do so, this would be a difficult question to answer by way of a 'yes'/'no' response. (Try out both responses for yourselves and see what sorts of presuppositions are implicated.) As it happens both participants in this exchange are professional lawyers – as is the majority of British politicians – which may in part explain the 'legal sounding' discourse that characterizes political debate of this sort. A major difference here, however, is the absence of any control on the provision of a direct answer to the question. Blair is able both to ignore the terms of the question and to change the direction of the interaction, a discourse prerogative perhaps of the incumbent of the highest office in the land.

The legal profession's view of what exactly constitutes a leading question is rather more loosely determined and the jury is out, so to speak, on whether or not lawyers should use them as an examination strategy. For example, the advocacy manual for barristers practising in Northern Ireland encourages lawyers to avoid leading questions and instead to ask more flexible questions that give witnesses options in their replies (Lowndes 2004). Yet the manual's example of so-called 'flexible' questioning is none other than the presupposition-laden sequence 'Were you inside or outside the building on the night in question?' which we offered in Table B7.1 as an example of the *alternative question* pattern.

Interrogation and cross-examination

Interrogation and cross-examination are forms of discourse where pressure is put on a witness, suspect or defendant to elicit 'proof'. Generally more aggressive than the exploratory interview, an interrogation is designed to elicit a confession. Shuy elaborates thus:

> Interviewers make use of less of their power than do interrogators. An interview probes but does not cross-examine. It inquires but does not challenge. It suggests rather than demands. It uncovers rather than traps …. In contrast, interrogators make ample use of their power. They challenge, warn, accuse, deny, and complain. They are more direct. They demand and they dominate.
>
> (Shuy 1998: 12–13)

It is in the nature of interrogation and cross-examination that an unequal relationship of power exists, where those asking questions have authority and power (in our first sense of the concept, A1) and those interrogated or otherwise questioned are in a position of weakness. Given that both types of interaction can have a profound influence on people's lives, it is important to look a little more closely at some of the issues attendant on this relationship of inequality.

The literature in forensic discourse analysis abounds with illustrations of social asymmetries, embodied by differences in dialect, linguistic skill and oral proficiency, in the two sides of an interrogation or cross-examination. For example, Brennan (1994) discusses the cross-examination of children in court and notes that very different rules attend to the reliability of children's testimony. A stark illustration of the problems faced by children is the following exchange where a 9-year-old is clearly thrown by an absurdly tortuous question from Counsel:

Counsel: You went to, went and got into the car outside your home,
I withdraw that, whereabouts in relation to your home did you get into the car on this morning?
Child: Well on the, when?

(Brennan 1994: 214)

The difficulty faced by children in courtroom contexts was an important impetus behind the influential Youth Justice and Criminal Evidence Act (1999). The legislation contains special measures that can be taken when children are required to testify, such as through live link or in recorded testimony, giving evidence behind a screen. There are also now limitations on Cross Examination when children are the alleged victims of sexual assault.

Another issue relating to social asymmetry in courtroom interaction concerns dialect variation. We argued in A7 that legal discourse is best thought of as a montage of interconnected specialist registers. The grammatical framework for the transmission of this compound register is Standard English. The prestige dialect of English, Standard English is the default variety used in formal written communication – to the extent that court stenographers in their transcription of proceedings often level out the regional dialect differences heard in the speech of witnesses and defendants. The lack of recognition of regional differences in speech has some far-reaching consequences for the legal process. For example, one of the present authors (Simpson) was involved some years ago in the Appeal of a homeless alcoholic Irish woman who had been convicted of murder in the West Midlands of England. The suspect, from County Clare (let us call her 'Mary'), had allegedly started a fire in an unoccupied house which led to someone's death. The sole evidence for her conviction was the following utterance, reported to police by two witnesses who arrived at the scene:

'We've a good fire goin' here'

It was argued at the initial trial that Mary's remark constituted an admission of guilt, on the grounds that the speaker was indicating that she herself was responsible for starting the fire. What was patently not taken into account was that the alleged utterance was couched in a dialect system that was markedly different from Standard English. A notable feature of Irish English (Mary's native dialect) is its complex tense system, where, under the substratum influence of Irish Gaelic, a range of alternative expressions and meanings replace Standard English constructions (Harris 1993; Filppula 1999). This particular utterance has a resultative-perfective aspect, which signals that a fire was certainly burning at the time of speaking but without implicating the speaker of the sentence as the Agent of the process – an aspect of meaning that most speakers in Ireland would grasp.

At the Appeal stage, Mary's conviction was overturned, but not because of this linguistic evidence. As it happened, the dialect evidence was not needed because her barrister uncovered anomalies in the initial prosecution case. The two persons who had 'heard' Mary's utterance were discovered to be itinerant alcoholics whose evidence and recall, in the absence of a proper police breath analyser test, was felt not to be credible.

Cross-cultural asymmetries feature in interrogation transcripts examined by Gibbons (2003), who looks at the ways in which traditional Australian Aboriginal communities are treated by the legal process and at the numerous injustices that have befallen them in consequence. Because of the value that is placed on tribal knowledge, questioning in Aboriginal societies is done indirectly and with caution (Gibbons 2003: 206). The courtroom practice is of course the diametrical opposite of this, where, in contrast to traditional tribal routines, questions are direct and interpretations of silence are understood as incriminating. Moreover, Aboriginal culture does not use measurement expressions to refer to time, and so a date is therefore captured not by clock or by calendar, but by a significant event that happened around the time in question. This helps explain the difficulty experienced by this Aboriginal witness in the transcript below, when asked about his activities:

Counsel: What time did you go to the hotel?
W: About ten o'clock at night
Counsel: What time did you leave the hotel?
W: About ten o'clock that night
Counsel: How long had you been there?
W: I was there for a couple of hours

(after Gibbons 2003: 207)

Rather than indicating an 'unreliable' witness, this series of exchanges simply highlights the collision between two different linguistic and cultural orders.

The Electro-static Detection Apparatus (ESDA)

In the mid-1980s, a major change in English law came about in the form of the Police and Criminal Evidence Act (PACE 1984). This required the police to make a contemporaneous audio or video recording of verbal evidence rather than relying on their own written record of what the accused said. The quality and reliability of the written evidence presented by the police at trial had been increasingly called into question, with many suspects alleging that they had been 'verballed' because the verbal evidence had been fabricated by police officers (Coulthard 2002: 19; and see D7). Increasingly, witness 'statements' that had led to convictions were found to lack credibility because they had been embellished in some way, in such a way that the version of the statement that was signed by the accused did not square with the version produced at trial. At the forefront of investigations into these disputed texts was a particular technique, now canonical in the development of forensic linguistic analysis. This technique was known as the Electro-static Detection Apparatus (ESDA) and a key paper outlining the history (and success) of its application is provided by Davis (1994).

How does ESDA work? Basically, ESDA is a documentation procedure that involves an application to an undersheet, over which an imprint of the page above has, invisibly, been laid. For example, if you take notes during a lecture using a file pad or similar block of pages, each time you complete a page, the imprint of that page, a kind of ghost version, is left on the pages immediately and further below it. An ESDA test enables an electronic image to form of the page above by taking indentations from the lower sheet, and this creates an 'ESDA lift'. The lift is then superimposed onto the higher sheet containing the original printed text and if the ghost version and the higher sheet do not match perfectly then the higher sheet has been embellished in some way since its original composition.

The issue of course is that the ESDA lift shows if a police statement has been tampered with. Before PACE, the 'rewriting' of witness statements was absolutely forbidden in law, so the importance of ESDA lay in its capacity to show uncontrovertibly that improper procedure had taken place, and this was shown time and again in Appeal cases where particularly compelling evidence was needed. As Davis (1994: 74) notes with respect to these Appeals, an allegation made by a suspected criminal against forces of law and order requires particularly convincing evidence to support it.

The following example is one of many contentious cases involving England's West Midlands Serious Crime Squad. The chain of miscarriages of justice that resulted from this unit's operations revealed an endemic malpractice that was to lead to its disbandment in 1988 (Davis 1994: 71). The following episode, which involves the case of Paul Dandy who was convicted of armed robbery, is one from a number of cases that went to Appeal and resulted in the overturn of a long prison sentence. Below is the 'admission' elicited from the interrogation of Dandy that was submitted in court, and that led to his prosecution. The subsequent ESDA lift, however, revealed that two incriminating sentences had been inserted *after* the interrogation. As you read through this reconstructed interrogation transcript, it might be worth trying to work out which bit of the text was *not* present in the ESDA lift:

Police: Have you got a brother named Roy?
Dandy: Yes.
P: On the 31st October 1986 you deposited £1,000 into the T.S.B. Where did that come from?
D: The sale of the GTI with 'Rabbit Injection' on the back.
P: Will you sign an authority for us to look at your bank account?
D: No.
P: I take it from your earlier reply that you are admitting been (sic) involved in the robbery at the M.E.B.?
D: You'se are good, Thursday, Friday, Saturday, Sunday and you've caught me, now you've got to prove it.
P: Do you want to read over the notes and caption them.
D: I'll initial the mistakes, but I won't sign them.
                                        (after Davis 1994: 81–2; Coulthard 1992: 244)

Even in terms of consistency with the overall tenor of the interrogation, there is clearly something odd about the sequence that begins with 'I take it from your earlier reply …' and ends at '… now you've got to prove it'. Davis's ESDA lift did indeed confirm that these two sentences had been inserted into the text after the interrogation and when confronted with this evidence at Appeal, the judge dismissed the case against Dandy immediately.

ADVERTISING DISCOURSE: METHODS FOR ANALYSIS

Social semiotics and Multimodal Discourse Analysis

As pointed out in B1, the initial analytical thrust in Critical Discourse Analysis (CDA) was towards examining linguistic structures, and attributing to them a crucial function in the social production of inequality, power, ideology and manipulation. Contemporary CDA recognizes that people rarely communicate monomodally, through language alone, but *multi*modally, through a combination of visual images, languages, sound and even body language. As different modes of communication have become used in a much more integrated fashion, they have also become an important focus of research in what is now often referred to as *multimodal* Critical Discourse Analysis (see B5 above). Just as with language, choices in visual communication can be equally ideological, can shape our world views and negotiate social and power relationships.

The work of scholars such as Hodge and Kress (1988), Kress and van Leeuwen (2006), van Leeuwen (2005), Forceville (1995, 2006, 2013) and Machin (2007a) has consistently emphasized the importance of incorporating visual images into textual analysis, arguing for a broader multimodal conception of discourse. Social semiotics, in this sense, is concerned with the multi-semiotic or multimodal character of many texts in contemporary society and explores ways of analysing visual images (such as press or online news photographs) and the relationship between language and visual images. Kress, for example, states that it 'is now impossible to make sense of texts ... without having a clear idea of what these other features might be contributing to the meaning of the text' (2000: 337). We have already pointed out in various places that the political and ideological views of newspapers can be expressed in the choice of different vocabularies (e.g. 'resistance fighters' vs. 'insurgents') and different grammatical structures (e.g. active vs. passive constructions). The same is true of the visual representation of events, of what Kress and van Leeuwen (2006) have termed 'the grammar of visual design', which means that just like linguistic structures, visual structures also express meanings and contribute to the overall message of a text. Analysing visual communication is therefore an important part of critical analysis, be it in the media, advertising, or any other texts accompanied by visual designs. According to Kress and van Leeuwen (2006: 13), images are 'entirely within the realm of ideology, as means – always – for the emergence of ideological positions'.

There is, of course, no universal grammar of visual design. Just as with language in general, visual language is not transparent and universally understood, but culturally specific. Western visual communication is influenced by the West's convention of writing from left to right, whereas other cultures write from right to left or top to bottom and will therefore produce different visual meanings. An important concept in the analysis of Western visual communication is the idea of 'Given' and 'New' (Kress and van Leeuwen 2006) which refers to the way visual and verbal language is placed in a newspaper, magazine or advertisement. In these contexts, the right of the page often appears to be the side for key information, the 'New' (often embodied in large photographs) to which the reader must pay special attention; the left of the page often by contrast contains mostly verbal texts, the 'already Given', something the reader knows already as part of the culture or at least as part of the culture of the magazine or newspaper. Another concept Kress and van Leeuwen introduce is the idea of 'Ideal' and 'Real'. This is the notion that information (linguistic and pictorial) that is placed at the top of a page is more generalized and idealized, while the information placed at the bottom is more everyday (and often more serious) in tone. The 'Ideal' can therefore be more 'frivolous', while the 'Real', by offering more factual information, is more down to earth. In Kress and van Leeuwen's formulation, what is at the top of a composition is the Ideal and what is at the bottom is the Real.

The front pages of Britain's red-top tabloid newspapers, for example, often display a fundamentally left–right, Given–New structure. There is usually one story, with the image on the right (usually in colour) as the New, and the written text on the left as the Given. Many printed advertisements follow the same convention, but by no means all. We shall show this in a printed advertisement later but here Figure B8.1 provides an example of the 'tabloid' Given–New and Ideal–Real structure.

Figure B8.1 Front page, *Daily Mirror*, 7 September 2017

On this front page from the *Daily Mirror* (7 September 2017) we can see both compositional structures at work: we have the Ideal at the top (about controversial Tory Member of Parliament Jacob Rees-Mogg, and actresses Catherine Tyldesley and Kym Marsh from British television soap opera *Coronation Street*); at the bottom the Real, oriented towards the more 'hard news' information. This top part itself is divided into a Given–New structure: the text to the left is the Given. This refers to an ongoing 'soap opera' in British politics at the time, the fascination with the contentious views of Jacob Rees-Mogg in a period when British Prime Minister Theresa May's leadership was less than secure. The New information on the right informs readers that in another soap opera lengthier 60-minute storylines would be somewhat racier, the pun '*sixy*' cleverly connecting the 'sexy' plots with the longer 60 minutes of nightly viewing for fans of the programme. The bottom part of the page refers to a Real hard news item, and one that readers might think about in terms of the analysis in Strand 4, reporting on the highly publicized decision of a school in East Sussex in England to prohibit Year 7 pupils from wearing skirts as part of their school uniform in an effort to improve 'gender neutrality' in the school.

We need to point out here that although the criteria developed by Kress and van Leeuwen (2006) offer useful tools to start us thinking about page layout and positions, they should not be seen as categorical absolutes. There are many visual representations in the print media and advertising that do not adhere to these patterns. For one thing, journalists often change a whole page layout at the last minute to accommodate a new advert or snippet of information, so a picture may move sides for balance – and in such a way that runs counter to the model of visual design.

With this caveat in mind, we shall look shortly at a print advertisement from two modes of communication, linguistic and visual, applying Kress and van Leeuwen's (2006) and van Leeuwen's (2005) method for a multimodal analysis. In C1 we provide a sample linguistic analysis of a text from the *Daily Mail* which reveals that modality is a linguistic resource for communicating degree of commitment, about *how* true or *how* real a representation should be seen (Machin 2007a: 46). However, modality is not restricted to language, and it was Kress and Hodge (1979) who first pointed out four decades ago that modality is a multimodal concept that can be applied to photographs or any kind of visual representations.

Looking at what is hidden or made less important or what is enhanced (e.g. colours) can tell us about the world that is created for us. This is as true for the language used as it is for images, advertisements and news photographs. As with linguistic modality, visuals can be of high modality ('is', 'certainly') or low modality ('might', 'possibly'). High modality in visuals means that things or people look 'realistic' – the way they would look if we saw them in real life (e.g. in a family photo). Photographs that do not appear to be realistic or naturalistic, that do not represent the world as it is had we been there, are of low modality. Advertisements and other promotional texts (e.g. for banks) and lifestyle magazines are full of visuals that have been modified in terms of colour, brightness and saturation and therefore have been lowered in modality. For example, Machin and Thornborrow (2003) show that women's lifestyle magazines use low-modality decontextualized settings (i.e. reduction of detail and background) with a greater focus on postures and participants to create a symbolic or fantasy world in which it is easy for women to have power and fun.

The ad we are going to look at is about a skin care product for men, and it takes its cue from others by a well-known multinational cosmetics conglomerate. Critical linguists have focussed increasingly on cosmetics advertisements aimed at men in recent years (Harrison 2008, 2011). The problem with powerful conglomerates is that they are ferociously protective of their 'brand' and they have teams of highly paid lawyers to enforce this injunction. Thus, what follows is an advertisement of our own that is modelled on the type of discourse strategies employed to market cosmetics for men. Although typical of cosmetics industry products, it of course bears no relationship to any actual proprietary brand currently on the market.

Appearing in many of the British lifestyle magazines for men, the ad (let us assume) is by *Aurore*, from their *Homme executif* line of products, and it markets a moisturizer cum self-tanner (Figure B8.2). The features we will focus on first are visual modality, composition (Given–New, Ideal–Real) colour and typeface.

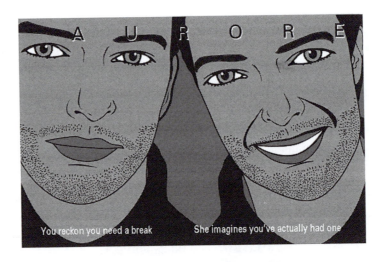

Figure B8.2 Aurore advertisement

The top part of the composition has two decontextualized photographs, which together with the absence of any imperfections in the model, mean they are of low modality. This idealizes the subject of the photograph. The advertisement displays both a Given–New and an Ideal–Real composition (Kress and van Leeuwen 2006). The top part of the page, the Ideal, is divided into two pictures; on the left we see the Given, a pale, rather serious-looking young man with stubble, whereas on the right, the New, he is visibly (self-)tanned and smiling confidently at us. In both pictures, he is looking directly at the reader (a so-called 'demand' picture).

The bottom part provides the factual detail and a picture of the product itself. In other words, the modality of the top and bottom part is different. The top right picture(s) show(s) what you *might* (low modality) look like when you buy the moisturizer. It is placed in the Ideal. The bottom part shows what *is* (high modality) and what you can actually do to achieve this ideal look; that is, buy this skincare product (high modality). It is, in other words, the Real.

The predominant colours in the ad (you'll have to take our word for it!) are dark blue, white and orange, which is somewhat ironic given that the ad is at pains to stress that the self-tanner does not produce an 'orange result'. The 'smiley' icon (orange in the original) next to the text in dark blue letters may serve to reinforce the 'scientific' claims made. The product itself is a mixture of orange, white, a silvery blue and a bit of grey. These colours can be said to be more common in ads for men.

The ad's typography is angular and rather 'blocky' in character, and is surrounded by much empty white space. Machin (personal communication) has suggested that this use of space is more common in ads for men, connoting perhaps a minimalist form of interior design, in contrast with a more homely and 'feminine' physical design and layout.

Let us now discuss the linguistic features of the ad in some detail. There is the headline, which interacts with the images and simulates a dialogue with the reader (*You reckon you need a break. She imagines you've actually had one*), the body copy, which takes up the bottom part of the ad with the product itself and which does the main persuasive 'selling' bit of the advertisement, the signature (*Aurore, Rome, Homme executif*), and the slogan (*Because you want to look good too*). If we take a closer look at the ad, particularly its body copy, we can see that it employs some widely used linguistic features in advertising, namely direct address, evaluative adjectives, repetition, disjunctive syntax and parallelism (see Delin 2000: 128–146). We discuss these in turn.

Direct address

Advertising makes a great deal of use of direct address (second-person personal and possessive pronouns, 'you' and 'yours') for both ideological and practical reasons. Ideologically, it seeks to address the reader or viewer personally with *you* in order to transcend its nature as a mass medium.

> '*You* reckon *you* need a break' – 'She imagines *you've* actually had one.'
> '*Your* skin looks bland and lifeless?'
> 'Because *you* want to look good too'

People do not like being addressed as part of a mass audience, as individuality is something that is culturally highly valued in Western societies. Fairclough (1989: 62) has referred to this attempt to 'handle' people on an individual basis as 'synthetic personalization'.

Practically, ads need to persuade readers and viewers to buy or do certain things and therefore they often contain imperatives. Our ad has only one example of an imperative: *Deal with it!*, demanding action from the reader. At the same time, the imperative (and questions) serves to set up a personal relationship between advertiser and consumer by simulating an 'intimate, interactive addressing of the reader … in order to engage the reader rather than simply conveying information' (Toolan 1988: 54). By using questions and the imperative (*Your skin looks bland and lifeless?*; *Deal with it!*) the advertisers are simulating the informality of a conversational speaking style. This more conversational style has also been deliberately introduced to other forms of public communication, written and spoken (e.g. political interviews and speeches, spoken institutional discourse, health and promotional leaflets) to simulate equality and informality between speaker/writer and the public.

Disjunctive syntax

Yet another strategy to mimic a conversational style in ads is the use of disjunctive syntax (Delin 2000: 129); that is, the use of sentences without verbs or subjects, or sentences consisting of one or two grammatical elements only. Examples from our ad are:

> *Aqua Mobile*
> *Counter-grey skin*
> *No orange!*
> *Natural-looking tanner*
> *Effective moisturizer*
> *Time-lag tanning and light hydration system*

Adjectives

Adjectives play a key role in advertising because they often convey 'positive or negative affective meaning' (Delin 2000: 133). Affective meaning displays the speaker's or writer's positive or negative evaluation of the item referred to. The *Aurore* ad contains few adjectives with negative connotations: *bland*, *grey* and *lifeless* as opposed to the positive ones: *Aqua Mobile*, *light*, *effective*, *good*, *natural-looking*. The negative adjectives are associated with the problem of working too hard and not having time for a holiday, which will show on your skin, whereas the positive adjectives are all associated with the qualities of the product. The way in which positive associations of the product are inserted in the mind of the reader has been referred to as 'fusion', which will 'imbue the characterless product with desirable qualities' (Cook 2001: 108).

Parallelism

Another common device in printed ads is parallelism, which is the repeated use of similar grammatical structures. The following features are linguistically parallel:

> *You reckon*   *you need a break?*
> *She imagines*   *you've actually had one*

The typography of these two sentences is also parallel in the sense that both use the same fonts and white letters. Another example of parallelism is *anti-grey, counter-orange*.

Repetition

Repetition through synonyms or near-synonyms and parallelism (*bland – lifeless; tanning – tanner; hydration – moisturizer*) characterizes also some of the text in the ad with these features all serving to intensify meaning.

Finally one could argue that having 'bland and lifeless skin' and not having time to take a break (hence the need to 'fake' a tan) are all conditions of a busy and stressful work-life. Not only are the readers' anxieties about appearance played to here, but the ad can also be said to 'naturalize' modern consumerist lifestyles which revolve around working hard but also having 'fun'. As Machin (2007a) points out, many present-day advertisements emphasize not so much the use of the product, which takes up relatively little space in the ad, but its lifestyle association, which is often symbolized through the photograph of a model or some other potent cultural symbol (e.g. promotional materials showing pictures of confident business women).

Reason and tickle in advertising

Writing as a professional advertiser, Bernstein (1974) offers an engaging book-length account of the strategies and goals of modern marketing. Although Bernstein's account is largely anecdotal, he draws an interesting distinction between two principal copywriting gambits: 'reason' advertising and 'tickle' advertising. He notes that sometimes an advertisement should be simply and directly communicated, and should make some appeal to reason, while at other times the best route is an indirect one. He goes further, arguing that reason equals fact, clinical truth and needs, but tickle equals emotion, imagination and desires:

> the greater the appeal to reason, the more direct the route; the greater the appeal to emotion (tickle) the less direct the route … If everything is spelled out the only reaction may be indifference. But if people are intrigued, and comprehension is not immediate, they may go on to participate in the advertising … A message in which a recipient participates is far more likely to result in action than one in which she is regarded as a piece of absorbent material.
>
> (Bernstein 1974: 104–105)

Contemporary linguistic pragmatics (the study of what language means in context) offers a number of ways for exploring the continuum between directness and indirectness in language. Much of this work can also be interestingly applied to the reason/tickle distinction (Simpson 2001), some of the central principles of which are summarized here. First of all, reason ads, in keeping with the general 'anatomy' of ads outlined in A8, can be characterized prototypically by (i) conspicuous product placement along with brand name and (if available) company logo visually prominent and (ii) a clear and unambiguous slogan giving the principle reason to buy the product. This second feature, the 'reason to buy' element, parallels the concept of the 'Unique Selling Proposition' (see A8). Moreover, unlike tickle ads (which we shall consider below), the basic discourse pattern for reason advertising remains stable across different media. What seems to mark reason ads out more than any other characteristic, however, is their particular use of a set of text-building devices known as *conjunctive adjuncts* (Halliday 1994: 36). The main types are summarized thus:

- ❑ *additive*:   and; also; moreover; nor
- ❑ *adversative*:   but; yet; however; on the other hand
- ❑ *conditional*:   [positive] if … then; in the event of; when
                        [negative] otherwise; if not
- ❑ *causal*:   so; then; because; as a result; that's why; [that] means
- ❑ *purposive*:   in order to; for; to [+ infinitive]

The first two types create semantic 'extension' in that they involve addition or variation between propositions, with the adversative suggesting also that there is some affective contrast between the two conjuncts linked. The remaining types create 'enhancement' because they establish a relation of cause and effect between propositions (Halliday 1994: 325).

Although all five types are common in advertising copy, it is the conditional, causal and purposive types that form the semantic bedrock of reason texts. These adjuncts 'enhance', rather than 'extend', with the 'reason to buy' element becoming foregrounded through clear exposition of the positive consequences following purchase and, less commonly, the negative consequences resulting from failure to purchase. Here, first of all, is a selection of reason advertisements exemplifying the conditional conjunctive adjunct.

Conditional structures

(a) If pain strikes, then hit back with Solpadeine.

(TV ad for 'Solpadeine' pain killers)

(b) And if of course you're not satisfied, Lever Brothers will give you your money back.

(TV ad for 'Surf' washing powder, with testimonial from 'actor and Surf user')

(c) If he's wearing Pampers, he's staying dry.

(TV ad for 'Pampers Unisex Extra' nappies)

In spite of the range of products that they promote, these reason ads all exhibit the same basic underlying 'if p then q' structure. They are two-place conditionals with the conditional clause positioned in front of the consequent. In all cases, the 'reason to buy' element of the ad is developed by establishing that if a certain condition pertains (for instance, if the consumer happens to be struck by pain or happens to be dissatisfied with a product) then this condition carries with it a direct, positive and beneficial consequence (that is, the pain can be eased by Solpadeine, dissatisfaction can be redressed by a refund and so on).

The second category of enhancing conjunctive adjunct, the causal, constitutes another important connective type in reason advertising. In the following examples, notice how the principal operators that link the propositions expressed in each ad are either 'so', 'because' or 'that's why':

Causal structures

(d) Flash does all the hard work so you don't have to.

> (TV ad for 'Flash' floor cleaner)

(e) These children are desperate for your help, so call Plan now.

> (Billboard print ad for a registered charity)

(f) Because new Pampers have many more long soft fibres, they clean much more easily.

> (TV ad for 'New Pampers' babywipes)

(g) Kotex understands how it feels to be a woman. That's why we've created new Kotex ultra-thin.

> (TV ad for 'Kotex' sanitary towels)

Although there is some flexibility in the ordering of propositions and the precise type of connective used, all of these ads display, in some form or another, a basic reason-plus-result argument. For instance, the reason offered in the first clause of (d) is that 'Flash' does all the hard work – the result of which (specified in the second clause) is that the customer is able to avoid such work. The last two examples in this list illustrate two particular types of causal: those with 'because' as their central connective and those with 'that's why'. Interestingly, the structure displayed by these two sets is interchangeable in that the basic 'cause and effect' sequence can be reversed: 'New Pampers have many more long soft fibres. That's why they clean much more easily' or 'Kotex have created new Kotex ultra-thin because we understand how it feels to be a woman'.

The purposive form is closely related to the category of causal connectivity, but in purposive conjuncts the emphasis is placed on some recommended future course of action that is predicated upon a targeted purpose or need. In other words, purposive reason ads are principally concerned with the bringing about of a particular (and desirable) state of affairs and, inevitably, it is the product on offer that is understood to facilitate this process. This means that purposives are implicitly prospective in a way that true causals are not. In the selection of purposives that follow, the key operators are either 'in order to' or an infinitive verb phrase heading a non-finite clause:

(h) In order to reveal younger looking skin, I've found Plenitude Excell A3 with triple AHA fruit acids.

> (TV ad for 'Plenitude' skin care product)

(i) To find out how easy it is to get on the internet, Just phone BT on 0800 400 449.

> (TV ad from British Telecom)

(j) Scratch the card to see if you are one of our lucky winners.

(Local print media: ad for lottery)

The purposive function may also be carried out by the preposition 'for' when placed at the head of noun phrases, as in:

(k) For driest nappies ever, choose Pampers Unisex extra.

(TV ad for nappies)

(l) For a new outlook, try Kemira fertilisers.

(Print ad for agricultural products)

Overall, these three principal categories of conjunctive adjuncts form the bedrock of reason ads. Of course, interplay between the modes is possible and one can find a mixture of connectives within the confines of a single ad:

(m) New ultra-powerful enzymes in the blue layer *mean* that dirt is lifted straight away, *so* the white layer can leave a deep shine. Try new 'Finish', *because* our best just got better.

(our emphasis)

The principal aim of ads (a)–(m) is to bring to the fore the primary motive(s) for purchasing the product; one means of achieving this aim is by developing a semantic connectivity that relies heavily on a specific and restricted set of conjunctive adjuncts. The 'message' in reason ads is therefore invariably plain, simple and unequivocal – a message that, literally, leaves nothing to the imagination.

Tickle advertising by contrast is situated at the other end of the pragmatic spectrum. Tickle ads principally generate *implicatures* (Grice 1975) which are, broadly, meanings that unfold when it is clear that the factual content of an utterance is not a reliable guarantor of the meaning of that utterance in context. Implicatures therefore depend on the addressee's capacity to draw inferences when they realize that the 'literal' meaning of the utterance is *not* intended. Ways of doing implicatures include the strategies of being ostentatiously indirect or obscure, making remarks that are manifestly irrelevant in the context or saying things that are obviously false, contradictory or tautological.

Consider by way of illustration the following example, from a space-based billboard advertising campaign for Bushmills whiskey:

(n) If you want to drink whiskey, drink whiskey.

This rather cryptic message was written text in bold print and occupied most of the visual space available while the reproduction of the bottle (with brand name only inconspicuously displayed) was positioned in the bottom right-hand corner of the ad.

This provides a neat counterpoint to those ads classified as reason above. Although it might resemble a straightforward conditional of the type discussed earlier – it does, after all, proclaim a 'reason to buy' of sorts – it is a prime example of the sorts of tautologies Grice (1975: 52) contends speakers use to generate implicatures. It flouts Grice's maxim of 'quantity' because it provides less information than would be conventionally required and so it makes no new assertion; compare it with 'If you want to drink whiskey, drink Bushmills'. Confronted with its propositional noninformativeness, a potential consumer must do a bit more inferencing work to arrive at an interpretation that satisfies them. What seems to trigger the retrieval of a 'meaning' for (n) is first of all the repetition of 'whiskey' across the two clauses. Basically, a conceptual split needs to be made between these two references to 'whiskey': if the first is held to symbolize the generalized class of beverage that is whiskey, then the second suggests a specific, prime and essential exponent of that category. Deriving subsequent inferences, such as 'Bushmills epitomizes the essence of whiskey' or 'Bushmills is the best whiskey', requires us to form a 'bridging assumption' (Blakemore 1992: 75). This is an assumption to which the second reference for 'whiskey' can be assigned and in (n) this is supplied by the inclusion of the bottle of Bushmills as co-text. Notably though, the processing effort required for the assignment of 'Bushmills' to the second whiskey 'slot' is not minimal: 'Bushmills' as a brand name is not obvious in the ad, so we need to scan the label closely to match the product brand name with assumptions encoded in the written portion of the advertisement.

In sum, this short advertisement observes neither of the two prototypical criteria for reason advertising which require that product and brand name be conspicuously placed, and, perhaps more importantly, that there must be some expression of a clear and unambiguous 'reason to buy'. While (n) bears the superficial trappings of a well-formed conditional, with its conjunctive adjunct arguably playing off this pattern in reason advertising, its implicitly tautological formula warrants that the consumer put in greater processing input in order to retrieve a satisfactory interpretation. Tickle advertising therefore requires greater participation by the addressee and a greater expenditure of processing effort.

Finally, an interesting aspect of the decoding of tickle ads generally is that the process seems to involve reinterpreting the ad in terms of a basic selling proposition. In other words, processing a tickle ad may to some degree involve rendering it down into a reason formula. For example, when asked to write down what they made of ad (n), the advertisement for Bushmills whiskey, our own students tended to produce responses that generally recast the ad in reason terms: 'There are ordinary whiskeys but Bush (sic) is the best one'; 'Bushmills is the best Whiskey'; 'If you want to drink a really good whiskey, then Bush (sic) is the one for you' and so on. It may well be that in terms of the reason–tickle distinction, the reason category often acts as a kind of cognitive template upon which tickle ads are built.

LANGUAGE AND NEW CAPITALISM: DEVELOPMENTS   B9

In A9, we provided a brief overview of some key themes and features in the new capitalism and the importance of language in this area. The language of the free market is now firmly embedded in discourse practices employed in the workplace, in politics, the media and universities. We will present a number of linguistic studies that have dealt with these developments and start off with recent developments at universities. First though, whenever we describe discursive practices, it is necessary to describe 'the social, cultural and political environment in which they are embedded' so we can use this environment as 'an interpretative resource' (Mautner 2005: 97).

The socio-political context: enterprise culture and discourse

In recent decades universities in Britain and the rest of the world have been undergoing substantial changes which have been described as a trend towards the 'adoption of a free-market or corporate-business perspective' (Webster 2003: 85). These changes, first introduced in Britain by the Thatcher government in the late 1980s and early 1990s, were continued and expanded during the years of New Labour. The managerial rhetoric employed in these institutional changes, the 'discourse of enterprise' (Keat and Abercrombie 1990) has been transported from political discourse, mainly Labour's 'Third Way discourse' (Fairclough 2000) into the public services in general and Higher Education in particular. Although 'enterprise culture' is regarded as the symbol of economic reconstruction during Thatcherism, it has at the same time also been a cultural reconstruction. As former UK premier Gordon Brown put it (when he was Chancellor of the Exchequer): 'If we are to have *the deeper and wider entrepreneurial culture we need*, we must start in our schools and colleges' and 'spread the *spirit of enterprise* from the classroom to the boardroom'. He also stated that 'enterprising' and 'entrepreneurial' are the typical keywords that reflect the amalgamation of universities and even primary and secondary education with business and corporate models (often referred to by its proponents as a 'partnership', but by its opponents as a 'colonization').

The Government therefore sees its role in creating an 'enterprise culture' and in delivering through the state education system the skills and competences that are in line with new capitalism and its 'enterprising' employees.

> We want every young person to hear about *business and enterprise* in school, every college student to be made aware of the opportunities in business – and to start a business, every teacher to be able to communicate the *virtues and potential of business and enterprise*.
> (http://news.bbc.co.uk/1/hi/education/1394674.stm, 18 June 2001; our emphasis)

It is within the context of a wider enterprise culture that the 'enterprising' or 'entrepreneurial' university has to be understood.

The 'enterprising' university

The developments we have just referred to have received considerable attention from social scientists and critical discourse analysts who have identified in particular the linguistic features of the 'marketized' educational sector.

A study of contemporary higher education discourse across Europe by Mautner (2005) has employed a corpus-based method for the analysis of the occurrence of the keywords 'enterprising' and 'entrepreneurial', thereby strengthening considerably previous more qualitative studies of university discourses (e.g. Fairclough 1993). This method can essentially 'provide *systematic* evidence about the significance of … keywords in English' (Stubbs 2001: 145; our emphasis). We will therefore summarize

Mautner's study before we move on to two textual samples of current Higher Education discourses.

Rather than seeing the current relationship between Higher Education and the market as a one-sided 'colonization' (Fairclough 1993), Mautner (2005: 98) refers to it as a 'process of convergence', albeit one that is 'asymmetrical' and in which the market ultimately emerges as the stronger partner. Although Mautner (p. 97) is not entirely opposed to institutional changes that might bring innovation and less bureaucratization, she remains critical of other developments, such as 'research being subjected to commercial pressures', which she regards 'as a threat to disinterestedness, independence, and objectivity'. Mautner's corpus analysis shows that 'entrepreneurial' does not have entirely positive meanings: she points out that *elites* and *farmers* can be referred to as entrepreneurial, but so can *hucksters* and *inmates*. 'Entrepreneurial' is coordinated with *flexible, outspoken* and *innovative*, but also with *free-wheeling, unscrupulous* and *aggressive*. Whether positive or negative, entrepreneurship is always about commercial success, whereas 'enterprising' has a wider meaning. Like entrepreneurial it can be both positive and negative (*this enterprising and talented little group* vs. *an enterprising slum-trained coward*). But unlike 'entrepreneurial', it can also refer to a general adventurousness and innovativeness rather than commercial success and can even be applied to animals (*an enterprising monkey*).

The corpus evidence also shows that there is an academic argument against the entrepreneurial university, which is essentially an 'anti-capitalist and anti-bureaucratic critique' (Mautner 2005: 106) and mainly concerned with the clash between traditional academic values and the values of business. Individual academics, however, do not have the power to 'translate their anti-entrepreneurial sentiments into transformative action' so that 'the entrepreneurial juggernaut, propelled by its powerful supporters, rolls on' (Mautner 2005: 112).

We can now examine a text that exhibits some of the key motifs that emerged in Mautner's corpus and discourse analytical research. The text below is taken from the *Enterprise Strategy* (2015) document of the University of Leicester

Integral to the **outward-facing ambitions** of this strategy is the **infusion of an enterprising culture** within the University – a culture that builds capacity and supports researchers to **actively assess opportunities for the commercial** and social applications of knowledge, and to engage more broadly with the public. To draw the most out of our high-impact research, **enterprise must establish a higher profile and greater visibility internally**, and staff members need to be supported with practical advice and guidance, as well as reward and recognition [...] Academics have further been encouraged to **organise** into research themes to **strengthen cohesion** and build critical mass in areas of particular strength. Such cross-cutting themes encourage the interdisciplinary working that our public and **private sector partners** so value. The **Enterprise and Business Development Office** have responded by aligning **enterprise professionals** closely with the college structure in order to be more **responsive to emerging needs**, respecting the diversity of requirements while playing a key role in developing and **promoting wider collaborations and innovative ways of working**. A number of recent efforts have **yielded promising results**. For instance, an increase in **the return of consultancy**

revenue to academics resulted in a significant increase in **consultancy activity**. **Enterprise activity** is to be a **criterion to be recognised by promotion panels**, alongside research and teaching. We will improve communication to staff of the recognition and **compensation opportunities available to enterprising staff**. We will also step up our awareness-raising and training efforts to bring to staff a flavour of what **'being enterprising'** looks like in different contexts and disciplines, and develop skills, capabilities and **capacities in line with requirements**.

While the **enterprise agenda** has steadily gained more ground with the academic and support community at Leicester, there is still work to be done to **embed it in the thinking and culture of this University**.

(Enterprise Strategy 2015, University of Leicester [our emphasis] https://www2.le.ac.uk/offices/red/documents/enterprise-strategy-with-science-library-photos-removed/view)

One of the first things to notice in this text is that it is replete with business-related lexis (e.g. *'enterprising culture'*, *'commercial'*, *'cohesion'*, *'consultancy revenue'*, *'capacities'*, *'embed it in the thinking'*, *'private sector partners'*). Like a commercial company producing goods for profit, Leicester's mission is to produce a 'return in the consultancy revenue to academics'. In terms of the knowledge of the University, *'commercial applications'* come before *'social'* ones, and the University wishes to *'infuse'* and *'embed'* commercial *'enterprise'* activity into the *'thinking and culture'* of the institution, so that what is considered of value is defined by an economic, rather than an educational criterion. An academic's ability to be *'more responsive to emerging needs'* in terms of the University's vision of *'wider collaboration'* with profit-focussed institutions is tied directly to career progression in this document. Educators themselves are cast as 'stakeholders' – a popular term in 'enterprise' discourse, which is used on six occasions in the 15-page document from which the above passage is taken – in the University's *Enterprise Strategy*. What is missing here is a conceptualization of academics as educators or researchers who might have ambitions to contribute to more than the economy of an institution or of society in general.

Ideologically significant words and phrases are highlighted in the paragraph above, the number of enterprise-type words alone is clearly visible. The University stresses that *'enterprise **must** establish'* a central function within its structures, and you should also pay attention to the level of categorical assertion present here. Phrases that use the verb 'to be' and are not marked for modality present aspects of the *Enterprise Strategy* as certain, such as *'integral to the outward-facing ambitions of this strategy **is** the infusion of an enterprising culture'* and *'there **is** still work to be done to embed it in the thinking and culture'*. As Mautner (2005) points out, universities are now at pains to stress that they are no longer unaccountable and otherworldly 'ivory towers', but firmly rooted in today's world, the economic principles of Leicester's *'private sector partners'* for example.

This brief text has provided an example of the increasingly marketized orientation of British universities, which is produced and reproduced in a variety of their discourses. The justification for adopting entrepreneurialism and its discourses in Higher Education is based on the hegemonic discourses of enterprise and new capitalism which insist that any organization or business wanting to survive has to adapt to global market conditions. It is simply assumed that current market-oriented orthodoxies are applicable to business as well as universities. However, this market logic, according to which knowledge is increasingly judged on its market performance and which turns students into consumers and at the same time marketable products in the job market should maybe be resisted if the university still wants to be concerned with 'future visions as a maker of history' rather than 'simply struggle for survival in the free-market conditions' (Webster 2003: 88).

Our next text example to illustrate the increasing use of business models in Higher Education is taken from a 'Negotiation Skills' Course run for academic and non-academic staff at a British university. The skills taught included the ability to 'negotiate', demonstrating rapport and empathy, asking questions, 'active' listening, avoiding conflict and interpreting body language. These skills, which are the focus of many communication training courses designed for different audiences and purposes, are considered important for professional as well as personal life. They are therefore a typical example of 'discourse technologies' and taught as 'transcontextual techniques' (Fairclough 1992). Courses like this are often run by outside training consultancies that offer training in various communication, office and interpersonal skills. The excerpts presented here are from overheads used during the one-day course. In this particular training course, 'negotiation' was defined as

- ❏ the process by which a mutually acceptable solution is reached between 2 or more parties
- ❏ about getting the best possible deal in the circumstance
- ❏ a social as well as a business skill
- ❏ something that can be learned!

This definition of negotiation and what it is for ('getting the best possible *deal*') shows that it is based on a commercial sector model that is deemed to be transferable and universally applicable ('a *social* as well as a *business* skill'). The assumption that 'skills' are detachable from people's individual personalities and can be taught and learned is common in many prescriptive communication training materials (see reading in D9). But it is debatable whether this is possible or even desirable, as talk is an expression of people's individual personalities. It is precisely because many people believe that talk is an expression of their individual personality that they regard training in communication skills as only marginally useful (Cameron 2000). The trainer on this particular course commented that 'language and *how to use it is key*' in successful negotiations and that one had 'to use the *right language* to be attractive'. This goes to show that the training of negotiation skills, just as other communication skills training, is 'talk strategically designed and inculcated' (Fairclough 2001: 34). For Fairclough (2001: 35), the concept of 'skill', which is pervasive in the new capitalism, is only 'superficially ethically neutral'. He regards the application of skills 'in the conduct of social relationships' as 'ethically objectionable' as it 'incorporates and legitimizes a manipulative and instrumentalist relationship to others'. For example, to become 'skilful' negotiators, trainees are advised to show '*rapport* and *empathy*' by using several behavioural steps:

- ❏ open on a neutral subject to allay hostility
- ❏ assure the other party of your commitment to a mutually agreeable solution – especially when holding back

❑ demonstrate respect for the process and the opposition
❑ explain where you are coming from
❑ really put yourself in their shoes – understand where they are coming from.

In this way, by 'opening on a neutral subject to allay hostility', trainees are instructed to use small talk *strategically* to establish rapport. This can be done by claiming common ground, as people do in casual conversation, but ultimately serves to make communication 'effective', thereby achieving institutional goals. The last two instructions on the list ('Explain where you are coming from', and 'Really put yourself in their shoes') resemble discourse techniques used in counselling.

These 'therapeutic' models of communication have become institutionalized in workplace settings that have nothing to do with therapy. For example, in one 'new' service workplace, the call centre, workers routinely have to draw on the quasi-therapeutic language of 'customer care' as 'if it were a caring profession in its own right' (Cameron 2000: 128). Service workers, and particularly call centre operators, often are instructed to perform what has been referred to by Hochschild (1983) as 'emotional labour'; that is, they are engaged in the management and commodification of feeling as part of their work role. For example, some call centres instruct their operators to use overly emotional, 'above the line', language, such as the hyperbolic 'that's brilliant' and 'that's tremendous' (when customers confirm their details) to build rapport with customers.

However, how much of these communicative ideals are inculcated and reflected in actual practice is difficult to say. Whereas in some service contexts, such as call centres, language use is indeed policed, there may be more leeway for employees in other settings. Both du Gay (1996) and Cameron (2000) comment on the fact that people negotiate and resist (linguistic) behaviours imposed on them by linguistic prescription in the workplace. As Fairclough (2001: 28) points out, a new discourse may be introduced into an institution or organization without being enacted or inculcated. People do not simply assimilate discourses, but appropriate, resist and subvert them, not necessarily in an open way but through 'rhetorical deployment'. They often use these discourses strategically without necessarily believing in them, as studies of managers in Higher Education have shown (Trowler 2001). Fairclough mentions the example of the 'appraisal interview' for staff, which has been quite extensively enacted within British universities. The extent of its inculcation is rather limited though – many academics resist its managerial discourses. This should remind us of the ability of individuals and groups to negotiate, displace and resist institutional discourses imposed on them (Giddens 1976).

In this unit we have covered linguistic studies that have dealt with recent structural and discoursal developments in the new global order. We have referred to the neo-capitalist workplace, the globalization of the media and the creation of an enterprise culture in Britain that has involved the reconstruction of many institutions along business lines. The introduction of Government schemes such as 'Enterprise in Education' and of now widespread institutional practices for staff, such as counselling, student-centred learning, and assertiveness and management training, are in many ways congruent with the political rhetoric of new capitalism: the (discursive) construction of an active, self-motivated, 'enterprising' individual who monitors his or her performance on the road to success. In unit C9 you have the opportunity to perform for yourself an analysis of marketized discourse from the higher education sector, specifically in the context of British universities entering into international markets to increase profits further.

STUDYING POLITICAL DISCOURSE: DEVELOPMENTS

B10

Developing the issues raised in A10, we will in this unit look at two very different linguistic studies of political discourse. Further below, we examine an example of 'life-style politics' in a British context. Before that, we focus on Chilton's analysis (2004) of a well-known political speech, given 50 years ago by British Conservative politician Enoch Powell, which has since become known as the 'Rivers of Blood' speech. The title arose because Powell quoted the classical Roman poet Virgil to make an oblique reference to the supposed threat of interracial conflict posed by an ever greater influx of foreigners into Britain:

> As I look ahead, I am filled with foreboding. Like the Roman, I seem to see 'the River Tiber foaming with much blood'.
>
> (quoted in Chilton 2004: 110)

Here Powell uses an 'indirect-meaning strategy' (Chilton 2004: 110), leaving it to the listener to make the inference that immigration will lead to a race war. Powell was subsequently expelled from the shadow cabinet for the inflammatory nature of his speech.

In his analysis of parts of the speech, Chilton (2004: 111–116) focuses on three of the four strategic functions political language may have (summarized in A10). These are legitimation/delegitimation, coercion and representation/misrepresentation. Chilton focuses mainly on lexical items (in bold below), *interpreting* their possible strategic functions. His interpretation of the strategies in the 'Rivers of Blood' speech are in boxed italics and interspersed with the speech:

The **supreme function of statesmanship**
Speaker is a supreme statesman
is to provide against preventable **evils**. In seeking to do so, it encounters obstacles which are deeply rooted in human nature. One is that by the very order of things such **evils** are not demonstrable until they have occurred … whence the besetting temptation of all politics to concern itself with the immediate present at the expense of the future.
Above all, **people are disposed to mistake**
Speaker does not make mistakes

predicting troubles for causing troubles and even for desiring troubles: 'if only', **they love to think**, 'if only people wouldn't talk about it, it probably wouldn't happen'. Perhaps **this habit goes back to the primitive belief** that the word

I do not have this habit, and I am not primitive

and the thing, the name and the object, are identical. At all events, the discussion of **future grave** but, with effort now, avoidable **evils** is the most unpopular and at the same time **the most necessary** occupation for the politician. **Those who knowingly shirk it**, deserve, and not infrequently receive,

I do not shirk moral duties

the **curses of those who come after**.

A week or two ago I fell into conversation with a constituent, a middle-aged, **quite ordinary working man**

Therefore from a reliable source

employed in one of our nationalized industries. After a sentence or two about the weather, he suddenly said: 'If I had the money to go, I wouldn't stay in this country' …. '**I have three children**, all of them have been through grammar school and two of them married now, with family. I shan't be satisfied till I have seen them settled overseas. In this country in fifteen or twenty years' time the **black man will have the whip hand over the white man**.'

This is not the speaker's assertion, it's from a reliable source

I can already hear the chorus of execration. How dare I say such a horrible thing? … The answer is that **I do not have the right not to** do so. Here is a **decent, ordinary fellow Englishman**, who in broad daylight in my own town says to me, his Member of Parliament, that this country will not be worth living in for his children. **I simply do not have the right to shrug my shoulders and think about something else.**

There exist moral rights and duties that I observe

What he is saying, thousands and hundreds of thousands are saying and thinking

Therefore from a reliable source

– not throughout Great Britain, perhaps, but in the areas that are already undergoing the total transformation to which there

England is being totally transformed

is no parallel in a thousand years of English history.

In fifteen or twenty years, on present trends, there will be in this country 3½ million Commonwealth immigrants and their descendants. **That is not my figure. That is the official figure given to Parliament by the spokesman of the Registrar General's Office.**

Therefore from a reliable source

The **natural and rational** first question with a nation confronted

I am rational, and natural, and these qualities are good

by such a prospect is to ask: 'How can its dimensions be reduced?' … the significance and consequences of an **alien element** introduced into a country or population are profoundly different according to whether that element is 1 per cent or 10 per cent.

The answers to the **simple and rational question** are equally *simplicity and rationality are good; rationality is simple*

simple and rational: by stopping or virtually stopping, further **inflow**, and by promoting the maximum **outflow**. Both answers are part of the **official policy** of the Conservative Party.

Therefore I am uttering official Conservative policy

[...]

If all immigration ended tomorrow ... the prospective size of this element in the population would still leave the basic character of **the national danger** unaffected ... years or so. [sic] Hence **the urgency** of implementing now the second element of the Conservative Party's policy ... If such a policy were adopted and pursued with the determination which the gravity of the alternative justifies, the resultant **outflow** could appreciably alter the prospects for the future. It can be no part of any policy that existing **families** should be kept divided; but ... we **ought** to be prepared to arrange for them to be reunited in their countries of origin.

Repatriation reunites families, therefore it is a moral duty

In his analysis, Chilton explores the strategies of legitimation, coercion and representation. We present here the main points of his argument.

Legitimation

Chilton sees two basic kinds of legitimation at work in Powell's speech: one is the speaker's claim to have better knowledge of the 'real' facts and therefore to be more 'rational' and more 'objective' than his political opponents. This type of legitimation is often backed up by figures and statistics that the speaker thinks the listener/reader will accept as authoritative (e.g. 'In fifteen or twenty years, on present trends, there will be in this country 3½ million Commonwealth immigrants and their descendants').

The second type of legitimation is the speaker's explicit or implicit claim that he is also right in a moral sense. The speaker not only presents 'facts' but also evokes certain basic feelings, of anger, sense of loyalty (to people one can assume to have a cultural affinity with), protectiveness, security and above all fear of invasion and domination by immigrants. Chilton also (2004: 117) detects 'a covertly metaphorical mode of expression' to do with physical space: spatial containment, movement in and out of a containing space, and movement of bodies (of immigrants). Hence the recurrent mention of 'flow', 'inflow' and 'outflow' in the speech.

Powell's legitimizing strategies can therefore be summarized as establishing moral authority and common moral ground, and claiming superior rationality. He makes 'truth claims' by quoting *authoritative* sources, such as Virgil on the one hand, and the 'ordinary' working man and the 'decent' Englishman on the other.

Coercion

Chilton (2004: 118) makes the important point that identifying coercive strategies 'is heavily dependent on interpretation' and that an entire speech could be classed as coercive in that it attempts to persuade. However, he distinguishes two kinds of coercion in the speech, which can provoke either emotional or cognitive responses. With regard to the first type, emotive coercion, one possible effect of Powell's speech is the inducement of fear by predicting that uncontrolled immigration will lead to racial conflict. In terms of speech acts (Austin 1962), Powell issues warnings.

Emotive coercion can occur when 'some fearful response may be stimulated' through the use of lexical items such as 'urgency', 'national danger' and 'evils', terms that are dispersed throughout the speech. Emotive coercion may also be said to occur through the spatial schema mentioned above – the conceptualization that one's country is 'a closed container that can be sealed or penetrated'.

The second type, cognitive coercion, is propositional rather than emotive and involves the different forms of implied meanings (indicated in italics in the speech above). Importantly, these implied propositions (presupposition, implicature and presumption) may not occur to all readers/listeners. It is debatable what long-term cognitive effects they have on the reader, they may not even have any at all depending on the hearer/reader. But, as Chilton points out, from a pragmatic point of view it becomes clear that such propositions are not easily challenged even if hearers find them inconsistent with their own representations of reality. Powell's attribution of the quote 'the black man will have the whip hand' to an actual source, namely the 'decent ordinary fellow Englishman', also makes it possible to frighten and simultaneously legitimize by making predictions, while evading responsibility for the assertion.

Representation

Here, Chilton focuses on the following part of Powell's speech:

> But while, to the immigrant entry to this country was admission to privileges and opportunities eagerly sought, the impact upon the existing population was very different. For reasons which they could not comprehend, and in pursuance of a decision by default, on which they were never consulted, they found themselves made strangers in their own country. They found their wives unable to obtain hospital beds in childbirth, their children unable to obtain school places, their homes and neighbourhoods changed beyond recognition, their plans and prospects for the future defeated; at work they found that employers hesitated to apply to the immigrant worker the standards of discipline and competence required of the native-born worker; they began to hear, as time went by, more and more voices which told them that they were now the unwanted.
>
> (2004: 122)

One of the first things to notice about this extract is the preponderance of noun phrases and nominalizations, so that the actions, effects and recipients of actions are not always clear. In some cases the predicate is clear, but not the argument, so that the hearer has to guess their meaning. A possible implied proposition in the text is that 'immigrants prevent wives of the existing population from obtaining hospital beds', although the speaker could of course claim that he never said that.

The text also contains the 'non-specified Agent' of passive constructions. As Chilton points out 'an intended referent can only be inferred, by the hearer, by way of contextual knowledge and background knowledge about contemporary politics' (2004: 122–123). In all the passive constructions from the extract above, 'they' is the grammatical 'topic' of the sentence, and at the same time the patient of an unspecified agent's action:

> they were never consulted
> themselves made strangers
> their homes and neighbourhoods changed
> their plans and prospects defeated
> standards of discipline and competence required of the native-born worker
> they were the unwanted

It is left to the hearers to work out who performed all these actions and to their ability to make an appropriate inference based on their political background knowledge. The likely conclusion that hearers may come to is that the agents are either the politicians criticized by Powell or the immigrants themselves. In Powell's representation of the world, the British people ('they') are predominantly 'proto-Patients' (Chilton 2004: 123); that is, they are at the receiving end of actions, perceptions and feelings. For example, they passively 'find' that things have happened to them ('they *found* themselves made strangers in their own country'), whereas immigrants actively 'seek' an objective ('privileges and opportunities eagerly *sought*'). So in the world that Powell tries to evoke in his speech, the British native population is victimized by the immigrants.

As Chilton states, it is difficult to interpret the possible effects that a political speech may have on its listeners/readers. It should, however, be pointed out that Powell's name and what he stood for cropped up 25 years later in a racist conversation among the main suspects in the Stephen Lawrence murder case (see A5) gained from a surveillance video police had installed in the suspects' house. Confirming van Dijk's view (1993a, 1993b) on elite racism, Chilton concludes that xenophobic discourse by elite speakers enters 'a network of communicative interchanges, involving the media and chains of face-to-face interaction that spread into the everyday talk of non-elite networks in a community' (2004: 124–125).

More discussion of language and politics can be found on the web materials that accompany this book.

THE LANGUAGE OF A SOCIAL MEDIA CAMPAIGN B11

In this section we introduce another discourse paradigm in the tradition of multimodal Critical Discourse Analysis. Developed by Martin (2000), this is the interpersonal system of evaluation, known as *Appraisal*. Appraisal is primarily a system of semantic resources for describing emotional reactions (*Affect*), moral assessments (*Judgement*) and for making aesthetic evaluations (*Appreciation*). More recently, Appraisal has also been applied to media images and journalistic discourse analysis (e.g. Economou 2006; Caple and Knox 2012; Mayr 2009) and can be seen as an important expansion of

Kress and van Leeuwen's (2006) interpersonal image analysis framework and modality (see B8). According to Martin, the primary function of a prominent image in a multi-modal article is to provoke a *desired* audience evaluation of the text that follows. The system of Appraisal is therefore another interpersonal category that is concerned with:

> how writers/speakers approve and disapprove, enthuse and abhor, ap-plaud and criticise, and with how they position their readers/listeners to do likewise.
>
> (Martin and White 2005: 1)

Appraisal allows the speaker or writer to comment on the world. Here we will apply Martin's three Appraisal categories to the analysis of online (newspaper) communica-tion. This is in line with more recent research in CDA which has treated digital media as 'emerging sites of discursive struggles' (KhosraviNik 2014: 287) and as a form of political action (Kelsey and Bennett 2014; Mayr 2009). We examine one such example of political engagement, a Facebook campaign launched by young people in Rio de Janeiro in protest against police violence and its coverage in a Rio newspaper. The reason for choosing this case is that in Brazil 'online media activism' (Custódio 2014) of this kind is one of the most important civic phenomena emerging from *favelas*, the self-built communities of the urban poor. Online media activism is used mainly by younger citizens as a democratizing force for social change through participatory media (Willis *et al.* 2014).

'Eu não mereço morrer assassinado': social media activism by favela youth in Rio de Janeiro.

The case reported here is of a Facebook campaign that was launched by favela youth after a fatal shooting of a young man by police. It is one example of the many small-scale online protests initiated by favela residents against human rights violations, some of which have occurred in the wake of the Rio state government's policy of favela 'Pacification', an ambitious community policing approach that was introduced in 2008. Importantly, some of this user-created content is increasingly incorporated into Rio's mainstream press, as was the case with Douglas Rafael Pereira da Silva, who was shot dead by police in a 'pacified' favela near Copacabana in April 2014. An aspiring televi-sion star, da Silva (also known as 'DG') had become caught up in a shoot-out between police and drug dealers. The case happened in a famous tourist area only three months before the start of the 2014 FIFA World Cup and therefore received intense national and international media coverage. The killing sparked street protests by favela res-idents, and in clashes with police another young man was shot dead. It was during these protests that a well-known blogger from a favela in Rio's North Zone, René Silva, posted an image of himself with a piece of paper bearing the inscription *Eu não mereço morrer assassinado* ('I don't deserve to be killed') on Facebook (see Figure B11.2 for a cropped version of the image). In this post, Silva mourned DG's death and called upon others to start an online campaign:

> My thoughts are with friend DG … What cowardice … they killed yet another young worker. Share this post and take part in this manifesto. Write [the message]

on a piece of paper and let's strengthen this movement because this cannot continue!

In terms of Appraisal, the message above contains strong negative Judgement of the act ('cowardice', 'killed') and positive Judgement of 'DG' ('friend', 'young worker'). The use of 'young *worker*' rather than, for example, 'young man' by Silva is significant, as it confers legitimacy on the victim and distinguishes him from drug dealing criminals ('traficantes', 'bandidos'), who usually receive no sympathy when killed by police. The poignant campaign slogan ('I don't deserve to be killed') also contains strong negative Judgement. The fact that it is handwritten makes it personal and intimate. In terms of Kress and van Leeuwen's (2006) framework (see B8), Silva's image (see Figure B11.1) is 'high-modality' or naturalistic, as it contains details and depth, natural shading and a realistic background. The fact that it is black and white lends it a documentary feel of 'authenticity'. Affect is inscribed in his sad facial expression and is provoked by his direct gaze, what Kress and van Leeuwen (1996) call a 'demand' image.

Many young people followed suit, posting images of themselves using the hashtag #EuNãoMereçoMorrerAssassinado on online channels. Some of the postings were quite creative, using different fonts, capitals, exclamation marks or red droplets to connote blood. These messages were clearly also *aesthetic* interventions; their Appreciation value was therefore quite high (see Mayr 2009). The following post is from Fernando Barcellos from the favela City of God, who used the hashtag #LutoDG (#I mourn DG) for his emotional appeal:

Figure B11.1 *Voz da Comunidade* (courtesy of Fernando Barcellos)

The campaign was subsequently covered in Rio's popular newspaper *Extra*, which has a track record of campaigning against human rights violations.

The visual composition of *Extra*'s page is structured along what Kress and van Leeuwen (2006) call 'centre' and 'margin' dimensions, where one element, in this case the image of René Silva is made the central element (Figure B11.2). *Extra*'s editor, Fabio Gusmão, explained that the paper always uses one large central image to create reader impact.

Let us now look at which of Martin's three kinds of Appraisal may be provoked by the choices of composition and content in *Extra* we just pointed out. The headline ('Após a morte …') , which translates as 'After DG's death, young people demand an end to killings in favelas with a social media campaign', contains negative Judgement ('killings'). The image below the headline *positions* the reader to accept the negative Judgement contained in the headline. However, as we shall see from the reader responses below, although headline and image together may be intended for the reader to feel empathy, affectual responses do not necessarily lead to empathy in readers. This is because images have the ability to 'trigger' people's pre-existing values, stereotypes, and cognitions (Domke *et al.* 2003). In other words, a provocation of strong Affect caused by an image may trigger Judgement. Economou (2008: 258) suggests that while the depiction of emotion on people's faces produces Affect, Judgement is more likely to be produced by the stance and gesture of social actors. In Brazil, the image of the dark-skinned, bare-chested youth acts as a potent cultural and class symbol and is taken by many as an indication of favela residence and hence criminality. It shows

Figure B11.2 *Extra* online page, 24 April 2014 (courtesy of Editor Fabio Gusmão)

René Silva in an extremely close frontal shot, taken from a horizontal angle and largely occupying the frame of the image. This results in what Kress and van Leeuwen (2006) call 'intimate social distance' between viewer and represented participant. However, practically none of the 53 reader comments expressed any sympathy for the fact that a young man had been tragically killed by police, nor did they demonstrate understanding for the campaign. Instead, the comments revolved around the activities of drug dealers in favelas.

While the image is interpersonally charged, it alone may not necessarily align the viewer for or against the young man in the image. The linguistic message on the image ('I don't deserve to be killed') with its strong negative Judgement is at least as important for communicating 'affective resonance' (Caple and Knox 2012: 222). This appears to be borne out by the reader comments below, whose negative evaluation of the campaign message is illustrated by inversions of the original:

1. I DON'T DESERVE TO LIVE WITH DOPEHEADS!!!
   [EU NÃO MEREÇO CONVIVER COM MACONHEIROS!!!!]
   #IDon'tDeservetoLiveWithDrugdealers
   [#EuNãoMereçoConviverComTraficantes]
2. I don't deserve to have drug dealers in my area
   [Eu não mereço ter traficantes de droga de meu bairro]
3. I also don't deserve to be killed, therefore help to get rid of the drug dealers here, who kill, corrupt and torture everybody who crosses their path and only then will we have peace.
   [Nem eu mereço morrer assassinado, então ajude acabar com os traficantes que aí estão, já que eles matam, viciam e torturam todos que cruzarem por seus caminhos e só assim teremos paz].

These three posts contain negative Judgement of drug consumers ('maconheiros' or 'dopeheads') and of drug dealers ('traficantes') and their actions ('kill, corrupt and torture', 'killed'). The capitals and exclamation marks as well as the hashtag in reader comment 1 are used to signal an emotionally charged comment and can be said to construe Affect in terms of anger (Zappavigna 2015). Interestingly, there was no condemnation or negative Judgement of the police in the above comments or in any other of the 53 comments the paper received.

Discussion

Some scholars suggest that online media activism of the kind discussed here may indeed have its greatest impact when it is incorporated into mainstream news media culture. As a result of *Extra*'s coverage of DG's case and of the campaign, one police officer was charged with murder and another six with fraudulent manipulation of the crime scene. User-created content is often perceived by professional journalists as possessing greater 'discursive authority' (Andén-Papadopoulos and Pantti 2011: 10) because of a sense of authenticity and personal intimacy with events. At the same time, campaigns of this nature are ephemeral and tend to be forgotten soon (see reading D11). They are also highly selective in that some cases travel from 'digital subcultures' (Mortenson 2011) to mainstream media, whereas others, which might be equally worthy of attention, do not. In the case study analysed here, two young men were shot and killed by police, but only one, a well-known aspiring TV star, received most of the media and public attention. The killing of the other victim, a homeless man with learning difficulties, was mentioned by *Extra*, but it did not provoke the same outrage. His image was posted on Facebook by a favela resident, asking for money to cover his burial.

Perhaps the main problem with an online campaign and its newspaper coverage is, as Mortensen (2011: 11) points out, that even if violence is exhibited pedagogically to prevent further violence and to engage the viewer, as this Facebook campaign and its reporting in *Extra* was meant to do, the spectator 'is enrolled in the logics of violence and needs to position him- or herself in a difficult process of identification and distancing'. We also have to bear in mind that images hardly ever convey a fixed message, as they are 'polysemous': they contain what Barthes (1977) calls a 'floating chain' of signifieds from which the viewer can choose some and ignore others. Therefore, the presumption that images like the ones analysed here will afford a heightened sense of emotional identification is never guaranteed (see Chouliaraki 2008). The reader comments analysed above appear to confirm this problem.

In the context of today's 'participatory' networked communication (see A11, and further in D11) it is also important to note that internet campaigns like the one reported here may be a 'superficial mode of participation' (Moubray 2015: 24), where political action is limited to circulating contributions on the net and works as a substitute for real political engagement in the form of 'off-line' activism, such as street protests. The Appraisal analysis conducted in this section shows that 'favela online media activism' (Custódio 2014) can be an important platform for denouncing human rights abuses, particularly when taken up by mainstream media, but it also points to its limited potential to mobilize change in Brazil, a society with rampant social and racial inequality.

B12 POST-TRUTH AND CRITICAL LINGUISTICS

Over in unit A12 we noted that critical discourse analysts have always been interested in how 'truth', or, at least, in how different conceptualizations of '*the* truth' have been portrayed in different kinds of texts. We also acknowledged the rather special circumstances that were attendant on the emergence of 'post-truth' and we will suggest shortly some methods for studying this more recent 'discursive shift' in society. However, it is important not to lose sight of the broad principle, emphasized in many parts of this book, that the exploration of the veracity or authenticity of texts has always been a mainstay of CL and, moreover, that such exploration often has clear social or cultural impact. A compelling recent example of this kind of work is Canning's critical discourse analysis of the Hillsborough Football Stadium disaster in England where, in 1989, 96 Liverpool football fans were unlawfully killed in a fatal crush at the ground (Canning 2017).Using a broad range of critical-linguistic frameworks, Canning demonstrates how members of the South Yorkshire Police Force, the unit in charge at the time of the tragedy, constructed a 'hooligan' narrative that portrayed the Liverpool fans as 'drunk', 'ticketless' and 'disorderly', and as ultimately to blame for the crush. The construction of this narrative, which scandalously led to a verdict from the original committee of inquiry of 'accidental death', involved making deletions and amendments to witness statements so as to vilify the actions of the fans on the one hand, while extolling the actions of the police on the other. For instance, the house-to-house questionnaires that were conducted with local residents were framed with strong presupposition-carrying triggers (see B7). You can work out for yourselves the presuppositions that are embedded in the initial interrogatives in each of the following two examples, but notice also how the phrasing of the text following these interrogatives leaves no doubt that the negative actions – theft, drunkenness and disorderly behaviour – are assumed to have already taken place:

1. 'Did football supporters steal alcohol to your knowledge? Explain briefly and estimate quantity.'
2. 'Did you witness any incidents of drunkenness or disorderly behaviour of any of the fans? (Brief description). Include time of incident.'

(after Canning 2017)

In addition to these framing techniques, original statements that were elicited from members of the emergency services were often presented to the inquiry in amended versions. The first statement in the pair below was the original version, taken from a paramedic at the scene. The second statement is the amended form, and this was the version presented to the original inquiry into the disaster:

1. '… as I alighted from my car I asked a Policeman where the Control point was, he did not know.'
2. '… I asked the ambulance crew in the area where the control point was. The[y] said they did not know and they left with casualties. I do not know who that crew was.'

(after Canning 2017)

Although the actions of the South Yorkshire Police later came to be heavily criticized, Canning's analysis reveals the extent to which the evidence-gathering process was constructed as a narrative frame through which blame was attributed. This frame, which was obligingly disseminated by the right-wing press, became part of a broader institutional narrative. But this narrative was predicated on the existence of a flawed body of witness statements that had been patently subjected to a systematic process of 'review and alteration' prior to their submission to initial inquiry. Writing in his capacity as lead researcher and primary author of the subsequent Hillsborough Independent Panel's report, Scraton concludes that the police's tactic of blaming the fans while exonerating themselves was sufficient to establish 'a broad and seemingly legitimate constituency' (2004: 185).

Post-truth and 'universal pragmatics'
Here we narrow the focus to consider a particular model of language that not only has significant potential for the analysis of 'truth' in discourse, but also for the analysis of

the other cognitive and social variables that come into play when we try to understand and interpret texts. The model, which we introduce below, tends to be more about the analysis of responses to texts rather than of the patterns in the texts themselves. The method of analysis essentially involves going beyond the text to focus on people's structured reactions to the texts as they express them through various media. Thus, this approach has an important bearing on the study of what has come to be termed *mediated* (or sometimes *mediatized*) reactions to texts and discourse.

The method that we have in mind, and which has been adapted productively in various CL studies, is the model of 'universal pragmatics' proposed by the Frankfurt-School philosopher, Jürgen Habermas (Habermas 1979; and see also Montgomery, 2007: 217–219 for a short overview.) The task of a programme in universal pragmatics is, according to Habermas, to identify and reconstruct universal conditions of possible understanding; to account, in other words, for the general presuppositions of communicative action (1979: 1). Habermas goes on to argue that anyone acting communicatively must, in performing any speech action, raise universal validity claims and then assume that these claims can be vindicated. According to Habermas, there are three principal validity claims which we gloss here as *truth*, *sincerity* and *appropriateness*.

The validity claim of *truth* relates an utterance to external reality. External reality refers to the world of objects about which one can make true or false statements. More simply put, it expresses the accuracy of a particular utterance with respect to the actual state of affairs in the real world. Unlike the claim of truth, the claim of *sincerity* (or 'truthfulness' in Habermas's original terms) arises from the subjectivity of the speaker or hearer and is disclosed in 'internal nature'. Sincerity is therefore the internal reality that a speaker would like to disclose in the public sphere, such that the speaker's own world of internal experiences can be expressed either sincerely or insincerely.

The last of the claims, *appropriateness*, embodies the normative reality for legitimate interpersonal relationships. Governing this claim (sometimes referred to as 'rightness' by Habermas) is an attitude to the institutional systems of culture and society. Set against both 'the' world of external nature and 'my' world of internal nature, the validity claim of appropriateness centres on 'our' social life-world of shared values and norms, of roles and rules. Within the framework of appropriateness, utterances are themselves either right (that is legitimate, justifiable) or wrong (illegitimate, unjustifiable). Table B12.1 captures the core elements of Habermas's model.

While the theoretical tenets of the validity claim model may seem rather daunting and inaccessible, its application by critical linguists to real data makes it, in a sense, come alive. For instance, an early study by Edginton and Montgomery applies the model to two British election broadcasts from 1992 and to the mediated responses that followed them in the popular press (Edginton and Montgomery 1996: 114–120). The Party Election Broadcast (PEB) run by the opposition Labour Party (then under Neil Kinnock) featured a five-year-old girl suffering from glue ear who had to wait a year for a simple operation on the National Health Service (NHS). Her plight was paralleled in the PEB with the story of an obviously wealthier family who could afford to pay privately for their own daughter's treatment for the same condition. The PEB was designed to highlight the underfunding of the NHS by the Conservative government. In a very

Table B12.1 The Model of Universal Pragmatics (adapted from Habermas 1979: 68)

Validity claim	Domain of reality	Mode of communication	General speech function
Truth	'the' world of external nature	Cognitive: objectivating attitude	Representation of facts – so that the speaker can share their knowledge with the hearer
Sincerity ('truthfulness')	'my' world of internal nature	Expressive: expressive attitude	Disclosure of the speaker's subjectivity – so that the hearer can trust the speaker
Appropriate-ness ('right-ness')	'our' world of society	Interactive; conformative attitude	Establishment of legitimate interpersonal relations – so that the hearer can be in accord with the speaker in shared value orientations

different vein, the Conservative government's PEB featured incumbent Prime Minister John Major making a return visit, after many years, to his humble origins in Brixton, London. Directed by John Schlesinger, the PEB was filmed in Major's chauffeur-driven car with the camera picking up his reactions, both verbal and non-verbal, to seeing (apparently for the first time in years) his old home and neighbourhood.

The tack taken by Edginton and Montgomery is an interesting one because it uses the Habermasian model to detect an asymmetrical pattern in the emergent media reaction to these PEBs. This reaction essentially plays off different validity claims and it creates a very different structuring paradigm for the interpretation of each of the two PEBs. For instance, right-wing print media reaction to the Conservative PEB played down its claim to *truth* while foregrounding its claim to *sincerity*. The *Today* newspaper, for example, acknowledged that even though a director such as Schlesinger could still not make John Major a decent actor (implying a lack of conviction in the 'truth' of the broadcast), it still found itself able to laud Major as 'the ordinary bloke', and as 'your pal John who buys tomatoes'. The *Daily Mail* goes further, touching on Major's 'unassuming modesty' and declaring that 'it is impossible to dent his *sincerity*' (our emphasis). Ignoring its preposterous staginess and the debatable truth of what it portrays, other papers remark on the genuinely touching moments in this PEB, on even seeing 'the memories on John Major's face'.

Mediated reaction to the Labour PEB played to an altogether different configuration of validity claims. While no one could doubt Labour's passion about the running down of the NHS, the claim of sincerity was never raised. Instead, the tabloids played up the two other claims, *truth* and *appropriateness*. The most widely read anti-Labour tabloid, the *Sun*, ran with a headline that challenged directly the PEB's validity claim of truth: 'If Kinnock will tell lies about a sick little girl, will he ever tell the truth about anything?'. This appeal to truth was pursued vigorously by the tabloids such that it led to the tracking down of both the family and the medics who were involved in the case. Invading the privacy of both groups, the tabloid reporters attempted to tease out any aspect of the case (the precise length of the delay for the operation, for example) that could compromise the story's claim to truth. Appealing also to the claim of appropriateness, great play was made in the pro-Tory press of the ethics of the story. Even though the case was a genuine one, there was great indignity at the involvement of a young girl in a political broadcast. So vituperative and vociferous was this media campaign that it became known as 'The War of Jenny's Ear'. What it does show is just how mediated reactions bring into play very different interpretive paradigms and, in consequence, how resolutely behind the Tories were the British redtop tabloids. While the Labour leader was branded an unethical liar, the Tory leader emerged, untainted by the excesses of his predecessor Margaret Thatcher, as sincere and genuine, a man very much in touch with the ordinary people of Britain.

In a later study, Montgomery applies the Habermasian model to the verbal tributes offered in the aftermath of the death, in August 1997, of Diana, Princess of Wales (Montgomery 1999). In this classic study, Montgomery considers some of the linguistic properties of the speeches by the Queen, the (then) British Prime Minister Tony Blair, and by Diana's brother Earl Spencer, before focusing on the mediated reactions to the speeches by broadcasters and by members of the public. Montgomery highlights the interpretative frameworks through which these speeches are assessed and understood. However, in unit C12, we propose to build some practical exercises around the data and analysis in this article, so we will make no further comment on this particular study here.

A more recent study again is Montgomery (2017) which comprises a detailed analysis of the discourse of Donald Trump during his campaign for the US Presidency. Montgomery's core research question is how was Trump able to persuade a significant portion of the electorate to vote for him while saying things that were widely regarded as either deeply offensive or plain wrong? While many US voters rejected much of what Trump claimed as lies, a significant portion of the electorate nonetheless found his words acceptable on some basis. Montgomery attributes this success in part to Trump's cultivation of an aura of authenticity which was embedded in a discourse of 'vernacular folksiness' (Montgomery 2017: 627). Couched in terms of the Habermas model, while Trump's claims were subjected to close scrutiny on the basis of *truth*, and his behaviour deemed *inappropriate* by many commentators, the rhetorical emphasis on *sincerity* was crucial to the appeal of his public statements to his electorate.

With both objective facts and standards of behaviour becoming less influential in shaping public opinion, it seems that personal beliefs and appeals to emotion – appeals to 'my' world of internal nature in other words – have come to dominate the post-truth era. D'Ancona remarks that for many, emotional sincerity is the highest virtue, greater than 'the starchy pursuit of objective truth' (2017: 33). In this respect D'Ancona, like Montgomery, sees the election of Trump as a consequence, not a cause, emanating from different ways of seeing the world. D'Ancona offers a cautionary follow-up, pointing out that Trump's departure from political office, whenever that day comes, will *not* mark the end of the post-truth era and it is a grave error of analysis to think otherwise (2017: 33; our emphasis). Unit D12, a reading by Robin Lakoff, builds on these observations.

Section C

EXPLORATION:
ANALYSING LANGUAGE AND POWER

C1 BEGINNING ANALYSIS

All of the material in this vertical section of the book is concerned with the exploration of texts and discourses within the parameters of the models and frameworks developed across equivalent A and B units. However, rather than throw you in at the deep end, as it were, we propose to begin with a sample analysis of a text that applies some of the concepts developed in A1 and B1. We concentrate particularly on Fairclough's three-dimensional model, outlined in B1.

Before moving on to the text, here are some aspects of text that could usefully form the basis of a preliminary investigation (following Fairclough 1989: 110–112), although we need to stress that many of these features will be elaborated in greater detail in other parts of the book.

Vocabulary

❑ Are there words in the text that are ideologically contested, such as sexist or racist terms?

❑ Are there formal or informal words, or is there a mixture of the two?

❑ What expressive values do the words have? How, for example, are evaluative words used?

❑ What metaphors/idioms are used?

Grammar

❑ What types of verbs are used? For example, do the verbs describe activity or states?

❑ Is agency (un)clear? (see also B1)

❑ Are nominalizations used? That is, have some verbs been turned into nouns? (see A1 and B4)

❑ Are sentences active or passive?

❑ Are there important features of modality? That is, are statements made directly and with certainty or are they toned down or 'hedged'? Look out for modal verbs such as 'can', 'might' or 'may' or adverbs such as 'probably', 'obviously' or 'certainly', which all express the writer's/speaker's opinion.

❑ Are the pronouns 'we' and 'you' used and if so, how?

A sample CDA analysis

Read now the following article from UK tabloid paper the *Daily Mail* (17 February 2016) and our supporting commentary on it. Reflect upon the points raised in the commentary, which are designed to provide you with a clearer idea of the issues with which CDA is concerned and some of the methods it employs.

Criminal notifications for EU migrants leap by 40% in five years: now there are 700 every week in the UK but less than 20,000 foreign criminals have been deported

- Europeans involved in 146,100 notifications including murder and rape since 2012
- Poles and Romanians the worst offenders, fuelling fears over EU impact
- But the statistics show that only 19,227 foreign crooks have been deported
- Evidence the bloc's freedom of movement rules are routinely being abused
- Notifications are made to other countries when their citizens are convicted, appeal their convictions or break their court orders

British courts are dealing with more than 700 notifications involving European Union migrants every week in the UK – a rise of nearly 40 per cent in five years.

In a fresh blow for EU backers, figures show that Europeans have been involved in 146,100 notifications – including murder and rape – since 2012.

Poles and Romanians are the worst offenders, fuelling fears over the impact of EU expansion.

But the statistics show that only 19,227 foreign crooks have been deported in the past four years – many of whom will have originally come from outside Europe.

Critics seized on the figures as evidence that the bloc's freedom of movement rules are routinely being abused. Under an EU information-sharing system, British police forces notify counterparts in other member states if one of its citizens is convicted of a crime here. The figures were released by the National Police Chiefs' Council under the Freedom of Information Act, which has exposed numerous public sector scandals but is now under threat from the Government.

They showed that last year 37,079 notifications were made. This is equivalent to 713 a week – or 101 every day. It compared to 27,056 notifications in 2010 – meaning there has been a 37 per cent increase for EU citizens in the UK. A notification also includes an appeal or a breach of a court order, said criminal records office ACRO.

Experts suggest that the figures are evidence that the surge of migration sparked by Britain throwing open its doors to citizens from the former Soviet bloc has led to a rise in the number of crimes.

In 2015, there were notifications concerning 10,300 Poles and 6,249 Romanians. They were followed by citizens from Ireland (5,164), Lithuania (4,557) and Latvia (2,330).

Jack Montgomery, spokesman for Eurosceptic group Leave.EU, who uncovered the figures, said: 'Remain campaigners like to claim that the EU is a huge boon to security and public safety. Free movement is enabling tens of thousands of crimes to be committed every year. This is a dreadful trade-off, however you measure it, and the situation is clearly worsening.

'The public are being endangered and the law-abiding majority of immigrants are being given a bad name, which worsens tensions.'

David Green, director of think-tank Civitas, added: 'When we consider if immigration is a bad thing or a good thing we have got to remember that a lot of people who arrive here are criminals.'

And Conservative MP David Davis said: 'This is just a demonstration that freedom of movement means we can't keep out people who we would wish to keep out in the public interest, or expel people we would wish to keep out.'

There were no details regarding offences or sentences. But figures will include a convicted Polish rapist who changed his name and used false documents to enter the UK and rape two more women he met online. Rafal Bargiel, 40, was jailed for life last December.

EU citizens sentenced to jail will be eligible for deportation but officials must check if they are a threat to public security, public policy or public health.

In 2014, the last calendar year for which figures are available, 1.2 million offenders were convicted in Britain's courts. There are about 3 million EU citizens among Britain's 63.7 million population. This was a 34 per cent rise on 2010. A Britain Stronger In Europe spokesman said: 'Our membership of the EU keeps us safer from terrorism and cross-border crime.

'Those advocating an end to free movement would also end our membership of the single market – hitting British businesses hard and increasing prices in the shops.

'Leavers know they can't win the argument on the economy so they're reduced to scaremongering once again.'

Commentary: text, discourse practice and social practice

Text

Before looking at the article in terms of discourse practice and social practice, let us look at the first dimension, the analysis of discourse as *text*. The text itself is an example of 'tabloid' journalism and a piece of 'hard news' (Bell 1991). 'Hard news' reports immediate events, such as crimes and disasters, whereas 'soft news' is usually longer articles or commentaries, sometimes with the author's personal opinion and usually bylined by his or her name.

Starting with the headline, we can say that it aims to express the essence of the article, so that the reader can gain a fairly accurate idea of what the whole article will be about. Headlines also serve as an important strategic tool to control the way readers make sense of the text. In a genre of discourse where space is limited, such as print media discourse, words need to be carefully chosen for maximum effect. In this way, headlines often encapsulate the newspaper's political stance and analysing the lexical choices and syntactic structures can tell you about possible underlying ideological meanings.

Consider in particular the naming strategies used in the headline and sub-headlines, which operate to provide additional supporting points for the ideology prevalent in the main headline. *EU migrants* are represented as *foreign criminals*, *Europeans* are associated with *murder and rape*, with *Poles and Romanians* being the *worst offenders*. Vocabulary (lexis) is one of the most obvious means speakers/writers employ to express ideological opinions about people and events, and the choice of lexis in this headline is therefore very important in connecting immigration to criminality. In a strategy mirrored throughout the article, the actions of these *foreign crooks* are lent facticity by the inclusion of no less than five sets of statistics, emphasizing the scale of the supposed problem of criminality amongst immigrant groups.

Another important function of vocabulary is that it achieves lexical cohesion. Cohesion is achieved by repetition and reiteration of words that are linked in meaning. The starkest example of repetition in this article comes at the very beginning, with the first six paragraphs echoing directly and immediately the points made in the headline and sub-headlines. *Poles and Romanians are the worst offenders* is repeated verbatim, as is the classification of migrants as *foreign crooks*. Despite acknowledgement later in the article that there are *no details regarding offences or sentences*, the repetition of *rape and murder* strongly implies that many of the 146,100 notifications refer to very serious crimes. Statistics are used consistently throughout the article to emphasize exactness and to imply objectivity (remember that in media discourses very often these figures are accompanied by very little wider context – in this article the statistics are not compared to general crime figures provided by, for example, the Home Office, nor are they set against statistics that record relevant factors such as the number of immigrants residing in poverty in the UK). All of the statistics provided in the headline clauses are repeated at the top of the article, with additional figures used similarly throughout. Some subtle and strategic elaboration is also included amidst the reiteration at the beginning of the article, *EU migrants* and *Europeans* are now identified as *European Union migrants*, whilst *EU impact* becomes *EU expansion*. Both examples are important given the 'Brexit' context of this article, discussed further below.

Note also the use of synonyms or near-synonyms, as in *leap/rise/increase/surge, deported/keep out/expel, fresh blow/dreadful trade-off, criminals/crooks/offenders, endangered/abused, the bloc/the former Soviet bloc*, and see also antonyms, such as *freedom of movement/deportation*. The function of repetition and reiteration is to intensify meaning, with repetition having the strongest cohesive force. Fowler *et al.* (1979) have called this dense wording of a domain *overlexicalization* (see further, D1 and C3) which they consider a pragmatic strategy for encoding ideology in news discourse. Overlexicalization can therefore signal a certain (ideological) preoccupation on the part of the writer(s) with an issue, in our case criminality as connected to EU membership, and the 'threat' posed by immigration.

Ideology can also be expressed in *metaphors*; that is, through a figurative use of language (see further Strand 10). A metaphorical construction prevalent in media discourses about immigration is the 'building metaphor' (see Charteris-Black (2004) and unit D10), where migration being 'on the doorstep' of the State is described for example, or one country is represented as the supposed 'cornerstone' of democracy, constructing the notion of strength or security against some perceived threat. In our text, Britain is accused of *throwing open its doors to citizens from the former Soviet bloc*, which has apparently led to the increased crime figures referred to consistently. Charteris-Black (2004: 68) states that building metaphors often describe social conditions that are 'well-founded, solid, permanent and stable'; in this article the freedom of movement of EU citizens is constructed starkly in contrast to this stability – the policy has caused Britain to wantonly compromise security. The use of this metaphor is immediately followed in the article by more strategically selected statistics and a number of supporting 'expert opinions'. The crime figures in the article are also figuratively endowed with activity and immediacy, on two occasions they are *fuelling fears* over the European Union in an article published only months before Britain's vote to withdraw from the alliance.

According to Lakoff (1987), metaphors derive largely from our direct experiences with the environment and consequently frequently occur in everyday communication. The use of metaphorical/idiomatic expressions above results in a slight change from a formal to a more conversational tone in the text. This can be seen as an attempt by news providers to create solidarity with an assumed readership to whom they can mediate news in its own 'common-sense' terms. There is a degree of mystification about whose positions are being represented in the text; it is not expressed explicitly, for example whose fears are being *fuelled* by these statistics. If the positions of powerful people and groups are represented in a version of everyday speech (even a simulated and partially unreal one), then social identities and distances are collapsed. This is a point we will elaborate on in our discussion of the text as discourse practice below.

The use of *pronouns* is also worth looking at in a critical analysis of texts. We can see that there is little overt interaction with the reader in that they are not addressed directly, the statistics being presented as if they are objectively conceived facts. There are, however, some examples of inclusive 'we' and one of a more ambiguous 'you' in the quotations from 'experts' in the text. An example of 'inclusive we' would be 'Shall *we* go to the cinema tonight?', which involves both speaker and addressee.

> 'Freedom of movement means *we* can't keep out people who *we* would wish to keep out [...] or expel people *we* would wish to keep out.'
> 'This is a dreadful trade-off however *you* measure it, and the situation is clearly worsening.'

Use of the pronoun 'we' can be one strategy of 'positive self-presentation' (van Dijk 1993a; Caldas-Coulthard 2003: 287) with 'we', the British public, having to bear the consequences of EU membership through its apparent link to criminality. This contrasts with the 'negative other-presentation' that would be delivered through the use of a pronoun such as 'they', as in *officials must check if they are a threat to public security*. This article has a certain 'us' versus 'them' feel to it, note particularly the identification of *Poles and Romanians*, the list of nationalities in the eighth paragraph, and the repeated reference to the EU as a *bloc*. According to Reisigl and Wodak this is what in part exemplifies racist discourse: 'the generalized and absolute evaluation of differences that is advantageous to the accuser and detrimental to his/her victim' (2001: 5).

Another important means to make ideological meanings in texts is *grammar*. One feature you can look at is the types of verbs that are used in texts, as they have an important function in representing 'reality'. This text contains various patterns involving the verb 'to be' for example:

> There *are* 700 every week in the UK
> Poles and Romanians *are* the worst offenders
> The situation *is* clearly worsening

'To be', and indeed 'to have' in many other media texts, describe states rather than actions (see further unit B4). The possible ideological work achieved by the use of these verbs in the present tense is that they can be used to present as facts what are essentially ideologically driven and non-contextualized interpretations of the statistics.

Another noteworthy grammatical feature of this text is the extent to which the immediacy of the apparent threat is emphasized through the consistent use of verbs with a continuous aspect. These constructions reiterate the progressive and ongoing nature of a supposed problem, which will require some action to prompt cessation, in this case withdrawal from the EU policy on the free movement of people.

> The bloc's freedom of movement rules are routinely *being abused*.
> The public are *being endangered* and the law abiding majority of immigrants are *being given* a bad name.

Looking at nouns and nominalizations (see A1), a significant function of these lexical items is that they allow their referents to be specified, for instance through adding an evaluative or judgemental adjective. This has the effect of turning them into items with rather fixed, non-negotiable meanings, conveying the writer's opinion. Nominalization is not a very prominent feature of this particular article, although the following sentence from the ninth paragraph illustrates nominalization at work (in bold, with the evaluative term in italics):

> This is a *dreadful* **trade-off**, however you measure it, and the situation is clearly worsening.

Nominalization can also offer writers a wider choice of putting elements in sentence-initial position, as the subject or 'theme' of the sentence, thereby stressing what writers deem to be important information and making it more difficult for the reader to contest these meanings.

If we employ a fairly broad notion of modality, as in Fairclough (1992: 158–162), we may include any unit of language that expresses the writer's personal opinion of what s/he says, such as hedging (*I believe/think/suppose*), modal verbs (*can, may, must*) and modal adverbs (*obviously, clearly, probably, surely*) with their equivalent adjectives (*it is obvious/clear/probable*). In this article, the writer never appears in constructions such as *I think/believe*. Myers suggests that 'any implication that belief is personal weakens it' (1989: 14). The media generally claim that what they report are facts, knowledge and truth. In terms of modality, therefore, writers prefer more objective modalizing statements, such as *it is certain/clear* and so on, which allow partial perspectives to be universalized, suggesting that events can be categorically represented. This underpins the ideological work of the media in 'offering images of and categories for reality, positioning and shaping social subjects, and contributing for the most part to social control and reproduction' (Fairclough 1992: 161). Consider the following clauses: 'The statistics *show* that …'; 'We *have got to remember* that …'; 'This *is just* a demonstration that …'; 'But figures *will include* …'. Here we can see that what are essentially personal views or exercises in speculation have been turned into facts. These statements are presented as *categorical assertions*, presented as facts or certainties rather than being marked for modality. Indeed it is often the case that a statement is stronger if it is presented like this rather than being accompanied by a high modal adverb for example. Consider the effect of 'Poles and Romanians *are* the worst offenders' versus that of 'Poles and Romanians *definitely are* the worst offenders'. The categorical assertion sounds more factual.

Discourse practice

Approaching the text as an instance of discourse practice, we may wish to specify the processes involved in its production, distribution and consumption. Fairclough contends:

> The discursive practice dimension … involves various aspects of the processes of text production and text consumption. Some of these have a more institutional character [e.g. the editorial procedures of the *Independent* compared to *The Times*] whereas others are discourse processes in a narrower sense [the 'decoding' of texts by the reader/viewer].
>
> (1995b: 58)

We need therefore to consider the discursive processes of news discourse. This is by no means an easy task as in the written press texts never derive from a single source. According to Bell (1991), the production of a narrative involves a joint effort from multiple parties, including the work of the chief reporter, journalist, subeditors, editors, print setters and perhaps many others. As a consequence, the narrative undergoes many transformations and modifications, which, as Caldas-Coulthard (1992: 39) notes, mitigates responsibility for the text. It seems reasonable then to question to what extent the authors of the text were involved in its production and what was altered – regarding the quotations from Jack Montgomery or David Davis, or indeed from the ideologically unnamed *spokesman* for the group A Britain Stronger in Europe – or what was added and deleted by others. Moreover, newspaper organizations these days are driven more than ever by the economic imperative to retain their audience within a very competitive media market. This means that in practice institutional practices determine what becomes news more so than the events themselves. So to understand news texts and the ideologies they produce we need to understand them in part as a result of these routine practices and not simply as bias on the part of the author(s).

The most common form of intertextuality, an important index of discourse practice, is reported speech. Reported speech can be reported directly through the reproduction of actual speech or in indirect report or summary. The text contains examples of both. Paragraphs 9, 10, 11, 12, and 15 have direct reported speech (in inverted commas) and paragraphs 5 and 7 are examples of indirect report, attributed to *critics* and *experts*. Teo points out that the use of direct quotes is one device of newsmakers to give a 'semblance of facticity and authenticity', which is a 'powerful ideological tool to manipulate readers' perception and interpretation of people and events' (2000: 18–19). In this text three people are quoted – in support of these *critics* and *experts* – who offer Eurosceptical interpretations of the statistics, whilst only one *spokesman* represents any dissenting opinions. Note particularly that this contributor's opinions on criminality are not represented, hence he can be dismissed as someone ignoring the core issue of the article, despite the fact that this section of his commentary has been chosen by the *Mail*.

Interdiscursivity means that a text contains elements of different genres. Our text contains a mixture of formal and more informal language. Figurative language represented by the metaphors discussed above is an example of more informal language which operates to construct allegiances between writer and reader.

Social practice

Looking at our text in terms of social practice, we can ask what this text says about the society it was produced in and the society it was produced for. What impact could it have on social relations? For example, could it help to continue certain social practices (e.g. xenophobia) or help to break them down? It is at this point, when we start looking at the 'social and cultural goings-on' behind a text (Fairclough 1995b: 57), that discourse analysis becomes 'critical'. This article has been produced in a socio-political climate which was dominated by the impending 'Brexit' referendum of June 2016, when the UK voted by a slim majority so secede from the European Union. The text is representative of those in many right-wing publications in the UK which have consistently focussed on offering limited representations of immigration, focussing on such things as criminality. This article for example does not consider the fact that criminality is more accurately connected to poverty than it is to race or nationality for example (See Gabrielatos and Baker (2008) and unit B5 for an account of these limited representations). Much of the climate which marked a section of British politics prior to the Brexit vote had been ideologically sculpted by articles such as this one to be hostile to the idea of European integration and EU membership, and to view the EU as a corrupt, bureaucratic and excessively costly political venture. This 'moral panic' shared by sectors of the British public over EU membership *fuelled fears* connected to xenophobia and anti-integrationist stances which were ultimately manifested in the Brexit vote.

Summary

To summarize our analysis, Fairclough's three-dimensional model (discourse as text, discourse as discourse practice and discourse as social practice) is based on three components: *description*, *interpretation* and *explanation*. In this analysis of the text from the *Daily Mail*, we have *described* some of the linguistic properties of the text, we have attempted both to *interpret* the relationship between text and discourse practice and to *explain* the relationship between discourse and social practice.

The following unit develops these issues further, offering a series of practical activities centred on the discourse of institutions.

Activity C1.1 ✪

❑ Select an article from a newspaper that refers to the 2017 election in the Netherlands, where the Freedom Party of Geert Wilders was a strong presence, or from France before the 2017 election, in which Marine Le Pen of the *Front National* party was eventually defeated by *En Marche!* candidate Emmanuel Macron.

❑ Conduct a Critical Discourse Analysis of how EU membership is represented. Can you expose ideological leanings in the text you have chosen?

C2 EXPLORING REGISTER AND IDEOLOGY

Across this Strand the focus has been on the language of organizations and institutions, and in particular, on the use of specialist registers by those institutions. The reading which accompanies this Strand in D2 looks specifically at bureaucracy as social control, and it fleshes out a number of the issues touched upon in B2. For now, here are some activities based around the issues raised in both A2 and B2.

'Officialese' and political institutions

The following two extracts report the death of a 33-year-old Birmingham man while in police custody. The first extract is the Home Office statement on the event, representing the British Government's official position. The second is the report of an independent pathologist on the same incident.

1. Following an assault on a custody officer, Mr X was being moved from one part of a prison to another when he became unwell. Medical assistance was called. He was pronounced dead at 21.21 hours.

2. The appearance of Mr X's body is definitely that of an asphyxial death. In my opinion death was due to the way he was handled. I am very concerned by the similarities of this case with that of Mrs Y, who died while a police squad was attempting to deport her.

A number of linguistic models lend themselves to this sort of analysis, many of which were elaborated across Strand 1, while unit B4, on transitivity, is also helpful.

Activity C2.1 ✪

❑ What are the main differences in the language of the two extracts, and what underlying positions are revealed in the texts?

❑ To be more blunt, if you were a member of the dead man's family, which report would *you* consider the more helpful?

'Congruent' and 'metaphorical' discourses

In discussing the way certain actions are depicted in the media, Fairclough talks of *congruent* and *metaphorical* discourses (Fairclough 1995b: 94–97). A congruent discourse is one that relays the sorts of experience it most usually signifies; a metaphorical discourse is the extension of a discourse to signify experience *other than* that which it normally signifies.

Consider the following headlines and opening texts (provided in Fairclough's analysis) from two newspapers of 13 January 1993 (two years after the 'first' Gulf War):

> *Spank You and Goodnight*
> *Bombers Humble Saddam in 30 Minutes*
> More than 100 Allied jets yesterday gave tyrant Saddam Hussein a spanking –
> blasting missile sites in a raid that took just 30 minutes.
>
> (*Sun*)

> *Saddam's UN Envoy Promises Good Behaviour After Raid by US, British and French*
> *Aircraft Gulf Allies Attack Iraqi Missiles*
> More than 100 aircraft blasted Iraqi missile sites last night after the allies' patience
> with Saddam Hussein's defiance finally snapped.
>
> (*Daily Telegraph*)

❑   What elements of the discourse of military attack are *congruently* applied in these two texts? Are there cases of *non-congruent* (*metaphorical*) application also, and if so, what effect does this have?

 Activity C2.2

❑   As a related activity, consult the website material which accompanies the book. For unit C2 you will find an excerpt from an American Department of Defense newsletter on the use of new laser weaponry. Consider the questions focussed on the concept of register which follow this text.

POWER AND RESISTANCE IN SPOKEN DISCOURSE   **C3**

In A2 we mentioned that whenever the exercise of power in discourse meets with resistance, this may take a variety of forms. People can and do contest institutional discourses, some of which are more active than others. In institutional contexts where the overt expression of power by the more powerful participants has been toned down, such as in the workplace, active resistance in discourse is more likely to occur. However, overt resistance to institutional discourse practices is unlikely when people's economic survival is at stake; for example, when they are dependent on state support. In such circumstances, milder 'everyday forms of resistance' (Scott 1985) are the strategies of the 'disempowered'. These are the kinds of 'dissent that are practised in the mundane, day-to-day process of living', which very often take the form of 'hidden transcripts'; that is, protest that occurs 'backstage', away from those with institutional authority, or is disguised so that members of the dominant group can only suspect their meaning.

Reverse discourse

People engage in the forms of resistance noted above through talk and they do so, for example, by rejecting often derogatory labels to classify them. For example, Pelissier Kingfisher (1996), in her study of a group of American 'welfare mothers' found that these women resisted stereotypes that branded them as lazy and promiscuous by making use of 'reverse discourse' (Foucault 1980). Reverse discourse 'draws on the very vocabulary or categories of dominant discourses in order to make a case for oppressed groups' (Pelissier Kingfisher 1996: 541). An example of reverse discourse can be seen in the following excerpt, where three 'welfare mothers' discuss a meeting they had with the aide to a local legislator:

```
1   S:   I told him, I said EVERY chi::ld NEEDS a safe
2        environment, NOT the rich, NOT the middle class, but
3        ALSO WELfare mothers
4   R:                          yep
5   S:                               and we are having to leave
6        Our kids with ANYbody and everybody that'll take 'em
7   C:   yep
8   S:        THAT'S not ri:ght
9   C:                    no it's not right
10  S:                                 that's
11  (   )
12  [
13  R:   'cause they're our FU:Ture
```

These three women not only insist that 'welfare mothers' should have the same rights as more well-to-do mothers but they also use reverse discourse by arguing that *all* children deserve to be looked after properly and by expressing concern for the next generation ('they're *our* future'). These are notions appropriated from mainstream discourse and probably very few people would argue with them. Linguistically, the women use overlapping speech and minimal responses ('yep') to indicate solidarity with each other. According to Goffman (1963: 112) one of the ways for stigmatized individuals to counteract stigma is through loyalty with 'like-situated individuals' which allows their otherwise stigmatized identity to gain self-worth and legitimacy. The women also attempted to contest their 'spoiled identities' (Goffman 1963) by refusing to see their poverty as a result of their personal deficits and replacing them with explanations based on class structure or the interests of the dominant classes. Pelissier Kingfisher found that 'resistance to a dominant discourse of necessity partakes of that discourse, while apparent accommodation may be a tool of subversion' (1996: 540).

Similarly, Houghton's study of female Latino adolescents on a compulsory therapeutic programme (1995) which attempted to address their refusal to endorse mainstream American values of work, material acquisition and productivity, showed that these young women knew very well that they would gain little from overt resistance. Instead they resorted to linguistic strategies that were difficult to confront by the therapists, such as mimicking the therapists' language or engaging in 'girl talk' – talk about their relationships and sexuality – which were basically consistent with topics of their group therapy. However, these were introduced into the therapeutic setting by them as a form of resistance, for instance by them talking at length about their relationships during the therapy sessions with the therapists struggling to keep them 'on topic'. Sometimes resistance was even overt, for instance when the rules of conversation were challenged by the young women demanding of the therapist 'Why do you get to interrupt and I don't?' (Houghton 1995: 137).

In the light of the foregoing discussion, consider below an excerpt from a Northern Irish radio phone-in programme, hosted by Stephen Nolan, in which the topic is women referees in football. In analysing the excerpt try to employ the linguistic categories discussed in units A3 and B3, both for CDA and CA, and keep the following questions in mind:

❑ What linguistic control strategies does the host employ?
❑ Are these control strategies successful?
❑ How does he attempt to manage topic control?
❑ Does the caller resist in any way and if so how?

★ Activity C3.1

> Host: Are women not a lot not a lot more emotional … though Linda [L: no] on the pitch? Are we really gonna say I'm not saying here that women are unacceptable on the pitch but should we not at least concede that women are going to be different referees on a football pitch than men
>
> Linda: I wouldn't agree with that because I know that ehm when you go up one step and you're umpiring at a higher level you are very focused on what you're doing and really emotions don't come into it I mean I played at a high level and and umpired [
>
> Host: [But so what you're saying are you saying to me that women are the same as men in temperament [L: of course] and decision-making [L: of course] is it really [?] and sports
>
> Linda: yes I mean in in Ireland we have a lot of men who umpire ladies' Hockey [H: Are you telling me] and I can't say to you that they are less emotional they are not emotional if you go out and you abide by the rules [
>
> Host: [But the very top of the premier league football game are you telling me that a woman is going to be as fast on the pitch [L: yes] as a man [L: yes I mean it] really?
>
> Linda: In football [
>
> Host: [Women aren't as fast as men

Antilanguages

Another form of oppositional discourse that can be used by subordinate groups as a moderate form of counter-power is the use of an *antilanguage*. Antilanguages are those ways of talking that are developed by subcultures as a conscious alternative to the language of the dominant or mainstream society. Although antilanguages are commonly found in the prison system or in the criminal underworld, they may also occur in any subculture in society, such as youth subcultures. The term goes back to Halliday, who defines an *antilanguage* as:

> a language of social conflict – of passive resistance or active opposition; but at the same time, like any other language, it is a means of expressing and maintaining the social structure – in this case the structure of the antisociety.
>
> (1978: 185)

The antilanguages developed in prison and criminal 'antisocieties' are the most clearly defined alternatives to the over-language as they often serve as secret languages and professional jargons in the subculture. As such they are characterized by both *relexicalization*, which is the process of creating from existing forms new names for things and people, and *overlexicalization*, which is the creation of new expressions for particular areas of interest and relevance to the antisociety. In prison, there are far more words for prison officers, drugs and alcohol, the police, violence and doing time than in the 'outside' world. During her fieldwork in several English prisons Devlin (1996) compiled 25 slang expressions for the police, 32 for prison officers, 22 for informers, 30 for sex offenders and 36 for male homosexuals. This reflects the importance of these categories in prisoners' lives. Slang terms like these enable prisoners to identify with each other and an alternative reality, the inmate social system, which helps them to avoid turning social rejection into self-rejection. In the words of McCorkle and Korn 'it [the inmate social system] permits the inmate to reject the rejectors rather than himself' (1954: 88).

Halliday's original study identifies a number of similar linguistic patterns in Calcutta Underworld Language, an antilanguage spoken on the Indian subcontinent. This antilanguage contains 41 words for police officers and 21 words of different types of bomb. What is of particular interest are the sorts of overlexicalization strategies that this underworld subculture uses. For instance, the antilanguage word 'ghot', which has no direct counterpart in the dominant Bengali language, means to swallow a stolen thing to avoid detection. 'Ulti', which is the name for the Calcutta antilanguage itself, is derived from Bengali 'ulat' meaning 'to turn down', while the word 'cukru' (from Bengali 'curi' meaning 'theft') is an alarmingly specific name for a kidnapper of a sleeping child. Capturing again a disconcerting degree of exactitude in meaning is 'guana' (metaphorically derived from Bengali 'gaha' meaning secret), which is a hidden cavity inside the throat to hide stolen goods, while 'dabal-deker', referring to a plump woman, illustrates a common feature of antilanguages which involves lexical borrowing from other languages, here from English 'double-decker'.

In addition to their emphasis on secrecy, antilanguages are characterized by prominent and often amusing verbal play. In Britain, there is a long and established history of antilanguages going back four hundred years to Elizabethan 'Pelting Speech', evidenced in the language of Falstaff and his cronies in Shakespeare's plays. 'Gobbledygook' was an antilanguage that developed among the Victorian working class in London ('erectify a luxurimole flakoblots' for 'erect a luxury block of flats'), but perhaps the best known contemporary antilanguage in modern Britain is *Cockney rhyming slang*. Like its French equivalent *Verlan* (from 'l'envers', meaning 'the reverse', and see the exercise in the website materials), Cockney rhyming slang (CRS) has spread outwards from the marginal groups of the antisociety which generated it into mainstream, middle-class culture. As its name suggests, this Cockney rhyming slang relexicalizes through rhyming, so existing English words are replaced by complex, even tortuous, rhyming phrases thus:

Existing word	Antilanguage word	Example
Believe	Adam and Eve	'I don't Adam and Eve it!'
Tenner (£10)	Ayrton Senna	'Lend us an Ayrton'
Hair	Barnet Fair	'He's got his Barnet chopped'
Mate	China Plate	'How's me old China?'
Yank	Septic Tank	'He's a Septic'
Look	Butcher's hook	'Let's have a butcher's at it'

An interesting feature of antilanguages is the constant push on the part of their speakers to rejuvenate the vocabulary of the language, creating ever more inventive and opaque terms. In CRS, contractions or secondary rhymes often appear, and in such a way that the original rhyme becomes opaque. Thus, 'porkies' (from 'pork pies' rhyming with 'lies') has lost the original rhyming connection, so someone who has been lying has been 'telling porkies', while 'syrup of figs', for 'wig', has been contracted to 'syrup' ('Check out the syrup on that bloke's head'). Secondary rhymes also exist for words, so 'garden gate' supplements 'China plate' for 'mate' (see above) while both 'dog and bone' and 'eau de cologne' double up as possibilities for 'phone'. In sum, the incentive to maintain group solidarity and to resist outsider influence is strong among users of antilanguages, and this is why these vibrant varieties of languages are marked by ever-evolving linguistic innovation and linguistic play.

The impact of Cockney rhyming slang on the vocabulary of modern-day English should not be underestimated. Indeed, many expressions from this antilanguage have entered mainstream language usage although their use is admittedly restricted to informal registers of discourse. For example, 'losing one's bottle' comes from 'bottle and glass', a rhyme with 'ass', while the financial sense of the word 'bread' comes from 'bread and honey' the second part of which is the rhyme with 'money'. To 'have a barney' with someone comes from 'barn owl', which in many London accents rhymes with 'row'. Using 'your loaf' has its origins in 'loaf of bread' (for 'head'), while not hearing 'a dicky bird' is a rhyme with 'word'.

Look now at the partially completed set of CRS words below. In some cases, the word has moved to a second stage (through a contraction or secondary rhyme, see above) and this has been indicated:

⊗ Activity C3.2

'Standard' term	CRS (phase 1)	CRS (phase 2)
wife	→ trouble and strife	
kid	→ ??	→ saucepan
stairs	→ apples and pears	
Flying Squad	→ Sweeney Todd	→ ??
bent (criminal)	→ Stoke-on-Trent	
?? (as in steal)	→ half inch	

time (in prison)	→ ??	→ bird
teeth	→ ??	→ Hampsteads
thief	→ tea leaf	

Can you guess/fill in the missing stages indicated by questions marks?

1. What linguistic features govern the process of relexicalization in the examples?
2. In terms of register, do you notice a particular *field* of discourse (see B2) that tends to recur in the examples?
3. Related to (2), why are these varieties of language constantly changing in this way?

The best known French antilanguage is *Verlan* whose process of relexicalization involves reversing standard French forms (of spellings and/or syllables) and then recombining them (thus, 'voiture' → 'turevoi' or 'café' → 'féca'). Although the origins of Verlan can be traced to the late 1940s and 1950s, the main impetus behind its development came around 30 years later, through the marginalized groups of the lower status housing projects (les banlieues) surrounding France's main cities. Verlan thus served as a language expressing alienation among that country's poorest immigrants, mainly Africans and Arabs. For instance, much of the dialogue of the 1995 film *La Haine* (meaning 'the hate') was heavily influenced by Verlan, and with its subsequent appearance in advertising and popular music also, there are few French people today who do not know of the existence of this antilanguage.

In the website material you will find some examples of Verlan, and a similar activity for the CRS example above. You can practice working out the processes of relexicalization of the standard French used to create this antilanguage.

C4 ANALYSING GENDER

Here we wish to explore further some of the themes we discussed in A4 and B4, particularly gender representation in the media, with a range of texts from the print media. We have already seen that an analysis of lexis and grammar in a text can potentially tell us something about the perpetuation of certain gender stereotypes. However, we only briefly touched upon the important function of lifestyle magazines in the discursive construction of gendered identities for consumption by readers and this is what we are turning to now. We should maybe point out that our conclusions about the functions of these magazines differ somewhat from Benwell's article (2002) on the functions of men's lifestyle magazines which is found in D4.

The construction of gender in men's and women's fashion magazines

The long-established market for women's magazines in the UK ranges from monthly fashion and lifestyle magazines ('glossies' such as *Marie Claire*, *Vogue*, *Elle*,

Cosmopolitan, Glamour) to weekly publications (either fashion-oriented, such as *Grazia* and *Look*, or focused on celebrities and 'real-life' stories, such as *Ok, Hello!*, and *That's Life*). Lifestyle magazines for women have been widely criticized for upholding traditional notions of femininity and undermining feminism by appropriating and accommodating its discourses, thereby limiting women (e.g. McRobbie 1991; Talbot 1992, 1995; Machin and Thornborrow 2003). In her study of the textual construction of the female body in women's magazines, Jeffries (2007) likewise argues that these magazines reinforce women's insecurities about an idealized body shape.

These critical accounts, however, do not explain the immense popularity of these magazines with their readers. Some of the older studies (e.g. McRobbie 1991) worked on the assumption that the ideological content of the magazines would be absorbed uncritically by its readers. Studies of reader reception (e.g. Frazer 1987; Hermes 1995) have, however, shown that female readers, far from taking in the contents wholesale, pick and choose, connecting with some parts of the magazines but not with others. Interviewing teenage girls about stories from *Jackie*, Frazer (1987) found that these girls regarded some of its contents as unrealistic fantasies. Although this does not prove that readers are not influenced by magazine contents, it does show that their possible effects cannot be assumed or predicted.

From readers' receptions studies we also know that many readers feel that at least some magazines convey a picture of assertive, independent and (sexually) confident women. One could therefore argue that women's magazines have at least responded to feminism, which 'exists as a productive tension in these pages' (McRobbie 1999: 55), although it cannot be denied that the emphasis on consumerism and on looking stylish and beautiful is equally strong. McRobbie has since criticized what she calls 'commodity feminism' which harnesses feminism to its own sinister capitalist ends. We, however, still argue that these magazines do show the impact of feminism. For example, the advice pages consistently exhort women not to put up with a man who is a nuisance. By and large the magazines are more 'anti-traditional' than traditional and encourage women to adopt a certain kind of 'liberated', if commodified, identity (although not always consistently, as Machin and Thornborrow (2003) point out). In these pages, femininity is artifice and performance, offering women the opportunity to play with different kinds of identity, which is in line with Butler's proposition that gender is performance.

In addition to women's magazines, critical (feminist) linguist studies of language and gender have in recent years also turned to men's lifestyle magazines (e.g. Benwell 2002, 2003, 2005). The men's magazine market, small in comparison to the women's market, only started in the late 1980s and early 1990s with the launch of *Arena, GQ* (Gentleman's Quarterly) and *Esquire*, all rather upmarket publications, which propagated an alternative form of masculinity, the 'new' man (Edwards 1997). This 'new' man was essentially a white, heterosexual, middle-class professional, with an active interest in fashion and consumption. He was even feminist-friendly, although these ideas about a 'new' masculinity have been dismissed as only superficial and leaving existing gender practices and politics unchanged (e.g. Litosseliti 2006).

In 1994, the launch of the more mid-market *Loaded* marked the beginning of yet another media-created male identity, the modern British 'lad', opposed to the 'new' man, and reverting to a more traditional stereotype of masculinity, interested mainly in beer, football and sex (Jackson *et al.* 2001). According to Benwell (2003), the discursive construction of the 'new lad' stresses the essential difference between the sexes, the need to reassert traditional or 'hegemonic' masculinity (for example by distancing itself from homosexuality), and through contradiction, ambiguity and irony. For Jackson *et al.* (2001: 77–78), the use of irony in men's magazines has two functions: first, advice on relationships, sex, health and appearance has to be laced with humour to make it palatable to men; second, the humour and irony employed in men's magazines work 'to subvert political critique', so that ideas that may be found potentially objectionable and sexist by some people can therefore be dismissed as harmless fun.

However, a somewhat different interpretation of the functions of men's (and women's) lifestyle magazines is also possible. While these magazines' representations of masculinity can be 'regressive' and sexist, this may not be their primary purpose and selling point. Instead, they are a cultural phenomenon that can tell us something about today's masculinities (Jackson *et al.* 2001; Gauntlett 2008). While some (e.g. Benwell 2002; see also reading in D4) have argued that men's magazines are unaware of the constructed nature of masculinity, Gauntlett argues that they are '*all about* the social construction of masculinity' (2008: 179; original emphasis). Like women's magazines, they are complex and offer contradictory advice, but far from wanting to reassert traditional and repressive masculinity, they show men as 'seeking help and *reassurance*, even if this is (slightly) suppressed by a veneer of irony and heterosexual lust' (Gauntlett 2008: 176). While they do on some pages convey an idea of manhood built on the laddish values of no strings attached sex, booze and irresponsibility, they do on other pages cover issues that belie this 'constructed certitude' (Jackson *et al.* 2001: 68) of masculinity and at least offer 'the *potential* for new forms of masculinities to emerge' (Jackson *et al.* 2001: 23; original emphasis). This can be seen in the advice they offer in relation to women and some of the topics they cover:

> Look Good naked the FHM way: How to look more beach god than beached whale
>
> > (*FHM*, August 2008)

> Build Beach Muscle – Bonus Poster Inside
>
> > (*Men's Health*, June 2013)

> The Exposé: Explore Like a Billionaire
>
> > (*Maxim*, January 2017)

> Make Good Sex Great
>
> > (*Men's Health*, March 2017)

The language used to give advice may be 'blokeish' and ironic, but men are given advice on their looks, sex life and work, just as women are. As for the argument that men and women are presented as polar opposites in terms of sexual identities and desires in magazines (Jackson *et al.* 2001; Benwell 2003), a mere glance through them reveals that they look increasingly similar, with advice sections, features on fashion, and sex objects for the delectation of the reader.

To demonstrate this trend, we offer a brief comparative analysis of two short texts from two lifestyle magazines, one for men, one for women. The first is from a feature on actress Natalie Dormer in *GQ* (December 2014); the second from an interview with actor Kit Harington in *Elle* (January 2017). Both subjects star in the hit TV series *Game of Thrones* (the eighth series of which will air in 2018), Dormer as cunning noblewoman Margaery Tyrell and Harington as warrior king Jon Snow.

The *GQ* article about Dormer opens thus:

NATALIE DORMER: KILLER QUEEN

Nobody looks better in the whole Ren Faire-damsel rig than *Game of Thrones'* soon-to-be-queen, Margaery Tyrell. But actress Natalie Dormer—who sums up her recent string of period roles as a bunch of "elegant, long, flowing, gentrified *skirts*"—sometimes just wants to rip 'em all off. We'd call *this* look a first step. Shout-out to the clipper-happy groomers at *The Hunger Games: Mockingjay,* who shaved half of Dormer's head for her role as "badass" documentarian Cressida. (She'll be in both finale installments.) She didn't mourn very long for her lost mane before moving, she says, into "Phase 'Rock It Out.'" In other words, despite her milkmaid face and her rosebud mouth—usually fridge-magnet askew—the buzz cut gives her "a *shitload* of attitude." Which is good, because that's kind of her thing.

The text is accompanied by five images (not included here) of Dormer looking seductively at the reader. Each photograph is highly sexualized, with Dormer topless in two and clad in lingerie and stilettoes in the others. All pictures are therefore 'demand' pictures (Machin 2007a). The captions provide details of the designers and each piece of clothing.

In this accompanying paragraph the reader perceives Natalie Dormer as a sexualized and alluring object to be admired, and indeed desired. This effect is doubtlessly encapsulated by the images, but also reinforced in the text. Dormer is represented initially through a Relational Process focussing on how good she *looks*, before the Material *rip 'em all off* ramps up the sexual innuendo of the article, supported by reference to Dormer's *milkmaid face and her rosebud mouth—usually fridge-magnet askew.*

In this text Dormer is not just performing the role of a beautiful sex object, the seeming passivity of her highly suggestive poses in the images is counterbalanced by the *shitload of attitude* she possesses in the text. Dormer's active Material presence is reinforced in the subsequent paragraph:

The recovering tomboy and adrenaline junkie lives like the action-movie lead she hopes to be someday. She's currently training for the London Marathon, would rather you *not* open difficult jars for her, thanks, and picked up a scuba-diving addiction after filming an underwater crash scene at some "post-Iron Curtain leisure center" (her phrase) in the Czech Republic. "I love going out of my comfort zone—I *live* to go out of my comfort zone," she says. "Obviously, you have quieter years than others—you don't go jumping out of a plane every day." At the thought, she sounds faintly bummed. Only on the occasional Sunday does she take a break from badassery: "I'm a bed monster," Dormer says. So fetch her the Sunday paper, serf, and some egg-inclusive foodstuffs, and she's yours

Dormer is named as a *recovering tomboy* and an *adrenaline junkie*, who runs marathons and scuba-dives, and all with a certain unconventional 'edginess' represented by mildly risqué political incorrectness and *badassery*. Of course sexuality is never far away, *bed monster* referring the reader directly back to the images of the topless Dormer in bed where she can be *yours*.

This text has much in common with traditional lad's magazines, with Natalie Dormer performing highly sexualized suggestiveness; however, it cannot be blamed for casting her only in terms of her physical attributes, indeed her physicality is granted a certain independent attitude later in the text.

Let us now compare this with the text from *Elle* magazine on Kit Harington. The text opens thus:

KIT HARINGTON REALLY, REALLY WANTS TO BE ON *SESAME STREET*

As much as we love Kit Harington with a man bun, we've got only two more seasons to lust after the romance novel–long mane and the character to whom it belongs: brooding bastard Jon Snow of *Game of Thrones*—currently filming its seventh season (to premiere this summer) in Belfast. Plot spoilers for the HBO epic are notoriously hard to come by, but this one tidbit recently slipped out: Harington and four other principal castmates banded together to negotiate a $1.1-million-per-episode salary for each.

There are three pictures accompanying the article, all of which are 'demand' pictures. In the first, a studio shot, a rugged Harington looks broodingly at the reader in a manner replicated often by action actors in women's magazines. In the second Harrington is pictured with his partner and *Game of Thrones* co-star Rose Leslie – the so-called 'it couple' are frequently the focus of certain celebrity-obsessed media – and in the third he is pictured at the *Emmys* with a larger group of co-stars.

As in the article on Natalie Dormer, *Elle* focuses significantly on Harington's appearance, *lusting over* his *romance novel–long mane*. Later in the article he is admired for his *pursed lips and sculpted abs*. This could be seen as an indication that nowadays women's magazines objectify men as much as men's magazines have objectified women for decades, using similar language and imagery. For example, the UK edition of *Cosmopolitan* has a regular '*Cosmo* centrefold' feature with naked men, often sports stars and other minor celebrities, whose pictures are downloadable ('download a center-fold for your desktop at www.cosmopolitan.co.uk').

Harington is possessed of somewhat more professional status, however. Whilst Natalie Dormer's acting attributes are linked to her hairstyle, in Harington's case it is the *$1.1-million-per-episode salary* he has managed to secure. His prestigious acting training and *top-notch film roles* are the subsequent focus of the feature, reinforced by the images of him on the red carpet at the *Emmys*. In Critical Discourse Analysis very often the analyst must also be mindful of what does *not* form a theme of a piece of discourse; Natalie Dormer also boasts an impressive filmography and record of high quality television work which are absent in the piece from *GQ*.

Whilst these articles demonstrate the complex constructions of femininity and masculinity in lifestyle magazines, as a medium these magazines have not been immune to the effects of falling sales in the print media arena in general. *Loaded* ceased print publication in March 2015, although was re-launched online six months later in what editor Aaron Tinney described as an attempt to move away from 'Page 3 type stuff'. *FHM* – perhaps most famous for its annual '100 Sexiest Women' edition – ceased trading in November 2015. Whether or not these moves are solely the result of the decline in print sales as a result of the proliferation of online content, or whether they might indicate some wider shift in attitudes to the content itself remains to be seen. Certainly the above articles demonstrate that traditional features of femininity and masculinity remain important, and magazines such as *Esquire*, *GQ* and *Maxim* – with its '*Maxim*'s Hot 100' league table of female attractiveness intact – remain solidly on the market.

❑ Try to replicate the sort of comparative analysis we have just undertaken, by contrasting the linguistic and visual patterns in two short passages taken from male- and female-oriented lifestyle magazines.

❑ In B4 we saw that an analysis of transitivity and naming patterns can reveal that much media discourse is constructed around stereotyped notions of women (Jewkes 2011). Women who fail to conform to the cultural stereotypes of the maternal, caring and monogamous woman or who are in some way involved or implicated in a very serious crime are often 'punished symbolically by the media' (Jewkes 2011: 114). The material on the web provides you with an activity to investigate the construction of 'deviant' women in the tabloids.

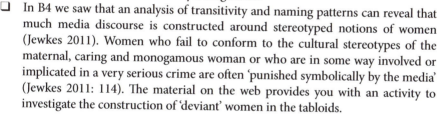

A WORKSHOP ON THE REPRESENTATION OF SOCIAL ACTORS

C5

This unit is designed for you to explore Social Actor Analysis and draws mainly on the concepts introduced and developed in unit B5. Social Actor Analysis is a method for studying, both linguistically and visually, how people are represented in texts.

Figures C5.1 and C5.2 show images from an article in the *Daily Mail* (11 August 2015). On 09 August 2014 Michael Brown, an 18-year-old African American, was shot dead by police officer Darren Wilson in Ferguson, Missouri. Violence followed the shooting and the later acquittal of Wilson by a Grand Jury. The so-called 'Ferguson Unrest' should be viewed in the context of several similar incidents that have taken place in the United States in recent years. These shootings have collectively given rise to the Black Lives Matter activist movement, established in 2013 in response to

Figure C5.1 Daily Mail, 11 August 2015

Figure C5.2 Daily Mail, 11 August 2015

the shooting of African American teenager Trayvon Martin in Sanford, Florida in February 2012, where member of a local neighbourhood watch group was acquitted of the killing.

Activity C5.1

Attempt a visual Social Actor Analysis of these images. You should consider in particular what is depicted through collectivization and/or individualization, as well as identification and functionalization. The effect of gaze will also be important, do these social actors challenge the viewer or other represented participants?

Remember that as a tool for Critical Discourse Analysis, Social Actor Analysis should be carried out in context rather than in isolation. Whilst images like these were by no means the only visual representations of the Ferguson Unrest or the wider Black Lives Matter campaign, how might they operate as a form of Social Practice? You might wish to extend this analysis to consider more widely different media representations of these incidents.

For further practice, consider the following article and image (Figure C5.3), taken from the website of Belfast City Council (2006). According to anti-racism campaigners in Northern Ireland, racism is just one manifestation of a sectarian community that is still deeply divided. (The written text precedes the visual accompaniment.)

Figure C5.3 Belfast City Council, 'Kicking racism out of football', 2006

Kicking racism out of football

Children from Belfast primary schools put the boot into racism today after participating in a multi-cultural football festival organised jointly by Belfast City Council and the Irish Football Association.

The youngsters underwent football skills training as well as learning about racial awareness and race hate crimes, and how other cultures have integrated into Northern Ireland society.

Held at Queen's Physical Education Centre and backed by Belfast Lord Mayor, Councillor Pat McCarthy, who joined the children at the event, and said: 'These children are having a great time and it doesn't matter to them who their opponent is, they are out to enjoy themselves and have a good time playing sport.

'I think the football coaches who are taking part are to be congratulated because racism in sport needs to be nipped in the bud and what better time to do it than when children are young and open to new ideas.

'We want to encourage them too to become active at an early age and to understand that football can be a unifying force no matter our creed, colour or gender.'

Sean Paul Murray, one of the organisers of the day and an IFA Grassroots Development Officer, said 'Everyone taking part is being made aware of the different cultures that share Belfast and some of the difficulties that can be encountered. We want to make people realise the difficulties immigrants face and how sport can be a common bond.

'Today will also help the children overcome barriers they face in their day to day lives. We also hope to encourage friendships among the children who are all from different primary schools,' he added.

In your analysis of social actors, you might find it useful to ask the following questions:

Activity C5.2 ✪

- ❑ How are the social actors defined linguistically and visually?
- ❑ Are they defined in terms of their ethnicity, and if so, why?
- ❑ Are social actors *individualized* and/or *categorized*? And does this contribute to their positive evaluation?
- ❑ Who is *nominated* and why?
- ❑ Why are the social actors represented in a *demand* image?

ANALYSING HUMOUR AND POWER

Across this Strand we have been examining the ways in which the analysis of verbal humour can play a part in the broader study of language and power. A number of the cases we examined in the Strand can be located on the web, and stories and incidents involving humour and its sometimes controversial or legal outcome break regularly in the media. For instance, we touched in B6 on Silvio Berlusconi's controversial comments on a member of the European Parliament. Following that event, Berlusconi welcomed the 2009 Presidency of Barack Obama, complimenting the new USA president as nicely 'tanned'. There followed again a similar outcry at the right-wing billionaire's remarks, whose defence predictably was the same complaint, that his detractors had no sense of humour.

One activity we encourage is that readers should collect instances of humour over the course of a whole day and think about the amount of contact that they have with 'humour events'. We include here humour and irony on television, in film, in print and broadcast media, and, of course, in everyday conversation. Think about the (often very different) forms and functions that humour has in everyday social life (and see further, web materials). Other more-targeted activities follow.

Humour and register mixing

Below is part of a 'politically correct Christmas card' that has been doing the rounds on the internet over the last few years.

> Please accept with no obligation, expressed or implicit, my best wishes for an environmentally conscious, socially responsible, low stress, non-addictive, gender neutral celebration of the winter solstice holiday, practised with the most enjoyable traditions of religious persuasion or secular practices of your choice with respect for the religious/secular persuasions and/or traditions of others, or their choice not to practise religious or secular traditions at all.
>
> I also wish you a fiscally successful, personally fulfilling and medically uncomplicated recognition of the onset of the generally accepted calendar year 2007, but not without due respect for the calendars of choice of other cultures and without regard to the race, creed, colour, age, physical ability, religious faith or sexual preference of the wishee.
>
> By accepting this greeting, you are accepting the following terms:
> This greeting is subject to clarification or withdrawal at any time by the wisher.
> It is freely transferable with no alteration to the original greeting.
> It implies no promise by the wisher to actually implement any of the wishes for him/her or others, and is void where prohibited by law, and is revocable at the sole discretion of the wisher.
> This wish is warranted to perform as expected within the usual application of good tidings for a period of one year or until the issuance of a subsequent holiday greeting, whichever comes first.

This warranty is limited to the replacement of this wish or issuance of a new wish at the sole discretion of the wisher.

In A6 we touched on the significance of register or style mixing as a mechanism in humour production. We also suggested that although writers in CDA talk of 'hybridity', 'manifest intertextuality' or 'non-congruent discourse', they have tended to overlook the function of this discourse feature as an incongruity-creating device, and therefore its comic potential.

Activity C6.1 ✪ ❏ Can you develop these observations to explain how the humour of the spoof Christmas card works? Also, is there any *target* in this particular humour genre, or is it just word-play for the sake of word-play?

Appropriateness and humour

A feature of incongruous or 'spoof' texts is that they violate the *validity claim of sincerity* (see further unit B12). Our model of irony (B6) shows, for example, how irony is negotiable, and how we can claim retrospectively that we were being ironic, and therefore insincere. However, this is not the only pragmatic issue at stake in the delivery and reception of humour. Another important validity claim is 'appropriateness', which also acts as an important constraint on the way we interpret humour, especially humour that is considered 'taboo' or 'red-flagged'. Whereas we may appreciate the central incongruity of a humour exchange, we may not necessarily feel that it is appropriate. Moreover, the appropriateness condition for humour is strongly integrated with social and cultural context, and changes in this external social environment will impact heavily on what a particular community deems 'appropriate' for humour.

Humour in the tabloids

In A6 we looked at some of the humorous resources used in the print media, especially punning. Punning introduces, among other things, a levity of tone. Now the important issue here, which relates to the discussion above, is whether such humour strategies are appropriate in the context of serious stories. Investigating this point further, we propose a short exercise in 'tabloidese'.

The story below, which appeared in the *Irish Times* of 4 February 2006, was covered in a range of papers, both broadsheet and tabloid. It relates the outcome of a harassment case involving a member of the Gardaí (the police force of the Republic of Ireland; singular, 'Garda'). The version here was typical of the general 'tenor' of the coverage in the broadsheets. The tone of the tabloids' coverage, which included the Irish versions of both the *Daily Mirror* and the *Daily Star* was, suffice to say, rather different in tone.

Garda found guilty of harassing woman

A jury at Waterford Circuit Criminal Court last night found a garda guilty of harassment of a woman and the theft of her underwear.

Garda Anthony Fennelly (39) … was found guilty of harassment on and between November 12th and 15th, 2003 …

He was also found guilty of the theft of underwear on September 16th, 2003. In September 2003, Garda Fennelly, claiming to be responding to reports of an intruder, gained access to Ms Cox's house through a neighbour. Ms Cox received reports that a Garda had jumped over the wall into her back garden. Items of underwear were understood to have been stolen from her washing line …

❏ Write a 'tabloid' version based of the story in the *Irish Times*. This should include (a) a headline, (b) a strapline and (c) opening text. The opening text is a paragraph, normally comprising a single sentence in tabloids, which gives as full a context and summary of the story as possible. Journalists often pare this down to form the headline. A strapline is a subsidiary headline, often in bold small case compared to the bold capitals of the headline.

> **Activity C6.2** ✪

❏ Without suggesting that tabloid stories are derivatives of quality broadsheets, what effect nonetheless does its transformation into *tabloidese* have on the story? Is the levity that it introduces *appropriate*? Thinking more seriously about this episode, which version of the report, the broadsheet or the tabloid, would the victim and her family feel more comfortable with?

❏ Follow the web material for further commentary on the 'real' tabloid versions of this story.

EXPLORING FORENSIC TEXTS

> C7

In this unit we present some exercises that involve a number of the issues in forensic linguistics raised across the Strand. While we encourage readers to try to obtain their own data from real legal contexts, we accept that this is not always easy to do – it is in the nature of a conservative and powerful profession that outside parties are not necessarily welcomed. Indeed, the literature in forensic linguistics reports numerous occasions where the presence of non-legal professionals in the courtroom is seen as an 'intrusion' by judges and other senior figures.

One way of accessing legal discourse without falling foul of the authorities is to draw on web resources. There are a number of useful websites that offer detailed summings-up, rulings on case histories and sometimes transcriptions of the trial proceedings. The All-England Law Reports database is a well-organized bank of legal data and case histories. In the USA, the 'Court TV Casefiles' site is also useful because it contains complete and detailed transcriptions of a number of high-profile trials – the case of 'Unabomber' Ted Kaczynski and the civil trial of O.J. Simpson, to name just two. (For more guidance, see further below, and also the Further Reading section that accompanies this Strand.)

Legal language as register

The comprehensibility of jury instructions has been an issue in forensic discourse analysis over the years. The indication is that jurors often have trouble understanding the judicial instructions delivered to them. For example, the presiding judge's five-part instruction in the inquest into the death of Princess Diana (31/3/2008) was extremely difficult to follow even in the watered-down versions disseminated through press releases. The complexity of these instructions may explain why jurors did not reach the verdict favoured by the court ('accidental death') while the verdict they did offer, 'unlawful killing', was not reached unanimously.

One concern is that the emphasis is on legal accuracy in the instruction, and not on comprehensibility to anyone outside the legal community. Understanding the concept of 'reasonable doubt' has proved particularly problematic, although steps have been taken to help explain this to jurors. The text below is an example of such a step, taken from the Tennessee Jury Instruction Manual (1995).

> Reasonable doubt is that doubt engendered by an investigation of all the proof in a case and an inability after such investigation to let the mind rest easily as to the certainty of guilt. Reasonable does not mean a captious, possible or imaginary doubt. Absolute certainty of guilt is not demanded by the law to convict of any criminal charge, but moral certainty is required, and this certainty is required as to every proposition of proof requisite to constitute the offense.
>
> (adapted from Gibbons 2003: 177–178)

Activity C7.1 ✪

❑ On the basis of its vocabulary and grammatical structure, how helpful is this manual as a guide for jurors? Can you suggest re-wordings that might make it more clear? A useful follow-up is to look at the website and information bulletins of the Plain English Campaign, an organization that has played an important role in the re-drafting of legal documentation.

❑ On a related issue, how effective are instructions by judges to jurors which (i) ask the jurors to ignore pre-trial publicity and (ii) ask jurors to ignore certain evidence they have heard that is deemed inadmissible? Are such instructions viable?

Electro-static Detection Analysis

In unit B7 we outlined the ESDA technique and assessed its impact on forensic linguistics. The exercise below is based on an application of the ESDA method in another, real Appeal case (Davis 1994: 78).

Text (a) is the written interview transcript that was presented in court, while the boxed text (b) is the ESDA 'lift' taken from the indentations on the lower page. [R = Respondent; Q = Questioner]

(a) R I was standing by the phone box keeping watch
    Q What did you all do then
    R We ran back to the car.

```
(b)
                            keeping watch
R   I was standing by the phone box
Q   What did you all do then
R   We ran back to the car.
```

❏ Comparing the two texts, the one submitted in court and the ESDA lift, can you piece together the story of how this suspect's statement was manipulated? Why is the version offered in court more incriminating? And what explains the misaligned sequence in the lift?

Activity C7.2 ✪

By way of footnote, when presented with the ESDA lift, the presiding judge in this Appeal case was heard to say 'It doesn't inspire confidence, does it?'

Questions and presuppositions during interrogation and cross-examination

❏ Working from our summary of presupposition triggers in unit B7, what difficulties (linguistically) might you experience in providing a YES or NO answer to the following question?

   'Would you care to tell me how the heroin ended up in your house?'

❏ And what difficulty might you experience in dealing with these two constructions?
   'Why did you return to the scene of your most recent burglary?'
   'Don't you now regret not calling the ambulance services earlier?

Cultural differences in police interviews

In B7 we drew attention to the significance of cultural difference as a factor in police interview and interrogation. The following encounter comes from the police record of an interview between Australian police (P) and an Aboriginal man (W). Judging by his replies, to what extent does the witness appear to understand the questions being put to him?

P: Right. Now Cedric. I want to ask you some questions about what happened at Jay Creek the other day. Do you understand that?
W: Yes.
P: Now it's in relation to the death of X. Do you understand that?
W: Yes.
P: Right. Now I want to ask you some questions about the trouble out there but I want you to understand that you don't have to answer any questions at all. Do you understand that?
W: Yes.

P: Do you have to tell me that story?
W: Yes.
P: Do you have to though?
W: Yes.
P: Do you, am I making you tell me the story?
W: Yes.
P: Or are you telling me because you want to?
W: Yes.
P: Now I want to understand that you don't have to tell me, right?
W: Yes.
P: Now do you have to tell me?
W: Yes.

(after Coldrey 1987: 84–85; Gibbons 2003: 209)

Gibbons describes this pattern in discourse as 'gratuitous concurrence' and it is only because the police officer checks the understanding of the witness that the problem comes to light. But what are the likely implications for a witness when this sort of concurrence is *not* detected?

Speech naturalism in transcripts of evidence

Here is a more general activity involving a transcript from a police interview which the accused claimed was totally fabricated:

K: I didn't mean to kill anybody you know. Fucking stupid to do it with my foot like it was.
PC: You're talking about your injured foot?
K: Yes.
PC: You alleged someone had shot you in a drugs deal sometime before this Dixon's job.
K: I don't know if I said that but I had my toes shot off in Newtown.

(after Coulthard 1992: 250)

Activity C7.3 ✪

❑   In his commentary on this passage, Coulthard draws attention to its *over-explicitness*. What features in the passage do you feel are unusually over-explicit and what are the implications for K of this information being brought to the attention of the court?

❑   The text implies that the police officer is *already* aware of the problem with the suspect's injured foot. Is the officer's first utterance then a natural response to K's disclosure about the crime? And to what extent is the police officer, in both of his utterances, telling the suspect something they both already know? (See further Coulthard 1992: 250.)

Legal language in everyday life

We suggested in A7 that we have good reason to be concerned about the power of legal discourse in its interaction with ordinary members of society. Some readers may be sceptical about this position. Students in full-time education may feel remote from the law's influence, where encounters with legally binding documentation are perhaps limited to, say, declarations of integrity on undergraduate essays or to the text of a rental agreement for accommodation.

So just how pervasive is legal discourse in your lives? This issue is worthy of investigation, so over the course of a working day you could try to collect and analyse as many instances as you can of contacts with legal discourse. This includes the small print found on the labels of various products. And remember, anyone who has downloaded iPod software for example will be bound by a licensing agreement, and the complex wording of this agreement will make a good place to start your analysis.

ANALYSING ADVERTISEMENTS   C8

This unit offers some practical suggestions for approaching advertising discourse. Below we suggest a checklist of features that can usefully be adapted to give shape to your analysis of advertising discourse. Although these features reflect the issues and developments covered in A8 and B8, there are many other aspects of ads that can be analysed; the Further Reading section that accompanies this Strand flags up a number of other approaches that are worth exploring.

A checklist of features

Among the many that could be asked, here are some questions that might inform a Critical Linguistic Analysis of advertising discourse. Where needed, refer to the context provided in A8 and B8.

(i)   What is being advertised? What goods and/or services are being promoted? Is the ad 'product' or 'non-product' oriented? How is the ad structured (in terms of body copy, slogan and so on)?

(ii) What ideological assumptions are encoded in the advertisement? Is there any ideological significance about the manner by which the commodity is marketed? For example, are certain wants and desires *naturalized* in the discourse of the ad?

(iii) How is the consumer/addressee positioned in relation to the text? Are specific gender roles projected onto the addressee through the discourse of the ad?

(iv) How are the claims made about the product justified or substantiated?

(v)   Are any aspects of vocabulary and grammar used as *mnemonic* devices? In other words, is the ad designed to sound 'catchy'? Is it presented as a 'jingle'? Look out for puns, marked grammatical constructions and striking collocations (combinations of words). Note also any significant phonological features such as rhymes, metre and alliteration.

(vi) What can be said about the ad in terms of visual and linguistic modality? Would you say the ad is an example of high or low modality? Are mixed media employed in the ad? If so, is the visual (and audio) structure of the text, in addition to its linguistic composition, significant to its overall meaning and interpretation?

(vii) In general terms, what communicative-cognitive techniques are used to market the product? What pragmatic strategies are being exploited? Does, for example, the *Reason/Tickle* distinction help explain how the text functions at a communicative level?

Advertising body copy

Here is a selection of 'one-liners' from advertisements that appeared in both print and broadcast media. Clearly, these texts are situated towards the 'reason' end of the *Reason/ Tickle* continuum drawn in unit B8. Read them through and consider the suggestions further below.

A. If you are experiencing anxiety, depression or feelings of anger, our experienced team of professional staff and counsellors can be of help to YOU.

B. If you still need a little more encouragement, you'll find lots of tips on the Special K public forum.

C. *Go Ahead!* can be enjoyed as part of a healthy diet and lifestyle, so you can relax and enjoy any of the range of great tasting snacks.

D. *Resound* is a radical improvement on hearing instrument and size because it uses a revolutionary design that combines invisibility and lightweight comfort.

E. If you can't taste the difference, why pay the difference.

F. This is the bread to greet any guest because it's the bread that mother knows best.

G. If you'd rather be relaxing than rinsing, then try new 'Flash Bathroom'.

H. Perri Pan Fried potato crisps are cooked in sunflower oil in order to give extra crunch and a fuller potato flavour. Mr Perri uses the finest potatoes and pure sunflower oil so choose Perri for quality and taste.

Activity C8.1 ✪

❑ Can you identify which type of conjunctive adjuncts underpins each ad? That is, can you say whether they are Causal, Conditional and so on?

❑ Are any of the patterns above enriched stylistically by rhetorical and other related devices? If so, what purpose does this rhetorical enrichment serve?

❑ Bernstein suggests that in the marketing of 'luxury' commodities 'the best route to take is an indirect one' (1974: 107). Going on your experience of advertising, and on the basis of the methods outlined in B8, what sort of marketing campaign 'suits' what sort of product? For example, whereas 'healthy' commodities (such as nappies, sanitary protection and pain killers, as in the ads above and in B8) lend themselves easily to a 'unique selling proposition', to what extent can a copywriter extol the virtues of cigarettes or alcohol in similar terms? Why, for example, in opting for a tickle-oriented campaign does a copywriter knowingly demand more cognitive processing from a potential consumer?

ANALYSING THE LANGUAGE OF NEW CAPITALISM   C9

As schools and universities are being drawn into new capitalist business practices and discourses, they are also compelled to adopt modes of learning and teaching that are in line with these practices. Gee *et al.* (1996), for example, note that many features of present-day school classrooms, such as their focus on team or reciprocal learning and teaching and the use of modern computer, telecommunications and network technologies, render them very much like new capitalist workplaces. The dominant view expressed in recent educational reforms in Britain is that education should be seen as a 'vocationally-oriented transmission of given knowledge and *skills*' (Fairclough 2005: 8; our emphasis). According to this view, students need to be taught a number of 'transferable' key skills, one of which is 'communication' (the others being numeracy, information technology and learning to learn). As we have seen in this Strand, the acquisition of an ever-widening set of skills is important for people if they want to succeed in the new capitalism. Fairclough (2005: 8–9) critiques the view of education as a transmission of skills as it regards knowledge as 'determinate, uncontested, and given externally to the learner' whereas in a critical view of education, knowledge and 'skills' are not just taught and learned but also contested. Below, we provide three texts that seem to exemplify the current 'official' position on education.

The first text is taken from the 'Careers, Employability and Skills' website of Queen's University, Belfast, and is aimed at students. Look at the text, drawing on any of the ideas brought up in this chapter and in Fairclough's critique above.

Courses to Enhance Your Skills

Graduate recruiters look for applicants who provide evidence of having developed a range of skills and abilities required in the workplace. These skills and abilities include:

- Intellectual ability
- Ability to be self-aware, to action plan, to understand workplace culture
- Leadership, teamwork, networking, communication, presentation, problem-solving, IT skills and strong business awareness

Certificate in Career Management and Employability Skills

Aimed at final year undergraduate and taught postgraduate students, this course:

- Helps students to better understand the graduate labour market and regional variations within it
- Enables final year students to make effective job applications

The second text is taken from the website of a secondary school in Northern Ireland. Consider the following questions:

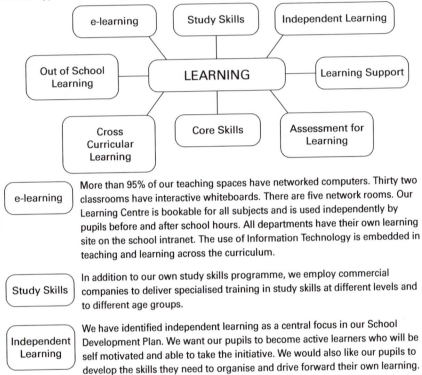

Learning

The modern world places many demands on young people today. They need to be competent in a range of different skills, independent, flexible, and yet able to work as a member of a team. We encourage our pupils to take responsibility for their own learning, to develop key skills and competences and to use modern technology as a tool for learning. The school's results show that our approach to learning is effective.

e-learning — More than 95% of our teaching spaces have networked computers. Thirty two classrooms have interactive whiteboards. There are five network rooms. Our Learning Centre is bookable for all subjects and is used independently by pupils before and after school hours. All departments have their own learning site on the school intranet. The use of Information Technology is embedded in teaching and learning across the curriculum.

Study Skills — In addition to our own study skills programme, we employ commercial companies to deliver specialised training in study skills at different levels and to different age groups.

Independent Learning — We have identified independent learning as a central focus in our School Development Plan. We want our pupils to become active learners who will be self motivated and able to take the initiative. We would also like our pupils to develop the skills they need to organise and drive forward their own learning.

Figure C9.1 Secondary school website, Northern Ireland

Activity C9.1 ✪
- ❑ In what way can this text be said to be in line with new capitalist work practices?
- ❑ What (enterprising) qualities are pupils expected to have?
- ❑ Do you feel that the range of skills the school offers to teach its students are useful? Why/why not?

Meeting the demands of the consumer has become the overriding institutional imperative in the new capitalism and even universities now tend to regard their students more as 'consumers' who get 'value for money' with the courses they choose, as discussed at length in B9.

British universities in particular have also sought to enhance their attractiveness globally by embracing opportunities in countries on the fringes of the English-speaking world, particularly in Asia, where the perceived prestige of a 'British education' is a highly marketable commodity. Many traditional British universities have established links, and indeed campuses, in the Far East. China, for example, is an economic powerhouse where the potential benefits for the 'missions', 'visions' and 'strategies' that mark the new outlook of these institutions are extensive. The third text is from the website of Nottingham University Ningbo, setting out the institution's 'Strategy 2020'.

Our Vision for 2020

A leading international university that is comparable to the Top 50 Chinese Universities. We transform the lives and livelihood of our students, staff and the local community through delivery of academic excellence with a global perspective.

Our Mission for 2020

- To provide a delivery model for higher education in China which is built on UNUK's expertise in British-style learning, management system, network and reputation but also localised with the Chinese context.

- To develop leaders and entrepreneurs to meet the challenges facing global society now and in the future; as well as educating responsible global citizens who are socially and environmentally aware.

- To develop core expertise in research and produce world-changing outcomes which improves human life and as well as to impact the socio-economic transformation and development in both the local and broader community. We will focus especially on key subject areas such as digital technologies, advanced materials and manufacturing, electrical drives, finance and economics.

- To promote international impact through broad collaboration and enhance significant local commitment through public service and community outreach.

(www.nottingham.edu.cn/en/about/strategy-2020/
vision-and-mission.aspx)

Consider the following questions:

❑ What linguistic strategies does the university use to promote itself to students? Can you detect features that are typical of advertising?

❑ How is the 'enterprising' or 'entrepreneurial' attitude that marks neo-capitalist education expressed in the text? Consider lexical items as well as grammar.

Activity C9.2 ✪

This unit offers some suggestions about how political discourse might be approached from the perspectives we outline in both A10 and B10. Further below, we develop some activities around a longer piece of text, from a presidential debate, but before that we look at forms of political metaphor in the media.

Political metaphor in the media

Below are 20 pieces of text taken from political discourse; that is, from the discourse of party manifestos, political speeches and pronouncements, and from commentaries *about* political activity. Before proceeding any further, you might want to remind yourself of the definition of metaphor provided in A10. After that, read through the examples and then go to the activities suggested.

1. What we need is a root and branch approach to the problem of teenage crime.
2. The moment was the high water mark of Michelle's time as First Lady.
3. [Trump's] obfuscated mind is causing China to haemorrhage money.
4. [The results] were said to signal the green shoots of economic recovery.
5. It was clearly a symptom of a corporate disease.
6. The attack on the pound took on dangerous momentum.
7. Britain needs a crusade against poverty and injustice.
8. The issue proved to be no more than a political football.
9. Jeremy Corbyn wants to harness union members' energies and experience.
10. The first job of a new government is to defend the value of the currency.
11. The foundations for recovery have been firmly laid.
12. We want small businesses to flourish.
13. This can only fan the flames of inflation.
14. This means amputating unprofitable departments.
15. We will ensure that NATO remains the cornerstone of our defence.
16. A one-off windfall levy will finance the project.
17. The Tories, with their dark past …
18. Today we stand on the threshold of a new era.
19. Defending freedom will light our country and all who serve it.
20. Fiscal rules and knock-about politics do not mix.

Activity C10.1 ✪ ❑ Below is a group of seven image schemata which form the source domains in the metaphorical expressions 1–20. Try to match up these source domain concepts with their target domains (that is, the topic being described through the metaphor), working out the underlying metaphorical formulae.

plants	*war*	*health*	
buildings	*light*	*sport*	*dimension (i.e. up–down)*

❑   What are the effects of these metaphors when constructed in this way? (See further D10.)

Inaugural address

The excerpt below is an edited version of the inaugural address of President Donald Trump, delivered in Washington D.C. on 20 January 2017. Read through the excerpt before proceeding to the activities below.

> [...]
>
> We, the citizens of America, are now joined in a great national effort to rebuild our country and to restore its promise for all of our people.
>
> Together, we will determine the course of America and the world for years to come.
>
> We will face challenges. We will confront hardships. But we will get the job done.
>
> [...]
>
> For too long, a small group in our nation's Capital has reaped the rewards of government while the people have borne the cost.
>
> Washington flourished – but the people did not share in its wealth.
>
> Politicians prospered – but the jobs left, and the factories closed.
>
> The establishment protected itself, but not the citizens of our country.
>
> Their victories have not been your victories; their triumphs have not been your triumphs; and while they celebrated in our nation's Capital, there was little to celebrate for struggling families all across our land.
>
> That all changes – starting right here, and right now, because this moment is your moment: it belongs to you.
>
> It belongs to everyone gathered here today and everyone watching all across America.
>
> This is your day. This is your celebration.
>
> And this, the United States of America, is your country.
>
> [...]
>
> Americans want great schools for their children, safe neighborhoods for their families, and good jobs for themselves.
>
> These are the just and reasonable demands of a righteous public.
>
> But for too many of our citizens, a different reality exists: Mothers and children trapped in poverty in our inner cities; rusted-out factories scattered like tombstones across the landscape of our nation; an education system, flush with cash, but which leaves our young and beautiful students deprived of knowledge; and the crime and gangs and drugs that have stolen too many lives and robbed our country of so much unrealized potential.
>
> This American carnage stops right here and stops right now.
>
> We are one nation – and their pain is our pain. Their dreams are our dreams; and their success will be our success. We share one heart, one home, and one glorious destiny.
>
> The oath of office I take today is an oath of allegiance to all Americans.

For many decades, we've enriched foreign industry at the expense of American industry;

Subsidized the armies of other countries while allowing for the very sad depletion of our military;

We've defended other nation's borders while refusing to defend our own;

And spent trillions of dollars overseas while America's infrastructure has fallen into disrepair and decay.

We've made other countries rich while the wealth, strength, and confidence of our country has disappeared over the horizon.

One by one, the factories shuttered and left our shores, with not even a thought about the millions upon millions of American workers left behind.

The wealth of our middle class has been ripped from their homes and then redistributed across the entire world.

But that is the past. And now we are looking only to the future.

We assembled here today are issuing a new decree to be heard in every city, in every foreign capital, and in every hall of power.

From this day forward, a new vision will govern our land.

From this moment on, it's going to be America First.

[…]

We will bring back our jobs. We will bring back our borders. We will bring back our wealth. And we will bring back our dreams.

We will build new roads, and highways, and bridges, and airports, and tunnels, and railways all across our wonderful nation.

We will get our people off of welfare and back to work – rebuilding our country with American hands and American labor.

We will follow two simple rules: Buy American and Hire American.

We will seek friendship and goodwill with the nations of the world – but we do so with the understanding that it is the right of all nations to put their own interests first.

We do not seek to impose our way of life on anyone, but rather to let it shine as an example for everyone to follow.

We will reinforce old alliances and form new ones – and unite the civilized world against Radical Islamic Terrorism, which we will eradicate completely from the face of the Earth.

At the bedrock of our politics will be a total allegiance to the United States of America, and through our loyalty to our country, we will rediscover our loyalty to each other.

When you open your heart to patriotism, there is no room for prejudice.

The Bible tells us, "how good and pleasant it is when God's people live together in unity."

We must speak our minds openly, debate our disagreements honestly, but always pursue solidarity.

When America is united, America is totally unstoppable.

There should be no fear – we are protected, and we will always be protected.

We will be protected by the great men and women of our military and law enforcement and, most importantly, we are protected by God.

Finally, we must think big and dream even bigger.

[...]

We stand at the birth of a new millennium, ready to unlock the mysteries of space, to free the Earth from the miseries of disease, and to harness the energies, industries and technologies of tomorrow.

A new national pride will stir our souls, lift our sights, and heal our divisions.

It is time to remember that old wisdom our soldiers will never forget: that whether we are black or brown or white, we all bleed the same red blood of patriots, we all enjoy the same glorious freedoms, and we all salute the same great American Flag.

[...]

In the context of the material outlined and analysed in A10 and B10, what political strategies can you detect in these exchanges? In answering this, you might want to consider the following issues:

❑ Are any of the strategies outlined and discussed by Chilton (2004) in evidence here?

> **Activity C10.2** ✪

❑ If so, what strategies does the new President use to legitimize his agenda? Think particularly of how politicians legitimate themselves by appealing to the opinions of members of the public.

❑ What examples of metaphor, parallelism, and presupposition can you locate in Trump's speech?

❑ What similarities are there in the discourse strategies of this speech and that of Enoch Powell, whose 'Rivers of Blood' speech we analysed in unit B10?

TWEETING POLITICS

As mentioned in A11, a social media presence is an integral part of contemporary politics, and social media platforms are used by politicians to disseminate everything from personal messages to political policies. Politicians and other institutional elites can also use social media to portray the public impression that they are more accessible and down-to-earth than perceptions that might be possessed by voters who traditionally view politicians in a more detached context. In this vein, political professionals will also tweet or post statuses on Facebook on a consistent basis, demonstrating to the public that they have their fingers on the pulse, as it were, and hoping that voters will view them more as a part of the 'real world' of 'ordinary people' than apart from it. Occasionally of course the preoccupation with ever-increasing public engagement can backfire. In November 2017 Arlene Foster, leader of Northern Ireland's Democratic Unionist Party (DUP), was among the first to congratulate Britain's Prince Harry on his engagement to American actress Meghan Markle. Unfortunately, and somewhat ironically given the DUP's staunchly pro-British political stance, Mrs Foster's tweet read 'Congratulations to HRH Prince William on his engagement to Megan Markle. Wonderful news this morning!' Whilst the misspelling of Miss Markle's first name might have been overlooked, the fact that Mrs Foster had instead congratulated Prince Harry's older and already married brother William was somewhat less easy to miss. Whilst instances like this may not be particularly serious and often provide some light relief in an age of consistently rehearsed political performance, they also raise a more serious consideration for those who feel that a social media presence indicates a more accessible brand of politics. When the inevitable apology came several hours later the tweet read 'Apologies to TRHs Princes William & Harry for tweet error on my account earlier. I stopped tweeting personally a long time ago. Genuine typo by a member of staff. Guilty of tweeting too fast. There goes any chance of an invite!! :-) AF'. For this politician, and we can safely assume for many others, social media is managed just like press releases and political speeches.

The power of the "Commander-in-Tweet": discussion

One politician who is perceived to have a somewhat more direct input into his Twitter account is US President Donald Trump, who is so active on Twitter that he has been dubbed "Commander-in-Tweet". Donald Trump uses social media to further his political agenda and to solidify the combative 'straight talking' reputation that brought millions of American voters to his banner in the 2016 presidential election campaign. Given his penchant for seemingly less polished language on social media (see further A11), it is perhaps unsurprising that Trump on Twitter is often a controversial place, with the President commenting upon, endorsing, and criticising other politicians and political actions.

One such controversial debate was sparked in November and December 2017 when the President retweeted three videos to his 44 million followers which were originally shared by Jayda Fransen, deputy leader of the ultra-nationalist party Britain First. The videos were titled 'Muslim migrants beating up a Dutch boy on crutches', 'Muslim destroys statue of Virgin Mary', and 'Islamist mob pushes teenage boy off roof and beats him to death'.

There are several important questions about the power of social media in general, and this incident in particular, which you should consider:

Activity C11.1 ⚙

❑ Unit A11 questions the empowering capacity of social media for individual citizens and independent groups, but what are the implications for power when the user is a member of a social or political elite?

❑ Jayda Fransen was convicted in November 2016 of aggravated harassment for abusing a Muslim woman wearing a hijab. She is facing charges of religiously aggravated harassment for her online activity following an investigation by Kent Police, and further charges for 'using threatening, abusive or insulting words or behaviour' during a speech in Belfast in August 2017. Does retweeting content posted by this individual in particular suggest that Donald Trump endorses her online activity and/or her political views? Remember that discourse has a social practice outcome – Jayda Fransen's Twitter account gained 20,000 additional followers in the hours following the retweets.

❑ The videos were tweeted with neither context nor commentary and their origin has not been independently verified. Given these facts, it is unlikely that a credible politician would refer to them in a speech for example. Are there different expectations about the validity of or the need to verify social media content? The defence of the White House regarding authenticity questions surrounding the videos was simply 'the threat is real'.

❑ Are there any positives to Trump's retweeting these videos? White House Press Secretary Sarah Sanders said that the tweets were intended to start a conversation about border security and immigration, saying the President intended to 'promote strong borders and strong national security'. You might consider issues raised in A5 and B10 in particular here.

❑ A spokesperson for British Prime Minister Theresa May accused Britain First of relying on 'hateful narratives which peddle lies and stoke tensions' in response to the tweets. In his rebuttal, again delivered on Twitter (initially to the wrong Theresa May), Donald Trump said 'don't focus on me, focus on the Radical Islamic Terrorism that is taking place within the United Kingdom. We are doing just fine!' With particular reference to Strands 5, 10, and 12, how would you classify the actions and responses of Donald Trump during this furore?

'TRUTH' AND MEDIATED REACTIONS

As anticipated in A12 and B12, we offer here some further suggestions about how Habermas's model of universal pragmatics can be applied to real discourse. We also noted in B12 that Montgomery (1999) is an exploration of the way validity claims are played out in the public discourse that followed the death, in August 1997, of Diana, Princess of Wales. Montgomery offers an overview of the tribute made by the (then) British Prime Minister Tony Blair and locates in the linguistic and paralinguistic structure of the speech the features that triggered the overwhelming public reception of this speech as being *sincere*. He then examines the verbal tributes offered by the Queen and by Earl Spencer (Diana's brother). He examines in detail the linguistic properties of these speeches, and readers are strongly encouraged to refer to the original article for these insightful analyses. However, Montgomery also focuses on the interpretative frameworks through which these two speeches were assessed and understood by members of the public, across a range of mediated contexts including studio discussions, interviews, vox pops and reports. Some of this material is reproduced here.

The first set of responses is from a variety of mediated reactions to the speech of Earl Spencer:

(i) BROADCASTER: … The most heartfelt perhaps moment was Lord Spencer's tribute to his sister which was both tremendously powerful and very very personal

(ii) MAN (vox pop): It was very emotional and the er as Christopher said Candle in the Wind and Earl Spencer's speech the Earl Spencer summed up the whole of the nation the whole of the country there with what he said …

(iii) CLERIC: ... we'd been searching all week for words to express what we feel and I think if there was one set of words that did it it was that ...

(iv) BROADCASTER: You were saying earlier some of what Earl Spencer had to say you thought might be a bit political
PUNDIT: yes and I felt when I was listening to it it didn't feel like er er a speech I expected at a funeral

(v) WOMAN (vox pop): but erm for me perhaps some of it would be better suited at another time
REPORTER: you think it was inappropriate
WOMAN: yes I do yes

Here now are some responses to the speech of the Queen. It should be noted that there had in the week preceding been much discussion in the tabloids about the absence of a tribute from the Royal Household, and pressure was mounting for some expression of public feeling by the Queen on behalf of the Royal Family.

(i) BROADCASTER: ... I think we saw the Queen speaking as we were promised genuinely from the heart she didn't stumble at all she's a real professional that was a live broadcast but she talked of William and Harry and she paid warm tribute to Diana ...

(ii) REPORTER: ... do you think the Queen struck a chord
BYSTANDER 1(vox pop): she sounded very sincere and she looked as though she was very moved and I think that will satisfy everyone
BYSTANDER 2 (vox pop): I thought she said everything she should have said can't think of anything that she left out at all

(iii) REPORTER: and Joan your thoughts as well she paid tribute to Diana she thanked everyone for their support so far
JOAN: Yeh I agree with Terry I think it was a very good speech yes I do agree (.) erm I hope (.) it's true that she feels it (.) you know and these are her words and nobody else's ...

(iv) BROADCASTER: ... do you think the Queen has in fact appeased the public mood?
LORD RUSSELL: yes I think she has I think she's produced a very good mixture of sincerity and good taste ...

Activity C12.1 ✪

❑ Re-acquaint yourself with the three claims from Habermas's model outlined in B12 and try to assess which (if any) of the claims are at the fore in the two sets of mediated reactions above. Remember, it is not a question of only one claim being in play in a text; rather, there can be a balance of claims in play, with one claim working perhaps in counterpoint to another.

❑ It may help to focus on some particularly telling sequences in the remarks above, such as the cleric's comment in set 1 that 'we'd been searching all week for words to express what we feel'. Contrast this to the vox pop comments in (v) in the same set. Consider also the somewhat unusual comment in set 2 on the Queen: 'she's a real professional'.

❑ One of the issues to emerge from Montgomery's article is that sincerity involves a kind of 'performative paradox'. Scannell (1996: 58) argues that if a person's behaviour is perceived by others as a performance, it will be judged to be insincere, for sincerity presupposes, as its general condition, the absence of performance. This connects in an interesting way with the study of British Party Election Broadcasts (by Edginton and Montgomery) which we surveyed in unit B12. We noted how the rather feckless attempt at 'acting' by the then Prime Minister John Major was received by the press. In a sense, it was Major's inability to carry off the 'insincerity' that would be demanded of an acting performance that seemed to engender the perception of his 'unassuming modesty'; an underlying sincerity therefore came out of his inability to feign a political performance.

❏ Funeral orations and similar tributes (such as those offered in the examples above) are clearly interesting if rather uncomfortable discourse events where the Habermasian validity claims are inevitably invoked. What kind of conflict between the validity claims might a person face when charged with delivering a tribute or paean to someone's life and accomplishments? In what ways are obituaries constructed when the deceased has, for instance, led a controversial life? Given that the obituary is traditionally understood to be a generally positive act of emotional disclosure, how do obituaries and funeral orations balance the validity claims of truth, sincerity or appropriateness? What happens when telling the 'truth' about someone is simply not straightforward?

Section D
EXTENSION:
READINGS IN LANGUAGE AND POWER

How to use these readings

Throughout this book, and in the Further Reading section in particular, emphasis has been placed on the importance of following up the introductory units by going directly to the original scholarly sources that inform them. As an intermediate step, we have assembled in this section 12 readings from the research literature, material that in our opinion best reflects the work of some of the key practitioners in the fields of Critical Linguistics and Critical Discourse Analysis. Each reading has been edited and anno-tated, and its significance to or connection with the Strand of the book to which it relates is made explicit in our introductory comments.

As with all of the books in this Routledge series, close and detailed reading of the work collected in Section D will pay dividends. The readings give an overview of the history of the discipline as well as demonstrating the methods and procedures of CL and CDA. They also collectively offer a model of good academic practice in terms of the writing skills they impart. Inevitably, some readings are more challenging than others, but they all address different (yet seminal) issues in CL and CDA and so merit inclusion here.

D1 **CRITICAL LINGUISTICS**

The following reading, by Roger Fowler and Gunther Kress, is from the pioneering vol-ume of essays *Language and Control* (Fowler *et al.* 1979) which, more than any other single publication, marked the inception of 'Critical Linguistics' as a field of academic enquiry. As we noted earlier in the Strand, Fowler and his co-authors were interested in the way language was used in real social contexts. While this emphasis on *language use* is now taken as a given in contemporary research, in its day the approach of Fowler and his colleagues made for an exciting new paradigm shift in the way we approach and understand language. Their book challenged the prevailing orthodoxies in linguis-tics, which, overshadowed by the work of Chomsky, assigned primacy of importance to the abstract rules of grammar and syntax. The vagaries and idiosyncrasies of real language in real social contexts were all but anathema to the Chomskyan tradition. While *Language and Control* is perhaps dated in many respects, its publication in the late 1970s marked a key and lasting turn in modern linguistics.

Although many of the chapters from *Language and Control* could stand as a useful first reading to this section, this particular piece, which focuses on swimming pool regulations, is a very good measure of the sort of micro-analysis that was conducted in early CL. It shows, among other things, how we can interrogate even the most seem-ingly innocuous discourses that unfold around us.

Roger Fowler and Gunther Kress

Rules and regulations

Roger Fowler and Gunther Kress (reprinted from R. Fowler, R. Hodge, G. Kress and T. Trew, *Language and Control*, London: Routledge and Kegan Paul, 1979, pp. 26–45)

Roger Fowler and Gunther Kress

[…] In this chapter we discuss an uncontroversial example of control: rules and regulations, and the language in which they are expressed. Rules are instructions for behaving in ways which will bring about an intended or desired state. Hence they presuppose a knower of the appropriate behaviour, who needs to transmit that knowledge to someone who does not have the knowledge. Knowledge is one source of power, and consequently, if both participants agree on their role-relationship, the application of power is unidirectional; there is no hint of negotiation for control. The source of the rules is in a hierarchical relationship to the addressees, in which it is assumed that he has the right to manipulate their behaviour. Superiority of knowledge and status gives the rule-maker the authority to issue commands, and we will shortly examine the syntax of commanding as it is manifested in our text. We will rapidly discover that a certain deviousness complicates expression of the power relationship, however. Though commanding presupposes inequality of power, it does not necessarily imply conflict of interests. The rules announced in the text below were drawn up by a member of a group for the communal benefit of that group. The group in question is a swimming club for children and their parents, run by the parents. The children all go to the same local school, and so both parents and children know each other independently of their membership of the swimming club. They are a community of friends; and the informal relationship of friendship seems to be in conflict with the more formal requirements of club organization. We argue that, in this text, the need for solidarity undermines clear expression of authority. To avoid alienating his members, the author of the swimming club rules resorts to a miscellany of syntactic stratagems to sweeten the pill.

Swimming club rules

1   Parents must accompany and take responsibility for their children at all times, unless the child is in the water in an instructed class. *Note* – In most cases this will mean one adult enrolling with one child, or, if they so wish, one adult with more than one child provided it is understood they are responsible for them.
2   Being absent for more than three consecutive sessions without explanation to the membership secretary means automatic expulsion.
3   No outside shoes will be worn when in the pool area.
4   Please respect the facilities and equipment, and take particular care with untrained children.
5   The age limits of the club are six months to eight years. For the six to eight years old instruction will he provided. Children may remain members for the completed term in which their eighth birthday falls.
6   There must be no more than twenty-four bodies in the pool at any one time.
7   Membership cards must always be carried and shown on request.

Here the author needs and seeks to direct the specific behaviour of his members. The speech act appropriate to this situation comes under the general category of *command*, and there are a large number of these in this text, with a variety of syntactic forms of expression. The most overt examples of command are 1 'Parents must accompany …' 4 'Please respect the facilities … and take particular care …' 6 'There must be no more than twenty-four bodies in the pool …' 7 'Membership cards must always be carried

Roger
Fowler and
Gunther
Kress

and shown'. Syntactically, 1, 6 and 7 are declarative sentences, while the two clauses in 4 are imperatives. Declaratives and imperatives express the relation between speaker and addressee in differing ways: the speech roles assigned in one case are 'giver of information' and 'recipient of information'; in the other 'commander' and 'commanded'. It is clear that the two forms are appropriate for two quite distinct kinds of power-relation: the imperative for one involving a considerable power differential, one where control may be exercised through the direct assertion of the roles of commander-commanded. The declarative, on the other hand, seemingly makes no specific claims about power-relations; the giving of information seems a neutral act. (This is in fact not the case: the giver of information also has the role of *speaker*, and there are conventions about who may and who may not be a speaker in any given situation – e.g. children should be seen and not heard; and everyone realizes when someone has 'spoken out of turn'. Also, a giver of information is a *knower* of information, and knowledge is a basis of power.) The 'command' in declaratives is not carried through speech-role directly, but modally, through the use of the modal verb *must*. In the imperative the source of the command is quite plain: I, the speaker/writer, command *you*, the addressee; but in the declarative with the modal 'must', the source of the authority is vague: it might be the speaker, equally it might not. The answer to the outraged question 'who says so?' is 'I' in the imperative, but in the declarative might be 'the committee', 'the people who own the pool', 'the caretaker', or 'I', or any number of other entities, 'common sense' included.

At this stage the unanswered questions are: where is the source of the vagueness, the need for obfuscation; second, why is there a switch, in just one case (4), from the modalized declarative form to the direct imperative form? We leave aside the first question for the moment, except to point out that it resides in the social relations between writer of rules and 'recipients' of the rules. The second question is illuminated by the conjunction of 'untrained children' and the age limit of six months at the lower end. 'Untrained' (explained as 'not toilet trained' in a later revision of these rules) hints that the dangers legislated against in rule 4 are critical and delicate. Non-toilet-trained babies could foul the pool; non-swimming-trained babies might drown. The serious-ness of both eventualities increases the authority, hence the distance, of the writer, so that he can call upon the weight of the direct imperative.

Note, however, that the authority structure indicated by rule 4 is still not straightfor-ward. 'Please' shows that this writer even at his most commanding is still negotiating for power – perhaps here also despairing, since what he requests, the close physical control of infants, is not really within the capability of parents.

As a general principle, we propose that the greater the power differential between the parties to a speech act of command, the more 'direct' the syntactic form (e.g. imperative) which may be chosen. Someone who enjoys absolute power can afford to be abrupt. The smaller the power distance the greater the amount of linguistic effort, of circumlocution (declaratives, particularly passives, e.g. rules 3 and 7). The swimming club rule-writer is in an ambivalent position of artificial authority, and needs to avoid curtness. He plays down even the very little power he does possess. The effect here is hesitancy. [...]

[A] passive declarative such as 3 'No outside shoes will be worn when in the pool area', or 7 'Membership cards must always be carried and shown on request' [...]

Roger
Fowler and
Gunther
Kress

involves deletion of agent. [...] There are two [...] important consequences of the passive. First, the naturally prominent first phrase in the sentence, which in actives is occupied by the agent of a process, is in passives occupied by the object. The object thus becomes focal: from an interest in 'parents carrying membership cards', attention is refocused on 'membership cards which must be carried'. Not only is the object given thematic prominence, but the agent is deleted as well. The persons become entirely uninteresting compared with the cards they must carry.

Second, the passive construction has a powerful neutralizing effect on the action or process being communicated. The auxiliary 'be' is introduced, so that 'carried' begins to look like an adjectival attribute of 'membership cards'. In the form 'will be carried' an attentive reader will see the passive form, and speculate about the deleted agent. The next stage from here would be 'membership cards *are* carried', in which the transformation from a *process* to a *state* is total. The point is that processes, being under the control of agents, imply the possibility of modification, decision; whereas states are perceived as unalterable and thus to be put up with. All 'be' forms classifying process as state are open to suspicion and should be inspected: cf. 'is understood', 'are responsible' in 1.

The deletion of agents in the truncated passive occurs not only in the main syntactic structure of rules such as 3 and 7, but also in phrases within sentences: 'instructed class' (1), 'untrained children' (4), 'instruction will be provided' (5) and 'completed term' (5). [...] The point at issue is that the uncertainty about agency spreads a general vagueness through the rules, and a vagueness precisely in the area of *who does what*. The readers of the rules are left in a situation of helpless ignorance: apparently the knowers know, but seem to keep the ignorant from knowing. A dissatisfied member can be left very frustrated by not knowing where to turn for specific action. Here the process merely confers the power derived from relatively trivial knowledge on those who have it, and creates a class of those who do not have such power/knowledge. In more important contexts it works as a powerful means of control. Anyone who has ever come up against 'faceless bureaucracy' will know what this is about. [...]

Agent deletion is pervasive throughout this text, and the syntactic reduction which accompanies it results in a number of new noun-like compounds: 1 'instructed class', 4 'untrained children', 5 'completed term' have already been commented on in the context of agent-deletion. These reduced passives [...] become potentially equivalent to ordinary dictionary words, in that their meanings can be regarded as unitary, unanalysed. 'Untrained children', having been coded in a compact linguistic form, serves to crystallize a new concept, and to make it memorisable. This process of coding experience in new ways by inventing lexical items is known as *relexicalization*. It is extensively used in the creation of specialized jargons, and significantly such jargons often involve *systems* of related terms, i.e. systematic classifications of concepts. Members of the club are required to accept a new classificatory principle for their children, one that is relevant and necessary in the system of concepts habitually employed by the club to categorize its members and their behaviour. Once this relexicalization begins, it may extend into a system that includes, say, 'trained', 'over-trained', 'under-trained', 'uninstructed', 'part-instructed', etc. The member cannot be sure how far the club's specialized classification system extends.

**Roger
Fowler and
Gunther
Kress**

There are relexicalizations which are based on syntactic structures other than nominalization through truncated passives. In 3 we have 'outside shoes', and no doubt its complement 'inside shoes'; there is the 'pool area', a word which exists in the language of the world outside this club; however, with a large range of new terms being created, the nervous member of the club will be wary of relying on any continuity between his normal language and the language of the club. The most complex new nominal created here is in 2: 'Being absent for more than three consecutive sessions without explanation to the membership secretary' – here is a concept to master! Notice that the rule-writer evidently regards this as a difficult lexical item which has to be defined for the innocent addressee: i.e. his use of the definitional verb 'means'. Now 'means' is often used to equate two mutually substitutable linguistic items: e.g. "amour" means "love", "avuncular" means "behaving like an uncle". In the club rules, however, 'means' equates actions in a consequential relation: 1 'this will mean one adult enrolling …'. The use of 'means' here suggests the inevitable unalterability of the consequence.

The effect of the relexicalization is control through the one-way flow of knowledge. This device is probably more powerful than the direct control exercised in the commands analysed above. Whereas an obstinate individual might offer resistance to direct interpersonal manipulation, he or she would find it difficult to evade the control exercised through the new terminology of this society. The only strategies available would seem to be withdrawal from this club, or the construction of an alternative vocabulary; which might in fact amount to the same thing. However, for any member of the club, these terms constitute the categories which describe possible entities of the conceptual system which defines the 'world' of the club: and in that sense they control the user of that language. […]

Issues to consider

This reading articulates a number of issues that resonate in contemporary CL and CDA. As is clear throughout, the emphasis is at the micro-analytic level of the text's construction, from which is adduced numerous interpretations of how these 'syntactic stratagems' enable the rule maker to exercise control through language. The idea of the 'agentless passive', for instance, comes under scrutiny (see B1). There is also an early outing for the concept of 'relexicalization' (see B3), although in linking it to constructions like 'outside shoes', 'pool area', 'instructed class' and 'untrained children', Fowler and Kress seem to be talking more about register-linked noun phrases than the more common sense of relexicalization as 'new words for old'. Nonetheless they make an interesting point about how these noun phrases help shape the conceptual system which defines the 'world' of the club.

Some suggestions for discussion follow.

❑ Work in early CL has been criticized for its tendency to see texts as products, without adequate attention being paid to the processes of producing and interpreting texts. Are there other aspects of the swimming pool regulations – aspects of *discourse* for example – that could be analysed? In general terms, do you feel that Fowler and Kress's interpretations of the text are justified on the basis of their analysis? Do you think non-academic readers of these regulations would have considered them 'faceless bureaucracy'?

❑ A counter-argument against the CL approach to 'agent deletion' in the passive (acknowledged elsewhere in the Fowler and Kress article) is that this grammatical feature is simply an economy in expression, and that, to be blunt, nothing sinister is intended by it. Is the syntactic reduction in the swimming regulations, contrary to what Fowler and Kress say, a simple 'economy' of style?

❑ In the section of the article which immediately follows the excerpt we have provided here, Fowler and Kress introduce the notion that other types of instructions, such as those given in recipe books, are syntactically much simpler than the swimming club rules they analyse. They argue that in recipe language imperatives are the only form of command used, as in 'Peel a large onion' or 'Add a sprig of thyme to the sauce' and so on. In your experience, is this really the case? Are recipes really grammatically restricted to imperative clauses, or are they more discursively complex than this?

❑ A general issue related to the two previous points is to do with other possible ways of representing the rules as both language and discourse. If CL takes issue with a particular textual representation this presupposes (often implicitly, and not addressed by Fowler and Kress) that there is another, 'better' way of writing the rules. In other words, in what other ways could the regulations have been written? Can you draft such a re-write? Or do you get the sense from their article that Fowler and Kress are really taking issue with the idea of authority and that in essence *all* rules are problematic?

❑ In considering this issue, you might find it helpful to read beyond this excerpt by accessing directly the seminal work from which it is drawn. Fowler and Kress continue their discussion by considering the 'functions' of the rules. They note that the rules are simultaneously *directive*, in that they must be practical enough to control the actions of those to whom they are addressed, and *constitutive*, in that they are important to the very notion of establishing a group as a club. The authors conclude that 'a club must have rules for it to count as a club: they are a token of its formal existence'.

BUREAUCRACY AND SOCIAL CONTROL   **D2**

The following reading is an excerpt from Srikant Sarangi and Stefaan Slembrouck's book *Language, Bureaucracy and Social Control* (2013). A significant expression of institutional discourse, bureaucracy is the scrutiny and categorization by state institutions of all areas of social activity. (This idea of a kind of 'state surveillance' of public and private life accords with Foucault's idea of power as outlined in A1 and elsewhere.) Sarangi and Slembrouck (2013: 3) argue that bureaucracy transcends printed documents, mechanical decision-making or concrete government buildings. It is rather best seen as an event or a process that happens to those involved, whether they are clients or bureaucrats. Citizens become 'clients' when they enter a bureaucratic process, and this process is driven by categorization and coding. Citizens therefore no longer exist as individuals but as fixed, named categories such as 'tax payer', 'job seeker', 'single parent' and so on.

This reading focuses on and examines a number of 'bureaucratic events'. The authors look at the ways in which institutional representatives address and construct clients, with particular emphasis on the leaflets and application forms that are central to this type of categorization. By collecting a number of actual cases where clients come up against the bureaucratic process, Sarangi and Slembrouck's study, like a number of the readings in this Strand, illustrates admirably the 'hands on' potential of discourse analysis, where asymmetrical relationships of power are explored through real instances of social interaction. Tellingly, the present reading shows how clients, through procedures involving rather rigid and mechanical form filling, become fixed categories in the bureaucratic process. Such is the nature of bureaucracy as a system of power that, in order to function, it needs to 'de-individualize' people into labels and codes.

The bureaucrat's perspective: citizens as clients

Srikant Sarangi and Stefaan Slembrouck

Srikant Sarangi and Stefaan Slembrouck (reprinted from Chapter 6 of *Language, Bureaucracy and Social Control*, by Srikant Sarangi and Stefaan Slembrouck, London and New York: Routledge, 2013)

[…] The bureaucratic process can be looked at as a process in which 'all' citizens can potentially become clients – a taxpayer, a registered patient, a licensed driver, an unemployed citizen. Within each category one can find clients with various kinds of experience and various kinds of literacy. What is more, someone who is a 'professional' client in one area may be quite 'naive' when it comes to another client category. In dealing with the public, bureaucracies conduct their routine work with certain client types in mind, which may vary according to the nature of the contact situation. For instance, there is the erring client who is a potential threat to the institutional norms, the foreign client who comes within the remit of the institution, the prospective applicant addressed in a leaflet. In this chapter we shall look at how these client types are constructed in 'bureaucratic' situations. […]

What sort of perceptions do institutional representatives bring to a situation where the client appears to be in the wrong?

The case we are discussing happened in a university library. ND, a visiting scholar, walks past the alarm point and the alarm goes. Knowing what the alarm means, ND returns to the counter and, unasked, she opens her bag to check its contents. She knew she had no borrowing rights, but only a card entitling her to use the on-site library facilities. An attendant arrives. By that time ND has already found out that she had a book in the bag which she should have left in the library. She says: 'oh I'm so sorry it's just like the size of my diary sorry extremely sorry'. Another library employee arrives and asks: 'How is this book with you?', a question which ND interprets as 'How did this come about?' She replies: 'along with these diaries this small book by mistake I have put it sorry for this'.

The second library employee asks for ND's library card, takes it and goes away to consult with a senior colleague. Meanwhile, ND asks the attendant: 'Shall I go and put

Srikant
Sarangi and
Stefaan
Slembrouck

the book on the shelf?' She shows the photocopies she has made of the book, which the attendant inspects.

The second employee comes back with the 'offender's form' and asks ND to fill it in. She says: 'generally we call the police in such cases you better fill it in'. ND is worried and says 'you see I'm a government servant in [country] I teach there it's not expected of me it's just a mistake will there be any problem in my service then'. ND was a visitor to the university but as she is employed by the government of her country she cannot afford to have a record. The offender's form was more alarming than the library alarm itself.

ND dutifully fills in the form (part 1). A third (senior) employee arrives and asks: 'Have you got any other identification where is your passport?' ND replies, 'I haven't got the passport here I've given it to the immigration for extending my visa and I'm supposed to get it back tomorrow but my brother is working in the university'. 'What is his name?' 'DR.' The senior employee picks up the phone to contact DR but he was out. The second employee then turns to ND and asks: 'what you have explained to me now how this book came with you you just write here' (part 2 on the back of the form).

By then, the senior employee comes back and says: 'I've left a message [for your brother] he's not there generally we call police in such matters but we will keep this pass and you may not use the library further.' The next morning, DR, having received the message from his answerphone, calls the senior employee to clarify the situation. The message on the answerphone included that 'she was trying to remove a book without issuing it'. DR stresses that it was a mistake and asks whether ND could retrieve her library card as she wanted to continue using the library resources during her stay. The card was returned to her the same day.

The sequence of events was clearly determined by asymmetrical perceptions of the situation ND is perhaps a 'naive' client. She tries very hard to cooperate and admits her mistake. The book indeed resembled the diary and she had taken photocopies of relevant sections. Her passport was indeed at the embassy. However, the fact that she was ready to expand and explain was treated with suspicion. Moreover her offer of remedial action was interpreted as coming from someone who had been caught and was trying to buy her way out. [...]

Let us analyse the library incident further from the bureaucratic perspective. The basic policy here is that the institutional representative has the benefit of the doubt. All library users are potential booklifters. From the library staff's point of view it is not possible to go on record as stating that ND had made a genuine mistake.

It is important to bear in mind that bureaucrats, in their day-to-day activities, can be held accountable by the institution which they are serving and where absolute power lies. Going through the procedure is their safety net. So the card was immediately withdrawn to see whether the client's statements were correct but also to allow the library staff to back up their actions. It is just possible that the staff actually believed the user from the start.

Likewise, the use of the 'offender's form' reveals the institution's premium on the meaning of actions (rather than a concern with the client's intentions). In the section marked 'for official use', the library staff is required to tick one of the two following boxes:

**Srikant
Sarangi and
Stefaan
Slembrouck**

ii. Item(s) was/were:

[ ] intentionally removed   [ ] unintentionally removed.

What matters is the library staff's assessment of the client's intentions. Even if the staff intended to return the card as soon as the user's explanation was confirmed, the offender's form had to be filled in, in order to be filed. This is also evident from the specification of the offence as communicated over the telephone: 'she was trying to remove a book without issuing it'. Let us look more closely at the part of the form under the heading of 'Details of offence':

Details of offence _____

Date of incident _____   Time of incident_____

Details of item(s) removed from the library without authorisation. Book(s)

call no_____   call no _____

barcode_____   barcode _____

author_____   author _____

title _____   title _____

_____   _____

_____   _____

Other item(s) _____   _____

Offender's statement: _____

I acknowledge receipt of this record and letter of warning.

Signature of offender:_____

Thus, filling in a form means that the client goes on record about an offence, an application, and so on. In the form above, ND becomes an offender by signature, irrespective of whether library staff later tick the box 'unintentionally removed'. As soon as a form enters a situation, the client is labelled (even before evidential information is processed). Forms are a major anchorage point for institutional classifications. Whether it is in the context of eligibility, or the context of disciplining, it is through forms that citizens are turned into 'clients' and their stories into 'cases'. […]

The information-seeking role of institutions through application forms and their information-providing role (through leaflets) is multi-functionally targeted at certain client types (e.g. to make sure that the 'old age pensioner' knows what the benefit is about, to make sure that the more streetwise client does reveal the information requested in [say] box 4a). Both these dimensions can be analysed in terms of client needs and bureaucratic perceptions of these needs – it is the latter which informs institutional provisions.

Application forms and leaflets are both text types which emanate from the institution but which have clients as principal addressees. […] one can examine what type of client is implied in leaflets, application forms, and so on. How does this relate to forms of social control? The fact that client needs differ from institutional provisions produces an asymmetry which makes the use of application forms inherently problematic. Thus, leaflets can be seen as moving ambivalently between, on the one hand, intended attempts at reducing this asymmetry and, on the other hand, having the normalising bureaucratic notions of clienthood.

[…] bureaucracy is all about processing people. Most of this processing takes place by examining information collected from clients through application forms, and turning this information into files on the basis of pre-existing categories which follow set institutional criteria. These categories inform institutional decisions.

Srikant
Sarangi and
Stefaan
Slembrouck

Let us first discuss a few general properties of application forms.

(1) Forms typically have names which reflect the subroutines, the labour division and the departmentalisation in an organisation in a way which is not transparent to clients (form names are there for the sake of bureaucrats).

(2) The layout of forms heavily constrains the client's activity in that it does not allow clients to tell a whole story. Boxes, dotted lines, multiple choice questions, pre-formulated answers, limited space (e.g. six letter spaces to fill in date of birth) all contribute to the packaging of the client's case. From a bureaucrat's point of view, this is tied up with the efficiency of processing information. There is, however, a recent trend to provide a space where the client can state things not accommodated by the form. This may appear as a move to minimise clients' constraints, but it is a double-edged sword, because it increases the possibilities that clients may give away information which could jeopardise their case.

(3) Forms have also temporal dimensions (deadlines and eligibility periods), which equally constrain the client's activities. Clients may be required to declare something ahead of a situation, whether or not it reflects the client's actual needs at that point in time.

(4) Forms are also used to provide information to clients; they have a 'leaflet function' through the occurrence of explicit information about the procedure, entitlements, and so forth, and there is also the implicit 'leaking' of information when clients work out aspects of the procedure and the decision making from the nature of the form.

(5) Forms also have sections for 'office use only' – boxes and diagrams which run parallel to the spaces used for clients' responses. This is where the decision making will leave its traces on the form and the categorisation of an applicant as 'a particular case' will become definite. This is usually done in a non-transparent way (with abundant use of abbreviations and non-transparent codes). This may explain why forms, once filled in and processed, remain the property of the institution and are seldom returned to clients.

The processing of information provided by clients by bureaucratic channels can be captured through the concept of '(re)formulation' (cf. Fairclough 1992). To (re)formulate a state of affairs is an act of classification but it also amounts to the imposition of a particular interpretation which informs subsequent action. (Re)formulation thus links up with situational power. It also successfully captures the asymmetry and the 'translation' element involved. Bureaucrats' (re)formulations take priority over clients' characterisations. Although forms reduce clients to category-types, this also entails a form of protection in the sense that a legitimate claim does not require more than what the form caters for.

Forms have an information-seeking function. They are often after the same information (e.g. personal particulars, education) but they vary when it comes to the amount of detail needed. For instance, one embassy may require certain personal details not required by another embassy, or embassies may require certain details not required by banks. The wide difference in what information is sought suggests that different institutions regard different types of information as essential and thus assign values to their 'preferred' types of information. Clients are very familiar with such differential treatment, but they rarely make this an issue and deny information that they deem 'irrelevant' on the basis of their prior experience with similar institutional processing. In fact, this reconciliation points to the fact that clients occupy a compliant cooperative role and turn their lives in to 'open books' for bureaucratic 'gaze'.

Srikant Sarangi and Stefaan Slembrouck

From the bureaucrat's perspective, it is easy to rationalise why certain bits of information are asked for. This may depend on the following factors:

> immediate processing: 'more information is always better', so that the bureaucrat can act on it without having to send reminders or having to seek further information from other sources. A form may also have a number of sections to be filled in by other institutions before it can be submitted. This reveals the hierarchies between and within institutions;

> traditions in record keeping, background statistical research;

> forms of legitimation (e.g. a client may be entitled to something following a verbal promise, but a form needs to be filled in for the record);

> records of information exchange with an implicit claim of 'objective' treatment (it carries the assumption that clients will be treated in the same way);

> devices to apply for and/or deny entitlement;

> face-redressive functions: apparent distancing from the institution when bureaucrats claim they do what forms require

One of the questions arising here is whether forms can be offensive in the way they probe and in the way they address a particular type of client. Or do they require of a client some understanding about their immediate functioning? The latter would mean clients must learn to 'distance' themselves from the information asked/provided in the form and not consider the forms as a 'moral grid'. But this also highlights the one-sidedness of information exchange and leaves clients with little power to 'challenge' bureaucratic practices. Forms can be described as a defence which bureaucrats use to protect themselves from accusations of partiality, bias and so on. An unsuccessful outcome is often blamed on the client, because the bureaucratic decision is taken in accordance with the information provided in the form. [...]

Institutions operate with certain assumptions about the clients they address and process. Institutional assumptions about client categories have implications for the kinds of application forms which are used and for the questions which are put to applicants in a particular form. Let us take the situation of claiming 'incapacity benefit' in Britain. An 'incapacity for work questionnaire' has to be filled in in order to claim this benefit. This questionnaire has various categories related to muscular activity, but there may not be room for people suffering from, say, a skin condition to be able to declare their situation. While client constructs have been built into application forms, the real clients may remain absent from the form.

The questionnaire elicits detailed information about everyday activities, such as 'getting up from a chair', 'walking', 'lifting and carrying' etc. Under 'walking' for instance, the form asks:

You cannot walk, without having to stop or feeling severe discomfort, for more than

> * Just a few steps
> * 50 metres, this is about 55 yards
> * 200 metres, this is about 220 yards
> * 400 metres, this is about 440 yards
> * 800 metres, this is about half a mile

Questions such as the above objectify (in)abilities and require clients to measure and express abilities in numerical terms. Additionally, there is a tension between 'an activity one ideally should avoid doing because of medical conditions' and 'what one manages to do, even against the medical odds, simply because daily living becomes impossible without it'. The applicant here has to grasp that the objectified measurement is the bit which is going to count – rather than a statement of the difficulties one experiences in coping with these things in daily life. […]

Srikant Sarangi and Stefaan Slembrouck

Clearly, self-assessment constitutes an important dimension of the filling in of application forms and clients may not only be inclined to under-estimate their needs, they will also be held responsible for the subsequent outcome of the decision-making. […]

Issues to consider

An important method in Sarangi and Slembrouck's study is the way they seek support for their position through the opinions of those who have direct contact with the bureaucratic encounters studied. Elsewhere in the same article, the views of a deputy manager of a Citizen's Advice Bureau are solicited in the context of a problematic income support form. This is an issue which we develop further in the web materials which accompany this book. We argue that it is important wherever possible in critical linguistic analysis to try to garner the views either of those who are directly affected by the discursive practice under examination or of those who have regular professional contact with that discursive practice. Some suggestions follow.

❑ 'Forms are a major anchorage point for institutional classifications', argue Sarangi and Slembrouck. To what extent does this reflect your own experience of 'form-filling'? Try to recount situations where you have been 'classified' or 'categorized' in bureaucratic terms. What stages were involved in the classification and what was the outcome of the process?

❑ Have you or someone you know experienced any difficult bureaucratic encounters like the ones described here by Sarangi and Slembrouck? That is, have you found yourself completing a document or application form that you know presents you in an unfavourable light (as in the 'library' example above)? Or has the form been worded in such a way as to make it impossible to present an accurate, true or realistic state of affairs (as in the 'incapacity benefit' and 'income support' forms discussed above)?

POWER AND RESISTANCE IN POLICE INTERVIEWS   **D3**

The following reading is from Kate Haworth's linguistic study of a police interview in which she employs a combination of Conversation Analysis (CA) and Critical Discourse Analysis (CDA) for an integrated approach to the investigation of institutional talk. Focusing on several linguistic features, her detailed analysis demonstrates that the balance of power and control between the participants is affected by their institutional status (one a police officer, the other a doctor), by the discourse roles assigned to them by the context and by their relative knowledge. Haworth also shows that power dynamics are constantly shifting and are open to contestation and resistance. Her wider consideration of the institutional context (in line with CDA), rather than with the immediate context of the police interview, reveals important aspects that have considerable influence on the interviewer's linguistic strategies. Haworth's study also illustrates that linguistics can make an important contribution to the improved use of police interviews in the UK criminal justice system, where interview transcripts may potentially distort the information in the recording through the omission of false starts, overlaps, discourse markers and so on. This area of study is particularly relevant for those with an interest in legal discourse and forensic linguistics (see further Strand 7).

Kate Haworth

The dynamics of power and resistance in police interview discourse

Kate Haworth (reprinted from *Discourse and Society* 17 (6) (2006): 739–759)

[In the data, P = police interviewer, S = Shipman and SOL = Shipman's solicitor. A key to the transcription symbols used in this reading is provided at the beginning of the book. The background on the Shipman case which forms the basis of Haworth's analysis can be found at https://www.gov.uk/government/organisations/shipman-inquiry]

Introduction

[...]
This study involves an analysis of power and control in an English police interview with a murder suspect. The data used here is of particular interest as it involves a high-profile and highly unusual interviewee: Dr Harold Shipman. Shipman was convicted in January 2000 of the murder of 15 of his patients, and a subsequent inquiry found that he murdered an estimated 260 people over a 27 year period. He evaded any suspicion until the death of Mrs Kathleen Grundy in 1998 and the appearance of a clumsily forged will naming him as the sole beneficiary. The interview used in this study took place at the early stages of the investigation and concerns the death of Mrs Grundy. Shipman maintained his innocence throughout the interview process and subsequent trial despite overwhelming evidence of his guilt.

[...]
In police interviews with suspects the role of each participant is clearly defined and restrained. Yet these roles are very unequal, especially in terms of the distribution of power and control. In addition to the asymmetric dynamic created by the ascribed roles of questioner and responder, the police have a considerable degree of direct power over the interviewee, controlling the setting in which the interview takes place and having the capability to make vital decisions about the interviewee's liberty and future based on the outcome.

Nevertheless, interviewees still have control over what they say, and that is the most crucial part of the interaction. The whole point of the interview process is for the interviewer to gain information from the interviewee. Thus although the police interviewer is ostensibly in control of the situation, the outcome of the interview is very much in the hands (or rather words) of the suspect interviewee.

The question of power and control is therefore an important aspect of police interview discourse. The interview material examined here is particularly promising for a study of this kind. Here we have a classic 'institutional discourse' context in that a representative of an institution (the police) is conducting a conversation as part of his institutional role with someone who is not part of that institution. But that person is a member of a different institution, and his presence in this context (as a suspect) is tied very closely to that institutional role (i.e. as a doctor being questioned about his patients).

Kate Haworth

[…]

An integrated approach to DA

A multi-method discourse analytic approach is taken in this study, combining Conversation Analysis (CA), Critical Discourse Analysis (CDA) and pragmatics. In particular I take CA's approach to data collection and analysis, using naturally occurring data and undertaking a close analysis of detailed transcripts. The analytical emphasis is on the micro features of the interaction and its sequential organization. However, the identification of power and control as potentially significant factors in the chosen interaction owes much to CDA, which allows a wider consideration of the significance of the institutional context and the social identities and status of the participants.

[…]

The approach taken here recognizes the methodological strengths and weaknesses of each. It thus aims to avoid the problem Fairclough identifies with CA of giving 'a rather implausible image … of conversation as a skilled social practice existing in a social vacuum' (1989: 12), while also avoiding the tendency of CDA to assume that power and status are pre-ordained and pre-allocated in a given context.

This approach thus recognizes the importance of including both micro and macro features in a sound analysis of power in discourse. It combines the analytical strengths of CA with the critical social stance of CDA, without sacrificing the pre-eminent focus on the data itself.

[…]

The data

The data analysed in this study represent one of several interviews conducted by the police with Dr Shipman. In a highly unusual move the police released the tapes of two of these interviews to the public. (I obtained the audio files used in this analysis from the BBC News website archives.) It should be noted that (despite the claim made on the website) these appear to have been edited. However, they are almost certainly the versions agreed by the Prosecution and presented as evidence at Shipman's trial. […]

My analysis reveals four features of particular significance in terms of the dynamics of power and control in this interview. These are: (1) topic; (2) question type; (3) the question-answer sequence; and (4) allusions to institutional status.

Topic

The significance of topic as a factor in the distribution of power and control in an interview setting is highlighted by Greatbatch in his study of news interviews. He comments that:

Kate Haworth

... news interviewers are effectively afforded sole rights to manage the organization of topics. For, in so far as they restrict themselves to answering, interviewees are obviously limited to dealing with the topical agendas which interviewers' questions establish for their turns and, as such, in contrast to interviewers, are not able to shift from one topic or topical line to another.

(Greatbach 1986: 441)

Thus it is expected that the person in the role of interviewer will set the topical agenda, leaving the interviewee in a restricted position discursively.

Question type

In considering the syntactic form and function of the questions used in these data, I follow the approach of Harris in her analysis of questions as a mode of control in magistrates' courts (1984; [and see A3]). She classifies questions by 'the nature of the responses requested' (p. 13). She found that the majority of questions used in the court require a minimal response, leading her to conclude that 'the asking of questions becomes a powerful means of controlling the discourse' (p. 14).

[…]

Question–answer sequence

This considers the basic expected sequence of the interviewer's turns as questions and the interviewee's as answers. Just as with topic, the role of questioner gives a large degree of power to that participant, allowing them not only to set what is an acceptable next turn from the other participant, but further to sanction the responder if their response is not deemed acceptable. It is open to the responder to comply with the expected sequence and co-operate with the interviewer, or to resist.

Institutional status

The fourth feature refers to participants' identification of themselves and each other in terms of their professional role. This is manifest in this interview in two ways: first, in appeals by participants to their own institutional status and, second, in attempts to undermine the other's status.

I found that patterns of these four features emerge through the sequence of the interview, with corresponding shifts in power and control as the interaction unfolds. These shifts occur precisely at the points at which the topic changes.

Results

Opening sequence

We have already noted that there is an expectation that the police interviewer will control the topical agenda. Yet right at the start we see something different. P goes through the formulaic opening to the police interview, namely the mandatory caution, and then starts to set up his agenda for this interaction. But as soon as P has completed

Kate
Haworth

enough of his utterance to make it clear that he is about to introduce topic, Shipman (S) interrupts:

P: … there's one or two points we'd like to pick up [on from]
S: [errr] can I clarify something first.
P: yeah
S: I've had the chance to mull over the questioning this morning. (.) and perhaps I've made clear what ha- happened when Mrs (.) Grundy asked me to witness the will …

P defers to S and lets him continue, thus abandoning his own topic introduction. S then introduces his own topic instead. Bearing in mind the expected balance of power in favour of P in terms of setting the topical agenda of the interview, this marks a significant breach of that order right at the start of the interaction.

This also represents a breach of the expected question-answer sequence of the interview, in that here S takes a turn which is not a response to a question from P.

[…]

P lets S continue with a fairly long turn, not intervening despite several pauses, and even encouraging him with back-channelling. By so doing he effectively hands S even more discursive freedom. But this introduces a highly significant feature of the police interview context: the overall aim is to get an interviewee to talk. Thus P is constrained by the institutional context into allowing S to talk 'out of turn' here.

In S's continuing turn there is also an element of implied criticism of P's role as questioner:

S: … that obviously didn't come out in this morning's interview, (.) and now I've clarified the situation.
      (21–22)

This is a challenge which P doesn't let pass

P: you were asked a question (.) this morning you had the opportunity to give that answer this morning. is there any reason why you didn't?
      (23–24)

Several features show how P is attempting to reassert his discursive position here. He directly addresses the implication that there was an omission in his earlier questioning: 'you were asked a question this morning' (23). Further, he clearly orients to the expected format of his turns as questions and S's as answers, by directly referring to S's turn as an 'answer' (24) despite the fact that, as noted, it does not occur as a response to a question. He thus reasserts the expected order and dismisses S's challenge.

We can see right from the start, then, that the question of control is a crucial one in this interaction, and that it is certainly not a straightforward matter of the participant with the role of questioner having an unassailable position of power. S has right away shown his unwillingness to comply with the restrictions imposed upon him by his role as responder, and has also displayed his ability to challenge P. P, meanwhile, has to continually assert his power in order to maintain it.

Kate Haworth

Mrs Grundy's medical records

P now gets to introduce the first main topic, namely Mrs Grundy's medical records. P makes it explicitly clear that he is unilaterally changing the topic:

> P: OK (-) I want to go back to the (.) computer (.) medical records … (33)

Throughout this sequence S picks up P's topic. However, that is not to say that his responses are straightforwardly co-operative. S's first response in this section simply does not answer P's question:

> P: the entry for (.) Mrs Grundy's visit on the 9th of June, (.) will you tell me why (.) there's no reference there (.) to you taking any blood from her. (-)
> S: normally (all) the blood results came back two days later.
> P: no but (can you tell me) why there's no (.) mention on that date.
> S: I cannot give you an explanation.

His answer does give the surface appearance of conformity, in that taken on its own it sounds like a legitimate and helpful answer – but not to the question asked. This is therefore a subtle form of subversion rather than a blatant challenge. The *illusion* of compliance is at least worth maintaining.

P recognizes this challenge and sanctions S, repeating his question (40). Failure to answer for a second time *would* have been a blatant challenge, and sure enough this time S replies. But although P maintains some control here, this demonstrates that his grip on it is by no means firm.

The chosen topic allows S to display his institutional status:

> P: … it doesn't actually say you'd taken a blood sample from her.
> S: errm (-) it's not the custom of most general practitioners to write, (.) 'I have taken a blood sample which would consist of this this and this' most general practitioners just write down what the blood test is that they're doing.
>
> (76–81)

This is another interesting evasive tactic, in that S does not address what he actually did, but instead refers to the 'custom' of his peers: he implies he has merely followed standard practice for his profession. He thus uses his professional status as a shield, shifting the focus of blame onto the institution to which he belongs, instead of on himself as an individual member.

> […]

Cause of death

The topic of the cause of death represents something of a crossover between the legal and medical domain, involving forensic evidence, but of a medical nature. It is therefore open to either P or S to dominate this section by steering it in the direction of their particular expertise. P begins by revealing that a forensic examination has detected fatal levels of morphine in Mrs Grundy's body, but then hands the initiative to S by using an open explanation-seeking question: 'do you have any comment to make about that' (287). This worked in P's favour on the topic of the will, as there was little scope

Kate
Haworth

for a plausible explanation from S. But here it hands the floor completely to S, allowing him to take the topic in the direction of his choosing.

He chooses to discuss Mrs Grundy's previous medical history, a subject over which he has sole knowledge as it is based purely on his own medical notes. He thus gets to speak at length here on his own version of events, namely that Mrs Grundy was a drug user and accidentally overdosed. Indeed there are several long pauses where P could have intervened, but instead he simply allows S to continue.

In fact P effectively only gets to ask one question in this whole 77-line sequence. He is twice interrupted by S before being able to complete subsequent turns. And, significantly, for several turns P is forced into the role of responder:

P: … if you're really suggesting that to us (.) [then-]
S: [may] I ask whether the house
        was searched?
P: yes, (.) no drugs whatsoever (.) that could cause a fatality (.) (are) the
        findings that we've got [from-]
SOL: [wh-] when was it searched (.)
P: I haven't got the date to hand that it was searched
S: well that's quite important (.)
P: are you suggesting though doctor, (.) [(?)]
S: [I'm not suggesting] anything I'm
        just telling you my fears and worries of this lady (.) er at that time.

This is another clear challenge to P, with S not only usurping P's position as questioner, but also implicitly criticizing his institutional status as an investigator.

Yet S still orients to the expected format which he is breaching with a 'request for permission to speak' ('may I ask …': 320), but this time the request is clearly 'token' as he continues without waiting for permission (Greatbatch 1988: 419). Thus S has by this stage moved to a much more challenging line of resistance than at the start of this interview.

With regard to the reversal of questioner–responder roles, Harris identifies such 'counter-questions' as a key mode of resistance to power and control (1989: 140–6). Thornborrow also observes this tactic being used in a police interview. She comments that:

> … it is the institutional roles occupied by the participants … that largely determine whether or not the outcome of these actions is successful or not. [The police officer] has no institutional obligation to participate as an 'answerer', and resists taking up this position when [the interviewee] puts him in it discursively … When a participant is placed discursively in a turn position that in some way conflicts with their institutional role, we can observe a degree of disruption to expected norms of interaction while the police interviewers re-establish their more powerful positions in the talk.
>
> (Thornborrow 2002: 53)

Yet the re-establishment of the police officer's power is not such a straightforward matter here. P does take up the role of 'answerer' (322–5), and when he subsequently tries to break out of this role and re-establish himself as questioner (329) he is interrupted by S and prevented from finishing his turn (330). This is indeed disruption, but it comes from S continuing his resistance and not from P reasserting himself. Control of this interaction is still very much under negotiation here.

[…]

Discussion

The interview

Through the above analysis several factors emerge as being of particular significance in the balance of power and control in this interview. The ascribed discursive roles of the participants are of paramount importance, providing the 'default' positions from which each participant must operate. As we have seen, these are very unequal in the resources they make available to each participant, giving P a considerable advantage in terms of power and control in this interaction. However, although this 'starting position' may be fixed, what each manages to achieve from there is not.

In line with the asymmetrical default positions, we have seen that P does have overall control of the interaction, whereas S is generally left in the position of attempting to resist that control, rather than being able to actually seize it for himself. Yet the level of resistance he manages to achieve is quite remarkable given the circumstances. Through his constant attempts to challenge and undermine P's position, he significantly reduces the default advantage with which P started out.

In addition, the institutional roles of the participants have been shown to have a strong influence on the interaction. S uses his professional status to bolster his discursively weaker position and place himself on a more equal footing with P. He also constantly undermines P's status, both as investigative officer and as questioner. It is interesting to note that P rarely alludes to his own institutional position – but this is hardly necessary in the context. His stronger discursive role as questioner is itself a manifestation of that status.

This leads neatly onto another key feature revealed in the analysis: the significance of the institutional context. We have seen that in several places S is left free to talk at some length in a direction apparently not of P's choosing, effectively handing him quite a degree of discursive control. But it must be borne in mind that the overall goal of the interaction is to get S to talk. P is therefore restricted by his institutional role into conceding discursive power and control at times in order to achieve the wider goals of the interaction.

[…]

Power and control can always be challenged by the use of discursive strategies, regardless of the subject matter, the status of the participants, or any other factor. However, although such challenges are indeed possible, they might not necessarily be wise in this context, and can in fact lead to a weakening of the challenger's position in the wider sense. Given the overall aim of building a case against S, it has been seen that P in fact gains the most when S does take discursive control. Thus it is just as important to know when to *relinquish* power and control in this context as it is to maintain it.

Issues to consider

In her analysis, Haworth interprets power in discourse as something that is constantly negotiated and constructed in interaction between speakers, even in institutional contexts where one would expect the person with institutional power (police officer, judge or doctor) to be automatically the more powerful interactant. But as we have just seen in the case of this police interview, it is paradoxically when the police officer *cedes* discursive control that s/he is able to achieve the most. This particular conception of power should help you to examine the power dynamics in spoken interactive discourse. Some suggestions follow.

❑ Although the author cautions against a deterministic view of power in institutional settings, she insists on taking the wider institutional context into account when analysing power dynamics between interactants. What factors other than language would you have to consider when analysing a police interview?

❑ Given that interview data that is presented in court often has a significant influence on the outcome of the trial, it is worrying that transcripts are routinely 'edited' in the judicial process, leading to potential distortion of crucial evidence. Looking at the transcripts presented in the reading above, in what ways do you think linguists can contribute to the enhancement of police interview data? (See also the issues raised in Strand 7.)

❑ Tape-record a casual conversation with your friends and record a political interview and transcribe a short excerpt. Analyse and compare the two transcripts in terms of the power dynamics expressed between the interactants. What are the main differences in terms of power in the two types of interactions? Can you detect any shifts in power and control as the interactions unfold? For example, what types of questions are asked and to what extent are they used as a means of dominating the interaction?

MASCULINITY AND MEN'S MAGAZINES   D4

In this chapter from Litosseliti and Sunderland's book *Gender Identity and Discourse Analysis*, Bethan Benwell argues that men's lifestyle magazines pursue a conservative agenda, attempting to reassert traditional masculine values rather than playing a more subversive role and challenging old-fashioned conceptions of gender. The main gender identity that is promoted in these magazines represents, according to Benwell, 'hegemonic masculinity', defined as the means by which 'particular groups of men inhabit positions of power and wealth, and how they legitimate and reproduce the social relationships that generate their dominance' (Benwell 2002: 158).

Although many texts on language and gender could qualify as a useful reading, this one was chosen because, alongside masculinity, it engages not just with magazine texts, but also with the wider issues of their production and consumption. In addition, the author refers to audience reception studies conducted with male readers as an important backdrop to her qualitative linguistic analysis of a small corpus of men's magazines. As such, this study demonstrates the contribution made to CDA by the increasing adoption of quantitative approaches.

Bethan
Benwell

'Is there anything "new" about these lads?' The textual and visual construction of masculinity in men's magazines

Bethan Benwell (from L. Litosseliti and J. Sunderland (eds) (2002) *Gender Identity and Discourse Analysis*, Philadelphia, PA: John Benjamins, pp. 149–174)

[...]

The discourse of the 'new lad' represented in data in this chapter, makes for a fascinating study of the way in which modern men's lifestyle magazines simultaneously celebrate and evade what some discourses would call 'political incorrectness'.

The main strategy of evasion employed by men's magazines takes the form of a cheeky knowingness and self-reflexiveness (commonly glossed as irony), which enables it to simultaneously affirm and deny its values. Indeed, it has been observed that irony preserves a quality of deniability (Stringfellow 1994). It allows a writer to articulate an anti-feminist sentiment, whilst explicitly distancing himself from it, and thus disclaiming responsibility from or even authentic authorship of it. This strategy corresponds closely to Talbot's observation concerning tabloid constructions of masculinity, that the stability of hegemonic masculinity might well lie in its very flexibility (Talbot 1997: 186). Similarly Connell makes the point that

> [i]t is important to acknowledge that there is an active defence of hegemonic masculinity and the position of economic, ideological and sexual dominance held by heterosexual men. This defence takes a variety of forms and it often has to yield ground or change tactics. But it has formidable resources, and in recent decades, in the face of historic challenges, has been impressively successful.
>
> (Connell 1995: 216)

This observation is reflected in the political endeavour of men's lifestyle magazines to preserve a narrow and conformist version of masculinity in the face of feminist and academic struggles to break down traditional accounts of gender relations. The tongue-in-cheek, self-aware quality (witness *Loaded*'s by-line: for men who should know better) might lead one to identify a space of genuine instability and ambiguity within men's magazines. Alternatively, this strategy can be seen as having your cake and eating it and not a genuine challenge to gender politics at all.

In my analysis of the discourse of men's lifestyle magazines, I shall attempt to chart the evasive, ambiguous and arguably strategic moves that define, endorse and give voice to this particular manifestation of masculinity. The discussion of the emergence of and response to *Loaded* (and its imitators) has suggested that the readers of the magazine constitute a relatively stable *discourse community* in which the language, values and meanings of the magazine are shaped by a complex dialectic between real readers and the production team. This is further reinforced by the interactive format of such magazines, in which readers' letters play a prominent and informing role, and where magazine staff pose as a modern day 'Everyman' in the form of intrepid volunteers for regular field trips to sample traditional or exotic masculine pursuits, or in the form of the highly interpersonal and self-revelatory nature of the features writing. Although it cannot be assumed that there is an unmediated relationship between text and reader (and instances of possible 'resistant' or ambiguous positions will be explored later in relation to the analysis), it can be assumed in this case that men (and women, who make up 25% of the readers) are voluntarily buying into a culture because of its broad appeal. Readers (to varying degrees) might be said to buy the magazine both to have their perceptions about masculinity confirmed, but also added to. [...]

Discourse and discourse analysis

[...]

Men's lifestyle magazines are an example of a discourse type which supports a set of 'regulatory fictions' (Butler 1999) concerning gender. Like most forms of mass media, lifestyle magazines, particularly those that explicitly address one sex rather than another, are a locus for a particularly exaggerated binary oppositional account of gender. Since gender norms, according to Butler, are 'discursively constituted, discourse analysis becomes a potent means by which the process of purportedly "natural" gender divisions and oppositions may be traced and decoded'.

[...] Where possible, I have attempted to address issues of discursive and sociocultural practice; for instance [...] I address the issues of both consumption and production of magazines by referring to the findings of Jackson *et al.* (1999, 2001), who carried out focus group fieldwork with male readers of men's lifestyle magazines, and to the work of Crewe (2001), who conducted in-depth interviews with the two founders of *Loaded*. Nevertheless, it should be stressed that my main focus is the strategic workings of the text in contributing to a particular construction (and sometimes evasion) of masculinity. [...]

An additional aspect of an account of 'discourse' which lays emphasis upon context is the non-verbal element which plays a constitutive role in the communication. Images are a ubiquitous form of communication within magazines, and it is impossible to ignore them in analysis. For this reason, part of my analysis focuses upon the significance of gaze in visual representations of men.

Identity of the male magazine

The magazine in general is described by Barthes as 'a prattling text ... an unweaned language: imperative, automatic, unaffectionate' (1983: 404). The short articles and features interspersed with bright and attractive images are aimed specifically at a busy readership which dips in and out of the text. Jackson *et al.* (1999), in their study of readers' receptions and attitudes to men's magazines, note (as Hermes (1996) [1995] did about women's magazines) that most respondents, even those buying the magazines regularly (committed readers), view them as superficial, disposable, and claim only to dip into them, rather than read them cover-to-cover (358–9). At the same time, such claims might be viewed with suspicion, since a consistent feature of men's attitudes to magazines is that they should not be seen to be highly invested in them. This is in part a function of their politically dubious image, but as much about the suspicion that they are unworthy vehicles of culture or opinion: trash, a waste of money, vacuous, silly and superficial (Jackson *et al.* 1999: 358). Therefore, it is worth noting Jackson *et al.*'s observation that one man who claimed to be only a 'casual' reader, in fact kept

**Bethan
Benwell**

a complete set of back copies of one particular title next to his bed. Such ambivalence threads its way, therefore, not only through *representations* and textual constructions of masculinity, but through the whole text-consumer interface. […]

Image, gaze, anxiety

[…]

Men's magazines largely avoid the objectification of men by means of a variety of strategies, examples of which will be explored shortly. It is significant that the narcissistic female gaze in women's magazines that acts as a point of identification and aspiration for women is not such a prevalent device in the male equivalent. As Simpson [1994] observed, the fashion for putting male bodies on display leaves them open to an *undifferentiated gaze* – i.e. it may be a homosexual one. Men who are surreptitiously observed (i.e. who don't meet the gaze of the reader), it is implied, might be objects of desire, and therefore the male image frequently involves a gaze that confidently, even challengingly, meets the reader's. On the other hand, the gaze that meets the reader's may imply that the reader himself is an object of desire – that a direct interaction is taking place. This observation about gaze also corresponds to Kress and van Leeuwen's thesis (1996) that represented participants whose gaze meets that of the viewer are establishing a direct relationship, even if only at an imaginary level. Kress and van Leeuwen describe this as a 'demand' image (1996: 122–123), because the gaze seems to demand something of the viewer, in the form of a particular social relationship. If a smile or pout is presented, social affinity or even desire may be demanded. The other type of representation, where the represented participant's gaze does not meet the viewer's, Kress and van Leeuwen term 'offer' (1996: 124), where the image is merely an object of contemplation, and the focalizing, observing role of the viewer is accentuated. In this case it is possible that the object in question may be an erotic, desirable one.

Images of men in men's lifestyle magazines therefore tread an uneasy line between occupying subject and object position. When a male represented participant is the object of the viewer's gaze, he tends to be active and nonsexual; when a male represented participant occupies a subject position, by gazing out at the reader, his gaze tends to be hostile and unsmiling. In both instances the key motivation behind the design of the image is to avoid homoerotic implications for both represented image and viewer.

However, this kind of prohibiting positioning of the reader often comes into conflict with other functions of the magazine. A certain kind of tension frequently arises between the norms of this narrow and defensive masculinity, and the demands and products of the advertisers whose revenue financially underpins the magazines. The need to promote anxieties in men about appearance and image sits uneasily with a dominant masculinity and all its phobias about sexuality. This is neatly put by Simpson: 'Men's style magazines, whose *raison d'etre* is to provide images of attractive men to be looked at by other men, are acutely aware of the imperative to disavow homosexuality' (Simpson 1994: 108). Once again, masculinity is forced to draw upon creative resources in order to retain its dominant position, whilst at the same time responding to pressure from consumer forces.

Bethan
Benwell

In *Loaded*, which offers perhaps the most conformist and defensive versions of masculinity, passive or sexualised images of men are almost entirely avoided and yet at the same time, strategies are in place to sell to men products or values which are implicitly 'feminine' in orientation; one advert (for Ultratone™ Bodyshaper) provides a useful example. A product such as this has inescapable connotations of vanity, concern or anxiety with appearance, and because its aim is to build up body muscles cannot avoid featuring a naked male torso, a possible object of homoerotic desire. In addition, the representation is an 'offer' image (to use Kress and van Leeuwen's term) which presents the man for contemplation or consumption. This image is, however, heterosexualised by the presence of an admiring woman (see Figure D4.1 below). Other images avoid directly confronting gazes (which might imply an interaction) or naked flesh, favouring rather whole body action shots with no clear view of the face, fashion shots which obscure the entire head of the model, or simply the product alone.

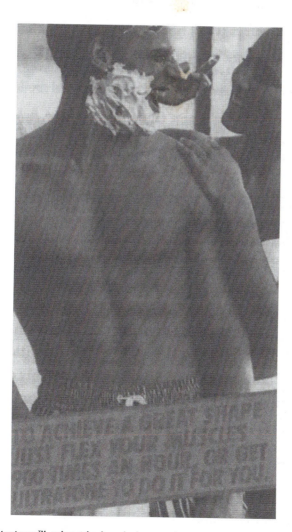

Figure D4.1 Ultratone™ advert in *Loaded* magazine

Bethan
Benwell

Humour and irony

Humour and irony are two other magazine masculinity's chief defences against sexual or gender ambiguity and are discussed in more detail in Benwell (2001). In my introduction I briefly discussed the role of irony in men's magazines, arguing that an ironic knowingness, a self-reflexiveness, a refusal to be clearly allied with stable positions, is used as a shield against the explicit markings of masculinity. Irony can be defined as a disjunction, opposition or contradiction between the surface form of an utterance and its underlying meaning or context, and is therefore a very useful strategy for disclaiming responsibility for politically unpalatable sentiments. Nothing can be more insinuatingly strategic than the ironic disclaimer, which anticipates various charges of sexism, racism or homophobia. For example, in *GQ* magazine's 'Home Front' article, a series of outlandish, exaggerated descriptions of manly 'domestic products' signal to us that the piece is meant to be read ironically and humorously:

> *Water for Men*: This isn't some fancy, foreign water, full of poncy minerals. This extra-butch bottled water contains just one mineral: salt, and plenty of it. And because it's oestrogen-free it won't turn you into a eunuch like tap water does.
>
> (*GQ* June 1997: 29)

[…]

The other role of irony and humour is to protect magazine masculinity from charges of taking on aspects of 'other' identities which might be seen to compromise its hegemonic masculine identity. This can be seen to good effect in an article in *Maxim* (April 1997) about facial, massage and manicure treatments entitled 'Shape your eyebrows, sir?' which is delivered with a detached, tongue-in-cheek tone throughout. The subject matter of the article raises the spectre of an 'unmanly' masculinity and embodies the tension discussed earlier that exists between traditional masculinity and the commercial needs of the magazine; for this reason it can be viewed as an exercise in reconciling this tension. The article is extremely explicit about avoiding connotations of the twin pariahs of magazine masculinity, femininity and homosexuality:

> A men-only grooming shop for normal, everyday, nothing-funny-about-my-testosterone-levels-thank-you-blokes who quite fancy the idea of a de-stressing massage, with maybe a facial and, oh what the hell, a manicure while I'm here.
>
> (*Maxim* April 1997: 106)

This telling opening description of the male beauty parlour is marked in a number of ways. The exclusive, ultra-male environment is signalled by a hyperbolic plethora of adjectives denoting both masculinity ('men-only', 'blokes') and ordinariness ('normal', 'everyday', again 'blokes') and explicitly rejecting sexual 'deviance' ('normal', 'nothing-funny-about-my-testosterone-levels'). Rather than simply being a description it is in fact a defence (one can detect the pursed-lipped tone of 'thank you' – meaning 'I'll thank you not to think otherwise') and reflects a trend in men's magazines for rare visits into the realm of male health and beauty to be handled with kid gloves. Dougary (1994) suggests that men's magazines with features on fashion, beauty, accessories, sexuality and emotions, are narrowing the divide between men's and women's interests.

However, the 'need' to promote a distinctive gender identity means that these subjects are treated very differently in the respective magazines. [...]

Bethan
Benwell

The tendency for men's magazines to relentlessly insist upon the 'otherness' of women, whether in a positive or negative way, is part of the wider cultural phenomenon of 'gender dichotomizing'. Although such a phenomenon is hardly new, it is a particularly salient feature of both men's and women's lifestyle magazines [...]

Conclusion

[...] My analysis of instances of men's magazine discourse attempts to demonstrate how discourses reproduce and reinforce a social order and how repeated and recognisable discursive strategies may be employed in the pursuit of gendered identities and relations. Whilst a more dedicated adherence to Fairclough's *Critical Discourse Analysis* would attempt to describe the totality of discursive and sociocultural practice in relation to texts, the brief engagement with possible reading positions, as well as observations about known conditions of production and reception, offers a more complex interpretation of discursive identities than would have been gained by a singular focus on the text. [...]

Humour and irony, [...] like the negotiation of gaze and image, may be yet another means by which hegemonic masculinity is able to accommodate social change. The stylised repetition of acts is a crucial prop in the upholding of stable gender identity, but it is nonetheless in conflict with the imperatives of a consumer magazine which is continually in search of the creation of new identities, new markets. Humour and irony (and also gaze) are thus chiefly employed in making these necessary adaptations and additions to masculine identity palatable and congruous with a more traditional model. Arguably then, they serve a reactionary, conservative role, rather than a subversive, unsettling one.

Issues to consider

This article makes some interesting observations on the use of irony in men's magazines and readers can track more general issues to do with humour and irony (as it intersects with power and discourse) across Strand 6 of this book. Benwell contends that irony in men's magazines tends to be pervasive and that its main function is to act as a defence against accusations of sexism. So those who criticize the contents of these magazines can be said 'not to get the jokes', making criticism redundant. Also consider the following:

❑ One argument in this and other articles on men's magazines is that men's, and by extension, women's magazines are essentially about constructing men and women as profoundly different and as locked in an eternal 'battle of the sexes'. You will have noticed that in units B and C of Strand 4 we have taken a somewhat different view and given cautious endorsement to the idea that men's and women's magazines are becoming increasingly similar in many ways. From your experience (as a reader of these magazines perhaps), which of the two views strikes you as more accurate?

❑ The article stresses the importance of including the views of (non-academic) readers, and reader-response based analysis is increasingly important in several areas of linguistics. How would you go about conducting audience research? Finding large numbers of people to interview might be quite laborious, so what other means of interviewing readers would there be?

D5 DISCOURSE AND THE DENIAL OF RACISM

The following reading, from a seminal article by Teun van Dijk, examines the prominent role of discourse in the (re)production of racism. It focuses in particular on one rhetorical strategy, the denial of racism, in many contemporary discourses about ethnic relations and ethnic minorities. Van Dijk examines various types of denial in everyday conversation and press reports. Among these forms of denial are positive self-presentation and negative other-presentation, mitigation, blaming the victim and other moves of defence in negative discourse about minorities and immigrants (see A5). Van Dijk also challenges the notion of 'racism from below', contending instead that it is mainly through political, media, academic, corporate and other elites that racism is (re)produced and that racism is denied.

Discourse and the denial of racism

Teun van Dijk

Teun van Dijk (reprinted from *Discourse and Society* 3 (1) (1992): 87–118)

[…]

One of the crucial properties of contemporary racism is its denial, typically illustrated in such well-known disclaimers as 'I have nothing against blacks, but …'. This article examines the discursive strategies, as well as the cognitive and social functions, of such and other forms of denial in different genres of text and talk about ethnic or racial affairs. […]

The guiding idea behind this research is that ethnic and racial prejudices are prominently acquired and shared within the white dominant group through everyday conversation and institutional text and talk. Such discourse serves to express, convey, legitimate or indeed to conceal or deny such negative ethnic attitudes. Therefore, a systematic and subtle discourse analytical approach should be able to reconstruct such social cognitions about other groups.

It is further assumed in this research programme that talk and text about minorities, immigrants, refugees or, more generally, about people of colour or Third World peoples and nations, also have broader societal, political and cultural functions. Besides positive self-presentation and negative other-presentation, such discourse signals group membership, white in-group allegiances and, more generally, the various conditions for the reproduction of the white group and their dominance in virtually all social, political and cultural domains.

[...]

Political, media, academic, corporate and other elites play an important role in the reproduction of racism. They are the ones who control or have access to many types of public discourse, have the largest stake in maintaining white group dominance, and are usually also most proficient in persuasively formulating their ethnic opinions. Although there is of course a continuous interplay between elite and popular forms of racism, analysis of many forms of discourse suggests that the elites in many respects 'preformulate' the kind of ethnic beliefs of which, sometimes more blatant, versions may then get popular currency. Indeed, many of the more 'subtle', 'modern', 'everyday' or 'new' forms of cultural racism, or ethnicism, studied below, are taken from elite discourse. This hypothesis is not inconsistent with the possibility that (smaller, oppositional) elite groups also play a prominent role in the preformulation of anti-racist ideologies.

[...]

The denial of racism

The denial of racism is one of the moves that is part of the strategy of positive in-group presentation. General norms and values, if not the law, prohibit (blatant) forms of ethnic prejudice and discrimination, and many if not most white group members are both aware of such social constraints and, up to a point, even share and acknowledge them (Billig 1988). Therefore, even the most blatantly racist discourse in our data routinely features denials or at least mitigations of racism. Interestingly, we have found that precisely the more racist discourse tends to have disclaimers and other denials. This suggests that language users who say negative things about minorities are well aware of the fact that they may be understood as breaking the social norm of tolerance or acceptance.

Denials of racism, and similar forms of positive self-presentation, have both an individual and a social dimension. Not only do most white speakers individually resent being perceived as racists, also, and even more importantly, such strategies may at the same time aim at defending the in-group as a whole: 'We are not racists', 'We are not a racist society'.

Whereas the first, individual, form of denial is characteristic of informal everyday conversations, the second is typical for public discourse, for instance in politics, the media, education, corporations and other organizations. Since public discourse potentially reaches a large audience, it is this latter, social form of denial that is most influential and, therefore, also most damaging: it is the social discourse of denial that persuasively helps construct the dominant white consensus. Few white group members would have reason or interest to doubt, let alone to oppose, such a claim.

[...]

Let us examine in more detail how exactly the press engages in this denial of racism. Most of our examples are taken from the British press, but it would not be difficult to find similar examples in the Dutch, German and French press.

Racism and the press

The denial of racism in and by the press is of course most vehement when the press itself is the target of accusations. Reflecting similar reactions by the editors of Dutch newspapers to our own research on racism in the press, the editor-in-chief of a major elite weekly, *Intermediair*, catering especially for social scientists and the business community, writes the following in a letter:

> (9)   In particular, what you state about the coverage of minorities remains unproven and an unacceptable caricature of reality. Your thesis 'that the tendency of most reports is that ethnic minorities cause problems for us' is in my opinion not only not proven, but simply incorrect.
>
> *(Translated from the Dutch)*

This reaction was inspired by a brief summary of mostly international research on the representation of minorities in the press. The editor's denial is not based on (other) research, but simply stated as a 'fact'.

[…]

With such an editorial attitude towards racism, there is a general reluctance to identify racist events as such in society at large. Let us examine the principal modes of such denials in the press. Examples are taken from the British press coverage of ethnic affairs in 1985 (for analysis of other properties of these examples, see van Dijk 1991). Brief summaries of the context of each fragment of news discourse are given between parentheses.

Positive self-presentation

The semantic basis of denial is 'truth' as the writer sees it. The denial of racism in the press, therefore, presupposes that the journalist or columnist believes that his or her own group or country is essentially 'tolerant' towards minorities or immigrants. Positive self-presentation, thus, is an important move in journalistic discourse, and should be seen as the argumentative denial of the accusations of anti-racists:

> (11)   [Handsworth] Contrary to much doctrine, and acknowledging a small malevolent fascist fringe, this is a remarkably tolerant society. But tolerance would be stretched were it to be seen that enforcement of law adopted the principle of reverse discrimination.
>
> *(Daily Telegraph, editorial, 11 September)*

> (12)   [Racial attacks and policing] If the ordinary British taste for decency and tolerance is to come through, it will need positive and unmistakable action.
>
> *(Daily Telegraph, editorial, 13 August)*

> (13)   [Racial attacks against Asians]. Britain's record for absorbing people from different backgrounds, peacefully and with tolerance, is second to none. The descendants of Irish and Jewish immigrants will testify to that. It would be tragic to see that splendid reputation tarnished now.
>
> *(Sun, editorial, 14 August)*

[…]

(15)   We have racism too – and that is what is behind the plot. It is not white
       racism. It is black racism … But who is there to protect the white majority?
       … Our tolerance is our strength, but we will not allow anyone to turn it
       into our weakness.

                                                                (*Sun*, 24 October)

These examples not only assert or presuppose white British 'tolerance' but at the same
time define its boundaries. Tolerance might be interpreted as a position of weakness
and, therefore, it should not be 'stretched' too far, lest 'every terrorist', 'criminal' or
other immigrant, takes advantage of it. Affirmative action or liberal immigration laws,
thus, can only be seen as a form of reverse discrimination, and hence as a form of
self-destruction of white Britain. Ironically, therefore, these examples are self-defeat-
ing because of their internal contradictions. It is not tolerance *per se* that is aimed at,
but rather the limitations preventing its 'excesses'. Note that in example (15) positive
self-presentation is at the same time combined with the well-known move of reversal:
'They are the real racists, We are the real victims.'
   […]

Subtle denials

Denials are not always explicit. There are many ways to express doubt, distance or
non-acceptance of statements or accusations by others. When the official Commission
for Racial Equality (CRE) in 1985 published a report on discrimination in the UK,
outright denial of the facts would hardly be credible. Other discursive means, such as
quotation marks, and the use of words like 'claim' or 'allege', presupposing doubt on
the part of the writer, may be employed in accounting for the facts, as is the case in the
following editorial from the *Daily Telegraph*:

(21)   In its report which follows a detailed review of the operation of the 1976
       Race Relations Act, the Commission claims that ethnic minorities continue
       to suffer high levels of discrimination and disadvantage.

                                                          (*Daily Telegraph*, 1 August)

Such linguistic tricks do not go unnoticed, as we may see in the following reaction to
this passage in a letter from Peter Newsam, then Director of the CRE.

(22)   Of the Commission you say 'it claims that ethnic minorities continue to suffer
       high levels of discrimination and disadvantage'. This is like saying that someone
       'claims' that July was wet. It was. And it is also a fact supported by the weight
       of independent research evidence that discrimination on racial grounds, in
       employment, housing and services, remains at a disconcertingly high level.

                                                          (*Daily Telegraph*, 7 August)

Denials, thus, may be subtly conveyed by expressing doubt or distance. Therefore, the
very notion of 'racism' usually appears between quotation marks, especially also in the
headlines. Such scare quotes are not merely a journalistic device of reporting opinions

or controversial points of view. If that were the case, also the opinions with which the newspaper happens to agree would have to be put between quotes, which is not always the case. Rather, apart from signalling journalistic doubt and distance, the quotes also connote 'unfounded accusation'. The use of quotes around the notion of 'racism' has become so much routine, that even in cases where the police or the courts themselves established that racism was involved in a particular case, the conservative press may maintain the quotes out of sheer habit.

Mitigation

[…] In the same editorial of the *Daily Telegraph* we quoted above, we find the following statement:

(23)   [CRE report] No one would deny the fragile nature of race relations in Britain today or that there is misunderstanding and distrust between parts of the community.

(Daily Telegraph, editorial, 1 August)

Thus, instead of inequality or racism, race relations are assumed to be 'fragile', whereas 'misunderstanding and distrust' is also characteristic of these relations. Interestingly, this passage also explicitly denies the prevalence of denials and, therefore, might be read as a concession: there are problems. However, the way this concession is rhetorically presented by way of various forms of mitigation, suggests, in the context of the rest of the same editorial, that the concession is apparent. Such apparent concessions are another major form of disclaimer in discourse about ethnic relations, as we also have them in statements like: 'There are also intelligent blacks, but …', or 'I know that minorities sometimes have problems, but …'. […]

Defence and offence

On the other hand, in its attacks against the anti-racists, the right-wing press is not always that subtle. On the contrary, they may engage precisely in the 'diatribes' they direct at their opponents:

(24)   [Anti-fascist rally] The evening combined emotive reminders of the rise of Nazism with diatribes against racial discrimination and prejudice today.

(Daily Telegraph, 1 October)

(25)   [Black sections] In the more ideologically-blinkered sections of his [Kinnock's] party … they seem to gain pleasure from identifying all difficulties experienced by immigrant groups, particularly Afro-Caribbeans, as the result of racism …

(Daily Telegraph, editorial, 14 September)

[…]

These examples further illustrate that denial of discrimination, prejudice and racism is not merely a form of self-defence or positive self-presentation. Rather, it is at the same time an element of attack against what they define as 'ideologically blinkered' oppo-

Teun van Dijk

nents, as we also have seen in the move of reversal in other examples. Anti-racism is associated with the 'loony left', and attacking it therefore also has important ideological and political implications, and not just moral ones.

'Difficulties' of the Afro-Caribbean community may be presupposed, though not spelled out forcefully and in detail, but such presuppositions rather take the form of an apparent concession. That is, whatever the causes of these 'difficulties', as they are euphemistically called, they can not be the result of racism. Implicitly, by attributing 'pleasure' to those who explain the situation of the blacks, the newspaper also suggests that the left has an interest in such explanations and, therefore, even welcomes racism. [...]

Conclusion

Whether in the streets of the inner city, in the press or in parliament, dominant group members are often engaged in discourse about 'them': ethnic minority groups, immigrants or refugees, who have come to live in the country. Such discourses, as well as the social cognitions underlying them, are complex and full of contradictions. They may be inspired by general norms of tolerance and acceptance, but also, and sometimes at the same time, by feelings of distrust, resentment or frustration about those 'others'.
[...]
However, negative talk about minority groups or immigrants may be heard as biased, prejudiced or racist, and as inconsistent with general values of tolerance. This means that such discourse needs to be hedged, mitigated, excused, explained or otherwise managed in such a way that it will not 'count' against the speaker or writer.
[...]
It is interesting to note that despite the differences in style for different social groups, such discourse may be found at any social level, and in any social context. That is, both the 'ordinary' white citizens as well as the white elites need to protect their social self-image, and at the same time they have to manage the interpretation and the practices in an increasingly variegated social and cultural world. For the dominant group, this means that dominance relations must be reproduced, at the macro- as well as at the micro-level, both in action as well as in mind.

Negative representations of the dominated group are essential in such a reproduction process. However, such attitudes and ideologies are inconsistent with dominant democratic and humanitarian norms and ideals. This means that the dominant group must protect itself, cognitively and discursively, against the damaging charge of intolerance and racism. Cognitive balance may be restored only by actually being or becoming anti-racist, by accepting minorities and immigrants as equals, or else by denying racism. It is this choice that white groups in Europe and North America are facing. So far they have largely chosen the latter option.

Issues to consider

☐ Van Dijk presents several linguistic strategies that speakers/writers can use in denying racism. Have you come across some of these yourself in everyday conversations, newspaper articles, news reports and so on? Do you feel that van

Dijk's conclusions regarding the denial of racism are justified on the basis of his analysis, and are they still valid?

HUMOUR AND HATRED

Exploring a topic that in our opinion has often been ignored by researchers of language and racism, Michael Billig examines in this reading the links between humour and hatred. He focuses on three websites that present racist humour and display sympathies with the Ku Klux Klan. We should point out at the outset that his data contains the most racially insulting terms possible and we anticipate that readers (outside the limited political circles of the Ku Klux Klan and the extreme right) will find these 'jokes' deeply unfunny and utterly distasteful. This material does, however, underline our position, argued throughout this Strand, that a description of verbal humour, especially in such a hostile and aggressive form, has a serious place in the study of language and power.

Billig's analysis emphasizes the importance of examining the 'meta-discourse' of the sites' strategic disclaimers (that is, their justification that a joke is 'just a joke') which present and justify the humour. Billig concludes that the extreme racist humour of the KKK is not just a joke, even in terms of its own meta-discourse of presentation. The meta-discourse also suggests that the extreme language of racist hatred is indicated as a matter for enjoyment. In a survey of disturbing and often horrific material, Billig makes a convincing case that there are integral links between extreme hatred and dehumanizing, violent humour.

Humour and hatred: the racist jokes of the Ku Klux Klan

Michael Billig

Michael Billig (reprinted from *Discourse and Society* 12 (3) (2001): 267–289)

[...]

Extreme politics of hatred

In order to understand the relations between hatred and humour, it is important not to consider ethnic or racial jokes in the abstract. Davies (1990) is correct in arguing that the structure and content of a joke should not be taken as necessarily reflecting the joke-teller's state of mind. The fact that someone might repeat a joke against a particular ethnic group, or laugh when hearing such a joke, is not in itself conclusive evidence that they hate, or even dislike, that particular group. It would be circular to explain the joke-telling in terms of hatred if the joke itself is the only evidence for that hatred. Other indications of hatred beyond the content of the joke are necessary if the link between hatred and humour is to be established. For this reason, the present study looks at jokes in the context of the extreme politics of racism, namely that of the Ku Klux Klan.

Any study that looks at the ideology of the racist right needs to be aware that the language of the extreme right is not straightforward. Denials and self-definitions cannot be taken at their face value. Often, extreme right-wing groups, seeking widespread support, operate according to a dual strategy. They take a high road in public, claiming to be respectably democratic, while in private a more extreme message is circulated. Analysts have demonstrated that contemporary fascist groups often conceal the full nature of their ideological extremism, while giving coded messages to hard-core supporters that the lower road has not been abandoned [...] In this way lip service might be paid to wider norms against appearing too openly racist or anti-Semitic, while, at the same time, these norms might be mocked in coded ways. This dual strategy of high and low roads can be detected in the politics of the FN in France and the FPÖ in Austria (Reisigl and Wodak, 1999; Wodak, 2000), as well as in the modern Ku Klux Klan (Wade, 1987) [and see Strand 5 also].

In consequence, one should not expect that the propaganda of the extreme right will express a simple position in relation to contemporary constraints against racism. Racist groups might seek to destroy the social basis of such restraints while at the same time they may be operating partly within such restraints. In propaganda designed for a wider audience, such groups might wish to be seen to disavow uninhibitedly racist jokes. However, within the more private confines of the group, and in internally circulated material, the humour of hatred might be enjoyed. What this would indicate is that the presentation of racist humour – or its meta-language – might have a complex and dissembling rhetoric.

Some preliminary words about terminology are necessary. The terms 'joke' and 'humour' will be used, but no aesthetic judgement is implied by these terms. It is not suggested that any material so described is actually funny. A social constructionist position is taken here. 'Humour' and 'jokes' are indicated by the claims of participants, not the preferences of the analyst. If someone is claiming to be telling a joke then this activity is treated as an instance of joke-telling, irrespective of whether or not the analyst finds the joke amusing. It may be the case that humour is found in all cultures (Apte, 1983), but not all cultures, sub-cultural groups or even individuals within sub-cultural groups find the same things funny. [...] In consequence, there will be social, political, cultural and moral reasons why the jokes that one group enjoys might not be shared by another group. In examining such phenomena, analysts should not restrict the labels 'humour' and 'jokes' to their own preferences in humour. Instead, they should treat the condemning and celebrating of particular forms of humour as topics for investigation. [...]

Materials

The materials to be studied are three websites, which provide racist jokes and promote links with Ku Klux Klan groups. The sites are not official KKK sites. The Ku Klux Klan

Michael Billig

is not a single organization, but there are a number of KKK groups and networks in the United States with connections abroad [...]

The three sites are:

1. 'Nigger Jokes KKK' (NJKKK), provided by Whitesonly.net. The site, on its home page, declares itself to be 'Humor jokes about nigger meant as a kkk comedy Ku Klux Klan' (here and elsewhere, no attempt is made to correct spelling, grammar or phrasing when quoting from the sites – no 'sic' will be given following misspellings etc, for 'sic' would imply that the transgressions of language are occasional rather than continual). This was the largest of the three sites. [...]

2. 'Nigger Jokes' (NJ), also provided by Whitesonly.net. This home page does not have a formal title, but has the running head 'Nigger Jokes'. The home page announces its humorous nature: 'Not everything must be deadly serious. Nigger Jokes and more Politically InCorrect Fun'. This is the nearest the page comes to having a formal title. The page also includes its own self-recommendation: 'I haven't laughed so hard in years! I'd forgotten how much fun Political Correctness took out of the world'. [...]

3. 'Nigger Joke Central' (NJC) provided by Whitepower.com. The index of this site provides links with 14 pages, the majority of which are lengthy lists of short jokes. The site does not merely specialize in the type of jokes suggested by its own title. In addition to headings such as 'Nigger Jokes' and 'Tons of Nigger Jokes', there are also headings such as 'Faggot Jokes' and 'Hispanic Jokes' and 'coming soon – Jewish Jokes!!' [...]

Not just jokes

On their home pages, all three sites declare themselves to be sites of humour. Connected to these declarations are disclaimers, whose nature and function need examination. NJ declares: 'Please keep in mind that these links are here for humor sake, all be they in bad taste. No one is condoning violence against anyone'. NJKKK contains a lengthy 'Legal Disclaimer' on a separate page. On the index page and also at the end of many items, it says 'please read our legal disclaimer'. This disclaimer contains statements such as: 'The site is meant as a Joke'; 'And you agree by entering this site, that this type of joke is legal where you live, and you agree that you recognize this site is meant as a joke not to be taken seriously'; 'And you agree that this site is a comedy site, not a real racist site'; 'we ARE NOT real life racists'. NJC does not have a separate page acting as a disclaimer. It simply declares on its home page: 'YOU MUST HAVE A SENSE OF HUMOR. IF YOU ARE OFFENDED, THEN FUCK OFF!!!'

[...]

The disclaimers, however, do not principally contrast comedy with 'real racism'. The force of the denial is primarily directed against the charge of inciting violent behaviour. Thus NJ, having declared that the site is for 'humor sake' follows this with the sentence that 'No one is condoning violence against anyone'. Accepting the 'maxim of relevance' that the following sentence is generally presented as relevant to the preceding one (Grice, 1975), the defence, or disclaimer, 'this is humorous' implies the claim 'we are not advocating actual violence'. [...]

Michael
Billig

Even without the disclaimers, this humour cannot be considered as *'just* joking'. It is displayed as humour with a surplus. As the NJC page declares: 'this site contains racial jokes, slurs and an overall negative view to the black race'. The overall negative view is not claimed to be a joke. The jokes themselves are not presented as 'just jokes', but they are labelled as 'nigger jokes'. The category labels the jokes and is not part of the jokes. It belongs, as such, to the meta-discourse of the joke. The appellation itself cannot be justified as 'just a joke': it is a serious label whose semantics are not neutral. The extra word, as the ultimate word of racist hate, comes with ideological, historical and emotional baggage. […]

No joke

On many of the pages of NJKKK and NJ the boundary between seriousness and joking is not clearly drawn (see Mulkay, 1988, for a discussion of the ambiguity of the boundaries of humour). In this respect, the pages present themselves as being more, or less, than jokes, despite what the legal disclaimers suggest. Thus, by the details of their presentation, not merely by their categorization, these jokes are not just jokes.

'Definition of a Nigger', which is to be found on both NJKKK and NJ, illustrates many of the features contained in these pages in which joking and serious claims are intermixed. Ostensibly the page parodies a dictionary entry. Thus, it starts as if humorously defining the ultimate word of racist hate:

> Nig-ger (nig'er) n. An African jungle anthropoid ape of the primate family pongidae (superfamily cercopithecoidea). Imported to the United States as slave labour in the late 1700's–1800's, these wild creatures now roam freely while destroying the economic and social infrastructures of American and various other nations. These flamboyant sub-human love to consume large quantities of greasy fried chicken.

Below the entry is a picture of an African-American male with a speaking-balloon: 'I be heer to pik up da welfare check, sucka'. As De Sousa (1987) has argued, jokes, especially sexist and racist ones, express stereotyped assumptions. The person finding the joke funny is implicitly accepting these stereotyped assumptions about the nature of the other. The imitation dictionary format, of course, spells out these assumptions and presents them as if facts. The use of the ultimate hate word as a technical dictionary entry, which is presented as if referring to biological, historical and anthropological 'facts', mocks the conventional tabooed nature of the word. For the joker, the so-called 'facts' are not the joke, but it is the incongruity of mixing the language of prejudiced stereotypes (that is, the greasy fried chicken) with the sombre language of the apparently unprejudiced dictionary.

The message that there are serious 'facts' is underlined by the next part of the page. The dictionary parody ceases and the page then presents statistics comparing rates of black and white crime. The statistical tables are not presented as parodies in the way that the dictionary entry is. The figures are ostensibly taken from the FBI crime statistics. Interpretations are offered for the figures: 'in every negative category niggers lead the way'. There is no attempt at humour here. Nor is there overt parody in the following section, which uses quasi-biological language. Again the ultimate word is retained

Michael
Billig

long after the joking has stopped: 'It's interesting to note that Niggers have the greatest variance in their DNA than any other group'. The joking definition of the dictionary entry is cashed in as 'serious' argument: 'What a greater variance means is, they are less evolved … Just like the monkeys at the zoo. The more you feed them, the more accustomed they come to believing they deserve it'. It ends with the declaration: 'Wake up America and Smell the Nigger!' Again, the joke is not even a joke.

Lynching as a joke

[…] Lynching, which has played such a major part in the history of the Ku Klux Klan, is celebrated jokingly on these pages. In these celebrations the distinction between the imaginary and the historically real is blurred, as once again joking and seriousness are combined.

One of the […] logos used by Whitesonly, […] is a rope, knotted into a noose. The accompanying legend reads 'Bring your nigger … we got the rope'. One page of NJKKK provides 'The "Noose Leroy" cyber hanging game'. The game is set in a cotton field and involves the player moving an image of a noose: 'Pin the noose on the Nigger! Pick him up, close your eyes and Noose him!' The winner is the player 'comes closest to putting the noose around the Nigger's neck'.

Both the logo and the game involve imagining lynching as fun. NJKKK also includes pictures entitled 'Lynching Tribute', accessed under the headings 'Origin of word "Lynch"' and 'Hanging Pictures'. These pages consist largely of photographs of actual historic lynchings. For the most part they depict the corpses of dead black men hanging. Commentaries are provided. Some are jokey, indicating that the expected reaction is not shock or disgust, but enjoyment of the violent images of lynching. On 'Lynching tribute Page II', accessed by 'Hanging Pictures', can be found a photograph of a black man being burnt, which is accompanied by:

> Another one bites the dust. You know how bad they smell alive, can you imagine a nigger burning? Ewww (God made niggers stink, so even blind people could hate them).

Regarding another burning, the commentary declares 'I bet their greasy skin crackles when burning!'

The page finishes with a disclaimer that it is not inciting violence. But the disclaimer itself becomes part of the joke: 'Remember don't kill niggers, they are a protected species under affirmative action laws!'. The notion of 'protected species', of course, replays the joke of blacks being a separate and lower form of life. However, the disclaimer cannot totally parody itself, for the page still needs to claim legal protection. There follows a longer disclaimer that seems to disavow the violence of lynching:

> This page is meant as a joke! don't do anything illegal. What has occurred in these pages is terrible. And if you even think about doing such an act, you are a moron. Hopefully after looking at these pictures, you'll see how terrible such activity is. And this page will make you realize how terrible violence is. Now let's work together to end the death penalty. It's no different that what has occurred in the pictures above.

Michael
Billig

The 'tribute page' accessed by 'The origin of word "Lynch"', also finishes with a dis-claimer that makes the connection between the photographed lynching and current executions: 'Your hands are as bloody as the executioners in these pictures, if you don't stand up today, against the death penalty.'

The levels of joking are complex. An overtly joking disclaimer has been provided. 'The protected species' disclaimer with its use of the ultimate hate word subverts by parody any notion of disclaiming. This parody, then, for legal reasons needs to be subverted by an apparently serious disclaimer. The claim is that the preceding content 'is meant as a joke'. The claim directly precedes the command not to do anything illegal, thereby again showing the rhetorical function of the joke-claim: it is being used as a defence against any charge of incitement to actual violence.

Concluding remarks

The major point of the present study has been to underline the connections between hatred and humour. These connections are strongly shown in the websites that have been studied. The results support Sartre's general point that humour can provide a means for expressing hatred and, thus, bigotry can bring its own pleasures to the bigot (see also Billig, 2005). Not only can the targets of hatred be savagely ridiculed but, by using the discourse of humour, the bigot can simultaneously mock the demands of reason.

The type of humour displayed in the KKK-supporting web sites is extreme, as is the politics of which they are a part. As such, this extreme racist humour may have different characteristics from other types of humour. It is common among theorists of humour to follow Freud's point that jokes permit tabooed desires to be expressed [Freud (1976) [1905]]. If today there are taboos against the outward expression of racism, then the racist joke becomes a way of saying the unsayable. Teller and recipient can deny that they are racist; they can protect their own sense of their non-racist selves by claiming that they are 'just joking'. Clearly, this type of explanation does not match the joke-telling of the extreme racist. The extreme racist has no *crise de conscience* about being racist. The joke sites, described above, openly parade their racism. The ultimate hate word is used again and again. The joking provides a context, not only for its use, but for opportunities to signal the enjoyment of its use.

The Freudian type of explanation depends upon the joker being able to believe that the joke is just a joke: it is not a 'real' expression of sexual or aggressive desire. The extreme racist jokes, as has been seen, are not presented as 'just jokes' – they are always more than jokes. However, the Freudian explanation is not totally inappropriate. The joking still permits freedom from restraint.

First, as has been mentioned, there is the freedom from the demands of logical and factual argument. The jokers know that blacks are not gorillas or apes. They know that the stereotypes are exaggerations. It is this knowledge that permits the jokes to be enjoyed as jokes and the targets to be dehumanized. Constantly in these sites, 'factual' claims intrude on the jokes. Apparent statistics and pseudo-biology remind the reader that the joke is not just a joke. At the same time, the pictures of primates, the extreme exaggerations and the parodies knowingly mock the world of cautious fact and reasonable argument.

Michael Billig

Then, there is the type of restraint that follows from denial. KKK groups might not deny that they are racist, but they publicly deny that they hate blacks. In these denials, the ultimate hate word is avoided. The jokes – the very label 'nigger jokes' – not only throw off all such restraint with gusto but they mock the restraint. However, this cannot be done openly. The jokes do not, and cannot, take the KKK as their target, in order to mock openly the public restraint of the denial of hatred. The politics of the extreme right demands a limited discipline, which the jokes evade but cannot express directly. The joker cannot state openly: 'Look, we are contradicting what our leaders tell us to say publicly – we do hate'. The jokes achieve this, especially as the political ideology overflows the context of joking. Thus, political loyalty is asserted through the joking: these are, to use the terminology of NJKKK, 'KKK jokes'.

Most importantly, these jokes, that are not just jokes, mock restraints against racist violence. They celebrate such violence, encouraging that it should be imagined as enjoyment without pity for the dehumanized victims. The harm of such violent fantasy can be denied – it's not real after all. As with much humour, there is ambivalence, as assertion and denial both are present with no need to resolve contradiction. On these joke-pages, the KKK supporter can find fantasies of violence that are not to be found on the 'serious' pages of official KKK groups. There are games in which nooses can be placed around dehumanized figures of blacks; there are pictures of lynchings with gloating comments. The supporter can laugh at the death of blacks, who, seriously, are depicted as less than human. And this depiction calls for more laughter and violent fantasy.

On these pages, the extreme racist can be brave without acting. They can be murderers in their imagination. There is no need for conscience: these are jokes and the targets deserve their fate. The contradiction between the two justifications does not matter. Thus, racists are invited to join the fun of the lynch mob without moving from their computer. They can have blood on their hands, but the blood will not drip messily onto the keyboards. Far from saying to themselves that it is only a joke, they can assert that this is not just a joke. And if they do say this, then they will, at last, have said something that is accurate.

Issues to consider

Billig's thought-provoking article shows, among many things, how the analysis of (racist) verbal humour can play a part in our wider understanding of language and power in the context of ethnicity and race. It also highlights the paradox that confronts the analyst in critical humour studies in that the data examined is often disgusting and malevolent, and a long way from being either sophisticated or even 'funny'. As Billig (2005: 272) remarks elsewhere in his piece, only by 'retaining the words "joke" and "humour" to describe such material is it possible to pursue the links between humour and hatred'.

It is also worth noting how the mechanics of humour production come into play in the KKK materials. Billig talks of the 'disclaimers' used (see further B6). Also, some of the basic parodic techniques we surveyed in A6, such as register and style-mixing, are employed in these websites: a case in point is the spoof dictionary format which 'defines' prejudiced stereotypes and presents them as if facts.

More suggestions follow.

❑   Many jokes work on the same incongruity template which means that the basic underlying formula can be extended to incorporate many different targets. The following is a common variant on one of the racist jokes examined by Billig (2005), except that here the 'ultimate hate word' has been replaced.

1. What do you call three lawyers at the bottom of a river?
2. A good start.

Common wisdom presumably concedes that this joke is not as offensive to its target group as those found in the racial hatred material. But given that it employs the same joke formula and makes explicit its target in the same way, why is it not so offensive?

❑ The popular black American comedian Chris Rock is well-known for his edgy, taboo humour, and issues of race and identity feature prominently in his comic routines. Here is a transcript from a section of one of his stand-up performances, played in front of a mixed (though largely black) audience:

> Now we've got a lot of things, a lot of racism in the world right now
> Whose more racist? Black people or white people?
> Black people … You know why? Cause we hate black people too
> Everything white people don't like about black people
> Black people really dont like about black people
> There some shit goin on with black people right now
> There's like a civil war goin on with black people
> And there two sides …
> There's black people, and there's niggas
> And niggas have got to go
> Everytime black people wanna have a good time
> Ignorant ass nigga fuck it up
> Can't do shit, can't do shit, without some ignorant ass nigga fuckin' it up
> Can't do nothin'
> Can't keep a disco open more than 3 weeks
> Grand opening, grand closing
> Can't go to a movie the first week it comes out
> Why? Cause niggas are shooting at the screen!
> What kind of ignorant shit is that?
> Hay this is a good movie, this is so good I gotta bust a cap in here
> Hay I love black people, but I hate niggas boy, boy I hate niggas
> Boy I wish they'd let me join the Klu Klux Klan
> Shit, I'd do a drive-by from here to Brooklyn
> I'm tired of niggas man
> You can't have shit when you around niggas …

Is it the case that Rock, to be blunt, is telling 'nigga' jokes here? If you found the KKK website 'humour' distasteful, we wonder if you (as Rock's audience obviously, do) find Rock funny. The question is, why? Is Rock's skill in the delivery of humour, with all the craft and timing that this implies, simply superior to that of the racists? Or is Rock himself racist? And how is it that the 'ultimate hate term' can, in this context, be turned on its head so markedly?

FORENSIC LINGUISTICS

The following reading, by Malcolm Coulthard, is from a collection of important essays covering all aspects of forensic linguistics. Coulthard's paper focuses on the famous case of Derek Bentley, the last man to be executed in Britain, who was found guilty of murder and hanged in 1953. This is one of a sequence of 'real time' publications by Coulthard on the case (for the first of which, see Coulthard 1992), and the series as a whole serves a good illustration of the very involved and 'hands-on' work of the forensic discourse analyst. In 1998, Bentley's case came before the Court of Appeal and his conviction was successfully overturned – but only 45 years after his execution and long after all of his nearest surviving family members had died.

Focusing on Bentley's disputed 'confession', which dates back to the time when police interviews were recorded contemporaneously in longhand, Coulthard demonstrates convincingly how the police were able to create a misrepresentation of the original interaction, which was subsequently presented to the Court, and which would significantly influence the outcome of the case. It was the disputed confessions from this and other notorious cases that prompted the English judicial system, in 1984, to introduce the tape-recording of police interviews and statement-taking (see further B7). Coulthard's analysis is, however, a salutary lesson for those judicial systems where both the police and the courts are still allowed to make written records of interactions without recourse to a taped record.

Whose voice is it? Invented and concealed dialogue in written records of verbal evidence produced by the police

Malcolm Coulthard **Malcolm Coulthard** (reprinted from J. Cotterill (ed.) *Language in the Legal Process*, London: Palgrave Macmillan, 2002, pp. 19–34)

[…] One November evening in 1952 two teenagers, Derek Bentley aged 19 and Chris Craig aged 16, tried to break into a warehouse. They were seen, as they climbed up onto the roof, by a woman who was putting her daughter to bed. She called the police, who arrived soon afterwards and surrounded the building. Three unarmed officers, two in uniform the other in plain clothes, went up onto the roof to arrest the boys. Bentley immediately gave himself up. Craig drew a gun, started shooting and eventually killed a police officer.

Bentley was jointly charged with murder, even though he had been under arrest for some considerable time when the officer was shot. At the trial, which lasted only two days, both boys were found guilty. Craig, because he was legally a minor, was sentenced to life imprisonment; Bentley was sentenced to death and executed shortly afterwards. Bentley's family fought for a generation to overturn the guilty verdict and they were eventually successful 46 years later in the summer of 1998. The evidence which was the basis for both Bentley's conviction and the successful appeal was in large part linguistic and will be the focus of the rest of this chapter.

Malcolm
Coulthard

In the original trial the problem for the prosecution, in making the case against Bentley, was to demonstrate that he could indeed be guilty despite being under arrest when the murder was committed. At this point it would be useful to read the statement which the police claimed Bentley had dictated shortly after his arrest. It is presented in full below – the only changes I have introduced are to number the sentences for ease of reference and to highlight in bold for subsequent comment a series of negative clauses:

(1) I have known Craig since I went to school. (2) We were stopped by our parents going out together, but we still continued going out with each other – I mean **we have not gone out** together until tonight. (3) I was watching television tonight (2 November 1952) and between 8 pm and 9 pm Craig called for me. (4) My mother answered the door and I heard her say that I was out. (5) I had been out earlier to the pictures and got home just after 7 pm. (6) A little later Norman Parsley and Frank Fasey [sic] called. (7) **I did not answer the door or speak to them.** (8) My mother told me that they had called and I then ran out after them. (9) I walked up the road with them to the paper shop where I saw Craig standing. (10) We all talked together and then Norman Parsley and Frank Fazey left. (11) Chris Craig and I then caught a bus to Croydon. (12) We got off at West Croydon and then walked down the road where the toilets are – I think it is Tamworth Road.

(13) When we came to the place where you found me, Chris looked in the window. (14) There was a little iron gate at the side. (15) Chris then jumped over and I followed. (16) Chris then climbed up the drainpipe to the roof and I followed. (17) Up to then **Chris had not said anything**. (18) We both got out on to the flat roof at the top. (19) Then someone in a garden on the opposite side shone a torch up towards us. (20) Chris said: 'It's a copper, hide behind here.' (21) We hid behind a shelter arrangement on the roof. (22) We were there waiting for about ten minutes. (23) **I did not know** he was going to use the gun. (24) A plain clothes man climbed up the drainpipe and on to the roof. (25) The man said: 'I am a police officer – the place is surrounded.' (26) He caught hold of me and as we walked away Chris fired. (27) **There was nobody else** there at the time. (28) The policeman and I then went round a corner by a door. (29) A little later the door opened and a policeman in uniform came out. (30) Chris fired again then and this policeman fell down. (31) I could see that he was hurt as a lot of blood came from his forehead just above his nose. (32) The policeman dragged him round the corner behind the brickwork entrance to the door. (33) I remember I shouted something but I forgot what it was. (34) **I could not see Chris** when I shouted to him – he was behind a wall. (35) I heard some more policemen behind the door and the policeman with me said: '**I don't think** he has many more bullets left.' (36) Chris shouted 'Oh yes I have' and he fired again. (37) I think I heard him fire three times altogether. (38) The policeman then pushed me down the stairs and **I did not see any more**. (39) I knew we were going to break into the place. (40) **I did not know** what we were going to get – just anything that was going. (41) **I did not have** a gun and **I did not know** Chris had one until he shot. (42) I now know that the policeman in uniform that was shot is dead. (43) I should have mentioned that after the plain clothes policeman got up the drainpipe and arrested me, another policeman in uniform followed and I heard someone call him 'Mac'. (44) He was with us when the other policeman was killed.

Bentley's barrister spelled out for the jury the two necessary preconditions for them to convict him: they must be 'satisfied and sure'

(i)   that [Bentley] knew Craig had a gun and
(ii) that he instigated or incited Craig to use it.

(Trow 1992: 179)

The evidence adduced by the prosecution to satisfy the jury on both points was essentially linguistic. To support point (i) it was observed that in his statement, which purported to give his unaided account of the night's events, Bentley had said 'I did not know he was going to use the gun', (sentence 23). In his summing up, the judge, Lord Chief Justice Goddard, made great play of this sentence arguing both that its positioning in the narrative of events, before the time when there was any policeman on the roof and also the choice of '*the* gun' (as opposed to '*a* gun') must imply that Bentley knew that Craig had a gun well before it was used – in other words 'the gun' at that position in the statement must be taken to mean 'the gun I already knew at this point in the narrative that Craig had'. In addition, the judge argued, this sentence also showed Bentley to be an unreliable witness, because he then contradicted himself later, in sentence 41, by saying 'I *did not know* Chris had [a gun] until he shot'.

The evidence to support point (ii), that Bentley had incited Craig to shoot, was that the police officers in their statements and in their evidence given in court, asserted that Bentley had uttered the words 'Let him have it, Chris' immediately before Craig had shot and killed the policeman. Bentley, supported by Craig, had denied uttering these words – a claim also supported years later by a fourth policeman, who was never called to give evidence at the trial.

Bentley's defence, in the words of the judge in his summing-up, was:

'I didn't know he had a gun and I deny I said "Let him have it, Chris". I never knew he was going to shoot and I didn't think he would.' Against that denial (which, of course, is the denial of a man in grievous peril), you will consider the evidence of the three main officers who have sworn to you positively that those words were said.

(Quoted in Trow 1992: 109)

So, as the judge emphasised, the strength of the linguistic evidence depended essentially on the credibility of the police officers who had collected it and then sworn to its accuracy. When the case came to Appeal in 1998, one of the defence strategies was to challenge the reliability of the statement. They felt that if they could throw doubt on the veracity of the police, they could mitigate the incriminating force of both the statement and the phrase 'Let him have it, Chris'.

The linguistic evidence

At the original trial three police officers swore on oath that Bentley's statement was the product of unaided monologue dictation, whereas Bentley asserted that it was, in part at least, the product of dialogue – in other words that police questions and his replies had been converted into a monologue attributed to him:

Q   Did you in fact dictate that statement as it is written down.
A   No Sir.
Q   How was it taken from you.
A   In questions sir.

(Trial transcript, pp. 100–1)

There is no doubt that this was a recognised procedure for producing statements at the time – a senior police officer, Chief Inspector Hannam, in another murder case, that of Alfred Charles Whiteway one year later, explained to the Court how he had elicited a statement from the accused in exactly this way:

> I would say 'Do you say on that Sunday you wore your shoes?' and he would say 'Yes' and it would go down as 'On that Sunday I wore my shoes'.

(Trial transcript, p. 156)

There are, in fact, many linguistic features which suggest that Bentley's statement is not, as claimed by the police, a verbatim record of what he dictated, and I have written about these elsewhere (Coulthard 1993); here I will confine myself simply to evidence that the statement was indeed, at least in part, dialogue converted into monologue. One of the first things that strikes one on reading the statement is that for most of the text the narrative of events is fairly coherent. However, this narrative seems to end with utterance (38) 'The policeman then pushed me down the stairs and I did not see any more'. What follows in sentences 39–42:

> (39) I knew we were going to break into the place. (40) I did not know what we were going to get – just anything that was going. (41) I did not have a gun and I did not know Chris had one until he shot. (42) I now know that the policeman in uniform that was shot is dead.

appears to be some kind of meta-narrative whose presence and form are most easily explained as the result of a series of clarificatory questions about Bentley's knowledge at particular points in the narrative, information which the police knew would be very important later at the trial.

At first one might not attach too much importance to these post-narrative questions – they certainly do not materially change the narrative which Bentley has already told – on the contrary, they allow him to clarify what he knew and did not know and also give him a chance to assert his lack of any pre-knowledge of Craig having a gun. Indeed, the fact that these may have been elicited, rather than spontaneously offered, did not seem to trouble the prosecution at trial. When Bentley was asked specifically about the sentence sequence (39–40) he replied 'That was [sic] an answer, Sir, to a question', to which the prosecution barrister replied 'I daresay it was in reply to a question' and then moved on immediately to a new topic.

However, this passing acknowledgement does reinforce Bentley's claim and prompts us to look for evidence of multiple voices elsewhere in the statement. We do so, of course, in the knowledge that there will always be some transformations of Q-A which will be indistinguishable from authentic dictated monologue. In the example quoted above, had we not been told that 'On that Sunday I wore my shoes' was a reduction

**Malcolm
Coulthard**

from a Q-A we would have had some difficulty in deducing it, although the pre-posed adverbial, 'On that Sunday', certainly sounds a little odd.

We can begin our search with the initial observation that narratives, particularly narratives of murder, are essentially accounts of what happened and to a lesser extent what was known or perceived and thus reports of what did *not* happen or was *not* known are rare and special – there is an infinite number of things that did not happen and thus the teller needs to have some special justification for reporting any of them to the listener, in other words there must be some evident or stated reason for them being newsworthy.

[...] We find examples of negatives being used in a [normal] way in Bentley's statement:

    (6) A little later Norman Parsley and Frank Fasey called.

    (7) I did not answer the door or speak to them.

When Bentley reported that his friends had called, the listener would reasonably expect him at least to have talked to them and therefore here there is a quite natural denial of a reasonable expectation.

However, there are, in Bentley's statement, some negatives which have no such narrative justification, like sentence (17) below:

    (16) Chris then climbed up the drainpipe to the roof and I followed.

    (17) Up to then Chris **had not said anything**.

    (18) We both got out on to the flat roof at the top.

Chris is not reported as beginning to talk once they got out onto the roof, nor is his silence contrasted with anyone else's talking, nor is it made significant in any other way later in the narrative. A similarly unwarranted example is:

    (26) He caught hold of me and as we walked away Chris fired.

    (27) There **was nobody else** there at the time.

    (28) The policeman and I then went round a corner by a door.

None of the possible inferences from the denial seem to make narrative sense here – for example, 'that as a result of there being no one else there ...'

    (a) it must be the policeman that Craig was firing at,

    (b) that it must be Craig who was doing the firing.

    (c) that immediately afterwards there would be more people on the roof.

So the most reasonable conclusion is that at this point in the statement-taking a policeman, trying to clarify what happened, asked a question to which the answer was negative and the whole sequence was then recorded as a negative statement. The fact that, like (27), other sentences in the statement may have been elicited in this way, becomes particularly important in relation to sentence (23):

    (23) I did not know he was going to use the gun.

which is the one singled out by Lord Chief Justice Goddard as incriminating. This sentence, too, would only make narrative sense if it were linked backwards or forwards to the use of a gun – in other words if it were placed immediately following or preceding the report of a shot. However, the actual context is:

(22) We were there waiting for about ten minutes.
(23) I did not know he was going to use the gun.
(24) A plain clothes man climbed up the drainpipe and on to the roof.

If it is accepted that there were question/answer sequences underlying Bentley's state-ment, then the logic and the sequencing of the information were not under his direct control. Thus, the placing of the reporting of some of the events depends on a decision by the police questioner to ask his question at that point, rather than on Bentley's reconstruction of the narrative sequence and this, crucially, means that the inference drawn by the judge in his summing-up is unjustified. If one were able to assume that the confession statement was Bentley's unaided narrative, then the positioning of 'I didn't know he was going to use the gun' would be significant, because there is no timing adverbial and so the observation would have to take its time from its position in the narrative. In that view Bentley appears to be reporting that, well before the gun was used, he knew about its existence. However, if this sentence is in fact the product of a response to a question with its placing determined by the interrogating police offi-cers, there is no longer any conflict with his later denial 'I did not know Chris had one [a gun] until he shot'. Nor is there any significance either in Bentley being reported as saying '*the* gun' – all interaction uses language loosely and cooperatively. If the police-man had asked Bentley about '*the* gun' Bentley would assume they both knew which gun they were talking about and the sensible interpretation would be 'the gun that had been used earlier that evening' and not 'the gun that was going to be used later in the sequence of events that made up Bentley's narrative'.

By a remarkable coincidence a parallel sequence occurred during the trial itself. Bentley's barrister, whilst eliciting a narrative of the evening's events from him, pro-duced the following set of questions:

Q   Well, after some difficulty did you then get on the roof and find Craig?
A   Yes sir, I went on Craig's drainpipe and got up.
Q   Up to that time did you know that Craig had a loaded revolver?
A   No Sir.
Q   When you got on to the roof what happened then?
A   Some lights in the garden; someone shone a light in the garden.

(Trial transcript, p. 97)

If this sequence of Q-A exchanges were to be turned into a monologue narrative, the 'knowledge' about the loaded gun would similarly be reported well in advance of its use, with a similarly misleading effect.

The judgement

Demonstrating that the statement was indeed a jointly produced document, in part authored by the police officers who wrote it down, both removed the incriminating value of the phrase 'I didn't know he was going to use the gun' and undermined the credibility of the police officers on whose word depended the evidential value of the utterance 'Let him have it, Chris'. In August 1998, 46 years after the event, the then Lord Chief Justice, sitting with two senior colleagues, criticised his predecessor's summing-up and allowed the Appeal against conviction.

Issues to consider

Those interested in researching further the Bentley case will find Trow's book (1992) useful. It not only describes the detailed circumstances of the case but brings to light much important new evidence that was never admitted at the trial in 1952. The sense of outrage that still surrounds the Bentley case has made it something of a *cause célèbre* for musicians and film makers, with songs by Ralph McTell and Elvis Costello, and with Peter Medak's 1991 movie *Let Him Have It*, billed with the tagline 'The shocking story of an unbelievable miscarriage of justice'. Some suggestions for discussion follow.

❑ As Coulthard himself has noted in other publications on the case, there are many more features of Bentley's disputed confession that can be challenged using the tools of forensic linguistics. One feature is the use of the temporal connecting word 'then' in constructions like: 'Chris **then** jumped over and I followed …'; 'Chris **then** climbed up the drainpipe …'. In these instances, the temporal connector is placed *after* the Subject but *before* the verb, whereas the linguistic evidence from concordances of everyday language suggests a different pattern with 'then' coming before the Subject: 'then Chris jumped' and so on. Coulthard (2001) claims that both the frequency of the word *then* and its grammatical position make it more like 'police speak' than normal usage.

Going on your experience of everyday narrative, is this claim justified? If you have access to a concordance, you could investigate the claim by keying in 'then' and looking closely at its collocates. (See the web materials that accompany this book for more discussion of corpus techniques in CDA).

❑ Another important aspect of the Bentley case was to do with the accused's own psychological and educational competence. In the days of the IQ test, Bentley recorded 66 on the scale which equated to a reading age of 4 and a half years. Indeed, in 1952 he could still not sign his own name (Trow, 1992: 64–67). He had also suffered, when younger, two serious head injuries, the second of which brought on epilepsy. Even the trial judge described him as 'three quarter witted'.

Look again at the disputed confession, asking yourself if this really is the 'language' of someone with such chronic learning difficulties. Are there any expressions in particular that strike you as being unusual or incongruous?

LANGUAGE, STYLE AND LIFESTYLE   D8

The following reading is taken from an article by David Machin and Theo van Leeuwen, in which the authors analyse the language style of a women's magazine, *Cosmopolitan*. This style consists of a mixture of advertising, conversational, expert and street styles through which *Cosmopolitan* globally disseminates lifestyle models for women. In this way the magazine attempts to secure women's allegiance to the *Cosmo* lifestyle of the 'fun fearless female', mainly through the way they dress and groom. The authors demonstrate how this language, through choice of phonology, lexicon and grammar, plays an important role in promoting a model of the self where personal characteristics can be bought through identification with consumer lifestyle models. For their research, the authors collected two monthly editions (October and November 2001) of 44 versions of *Cosmopolitan* magazine, translating a number of non-English versions and referring in the article mainly to the US, Dutch, Spanish, Indian and Chinese versions.

Language style and lifestyle: the case of a global magazine

David Machin and Theo van Leeuwen (reprinted from *Media, Culture and Society* 27 (4) (2005): 577–600)

David
Machin
and
Theo van
Leeuwen

[...]

We will begin by introducing the concept of style, and then show how the linguistic style of *Cosmopolitan* can be interpreted as 'lifestyle', thus investigating the 'possible parallels between the use of language and the use of symbolic markers in lifestyle practices' (Chaney, 1996: 46). [...] The three approaches to style that follow can help us to think about the way that this process works.

Individual style

The idea of 'individual style' foregrounds individual difference. Although the ways in which we speak and write and act are always to some extent socially regulated, there usually is room for individual difference, for 'doing things our way'. This kind of style is perhaps the oldest. The Romans already had a saying *stilus virum arguit* ('the style announces the man'), and the word 'style' comes from 'stilus', the Latin word for 'pen'. Handwriting is in fact a good example of individual style. As histories of handwriting (e.g. Sassoon, 1999) show, it has always been socially regulated, most recently through the ways it has been taught in the school system, yet everybody has their own recognizable handwriting, their own individual style. [...]

Social style

The idea of 'social style' foregrounds the *social* determination of style, the idea that style expresses, not our individual personality and attitudes, but our social position, 'who we are' in terms of stable categories such as class, gender and age, social relations

David
Machin
and
Theo van
Leeuwen

and 'what we do' in terms of the socially regulated activities we engage in, and the roles we play within them. Social style is not internally, psychologically motivated, and it does not follow from our moods or from our stable and consistent 'character'. It is externally motivated, determined by social factors outside our control. [...]

Lifestyles

'Lifestyle' combines individual and social style. On the one hand it is social, a group style, even if the groups it sustains are geographically dispersed, scattered across the cities of the world, and characterized, not by stable social positionings such as class, gender and age, or comparatively stable activities such as occupations, but by shared consumer behaviours (shared taste), shared patterns of leisure time activities (e.g. an interest in similar sports or tourist destinations), and shared attitudes to key social issues (e.g. similar attitudes to environmental problems, gender issues, etc.): 'People use lifestyles in everyday life to identify and explain wider complexes of identity and affiliation' (Chaney, 1996: 12). Lifestyles are also social because they are signified by *appearances*, so much so that just about any set of attitudes can be, and is, conveyed by styles of dress and adornment, interior decoration, and so on. [...]

Finally, 'lifestyle' is social because of the role it plays in marketing, where traditional social indicators such as class, gender, age, etc., have been replaced by lifestyle market segmentation techniques, which classify consumers through a mixture of consumption patterns and attitudes. [...]

Yet, lifestyles are also individual. [...] And although individuals can be made aware of the fact that their choices are also the choices of millions of 'people like them', across the globe, they nevertheless *feel* that their style is primarily individual and personal, and that they are making creative use of the wide range of semiotic resources made available to them by the culture industries. This is further enhanced by the fact that 'lifestyle' identities are unstable and can be discarded and re-made any time. [...]

Like writers, artists and actors in the past, people now create their identities quite deliberately, or 'reflexively' – perhaps this helps explaining the exalted status of writers, artists, actors, etc. in contemporary consumer society.

[...]

In the remainder of this article we will return to the example of *Cosmopolitan* magazine, and try to describe its linguistic style as 'lifestyle'.

Language style as lifestyle

In discussing the linguistic style of *Cosmopolitan* as 'lifestyle', we will concentrate on two questions. First, *how can this style be described as a 'composite of connotations', and what identities and values does it express?* We have seen that lifestyles are put together from existing styles which have lost their specific functions as regional dress, period dress, uniform, etc., and which are combined to form hybrid styles that express a particular combination of meanings which derive from connotations – from the associations we have, in the shared, global popular culture, with the places, times and other contexts from which the original styles originated. Thus sports dress is no longer

David
Machin
and
Theo van
Leeuwen

worn only on the sports field. It is worn elsewhere as well, and then stands for the values associated with sport, and its particular role in neo-capitalism [...].

The second question is: *how diverse is this style? How does it negotiate between the individual and the social, or, in this case, the local and the global?*

Lifestyle entails, on the one hand, a loss of uniformity and increased space for individual style, but, on the other hand, individual lifestyles draw on deliberately designed and globally distributed semiotic resources that are definitely not individual. *Cosmopolitan* magazine clearly contributes to increased global cultural homogeneity – comparing the magazine's Dutch, Spanish, Indian and Chinese versions to earlier women's magazines from these same countries leaves no doubt about this. On the other hand, the magazine is localized into 44 different versions, many of them in languages other than English. It has also created room for difference. [...]

Advertising style

Advertising style developed, not just to sell products and services, but also to model the identities and values of consumer society. It was the first 'corporate' language variety, and it played a key role in what Fairclough (1993) has called the 'marketization' of discourse. Now that consumer society is coming into its own, so is advertising style. It is rapidly spreading beyond the confines of actual advertisements and infiltrating other genres, for instance the 'advertorials' of magazines and the burgeoning lifestyle sections of the print media. Displaced from its original function, advertising style connotes a preoccupation with consumer goods and their meanings and attractions, and with the identities and values advertising has traditionally celebrated – glamour, success, hedonism, sensuality, sexuality. We will discuss three aspects of this style in a little more detail: direct address, evaluative adjectives and poetic devices.

Direct address. Advertising style makes a great deal of use of direct address [...]. This excerpt from Indian *Cosmopolitan* (October 2001) is not an advertisement, yet it is full of imperatives and instances of 'second-person' address, even though there are also remnants of 'proper' magazine reporting style (e.g. attributed statements such as "Too many accessories can kill your style ...", says hairstylist Jojo').

SUPERSLEEK STRANDS

'Too many accessories can kill *your* style. Sleek hair that is off *your* face looks really glamorous,' says hairstylist Jojo. *Fake* a poker straight mane with this simple tip from him. 'Before styling, *use* a good conditioner on *your* hair. *Blowdry* your mane using a round brush. Then spray an anti-frizz product on your dry hair. *Divide your* tresses into sections and *run* a straightening iron through the whole length. *Finish* with a spritz of a shine enhancing product,' he suggests. Jojo likes L'aurore Professionel's Tec-ni-Art Liss Control+, RS 339, Tec-ni-Art Spray Fixant Anti-Frizz, RS 399, and Tec-ni-Art Gloss Shine & Hold Spray, ES 399.

David
Machin
and
Theo van
Leeuwen

The Indian *Cosmopolitan* is published in English, but the same advertising-like features occur in non-English versions, for instance in the Dutch version (October 2001).

> Gebruik in plaats van een vloeibare eyeliner een potlood of oogschaduw die je mooi uitwerkt.
>
> (literal translation: '*Use* instead of mascara an eye pencil or eye shadow which *you* apply beautifully.')

Or in the Spanish version (October 2001):

> Aprovecha para exfoliar tu piel y recuperar su luz.
> (literal translation: '*Take* advantage to exfoliate *your* skin and recuperate its glow.')

Or in the Chinese version (October 2001):

> Fu yu pi fu tan xing, gai shan song chi qu xian.
> (literal translation: '*Give your* skin elasticity, *tighten* those loose curves.')

Adjectives. Adjectives play a key role in advertising style because many adjectives can apply both to the advertised product (the signifier) and to the values it signifies. For instance, in the US version (October 2001):

> Dramatic, passion-inspiring purple is the season's hottest hue. To instantly make any outfit feel more 'fall 2001', just add a taste of plum.

Here 'dramatic' and 'passionate' can both be seen as a description of the colour (the signifier) and as a 'mood' or 'personality trait' the reader can express by means of the colour. Similarly, in the Dutch version of the magazine (October 2001):

> Heerlijk warme, zachte stoffen, lieve bloemen en zoete pastels in combinatie met wit. Zo wordt je huis een op-en-top winterpaleis, voor het ultieme prinsessengevoel. ('Deliciously warm, soft fabrics, dear flowers and sweet pastels in combination with white. That's how your house becomes a winterpalace, for the ultimate princess-feeling.')

Clearly adjectives like 'warm', 'dear' and 'sweet' can apply to the fabrics as well as to the reader who chooses them to decorate her home, that is, the 'princess' in her 'winterpalace'. This ambiguity gives the adjective a key role in advertising. It welds together the signifier (the colour) and the signified (the personality traits of the user), making them seem like two sides of the same coin. Cook ([2001]) has commented in some detail on the referential ambiguity of adjectives in advertising.

Poetic devices. Advertising style also makes abundant use of poetic devices. Here is another example from the Indian *Cosmopolitan* (November 2001):

> Flaunt that gorgeous body:
>
> A sure shot way of upping your sinister sister image is showing off that bold bod – the right way. Give up the tedious treadmill at the gym for a sexy, stretchy session of yoga to attract attention to all the right places.

**David
Machin
and
Theo van
Leeuwen**

Note the alliterations and half rhymes: 'sinister sister image', 'bold bod', 'tedious tread-mill', 'sexy, stretchy session'.

This use of poetic devices has again both a practical and an ideological function. The problem of 'recall' is a major practical problem in advertising, and a major theme in its trade and research journals. How can we make sure that people will remember the brand, the product, the message?

Poetic devices (and music) can help. In societies without alphabetic writing, knowledge had to be stored in memory and therefore often took the form of epic poems, with standard metres and an abundance of poetic devices (Ong, 1982). [...] Advertising has revitalized this tradition with its ear-catching language and musical jingles.

But poetic devices also make advertising style more entertaining and pleasurable than, for instance, technical descriptions of products, or instruction manuals. Advertising style pioneered 'edutainment', the combination of instruction (for instance, on how to make yourself beautiful or how to keep your teeth white) and pleasure, thereby undermining the traditional split between the serious and the popular, between high art and low art – and between the higher and lower classes and their different tastes (think also of the way advertising has incorporated high art, classical music, etc.). Advertising's emphasis on pleasure is therefore not just expressed through the pleasurable activities it portrays or alludes to, but also through its linguistic style.

This theme is closely related to another aspect of advertising, its *transgressive* nature. Advertising is deliberately unconventional, deliberately bent on breaking rules and defying taboos, as in the above quote where women are encouraged to flaunt their femininity unashamedly.

Again this is not just a matter of content, but also of style. Advertising style also breaks rules of spelling ('*Mudd. Pure Inddulgence*'), grammar ('*B&Q it*'), and vocabulary – by concocting often punning neologisms: examples from the October 2001 US *Cosmopolitan* include '*bootylicious*' and '*denim-ite*'. The Chinese version of the magazine delights in creating such neologisms, for example:

> yan yi *zhen wo* mei li.
> ('Show me real charm.')
> *mi mei* du zhu.
> ('Gamble on glam.')
> yi tou hu mei de jon se juan fa ji yi shuang lan bao shi ban de yan tong.
> ('Foxy-charming curly hair and diamond-blue pupils.')

And so does the Dutch version. One of the present authors grew up in the Netherlands and can remember how neologistic compounds such as *winterbleek* ('winter-pale'), *natuurzacht* ('nature-soft'), and superlatives such as *krachtproteïne* ('power-protein') and *superlicht* ('super-light') were first introduced when commercials began to appear on Dutch television in the 1960s. [...] This breaking of rules is always tongue-in-cheek,

David
Machin
and
Theo van
Leeuwen

so that we can at once enjoy the transgression and dismiss it as 'not serious', 'only a joke', 'ironic'. The message is at once received and denied. Many lifestyle sociologists and cultural analysts see irony and self-parodying as a key feature of modern lifestyle identities, characteristic of postmodernity. In advertising they have played an important role for a long time, traditionally to allow advertisers to appeal quite openly to the consumer's greed, envy and lust – and get away with it.

But in this respect there are differences between the localized versions of the *Cosmopolitan* magazine. The Indian version takes the tongue-in-cheek approach to extremes, as if to make it absolutely clear that it's only a game, accompanied by much nervous laughter and giggling. Compared to the US and Western Europe, India is still very much a man's world, where the gospel of *Cosmopolitan* has by no means been fully accepted. The Spanish version, on the other hand, is more subdued and serious. The use of rhyme and alliteration is for the most part restricted to the headlines, and the body of the texts uses a more formal style. The subtitle of the magazine, for instance, is not 'Fun Fearless Female' as in the US and the UK, but 'The Woman who is Changing the World'. [...] Introducing elements of 'street language' into your speech is just not done in Spain. The Chinese version, on the other hand, has adopted the *Cosmo* style with enthusiasm: 'Let's compete to see who is more joyfully casual.' There are economic reasons for this, because they see it as a style that will attract advertisers. At the same time, in creating a Chinese version of *Cosmo* 'poetics' they draw on classical Chinese styles, such as the symmetrical arrangements of words in the 'antithetical couplet', rather than on Western poetic devices. Apparently market reform has been accompanied by a revitalization of traditional forms in China, for instance a return of traditional characters (Scollon and Scollon, 1998), even in popular culture texts imported from the United States, Hong Kong and Japan (Nakano, 2002). [...]

In conclusion, we have tried to show that *Cosmopolitan* style is a hybrid of different styles, chosen for the connotations they bring, for the way they help express the magazine's identity and values. Like the media styles of the 1920s and 1930s, this style has been quite deliberately designed. And although local versions adopt it in their own specific ways, overall it is a *global* style. [...]

Issues to consider

As we saw in the reading above, advertising language and style have moved beyond advertising itself and started to colonize other genres such as lifestyle magazines, but also many other print media as part of the commercialization of the press. Although not reproduced in the excerpt above, it is worth adding that the authors also undertook interviews with the editorial staff of these magazines to gain an insight into the strategies developed for particular types of dissemination in different cultures and countries.

LANGUAGE IN THE GLOBAL SERVICE ECONOMY   **D9**

In this Strand so far we have focused on several aspects of the phenomenon of globalization and new capitalism. One of these aspects is the 'new work order' (Gee *et al.*, 1996) in which new ('post-Fordist') ways of working are increasingly making new demands on the linguistic abilities of workers. Cameron (2000) notes that it is in the contemporary service sector of the economy, and particularly in call centres, that an increasing tendency for employers to regulate workers' communication patterns can be observed.

This article discusses some sociolinguistic characteristics of the speech style prescribed to workers for interacting with customers in service contexts, focusing in particular on the linguistic and vocal 'styling' prescribed for operators in telephone call centres in the UK. Cameron not only discusses the linguistic regimes that operate in many call centres but also focuses specifically on gender, drawing attention to the similarities between the preferred style of speech and what is popularly known as 'women's language' (see further Strand 4).

Styling the worker: gender and the commodification of language in the global service economy

Deborah Cameron

Deborah Cameron (reprinted from D. Cameron, *On Language and Sexual Politics*, London: Routledge, 2006, pp. 112–132)

[…]

Here I examine the imposition on one group of English-speaking customer service workers (telephone call centre operators) of a particular speech style as the norm or 'standard' for interaction on the job. As well as discussing the means used by organizations seeking to exert control over the speech of their employees, I will discuss some of the sociolinguistic characteristics of the speech style that is prescribed as a 'standard'. I will argue that its most salient features are not markers of class, region, or nationality/ethnicity, but symbolic markers of feminine gender (though they are not presented explicitly as gendered, and they are prescribed to workers of both sexes). The commodification of language in contemporary service workplaces is also in some sense the commodification of a quasi-feminine service persona. […]

The data

[…]

I chose to study call centres, in particular, for two reasons. First, they provide a prototypical example of a 'new' service workplace: the vast majority have existed for less than ten years, and their institutional culture has always incorporated the disciplines of globalized capitalism. […] Companies can cut costs by routing all customer enquiries

Deborah Cameron

to one point, and since its physical location is irrelevant – customers do not have to go there – it can be put where rents and labour costs are low. [...]

Second, language has a special significance in call centre work. The operator's job consists of little else but language-using [*sic*] – talking to customers on the phone and inputting/retrieving data using a computer – and her/his professional persona must be created entirely through speech. Typically, the speech of call centre operators is subject to intensive regulation and constant surveillance. Supervisors can covertly listen in on any call (known in the industry as 'silent listening'), while in some centres every call is recorded and may become the subject of 'counselling' (a worker and a supervisor or manager listen together to examples of the worker's performance and engage in critical assessment). Call centres, then, are a good example of service work as language work, and as such they are also a particularly rich source of insight into the commodification and regulation of language on the job.

I collected data relating to seven centres located in various parts of the UK (central Scotland, the north of England and London). The service functions performed in these centres were: providing directory assistance to telephone subscribers, logging faults in telecommunications equipment, dealing with auto insurance claims, processing personal banking transactions, authorizing credit requests, booking rail tickets and handling enquiries for a utility (gas) company.

[...]

Standardizing speech in call centres: scripting and styling

The institutional regime of the call centre exemplifies the hyper-rationalizing tendency that the sociologist George Ritzer (1996) has dubbed 'McDonaldization'. For Ritzer this tendency is defined by its drive to maximize four things: efficiency (the most output for the least effort), calculability (the measurement of quality in terms of quantity), predictability (as little variation as possible) and control (of workers' activities by means of technology).

[...]

Efficiency is maximized in call centres by designing interactional routines so that they consist of the fewest moves needed to complete a given transaction successfully. For example, in the directory assistance centre, the standard routine for processing a request for a phone number has the 'core' moves 'which name please', 'which town', 'which address'. This reflects the fact that the software used to retrieve phone numbers needs all and only the answers to these questions (preferably in the order just given) to trigger a search. [...]

Calculability is maximized by setting targets for the time taken to process calls, and judging the quality of employees' work in terms of the number of calls handled in a given period. [...] The use of standardized scripts for common routines enhances calculability as well as efficiency, since the duration of a prescripted routine can be estimated more accurately than if there is no script. Though the customer's moves are not scripted, it has been suggested that customers dealing with employees who follow scripts are apt to 'routinize' their own behaviour in response (Leidner 1993).

Not all call centre regimes use scripting proper ('scripting' being defined here as the provision of a full specification for every word uttered by the operator.) An alternative is to provide a 'prompt sheet', which specifies what interactional moves the operator should make in what order, but does not prescribe a standard form of words. Some centres do not even go that far, providing only general guidelines for the 'staging' of a transaction, leaving the exact number of moves in each stage to the operator's discretion. Others use some mixture of the strategies just described. These options exemplify differing degrees of emphasis placed on the *predictability* of call centre interaction. [...]

Finally, technological *control* over human operators is seen in various aspects of the call centre regime. Automated call distribution systems dictate the pace of work, while the software used for functions like retrieving telephone numbers, bank account details and rail timetables shapes the sequence and content of many routines. Perhaps the most striking instance of technological control in call centres, however, is hi-tech surveillance. [...] These surveillance practices focus more specifically on the operator's handling of the *interactional* task, rather than simply on her/his performance as measured by statistics. [...]

Call centre style and women's language

[...]

In the following discussion I will seek to show in more detail how various elements of the symbolic construct 'women's language' are appropriated and recombined in the call centre context to produce a particular service style. The discussion is based on materials (e.g. training manuals and appraisal criteria) I collected from four call centres in my sample, and it focuses on concerns that recur across those materials.

One concern that is highlighted in all the materials I collected is with the styling of the operator's *voice*. Two instructions on vocal performance are invariably given: that operators should smile – even though, obviously, they are invisible to their interlocutors – and that they should use an 'expressive' intonation. What the instruction to smile actually means is that the routine (or sometimes just part of it, e.g. the opening) should be performed 'with the lips in a smile posture'. 'Expressive' intonation means *emotionally* expressive, and is explicitly contrasted to intonation which will be heard as monotonous or uninvolved.

Smiling

❑ Does the member of staff answer the phone with a smile? (*credit authorization centre appraisal checklist*)

❑ Remember, smiling can be heard as well as seen. (*directory assistance centre employee manual*)

❑ Have a smile in your voice and avoid sounding abrupt. (*performance guidelines, auto insurance centre*)

'Expressive intonation' projecting attitudes/emotional states

❑ Our commitment is to give the caller an impression of excitement, friendliness, helpfulness and courtesy. Your telephone manner should sound as if you have been waiting for that particular call all day. You must never sound bored on a call. (*directory assistance centre employee manual*)

❑ The objective at the beginning of a call is to demonstrate sincerity and warmth. Try to make the caller feel you are there for them ... [avoid] a disinterested, monotonous tone to voice. (*performance guidelines, auto insurance centre*)

Deborah Cameron

It has been argued that both smiling and using expressive intonation are symbolically feminine behaviours. In the case of smiling, nonverbal communication researchers point out that it is not simply a spontaneous expression of pleasure but often functions, especially with non-intimates, to signal deference or appeasement. [...]

As for expressive intonation, it is both a stereotype and in some cases an empirical finding that female speakers exploit a broader pitch range, in other words tend less to monotony. This characteristic has been used in the past to label women as over-emotional and lacking in authority, tempting women like Margaret Thatcher to deliberately reduce the pitch range they use. The fact that vocal expressiveness is valued in service-work might suggest that authority is not among the qualities workers are expected to display.

[...]

Other recurrent styling concerns are to do with the management of interpersonal relationships through strategic choices at the level of discourse. One common instruction, for example, is to *create rapport* with callers, while another is to display *empathy* with them. In this example these (related) concerns are combined in the following, quite lengthy recommendation:

Rapport/empathy

❑ Creating a rapport and showing empathy is about adding the human touch to a business call relationship ... This means treating the caller as a person, recognising their situation and building a genuine conversation to reflect this ... Use language which conveys understanding of and empathy for the caller's individual situation, e.g. 'are you OK?' 'was anyone hurt?' 'that must have been very distressing for you.' (*performance guidelines, auto insurance centre*)

Here, two main discourse strategies are suggested. One is asking questions to show concern for the caller and encourage her/him to air her/his feelings about the incident that prompted the call (in this context, a traffic accident). The other is the technique known to communication trainers as 'mirroring', which means trying to demonstrate awareness of the interlocutor's mood and reflect it back to her/him in your own verbal and nonverbal behaviour. It is, of course, a common stereotype that women are better than men at inferring others' feelings from their outward behaviour, which is a precondition for successfully displaying empathy. The association of rapport-building with women's talk appears in many sources, notably Deborah Tannen's (1990) aphorism that men do 'report talk' and women do 'rapport talk'.

Another issue that is often addressed in call centre styling materials is the use of minimal responses. Concern about this aspect of interaction might seem to be motivated primarily by the need to make operators aware of specific constraints affecting telephone talk – that is, since there are no visual cues, verbal back-channelling is necessary to reassure the caller that the operator is still present and listening actively. However, the following example shows that the writer realizes there is more to the use of minimal responses than simply keeping the channel of communication open.

Minimal responses

❑ Use words of acknowledgement: yes, OK, thank you, I understand, I see ... [avoid] disruptive, disinterested or challenging use of listening acknowledgements, and using the same listening acknowledgement throughout the call. (*performance guidelines, auto insurance centre*)

Deborah Cameron

This is a recommendation to use minimal responses supportively: they should not be inserted where they will disrupt interaction, connote lack of interest or disagreement. It may be recalled here that some researchers (Fishman 1983; Reid 1995) have found women not only using more minimal responses than men, but also timing them more precisely, to coincide with or immediately follow the completion of the point they are responding to. The use of delayed minimal responses, which may suggest inattention, lack of interest or disagreement, has been associated more with male speakers. Once again, what is being recommended here would seem to be gendered, matching what is believed and what in some cases has been found to be women's rather than men's behaviour.

[...]

With the foregoing examples I hope I have shown that the ways of interacting recommended in training and appraisal materials for call centre operators bear a striking resemblance to ways of speaking that are associated, in the popular imagination and also in some instances by empirical research, with women speakers rather than men. This might prompt the question: do the style designers themselves make the connection?

In my view, the answer to this question is 'yes and no'. On one hand, there is evidence that many call centre managers regard young women, in particular, as 'naturally' suited to the work (Reardon 1996) [...] On the other hand, organizations do not present the ideal speech style explicitly as a gendered style: women may be considered 'naturally good at that sort of thing', but the 'thing' in question is not just (tautologically) 'being women', and the same style is also expected of men. What the preferred style of communication overtly signifies is not 'femininity' but 'good customer service'. [...]

Conclusion

[...]

One theme of the analysis presented above is the linguistic consequences of globalization. I have suggested that present-day corporate verbal hygiene practices may be analysed as part of a strategic attempt by organizations to maximize their advantages in a hyper-competitive globalized economy which is increasingly dominated by the provision of services. Yet it might well be asked whether current practices have precedents in the pre-globalization era. I certainly would not wish to argue that until the late 1980s (the moment of financial deregulation which is generally taken to have inaugurated the shift to today's global economy) workers spoke exactly as they liked, without norms or constraints. Clearly, for as long as 'work' has been a distinct domain of social practice, people have developed ways of acting and speaking peculiar to that domain, undergoing within particular workplaces processes of linguistic and other acculturation. [...] However, I would argue that there has been significant intensification, both

Deborah Cameron

of the desire of organizations to control employees' language-use and of their ability to do it with some degree of effectiveness (in the case of call centres, by using hi-tech surveillance). [This], of course, is the very opposite of what is usually claimed about the new global economy, which is frequently said to require highly skilled, self-motivating decision-makers and problem-solvers. [...]

Finally, the verbal hygiene practices which are the subject of this article are of interest for what they tell us about the relationship between language and gender. I have argued that the regulation and commodification of language in service work-places has resulted in the valorization of a speech style whose characteristics include expressiveness, caring, empathy and sincerity – characteristics popularly associated with the speech of women (if anyone doubts this, let them consult any example of the 'Mars and Venus' genre originated by Gray (1992), whose tenets have subsequently pervaded popular culture (cf. Cameron 1999; Talbot 2000)).

Issues to consider

❑ Below are two internet postings from two former call centre operators describing the character of their work (Blogs, *Guardian*, web 2008). The first one is male; the second did not specify his/her gender.

1 The problem with (most) call centres is: – The staff under trained, over worked and under paid. They also have little or no job security. I worked in a call centre for 9 months. By the time I left I didn't give a monkeys about the company or their customers. But then I suppose it's all our own faults for wanting the very best of everything but not wanting to pay for it.

2 I used to work at a call centre for a bank dealing with people's savings accounts. They didn't have any sort of pretence of wanting their employees to have 'fun' or be 'ker-azee'. Any sign of runaway individuality – like a slightly off the wall hairstyle (despite the fact that customers couldn't see you) or a sense of humour – was firmly stamped out, as was any attempt to assuage the mind numbing boredom in between calls by reading a book or magazine during quiet spells. (...) All this would have been bearable – the main problem was that it all seemed so pointless. As long as the caller wanted only information you were fine, but if there was any sort of problem – as an insignificant worker ant you had no power whatsoever to help them. The people that did were located at a different call centre and were pretty elusive – it was very hard to even get hold of them, and they tended to want all customer instructions submitted in writing (a requirement guaranteed to make any customer apoplectic with rage). Add to this a general attitude of total unconcern with people's problems. (...) Eventually I started skiving off and not really bothering to turn up on time – to be honest it was a massive relief when they finally sacked me.

Many call centres may have taken the philosophy of 'customer care' to extremes, expecting their operators to perform 'emotional labour' (Hochschild 1983); that is, using a language of feeling and caring for interacting with their customers. The comments above, however, seem to paint a different picture of customer 'care'. In what sense do you feel they endorse Cameron's conclusions?

❑ In interviews with a small sample of male call centre operators Cameron (2006b) found that these operators did not consider their gender an issue in their work but were unhappy with the artificiality and subservience imposed on them by scripts and styling. Do you feel that the prescribed 'feminized' service style could be problematic for men?

CRITICAL METAPHOR ANALYSIS

D10

In the reading for this Strand, Jonathan Charteris-Black undertakes a Critical Metaphor Analysis of a corpus comprising the party political manifestos of the two political parties, Labour and Conservative, that have dominated politics in Britain since the end of the Second World War. Manifestos state the intentions and policies of political parties and aim to persuade the electorate to vote for them. The importance of persuasion in all types of political discourse is likely to lead to more extensive and explicit use of metaphor to express systems of belief as well as communicating social objectives. Metaphors are inherently persuasive and are therefore very common in rhetorical and argumentative language such as political discourse. There is some support for the view that metaphors play a role in influencing our underlying political and social beliefs and in evoking a particular emotional response in the listener or reader (see further A10, for our definition and discussion of metaphor).

The following reading demonstrates that a corpus-based Critical Metaphor Analysis constitutes an important quantitative linguistic tool for revealing underlying ideologies, attitudes and beliefs in political discourse. It is therefore a useful and necessary addition to the qualitative approach of CDA. Whereas the qualitative analysis allows us to state what counts as metaphor, the quantitative analysis allows us to state the frequency of a metaphor in a corpus. Charteris-Black argues that if ideology influences metaphor use, we can assume that political parties will use metaphor differently and also that metaphor use changes over time according to shifts in outlooks and beliefs.

Metaphor in British party political manifestos

Jonathan
Charteris-
Black

Jonathan Charteris-Black (reprinted from Chapter 4 of *Corpus Approaches to Critical Metaphor Analysis*, Basingstoke: Palgrave Macmillan, 2004, pp. 65–85.

Researching political manifestos

[...]

The research was conducted employing a corpus of the post-war manifestos of the two major political parties that I will refer to as the British Manifesto Corpus; it can be accessed via a web site at http://www.psr.keele.ac.uk/area/uk/man.htm. The research questions that were addressed are as follows:

Jonathan
Charteris-
Black

1   What differences and similarities are there (if any) between the metaphors that are
    used in the political manifestos of each of the major parties?
2   What differences and similarities are there (if any) between the conceptual
    metaphors for which there is evidence in the political manifestos of each of the
    major parties?
3   How can we account for the choice of metaphor by each of the major parties?

To answer these questions I divided the more recent part of the British Manifesto Corpus (those written in the period 1974–97) into two separate corpora: Labour and Conservative manifestos. The size of the Labour corpus was 65063 words and the size of the
Conservative corpus was 67712 words. Another parameter of variation within a historical corpus of this type is time and I hoped to identify whether use of metaphor changes
within the same political party. I therefore split the British manifesto corpus into an
earlier and later post-war period. The earlier period was the sixteen manifestos written
by the two major parties in the period 1945–70 and the later period was the fourteen
manifestos written in the period 1974–97 to answer a fourth research question:

4   Has the choice of metaphor by either of the main political parties changed during
    the post-war period?

[…] The methodology combined qualitative with quantitative analysis of metaphor.
Qualitative analysis is necessary to identify metaphors; this is done with reference to
verbal context. Quantitative analysis is then used to see how typical such uses are.
Initially, qualitative analysis of a sample of three manifestos (those for October 1974,
1979 and 1997) revealed a set of metaphor keywords – these then formed the basis of
quantitative analysis. Key words are potential metaphors because they are words that
we would not normally expect to occur in the political domain. All morphologically
related forms of the keyword were included; so, for example, in the case of *build* the
following forms were searched: *build, building, buildings, builders, built, built-up*. Only
those forms that were used to refer to non-concrete entities were classified as metaphor since they create a degree of semantic tension between the original sense that
refers to physical construction and the abstract reference of the metaphor.

Metaphor in Labour and Conservative manifestos

Qualitative analysis of the British Manifesto Corpus showed evidence that metaphors
drew primarily from five source domains for metaphor. These were: conflict, journeys,
plants, religion and building. What is initially most striking is the similarity between
the two political parties as regards choice and frequency of source domain. There are
no important differences between the parties in the frequency of any of the source
domains of metaphors. This suggests that we may accurately speak of the conventional
metaphors of politics rather than the conventional metaphors of political parties. Nor
is there any marked difference in metaphor frequency – with a metaphor occurring
every 120 words in the Labour corpus and every 127 words in the Conservative corpus.
However, […] there is evidence of variation in the way that each party employs the
same metaphor to construe meanings that reflect its particular ideological stance. […]

Conflict metaphors

Jonathan
Charteris-
Black

Metaphors from this source domain included words such as *fight, battle, protect* and *threat* in a political context and conflict was easily the most common domain in the British Manifesto Corpus accounting for over 40 per cent of all metaphors identified. For this reason I propose a conceptual metaphor POLITICS IS CONFLICT. Politicians employ conflict metaphors because they highlight the personal sacrifice and physical struggle that is necessary to achieve social goals. They imply that some form of short-term hardship is necessary to attain worthwhile long-term goals. Conflict metaphors commonly have an important role in the evaluation of abstract social goals so that, for example, social ills can be conceptualised as 'enemies'.

[…]

Typically, both parties defend abstract social goals that are positively evaluated by their own party but are represented as under threat from the opposition, as in the following.

Defence of a valued social goal (both parties)

We will defend the fundamental rights of parents to spend their money on their children's education should they wish to do so. (Conservative)
[…]
While continuing to defend and respect the absolute right of individual conscience … (Labour)

Parties may also 'defend' particular social institutions or groups in society that are positively evaluated by their own party but represented as being under attack from the opposition.

Labour created the *National Health Service* and is determined *to defend* it. (Labour)

We will continue to *defend farmers and consumers.* (Conservative)
[…]

Conflict metaphors in the British Manifesto Corpus provide little evidence of difference between parties in terms of the underlying conceptual metaphor POLITICS IS CONFLICT. This may be because it is itself based on two fundamental conceptual keys that underlie much political discourse: LIFE IS A STRUGGLE FOR SURVIVAL and SOCIETY IS A PERSON. However, the rhetorical use of conflict metaphors for the communication of value judgement is rather different for each party. While both parties defend social goals or social groups, Labour attacks social ills while the Conservative Party defends valued social goals or social groups that are represented as being under attack by Labour.

Building metaphors

Metaphors from this source domain carry a strong positive connotation because they express aspiration towards desired social goals. It may be because of this that building

D10

Jonathan Charteris-Black

metaphors are used in very similar ways in both the Labour and Conservative corpora. In terms of frequency there is remarkably little difference between the two corpora. It seems that building metaphors are used invariably to represent a particular policy as well-founded, solid, permanent and stable as in the following:

Building metaphors for stability

It is the *foundation stone of a capital-owning democracy*. (Labour)
We will work with our allies to ensure that NATO remains *the cornerstone of defence*. (Conservative)

Building metaphors are motivated by a conceptual metaphor SOCIETY IS A BUILDING and invariably convey a positive evaluation because a valued outcome requires social co-operation between government and the people. Social goals are conceptualised as needing patience and effort. Because instant outcomes are not expected, there may also be a need to make sacrifices. Such highlighting of progress towards long-term social goals is evident in the use of *foundation* metaphors which invariably imply a positive evaluation of whatever follows.

'Foundation' metaphors for progress towards long-term goals

It must get the economy out of recession, it *must lay foundations for the future*. Recovery must be based on investment, for only investment will create lasting prosperity. (Labour)
The *foundations for recovery have been firmly laid*. In the next Parliament, we shall build on this … (Conservative)
Over the past five years the Labour government have *laid the foundations of a stronger economy*. (Labour)
It is on this that our chance of overcoming the country's economic difficulties and *laying the foundations of a new prosperity* for everyone will depend. (Conservative)

Both parties use the phrase *lay the foundations* to indicate an intentional series of actions that will form the basis of something that is positively evaluated: usually successful economic performance as this is taken as a precondition of other social and political policies. […]

Journey metaphors

Lakoff (1993) reformulated the journey metaphor as PURPOSEFUL ACTIVITY IS TRAVELLING ALONG A PATH TOWARDS A DESTINATION. […] Therefore, since politicians are concerned with goal-oriented social activity, I will incorporate this into a political conceptual metaphor: PURPOSEFUL SOCIAL ACTIVITY IS TRAVELLING ALONG A PATH TOWARDS A DESTINATION.

We find evidence of this in two of the most common metaphor keywords in the British manifestos corpora: *steps* and *forward* […]. These are conventional ways of talking about progress towards a goal and are employed in a similar way by both parties. However, there is a difference as regards time and space in the two corpora; Labour metaphors are typically spatial in that *forward* usually collocates with *bring, put*

Jonathan
Charteris-
Black

or *move*. However, in the Conservative corpus there is evidence of a time orientation so that movement forward is seen as progress in time rather than in space; consider for example the following.

Moving forward in time (Conservative)

Our history is the story of a free people – a great chain of people stretching into the past and *forward into the future.* (Conservative)

This manifesto sets out our vision for the Britain of the 1990s and beyond; a future based on the aspirations of millions of individuals and their families, their hopes, their needs, their security. For the first time in a generation this country *looks forward to an era of real prosperity and fulfilment.* (Conservative)

Here progress is conceived as occurring in time rather than in space [...]. This contrasts with the Labour use of *forward* which is invariably part of a series of actions that are thought of as occurring in *space* rather than in time; consider the following.

Moving forward in space (Labour)

We *put forward* in this manifesto a list of improvements we want to make in society. We put them forward in good faith; but many of them cost money. (Labour)

Second, we will introduce new legislation to *help forward our plans for a radical extension of industrial* ... (Labour)

Interestingly only in one of the New Labour manifestos is *forward* used as a time-based notion.

Moving forward in time (New Labour)

We aim to put behind us the political struggles of left and right that have torn our country apart for too many decades. Many of these conflicts have no relevance whatsoever to the modern world – public versus private, bosses versus workers, middle class versus working class. It is time for this country to *move on* and *move forward.* (New Labour)

There is an interesting shift in New Labour journey metaphors from the traditional Labour focus on progress along a path in space towards the Conservative conceptuali-sation of progress as movement forwards in time. This can be accounted for by the fact that the Conservative Party had held power for the previous nineteen years. The shift to time rather than space orientation suggests that the rhetorical use of New Labour is adapted from Conservative Party discourse. [...]

Plant metaphors

Metaphors from the domain of plants are an important group comprising 13 per cent of all metaphors in the British Manifesto Corpus. Many of these were accounted for by a conventional metaphor for *growth* that is used in similar ways by both parties in the context of describing economic expansion. We also find a similar use of *flourish*

**Jonathan
Charteris-
Black**

to imply a strong positive evaluation – although we can see from the agent of *flourish* (in bold) that different social phenomena are given a positive evaluation by each of the parties.

Evaluation of 'flourish' in Labour and Conservative manifestos

But **families** cannot *flourish* unless government plays its distinctive role. (Labour)
That is the only way that **democracy** can *flourish*. (Labour)
[…]
For **enterprise** to *flourish*, the state must get out of the way of the wealth creators.
(Conservative)
[…]
To build a responsible society which protects the weak but also allows the **family
and the individual** to *flourish*. (Conservative)

In each case a social entity is prioritised using the same metaphor by each of the parties – *flourish* identifies those social entities that are highly valued by each of the parties. In some cases these are the same, for example 'families', but in others they are specific to parties, for example 'business' is claimed to 'flourish' under the Conservatives and 'democracy' is claimed to 'flourish' under Labour.

There is also evidence of creative metaphor in the source domain of plants. For example, let us consider the use of the term *windfall* as in the Labour Party 1997 manifesto; it is always used in a nominal compound form *windfall levy*:

New Labour and the windfall levy

A **one-off windfall levy** on the excess profits of the privatised utilities will fund our ambitious programme. (New Labour)
This welfare to work programme will be funded by **a windfall levy** on the excess profits of the privatised utilities, introduced in this Budget after we have consulted the regulators. (New Labour)

The use of this metaphor is important in that it conceals agency: it is not clear that this is a tax imposed by the government of the day. The Bank of English corpus shows that the other familiar collocations of this word are *windfall tax; cash windfall; windfall profits*. Here public revenue is conceptualised as being obtained without any effort because it is through the natural process of the wind blowing. There is no victim and no effort involved in obtaining a social benefit. This is an example of a creative use of metaphor that deliberately construes an event as effortless – because there is no animate agent – and positive – as if it were a gift of nature. […]

Religious metaphors

While there was evidence of some religious metaphors (e.g. *vision* and *faith*) in both party corpora, the Labour corpus (especially New Labour) contains a much wider range of words from this source domain; I have illustrated some of these [above]. Here are some typical examples of *vision* metaphors from the New Labour manifesto.

Jonathan Charteris-Black

Labour party religious metaphors

But a government can only ask these efforts from the men and women of this country if they can confidently see a *vision of a fair and just society*. (New Labour) An independent and creative voluntary sector, committed to voluntary activity as an expression of citizenship, is central to *our vision of a stakeholder society*. (New Labour)

The use of 'vision' is based on the conceptual metaphor SEEING IS UNDERSTANDING (Lakoff and Johnson 1980: 48); it implies that there is an altruistic objective that is understood by the party and towards which its policies are directed. It is one that is analogous to spiritual progress because it claims that the objective is to make the world a better place to live in and is, I have argued, evidence of a conceptual metaphor POLITICS IS RELIGION. The idea of spiritual rebirth is activated by words such as *renewal, values, justice* and these words evoke earlier notions from religious evangelism that form a part of the origins of both the Labour and the Liberal parties. [...] perhaps the most interesting uses of religious metaphor are found in the New Labour election manifesto of 1997.

Summary

In this chapter I have analysed a sample of British political party manifestos for evidence of its metaphor content. [...]. There were no significant differences between the types of conceptual metaphor employed by either political party with five dominant domains in the corpus for each party. Both parties have a set of stock metaphors for positive evaluation based on conceptual metaphors such as WORTHWHILE ACTIVITY IS BUILDING and SOCIETY IS A BUILDING. There is also evidence of creative metaphor for positive evaluation in the source domain of plants with the use by the Labour Party 1997 of *windfall levy*. However, there has been a shift in metaphor use with metaphors of conflict becoming more common at the expense of building metaphors.

There were different discourse strategies between the two major British political parties; though 'conflict' metaphors were commonly used in the Labour manifestos, Conservative manifestos represent their policies as 'defence' against the 'attack' of Labour policies. It is argued that this reflects a different evaluation of direct governmental intervention since this is more likely to be undertaken by the Labour Party. There are also conceptual differences in journey metaphors as the Labour Party conceptualizes progress in spatial terms while the Conservative Party conceptualizes progress as movement forwards in time. [...] New Labour also makes much more systematic and extensive use of metaphors of religion and an ethical chain based on a conceptual metaphor POLITICS IS RELIGION. Therefore, metaphor serves a vital pragmatic role in providing the type of evaluation and expressive meaning required by both ideological conviction and by the genre of the party political manifesto. [...]

Issues to consider

One important question emerging from Charteris-Black's chapter is the extent to which speakers/writers use metaphors consciously or whether they are produced more intuitively as a result of unconscious rhetorical and stylistic conventions. Although this is difficult to assess, there seems to be at least a covert ideological motivation in the use of certain (political) metaphors. By combining qualitative and quantitative methods of analysis we are in a better position to reveal the covert and subliminal role of metaphor. While some linguists (e.g. Lakoff 1991) have provided excellent qualitative analysis of metaphors in political discourse, they have not used corpus data to support their claims. Critical Metaphor Analysis supports qualitative analysis with quantitative data on metaphor frequency and this provides a more robust account of the discourse role of metaphor. Some suggestions for discussion follow.

❑ Charteris-Black has used the party political manifestos of the Conservatives and (New) Labour in Britain for his comparative analysis of metaphor. What other types of political discourse (in your part of the world) could you include for a more comprehensive description of metaphor in political discourse? How would a corpus-based approach assist you in this task?

❑ The metaphors covered in this excerpt from Charteris-Black's study developed primarily from five types of source domain: conflict, journeys, plants, religion and building. Another important metaphor used in politics and economics is the 'disease' metaphor, which is embodied in descriptions of ailing economies and political systems through expressions like 'anaemic industry', 'a chronic deficit' or 'the best economic medicine' (see also C1 and C10). Try to find examples of the 'disease' (and its obverse, 'health') metaphor in print and broadcast media and think about what function it serves when used to describe politics and the economy. It may be worth comparing different media outlets with different political allegiances to see if the metaphor is spread uniformly across them. An intriguing observation from Boers (1999), again based on a corpus analysis of metaphor, is that the 'disease' metaphor is used more often by the European media between November and March than between April and October. Why should this be the case? And what does it suggest about the importance of metaphor in human cognition?

D11 SOCIAL MEDIA ONLINE CAMPAIGNS

The following reading is taken from an article by Innocent Chiluwa and Presley Ifukor, which uses critical discourse analysis to examine the language of a prominent social media campaign. In April 2014, the Nigerian terrorist group Boko Haram (BH) kidnapped 276 girls in Borno State, and as of January 2018, 113 are still missing. In this article the authors analyse the language of the #BringBackOurGirls campaign, which has been prominent across social media and has garnered international support from prominent individuals, such as former US First Lady Michelle Obama and former British Prime Minister David Cameron. The article applies the appraisal framework outlined in unit B11 to demonstrate that the campaign exhibits high levels of affect in its emotional representation of the event, whilst also acknowledging that if social media campaigns are not augmented by prominent offline actions they can lapse into 'slacktivism'.

'War against our children': Stance and evaluation in *#BringBackOurGirls* campaign discourse on Twitter and Facebook

Innocent Chiluwa and Presley Ifukor (reprinted from *Discourse and Society* 26 (3) (2015): 267–296)

[...]

#BringBackOurGirls social media campaign with accompanying photographs of protesters and graphic images of children and schoolgirls on *Twitter* and *Facebook* was no longer a local Nigerian affair; it became a global campaign for the release of the kidnapped girls as well as girls' rights to formal education. Initially, as a demand addressed to the Nigerian government and the armed forces, 'bring back our girls' later became an appeal to BH, and the entire world, including the UN. Having been tweeted thousands of times, the campaign also drew thousands of *likes* on *Facebook*, and attracted sympathizers from around the world, including celebrities and social activists, some who not only tweeted or commented on *Facebook* but also joined in offline protests. Civil rights groups, students and girls' rights campaigners in the United States, England, France, Canada, Malaysia, South Africa and so on joined the campaign. The social media slogan also attracted the likes of the US First Lady, *Michelle Obama*, [sic] and the British Prime Minister, David Cameron, calling for more to be done to free the missing schoolgirls. Also, Malala Yousafzai – the girl education campaigner from Pakistan – was among hundreds of people who tweeted and included a photo of themselves with a sign reading *#BringBackOurGirls* to show their support. Evidently, the campaigners actually believed that the general social media condemnation of BH such as those represented by the *#BringBackOurGirls* had the potential to achieve positive results.

[...]

Against this background of global terror and conflict discourse of fear, frustration, anger and helplessness, some general patterns of language use on *Twitter* and *Facebook* about the events are prone to convey intense emotions. Ellsworth and Scherer (2003) citing Arnold (1960) argue that '… certain ways of interpreting one's environment are inherently emotional, [because] few thoughts are entirely free of feelings, and emotions influence thinking …' (p. 527). Unfortunately, this also often puts commonsense at risk, because very often emotional language tends to exaggerate reality and misrepresent facts. We argue in this article that while emotional reactions and attitudes in discourse may reflect genuine general response to social realities, they are also in danger of negatively evaluating people and situations unjustly; discourses produced in a situation of global terror, especially reacting to some perceived 'war' or violence on children or a global campaign on security and children's rights to education in Africa such as *#BringBackOurGirls*, are most likely to ideologically (mis)represent facts, government or institutions. Emotional ideological evaluations of social actors and situations alone may achieve practically nothing, leaving the main problems of insecurity unsolved. In other words, they may end up as mere *slacktivism*. 'Slacktivism' (i.e. slacker and activism) is the low-risk, low-cost activity via social media whose

Innocent
Chiluwa
and
Presley
Ifukor

purpose is to raise awareness, or grant some emotional satisfaction to the persons engaged in the activity (Lee and Hsieh, 2013), such as clicking 'like' to show support for a group on *Facebook*, signing online petitions, or forwarding letters or videos about an issue. According to Morozov (2009), slacktivism is based on the assumption that, given enough awareness, all problems are solvable, when in actual fact they only make the participants feel good and very useful and important, but the efforts themselves have zero social impact. Morse (2014) further observes that 'the problem with hashtag activism is that information spreads very fast on social media and an inaccurate image or tweet goes twice around the world before the truth has time to put on his tie'.

[...]

We argue in this article that a social media campaigns [sic] can be highly successful if they are followed up simultaneously with offline actions like those of Tunisia, Egypt or Libya (see also Christensen, 2011). Our aim in this article therefore is to contribute to discourse stance literature by (1) showing how stance in social media discourse aids the spread of online protests and civil campaigns, (2) analysing how affective stance in this campaign exhibits ideological evaluations of social actors or governments and (3) revealing how affect expressed in this way can provide a cover for mere social media campaign 'supports', without practical efforts to solve the problems of insecurity and lack of freedom in Africa.

[...]

Methodology

Our data are derived from a corpus of 2500 tweets and 2500 *Facebook* posts comprising 24,983 words. A keyword analysis of the corpus was carried out using Wordsmith to determine the key lexical components of the corpus, especially key lexical items that express evaluation and affective stance. In compiling the keywords, the Nairaland corpus (compiled from the Cyber-Creole Project of the University of Freiburg) was used as a reference corpus. We examined the linguistic contexts within which key (evaluative) words occurred. Since it was difficult to draw examples of affect and judgement expressed in the data electronically following our method of analysis, we utilized only a qualitative method by analyzing samples from the raw data. The quantitative keyword analysis only gave us an idea of the kind of lexical items that are available in the corpus. Thus, our analysis is essentially qualitative since interpretive (critical) discourse analysis of the data is carried out in relation to the context [...] **FBP** stands for 'Facebook post', while **TWT** stands for 'tweet' [...]

Constructing the Crisis

[...] Since affect is an emotional reaction to behaviour, process or phenomena (Martin and White, 2005), it is natural that the *act* of kidnapping of the girls is generally constructed with negative emotions expressed in words such as 'despicable', 'shameful', 'disgusting', 'cowardly', 'outrage', 'brutality' and so on. The negative evaluations of the activities of BH reflected in the above words are instances of inscribed attitude and are used to explicitly express the writers' judgement, which also has the invoked attitude potential to influence the readers' evaluation of the crisis. As a matter of fact, these

SOCIAL MEDIA ONLINE CAMPAIGNS   239

D11

Innocent
Chiluwa
and
Presley
Ifukor

negative evaluations are mutually shared by all the campaigners given the context and situation of the crisis. The samples below show that negative evaluations of the situation are reactions to what has been read in the (social) media or heard people say about the crisis and not necessarily from what individuals already knew about the events in the country or their individual commitments to the events […]

> **FBP1.** Susan Scritchfield. *Shameful*, such *thievery* and *brutality* to try *to steal* the future from these beautiful young lives and their loved ones. *Cowardly* to *repress* human potential.
>
> **FBP3.** In the last few weeks we have seen a *horrific onslaught of violence* against women.
>
> **FBP4.** Grace Sim Auta. This is just *crazy* and *unacceptable*!
>
> **FBP5.** Kim Spellmon. Bring back our girls please and stop the *foolishness* of wicked men. This type of *sickness* among men is *despicable*. The very beautiful thing that you have *stolen in* the name of your sharia law is the Law of Life.

Discursive structure of the campaign

[…] most of the examples from the data below are the acts addressed to the campaign participants, urging them to get more involved in the campaign:

> **FBP6.** Four simple actions that will make a difference for the 300 Nigerian schoolgirls that were kidnapped: *Write/call* your government leaders, *demand* they help Nigeria *Share* this news with your friends and family *Organize* a rally; *march* or vigil and *spread* the news in your community. *Repeat …*
>
> **TWT1.** *Let the world know* that the #nigerianschoolgirls have not been forgotten. RT this and spread the message: #BringBackOurGirls

As highlighted in the literature above, affect is not only conveyed through words but also longer grammatical structures as well as paralinguistic information. In other words, affects expressed in the campaign discourse go beyond lexical items to include phrases and whole text samples, reflecting the general mood of the campaign/crisis. For instance, the verbs (or acts) such as *write, share, organize, raise* and so on express the general sense of urgency, anxiety and desperation in the tone of the entire samples.

Representing BH

In the appraisal of BH and their actions, certain evaluations are explicitly stated, for instance, referring to them as 'terrorists', 'kidnappers', 'rapists' or 'murderers', which are based on the general knowledge of the Islamist group and their activities. Some of the evaluations are implicit, again reflecting an invoked evaluation. For instance **FBP16** says: 'real men respect women everywhere in the world'. By implication, BH are not the '*real* men' of a cultured society in terms of their handling of women. This invoked attitude is indirectly inviting a negative evaluation of BH from the reader according to the writer's judgement. Other evaluations are encoded in rhetorical devices such as metaphor (e.g. referring to BH as '*orphans* of cultured learning'). In all the representations (e.g. below), negative affect is clearly expressed in the words used in the samples, most of which express sadness, anger and disapproval. For instance, in **FBP5** above, they are referred to as 'wicked men'. The noun phrase 'wicked men' referring to BH is a negative judgement but also a clear example of an inscribed evaluation, which presupposes how the reader should evaluate them. There is also an invoked attitude here, which the inscribed evaluation is implicitly inviting the reader to share. The same goes for all the negative evaluations of BH in the samples. Of course, all evaluations (negative or positive) reflect affect. For example, the adjective 'wicked' describing a subject is an evaluative judgement but at the same time implies negative emotion (e.g. anger, disgust or sadness) [...]

Representing the Nigerian government

Most of the representations of the Nigerian government involve the use of highly emotional evaluative words, many of them depicting disdain, anger and hate. Some of the negative evaluations were reacting to the general perception that the Nigerian government was not doing enough to rescue the girls; some campaigners attributed their ineffectiveness to indolence and incompetence.

> **FBP18**. Ernest Brown. *Damn fools*!!!! Spend that money on finding the girls, or on pplane tickets so real men can come and help!
> **TWT7**. #BokoHaram will end up kidnapping or killing all Nigerians bcos the *government doesn't care*! #Bringbackourgirls [...]

Representing the kidnapped girls as victims

[...] In the data, words and expressions that reflect appreciation are those that acknowledge the potentials of the kidnapped girls or to implicitly identify or align with their present suffering. Thus, there are expressions that reflect positive affect such as 'beautiful things' (showing admiration) and the use of rhetorical devices (e.g. metaphor), for example, describing them as the 'law of life' in **FBP5** above. This description probably alludes to their natural potential as wife and mother. In many African traditional contexts, women are viewed as the custodian of life because of their power to bear children; hence, anything that threatens them, threatens life. The feeling of sadness and sympathy is also expressed in words such as 'abandoned' or 'forgotten' in **TWT12** [...] They are also generally (and rightly so) constructed as the victim or the 'innocent', and this kind of evaluation is prompted in order to construct the gravity of (and possibly exaggerate) the criminal activities of BH. Referring to them as 'innocent' is a positive judgement, while the kidnapping itself is described as wickedness or 'sickness' in **FBP5** [...]

Representing the world

Since the BH problem was now viewed as a global 'tragedy', which is beyond what Nigeria alone can handle, the campaigners began to expect some decisive interventions by nations of the world regardless of some diplomatic or legal implications. Besides, the lukewarm attitude of world leaders who expected a formal invitation from Nigeria for assistance was criticized and generally viewed as irresponsible. As highlighted above, some campaigners interpreted Western inaction from a racial point of view, arguing that the world would have intervened if the crisis had happened in Europe or America. Thus, the world is generally constructed as a selfish and uncaring place to live in, especially because the kind of action expected of the entire world after three months of the girls' kidnap was not forthcoming. Affective stance, in the samples below, express disappointment, sadness, bitterness and anger expressed not only in individual words and phrases, but also in the general tone of the whole text samples [...]

Innocent Chiluwa and Presley Ifukor

> **FBP21**. Lorelei YolandaBcool Scott. *That's outrageous*! Can u imagine 200 schoolgirls being kidnapped in the UK? Or America? Or any civilised society? That would never be left until they were found! I hope those girls in the future somehow find their own way back to their families. Nigerian government, hang your heads in utter and disgraceful shame.
>
> **TWT18**. These girls are still kidnapped and we *just go on* and *move on with our lives*. Are we not humans anymore? #BringbackOurGirls [...]

Again notice an invoked attitude in expressions such as 'the world has forgotten', 'stopped caring', 'we just go on and move on with our lives', which not only evoke emotional responses from the reader, but also negative judgement of the global community. There is the constant question of why the 'bring back our girls campaign' had suddenly declined in its tempo. It was as if it was all over after the few months of the incident. In the samples below, the writers begin to assess the usefulness and relevance of all the social media campaign noise after all, and conclude that it was simply 'another day in twittersphere' [...]

> **TWT22**. I guess we now agree that #twitter won't #bringbackourgirls
> **FBP23**. So the world *stops tweeting* about #bringbackourgirls. 219 girls *still missing* and this is *just another day* in twittersphere.

Issues to consider

❑ Chiluwa and Ifukor's article demonstrates that both quantitative data gathering methodologies and qualitative close analysis of social discourses can yield fruitful research findings. As pointed out in B1, many CDA approaches to language now incorporate some level of corpus linguistic methods into analysis. The appendices attached to this article in the journal *Discourse and Society* contain the quantitative statistics upon which the discussions above are based. (See also the web materials that accompany this book for more discussion of corpus techniques in CDA).

❑ The conclusion of the extract above refers to a frequently cited issue regarding social media activism and whether or not it yields tangible results. You might think about this question further in the context of some of the commentary in A11 regarding the power of social media in general to act as an effective counterbalance to traditional power bases. The *#BringBackOurGirls* campaign saw initial success when it was aligned with and supported by the interests of powerful elites. Can we locate a correlation between the declining newsworthiness of the kidnapping event and the waning presence of the campaign which it sparked?

D12   POPULISM AND POST-TRUTH POLITICS

The following reading, by the internationally renowned linguist Robin Lakoff (see Strand 4), offers additional critical linguistic perspectives on the intersection between post-truth and the rise of populism, with specific reference to Donald Trump's election victory in 2016. Lakoff accounts for Trump's communicative strategies through a continuum that extends from 'lie', through 'post-truth', 'truthiness', and 'alternative facts', to 'truth'. Lakoff also asks the question: is Trump really a populist? In an entertaining and provocative reading, Lakoff interrogates Trump's many perceived idiosyncrasies in discourse, and discusses his supporters' seeming willingness to overlook them. Moreover, Lakoff probes in very interesting ways issues around gendered roles and stereotypes in the 'machismo' arena that constitutes contemporary politics.

Robin Tolmach Lakoff

The hollow man: Donald Trump, populism, and post-truth politics.

Robin Tolmach Lakoff (reprinted from *Journal of Language and Politics* 16 (4) (2017): 595–606).

[...] The Wizard of Oz

The most memorable aphorism coming out of the 2016 election has to be this: 'The press takes Trump literally but not seriously. Trump's supporters take him seriously but not literally' (Zito 2016). What exactly is this supposed to mean? Why is the 'right answer' the one Trump's supporters are offering? Is this the right choice – that Trump must be either 'serious' or 'literal'?

I don't think the epigram means anything. It is wrong to take Trump *either* seriously *or* literally: either choice would imply that Trump's utterances mean *something*, or are intended to mean something. What we are dealing with, and will probably be dealing with for the next eight years, is a 21st century Wizard of Oz – someone with no 'there' there [...]

The wise men

There are others than Trump who bear some responsibility for our predicament. First there are the 'elites', the public intellectuals and the media savants, who didn't take the Trump phenomenon seriously in the first place, but expended their wrath on his opponent. A few of them are now turning that anger back upon themselves, attacking intellectual 'elites', glamorizing and legitimizing his supporters, finding a putative nobility in their alleged reasons for supporting him.

What no one wanted to talk about during the campaign was what *really* elected Trump. It's true that the reasons for his victory, like any complex group phenomenon, are multiple. It's true that economic factors were important: the fact that the 'good jobs' working class people have expected as their due are vanishing with no solution in sight. But anyone listening seriously to Trump could tell that he didn't have a clue any more than anyone else. 'I'm going to create *millions* of *wonderful* jobs!' is no more a program or felicitous promise than 'I will be your voice!', and what needs to be explained, above all else, is why so many people, including many who should have known better, chose to hear it as if it were.

Robin
Tolmach
Lakoff

My own theory: it's very significantly about misogyny, a word seldom encountered in post-election analyses, and when uttered, usually dismissively. And why not? When pollsters asked voters why they had voted for Trump, they never said, 'Because I'd never vote for a woman for president', and virtuously offered the answers they were supposed to give, 'He tells it like it is. He will find us jobs'.

You have to assume that Trump voters are either unusually stupid, or remarkably evasive. I opt for the latter. *Of course* no one, speaking into a microphone, is going to identify himself (or herself) as a troglodytic woman-hater! But I suspect that, if so many of us didn't have deep worries about what it would mean for a woman to achieve the most symbolically powerful role in the world, Hillary Clinton would have been sworn in as president. Yes, certainly, voters wanted their candidates to recognize their economic distress and offer solutions for it. But (and it is here that the pundits fall parlously short) the fact is that neither candidate had the opportunity in our putative 'debates' to discuss at length any cure for the job crisis, but a lot of people, both Trump supporters and media analysts, heard Trump's empty rhetoric on the subject with more approbation than they heard Clinton's attempts to define her more serious perspective. She at least tried, but a remarkable number of political commentators and public intellectuals are on record as favoring Trump's blather over Clinton's trying.

Another part of the blame game were the incessant complaints about how Clinton was running a bad campaign. She wasn't 'spontaneous'. She was 'scripted'. She couldn't 'connect'. She was 'evasive'. There is a great deal to be said about these charges. One reason for Clinton's lack of 'spontaneity' is that, during her years in the public spotlight, she has been relentlessly mauled by the very critics who grumble about her non-spontaneity. When she shows spontaneity, her words are mercilessly subjected to microscopic inspection, giving them 'meanings' she never intended. As I have argued elsewhere (Lakoff 2000), this is a frequent way of silencing and demonizing public women. The natural response was hers, to become exceptionally cautious when speaking in public. So the pundits created this Clinton and then attacked her for becoming what they had forced her to become. Trump's emptiness, or hollowness, gets the most favorable interpretation; Clinton's meaningfulness is trashed.

Moreover, the tone of the discussion of Clinton, by both Trump and his supporters, went well beyond the usual overheated presidential campaign rhetoric in its vitriol. She was a 'traitor'. 'Hang her!' and 'shoot her!' became a common refrain at his rallies. He regularly described her as the 'worst' secretary of state we had ever had (no evidence provided), after previously calling her the best; he regularly described her as 'weak' and 'sickly'. Here too, analysis and critique were lacking.

Then there is the format of presidential debates in our time. Candidates are permitted only very short turns – a couple of minutes each. Suppose a candidate actually had a meaningful solution to our economic crisis. There is no way to express that in

**Robin
Tolmach
Lakoff**

two minutes. So presidential 'debates' necessarily become exercises in razzle-dazzle rhetoric as opposed to the serious examination of viable solutions But this campaign was unique in its persistent name-calling and infantile behavior, initiated and pursued by one candidate much more than the other, who was not subjected to nearly as much criticism for infantile style and substance as he should have been. But, generally covertly, Trump's performances were viewed as legitimate, because a man was performing them. Clinton's were derided and savaged, because as a woman, she had no right to speak publicly; no right to seek the position she was seeking; no right, most deeply, to ask for something, especially power, for herself. So any way she spoke, anything she said, was *wrong*. The explicit critiques were the excuses the critics found to rationalize their misgivings. The refusal to acknowledge the role of misogyny in this election is in itself deeply misogynistic, and an indication that the Oval Office door still has a sign on it: BOYS ONLY.

The 2016 election was persistently viewed as having as its theme Change vs. the Status Quo, with Trump representing the former. But in fact Clinton was the true 'change' candidate: had she been elected, our perceptions of the permissible relationship between gender and power, in existence since we became *Homo sapiens* if not before, would have had to change. That would have been (as is now all too clear) intolerable to too many Americans.

Moreover, the candidates themselves and how they were treated represented current and persistent gender stereotypes in peculiar ways. Trump wants desperately to be and to seem a macho man, a Super-Male. So he barks in sentence fragments; he recycles the same words and phrases over and over; he boasts; he bullies; he creates warlike antagonism; he always has to be Number One, bigger-than and better-than. His ratings, polls, crowds, hands, and other body parts have to be bigger than anyone else's.

And yet at the same time, when he isn't being careful, he shows himself to be not a man at all. His gestures are effeminate. His use of comparative and superlative forms (and especially *so* and *such*) is characteristic of stereotypical female speech; even the sneer that sometimes comes into his voice when talking about anyone other than himself has a stereotypically 'ladylike' edge to it, like gossiping. So he is not a Schwarzenegerian manly man; he is but a girly-man in manly clothing.

On the other hand, Clinton is perceived as an unlawful female. In her public speech she is not flirtatious or deferential. This, too, makes her scary to the insecure, male and female both. So Trump's gender insecurities work in his favor; Clinton's transcendence of traditional gender roles works against her. We will not see a female president unless and until American culture works its way out of this rathole.

[...] The popular Trump

A 'populist' by definition is someone whose political sympathies lie with the non-elite and marginalized. Trump has announced, rather peculiarly: 'I *love* the poorly educated!' Is this sufficient to establish him as a populist?

Well, no. Someone whose residences are noted for their gold-plated fixtures is not a populist; someone whose chosen companions (he seems to have no living friends) are plutocrats is not a populist; one who appoints only multibillionaires to cabinet

Robin
Tolmach
Lakoff

positions is not a populist. So the pundits' understanding of Trump as a 'populist' who goes up against the 'elites' (like themselves) in support of the 'regular' folks is based on nothing but that (a) he says he is and (b) he wears a baseball cap. The fact that someone speaks ungrammatically ('bigly') and in sentence fragments does not make him a populist; the fact that someone's utterances consist mostly of self-aggrandizing superlatives and playground insults makes him a narcissist, not a populist. Trump's frequent use of third-person self-reference ('If Putin likes Donald Trump, I consider that an asset') is not the language of a populist but rather of an egomaniac.

So Trump is not a populist, or indeed an anythingist. Populists, like all other politicians, have to have some set of core beliefs. To be an –ist, you need an –ism, and –isms are rooted in semantics. Trump no more believes in 'power to the people' than I believe in the Tooth Fairy. (He doesn't believe in 'No power to the people' either; he just doesn't have beliefs.) […]

The death of truth

Since Trump came into public notice, an astonishing level of interpretive effort has been lavished on his tweets and other utterances. For some commentators Trump functions as an unreliable Delphic Oracle: there must be some kernel of meaning whose truth value can be discerned by the cryptanalyst. But how to find it? And why does every cryptanalyst wannabe come up with a *different* Trump and a *different* truth (if any)? Many interpreters of the Trump phenomenon seem unable to accept the reality: America has installed a president who has no 'meaning'. His grammar does not contain a semantic component relating linguistic forms to extra-linguistic referents. He leaps nimbly over semantics, going directly from tortured syntax to objectionable pragmatics. He is not interested in making sense, or discerning truth (semantics); his only concern is how to win friends and influence people (pragmatics).

Hence Trump cannot be considered a 'liar', although he regularly says things that are demonstrably false. To be a lie, a proposition must: (1) be demonstrably false; (2) be known to the teller to be false; (3) be told to give some advantage to the teller. In the case of Trump's untruthfulnesses, (1) and (3) are certainly in evidence, but (2) is more problematic. It isn't just that Trump doesn't know when he is telling the truth, when a lie; it goes deeper than that: because Trump's grammar lacks a semantic component, he is incapable of even imagining a distinction between truth and falsehood; those concepts, and the distinction between them that is intrinsic to most human intercourse, are simply absent for Trump. This is not a good quality in anyone, and still less for a person with power. But it is worst of all in the president of the most powerful nation on earth. Negotiating with such a personage will be a very dangerous game indeed. Rather than feeling a need to justify his positions and plans with evidence, all Trump is concerned with in his public communications is whether people like him: he is desperate to be liked, and that is why he is president. Hence, too, his fixation on his numbers and sizes. They are as close as he gets to meaning; they constitute his meaning and identity, his semantics. So he gets frantic, threatening, and abusive when those 'likability' numbers aren't coming out right. Thus we see, quite disturbingly, at the recent news conference of Trump and [UK premier] Theresa May, Trump blandly giving his full (verbal) support to NATO, which during the campaign he repeatedly vowed to abolish. But at this discussion he clearly wanted to cozy up to May, and said what she clearly wanted to hear. There is no way to tell which of the diametrically opposite positions Trump actually espouses. The answer: neither. [...]

If Trump were merely a habitual liar, he would be less dangerous: liars almost inevitably are outed sooner or later; they give themselves away so thoroughly that even their perfervid supporters defect. But people like Trump, who simply open their mouths and out comes whatever, at that moment, for this audience, is *le mot juste*, cannot be discredited, or shamed, or forced to recant. And as long as Trump seems to his supporters to be saying what has to be said and telling it like it is – his are the nonverbal accompaniments of truth-telling – he will be secure in his office.

Functional democracy is predicated on mutual trust between governors and governed, as laid out in the Preamble to the U.S. Constitution. Someone whose truthfulness isn't even available for questioning destroys trust at every level. American democracy has survived many challenges over the course of its existence, but the current situation evokes new worries. [...]

What do Trump's supporters want?

Since every discourse, including voting, is cooperatively constructed, it makes sense to ask, What do Trump's supporters see in him? Why did working class voters vote for him, despite a plethora of unpresidential traits? Why did they see him as one of them, despite the mansions and the golf courses?

Well, they told the pollsters: he would get them jobs, he would restore their self-respect, he would MAKE AMERICA GREAT AGAIN. He would bring back a past Eden, a Golden Age.

Many cultures have a past Golden Age among their myths, and America has more than one: there is the Biblical story of Eden, and there is our foundational epic, in which George Washington never told a lie, Lincoln fought the Civil War to free the slaves, and we were and remain a most perfect union. America's most recent Golden Age was located somewhat fuzzily around the 1950s, after the war that made the U.S. the leader of the free world, and before all the disturbances of the '60s, when the laws changed to allow others than white males entrée into all the good things America had to offer: education, jobs, power, status. That was the snake in the Trump voters' Eden. For that brief shining moment between 1945 and 1973, America was Great for the Trump constituency. To Make America Great Again, the results of the Civil Rights and Women's Movements had to be undone.

The slogan itself is a coded message, recognized by Trump's supporters but not so much (explicitly) by the media analysts and the intelligentsia: bring America back to when white males could count on getting all the pie, not just their fair share of it.

Back then, straight white native-born men could talk and act just as Trump did in 2016: be as racist, homophobic, xenophobic, and misogynist as America had been back when it was Great. What seemed to his opponents embarrassingly antediluvian was to his fervent supporters evidence of his willingness to take us back to that Golden Age. Trump 'told it like it is' because he talked the talk of *Mad Men* and George Wal-

Robin Tolmach Lakoff

lace (the virulently segregationist governor of Alabama during most of the 1960s). People didn't vote for him (as the apologist intelligentsia would have it) despite his vile behaviors and utterances, but because of them. [...]

During the campaign, he [Trump] repeatedly used 'sarcastic' to describe a statement of his when an interviewer pointed out that it had a meaning antithetical to known reality. For instance, on August 12 he stated – reiterated several times – that Barack Obama had 'founded ISIS'. When the absurdity of the claim was pointed out, rather than apologizing, he said that he was only being 'sarcastic'.

He may have been being all sorts of things, but in the normal sense of 'sarcasm' ('1. a sharp and often satirical or ironic utterance designed to cut or give pain. 2a : a mode of satirical wit depending for its effect on bitter, caustic, and often ironic language that is usually directed against an individual', according to the Merriam-Webster Dictionary [see also Strand 6 of this book]), sarcastic was not what he was being. The use of that term throws the responsibility for the malapropism to the hearer/interviewer: 'You don't understand sarcasm? How stupid of you!' [...]

Truthiness and consequences

Humans believe in an antithesis: *truth* vs. *lie*. We understand that the latter is dangerous and in most cases intolerable in a social species whose continued existence depends on mutual trust. Hence the use of 'liar' can be dangerous. But that clear dichotomy is no more. In recent times American public discourse has evolved something closer to a semantic continuum or spectrum, obfuscating a clear distinction:

Lie … 'alternative fact' … fake news … post-truth … truthiness … truth/fact/reality

'Alternative fact' was offered by Trump's newly installed White House advisor Kelly-anne Conway on January 22, 2017, disputing the size of Trump's Inaugural Speech audience [see unit A12]. [...] 'Fake news', a term in common use at least since election day, refers to stories found on global web sites that masquerade as and use the format of genuine news but are deliberately manufactured fictions (one example being the story that a pizzeria in Washington functioned as the locus of a child-sex business run by Hillary Clinton). Recently, the Trump team has taken to using 'fake news' as a synonym for 'what is reported in the non-alt-right press' [...]. 'Post-truth' is defined by the Oxford Dictionaries, which selected it as their word of the year (2016), as statements 'relating to or denoting circumstances in which objective facts are less influential in shaping public opinion than appeals to emotion and personal belief'.

Just as 'post-racial' was (sincerely, if too optimistically) created in the aftermath of Barack Obama's election to describe an America in which a black man could be elected president, a 'post-truth' national discourse is defined (cynically) as one in which 'truthiness' (a word created and defined ironically by Stephen Colbert), is defined by Merriam-Webster (its 2006 word of the year) as, 'The quality of preferring concepts or facts one wishes to be true, rather than concepts or facts known to be true', very much in competition with 'truth' as what one does when not overtly 'lying'.

The whole set, of course, must take its place alongside older terms like 'prevarication' and 'equivocation', also devised to provide a semantic bridge between 'truth' and 'lie'; and newer ones like 'plausible/credible deniability', which describe ways of avoiding accountability.

The very fact that there is no universal agreement that there are illegitimate ways to construct an argument gives legitimacy to Trump and his supporters; it becomes harder to pin them down and justifies all kinds of slippage, verbal and otherwise. If you have a word for it, it must be legitimate.

When a powerful man has a faith in his own virtue and intelligence that is as unjustified as it is absolute, a quick and petulant temper, and a finger (however short) on the nuclear button, there is reason to be uneasy. When those who talk about him and hear about him daily and have to decide how to think about him can no longer have the confidence to determine whether he is speaking the truth or something else, there is reason to be really scared. [...]

Issues to consider

❑ At time of writing, president Trump is involved in an altercation with the president of North Korea, Kim Jong Un. After Kim asserted that he had a nuclear button at the ready, Trump tweeted (on 2/01/2018) that the U.S. button was bigger and more powerful than Kim's. The tweet was apparently designed to keep the North Korean leader 'on his toes'. To what extent are Lakoff's observations above germane to this exchange between the leaders? In particular, can you locate the exchange in her discussion of personality traits?

❑ Lakoff incorporates ideas from language and gender studies in her essay, and specifically, from her own work on the characteristics of 'female speech' (see Strand 4). To what extent are these ideas reflected in the political discourse of your own culture? That is, is this a recognizable pattern in the behaviour of politicians in your own country? Do the same 'machismo' practices exist? And if so, are these practices accompanied by (perhaps more subtle) 'non-macho' behaviour of the sort Lakoff identifies in her essay?

❑ Look again at the edited version of the inaugural address of President Trump which can be found in unit C10. Can Lakoff's observations be applied to (parts of) this text? And to what extent are Lakoff's provocative comments borne out by the discourse strategies that are embedded in Trump's speech?

FURTHER READING

Strand 1: Language and power

It would be remiss of us not to mention 'the competition' here, and there exist a number of useful textbooks that explore language and power in various ways. These include Bloor and Bloor (2007) which contains an accessible introduction to CDA and covers important topics such as gender, race, consumerism and law together with suggested activities at the end of each chapter. Similarly, Mooney and Evans (2015) provide useful introductions to contemporary issues in language, society and power (media, ethnicity, gender, language and age, global English).

Of course, Fairclough (1989; second edition 2001) remains the ground-breaking study in the more modern idiom of CDA, and Fairclough (2010) is a second edition of his lengthy text dedicated to CDA. A companion volume to Fowler and his colleagues' classic study (Fowler *et al.* 1979) is Kress and Hodge (1979), which is a good illustration of the older style approach of CL. Machin and Mayr (2012) provide a very useful practical instruction in Multimodal CDA, addressing a number of media also discussed in the present book. Wodak and Meyer (2015) outline CDA analysis of online and visual texts alongside more traditional approaches.

Young and Fitzgerald's book (2006) offers a theoretical introduction to both Systemic Functional Linguistics and CDA, along with a range of sample analyses from topics such as war, gender, racism, advertising and organizations. Van Dijk's volume (2008), in addition to serving as a useful introduction to CDA, brings together some of his most important writing on political discourse and on discourse and racism.

Strand 2: The discourse of institutions and organizations

Mayr (2004) offers a detailed linguistic analysis, from a combined SFL/CDA point of view, of the spoken and written institutional discourse within a prison. The study is also informed by a sociological description of social control discourse. Mayr (2008) offers a useful overview of the different conceptualizations of power and analyses a variety of institutional contexts, such as academia, prison, media and the military.

Drew and Sorjonen (1997), in a paper on 'institutional dialogue', provide a useful overview of previous work on institutional discourse while McHoul and Rapley (2001) offer a set of methods for analysing talk in institutional settings. Koester (2013) explores the characteristics of workplace conversations, and Mullany (2011) considers gendered workplace discourses.

Abousnnouga and Machin's multimodal analysis of British war monuments (2008) is an important investigation of the power of institutions to control discourses through visual texts, as is Machin's multimodal analysis of photographs of the Iraq occupation (2007b).

Strand 3: Power and talk

An extensive treatment of power dynamics in spoken institutional discourse can be found in Mayr (2004), a detailed linguistic study of classroom interactions in a prison (and see above). Thornborrow's analysis of British radio phone-ins (2003) is a useful addition to Hutchby's analysis of the same topic (1996). Another useful study is Thornborrow (2007), in which she applies CA to an examination of narrative discourse in the development of arguments in the British television talk show *Kilroy*.

Sarangi and Roberts (1999) focus on the discourse of medical, mediation and management settings. Finally, S. O'Halloran (2005, 2008) is the first to deal comprehensively with the spoken and written discourse of Alcoholics Anonymous (AA) meetings, challenging the notion that institutional discourse is always asymmetrical.

Strand 4: Language and gender

A key book-length study of language and gender is Cameron (2006b), which contains a collection of thought-provoking and insightful linguistic analyses of language, gender and sexuality combined with a feminist political orientation. Cameron (1985) remains a landmark contribution to the way gender intersects with theories of language and linguistics, while Cameron (1995) explores what she refers to as 'verbal hygiene' in respect of the way in which women are expected to use language. Cameron (2008) is a popular critique of what she refers to as the 'myth' of Mars and Venus. Cameron and Shaw (2016) is a shorter monograph specifically focussed on gender in political speeches in a single British election campaign. Litosseliti and Sunderland's collection (2002) is a useful survey of important topics in feminist linguistics, focusing in particular on the continuous construction of a range of masculine and feminine identities. Talbot (2014) is a second edition of a lengthy overview of language and gender studies, analysing speech in a wide range of scenarios.

Other significant edited collections on language and gender include Lazar's volume (2005) which brings together scholars writing from feminist perspectives within Critical Discourse Analysis. The theoretical structure of CDA is illustrated with empirical examples demonstrating the complex workings of power and ideology in discourse in sustaining particular gender(ed) orders. The areas studied range from parliamentary settings, news and advertising media, the classroom, community literacy programmes and the workplace. Benwell's edited collection (2003) explores constructions of masculinity in men's lifestyle magazines, their production and consumption, drawing on sociology, media studies, cultural studies and linguistics. A range of methodologies are explored, including interviews with magazine editors, focus groups with readers, corpus linguistics and discourse analysis. A recent chapter by Benwell (2014) in the second edition of Ehrlich, Meyerhoff and Holmes' influential collection on gendered identities explores the discourse of 'gross out', culturally associated with masculinity. Benwell (2005) and Page (2003) are important articles on gender.

Jeffries' critical discourse analysis of the textual construction of the female body in women's magazines (2007) offers a sobering account of how these magazines exert pressure to make women conform to the ideology of the perfect body, an issue taken up by Ringrow (2016) in analysing cosmetics advertising in English and French.

Strand 5: Language and race

A useful application of a CDA approach to the analysis of racism in the press can be found in Teo's investigation of two Australian newspapers (2000). Van Leeuwen's chapter on the *visual* representation of 'others' in a variety of Western media (2008) is a useful example of the visual application of his Social Actor model.

Wodak and Reisigl (1999) examine the discoursal representation of racism from a European perspective, while Gabrielatos and Baker's article (2008) is a significant recent investigation of the discursive construction of refugees and asylum seekers in a corpus-based analysis of UK tabloid and broadsheet newspapers, revealing a number of (mainly negative) categories of representation for asylum seekers.

An important analysis of racial prejudice can be found in van Leeuwen and Wodak's article on immigration control in Austria (1999), while Cottle's edited volume (2000) is a useful collection of (mainly) media-oriented papers on recent developments in the representation of ethnic minorities in the media. In the context of Cottle's collection, it is worth drawing attention to Husband's (2000) study of the media representation of multi-ethnic societies, whilst the monograph by Richardson (2004) examines the (mis)representation of Islam in British broadsheet newspapers which continues unabated. Buckledee (2018) examines the role of racism ('lite' and 'not so lite') in the 2016 Brexit referendum campaign. Orelus (2016) takes a CDA approach to analysing racial language in schools.

Strand 6: Humour, language and power

There exist a number of book-length treatments of verbal humour. The classic (and most accessible) study of the language of humour is Nash (1985), which offers an entertaining survey of its main devices and techniques. Ross (1998) is a textbook pitched at the most introductory level. The language of jokes is at the heart of Chiaro's introductory textbook (1992) while puns come under detailed scrutiny in Redfern (2000). A recent article by Weaver, Mora and Morgan (2016) examines humour and gender and provides useful, accessible introductions, whilst the collection edited by Chlopicki and Brzozowska (2017) applies models in discourse analysis, sociolinguistics and cognitive linguistics to examine humorous discourse.

Of the more advanced studies, Attardo's two books (1994 and 2001) are generally useful accounts of humour strategies in language while Simpson (2003) looks specifically at contemporary political satire in his study. Simpson's book also includes a case study of satire and the law which synthesizes some of the issues covered across Strands 6 and 7 in this book.

Mulkay (1988) approaches humour from the perspective of sociology and politics, and Apte (1985) from the perspective of anthropology. Lennon (2008a) is a study that looks specifically at the construction of non-verbal humour. Norrick (1993) examines joking in everyday spoken interaction and, as we have seen, Billig's book (2005) has of course particularly important significance for the study of humour and power. Davies (1990) is a study of 'ethnic jokes' from around the world which are classified into core typologies, and this more 'celebratory' treatment of ethnic humour is worth contrasting with the position taken by Billig. Weaver (2013) also examines the rhetoric of racist humour, whilst Tsakona and Popa (2011) consider the issue of political humour. A useful broad-ranging collection in this area is Routledge's *Handbook of the Language of Humor* (Attardo 2017). Finally, readers interested in the broader academic study of humour might find the international journal *Humor* useful.

Strand 7: Language and the law

The academic interests of forensic linguists are served by two important associations whose web pages are easily accessible: the International Association of Forensic Linguistics (IAFL) and the International Association for Forensic Phonetics and Acoustics (IAFPA). The key journal in this area is the *International Journal of Speech, Language and the Law* which, until 2003, was known as *Forensic Linguistics*.

As indicated throughout this Strand, numerous books have been published in the broad area of Forensic Linguistics, and most of these make for accessible and compelling reading, largely because of the hands-on involvement of their authors and because of the detailed recounting of real case histories they provide. An important collection of essays is Cotterill (2002), while Cotterill (2003) is a monograph that focuses on the civil trial of O.J. Simpson in 1994–95, whilst Cotterill (2007) contains articles that examine the language of sexual assault. As signalled in A7, work by the American linguist Roger Shuy has been a major scholarly influence in this area and good examples of his practice can be found in Shuy (1998, 2006). An important paper on the dilemma faced by forensic linguists about whether or not to testify in certain cases is Shuy (2002), while a particularly sensitive and compassionate exploration of the importance of language testimony in the judicial process is Shuy (2005). An ongoing series examines the language of a range of specific cases in which Shuy has served as an expert witness, focussed on the crimes of defamation (Shuy, 2010), perjury (Shuy, 2011), sexual misconduct (Shuy, 2012), bribery (Shuy, 2013), murder (Shuy, 2014), and fraud (Shuy, 2016). A collection edited by Solan, Ainsworth and Shuy (2015) pays tribute to the forensic linguistic work of the late Peter Tiersma.

Other important books on Forensic Linguistics are Coulthard, Johnson and Wright (2016), Gibbons (1994, 2003), Schane (2006), Solan and Tiersma (2005), Stygall (1994) and Tiersma (1999). Many of these books have appendices containing valuable transcriptions of court cases and related legal discourse. Matoesian (1993) concentrates on the discourse of rape cases in the USA, whilst Matoesian (2001) examines the language of a specific rape case. Olsson (2004) has, in addition to appendices of legal data, a useful collection of exercises and worked examples. Finally, Statham (2016) examines the process of trial by media, utilizing models in forensic linguistics, cognitive linguistics and CDA to propose a critical-forensic interface for the analysis of media language alongside trial language.

Strand 8: Language and advertising

Reflecting the widespread interest among linguists in this area of study, there are many good books on advertising discourse that come at the subject from a variety of scholarly perspectives. Myers (1994), Cook (1992) and Vestergaard and Shrøder (1985) are three very useful introductory books on the general characteristics of advertising discourse. More advanced book-length studies are Forceville (1995), which examines pictorial metaphors in ads, and Tanaka (1994), which uses a relevance-theoretical model to explore the pragmatics of advertising. Other important books include O'Barr (1994) and Ohmann (1996), and of course, as we pointed out in the Strand, Machin's introduction to multimodality (2007a) makes extensive use of adverts.

Older language-oriented books on advertising, some of which have been re-issued since initial publication, are Williamson (1978), Geis (1982) and Goffman (1976). Finally, useful articles and chapters in books include Thornborrow's study of gender positions in ads (1994), while puns in advertising discourse are the focus of Redfern's article (1982). The articles by Coleman (1990), Kress (1987) and Toolan (1988) are more general in scope, while Delin (2000) includes a helpful chapter, drawing on Fairclough's model, on the language of advertising.

Strand 9: Language in the new capitalism

Machin and van Leeuwen (2007) provides an accessible introduction to how globalization is changing the language and communicative practices of the media. Chiapello and Fairclough (2002) is an exploration of 'new management' ideology while Fairclough (2004) analyses the guidelines for an 'appraisal interview' in a university. Machin and van Leeuwen (2003) investigates the globalized and localized discourses of *Cosmopolitan* magazines in different countries, while Machin and van Leeuwen (2004) explores the increasing homogeneity of media formats and their role in the dissemination of global corporate values.

Lankshear (1997) is a useful overview of the impact of new capitalism on the 'new work order', on education reform and wider language practices, as well as on the wider changes at the level of state. Finally, Hansen and Machin (2008) analyses the promotion of visual discourses on climate change (globally operating Getty images) in advertisements and editorials, demonstrating that even climate change is now seen as a marketing opportunity in new capitalism.

Strand 10: Language and politics

Goatly (2007) is an important book which looks at the way metaphors are used ideologically in political discourse. Among other things, it examines metaphors that refer to 'race' (see our Strand 5) as well as exploring the metaphors that structure our conception of capitalist ideologies (see our Strand 9). Goatly's book therefore has resonance across a number of the issues we cover. Another significant book on language and politics is Fairclough (2000), which offers an analysis of the discursive strategies employed by the Labour party in Britain, while Chilton's study of political discourse (2004), referred to across the Strand, is an important contribution to our understanding of the ways in which politicians use language. Jeffries and Walker (2017) have examined the language of New Labour in depth.

Important articles in this area include Montgomery's study (2005) of the way the concept of 'war' was developed, post-9/11, as the dominant term in the media in the run-up to the conflicts in Afghanistan and Iraq. Van Dijk's volume (2008) also includes a study of 'war rhetoric', focusing on the Spanish government's legitimation of the war in Iraq, while Harris (1991) is an article looking at how politicians use evasive strategies in interviews. Metaphor features in Lakoff's study (1991) of the conceptual metaphor system used to justify the first Gulf war.

In a comparative study of British and Finnish data, Fairclough and Mauranen (2003) describe the conversationalization of political discourse, and the collection of essays in which this article is housed, by Blommaert and Bulcaen (2003), is generally relevant also. Lennon (2008b) uses corpus methods to examine changes in the political discourse of Northern Ireland. Finally, Machin and van Leeuwen's analysis of the political discourse of the film and computer game *Black Hawk Down* (2005a) uses verbal and visual Social Actor Analysis of the parties involved in the American intervention in Somalia in 1993 and its political history.

We anticipate that Britain's vote to leave the European Union will lead to a multitude of work in language and politics; Buckledee (2018) is one such publication referred to in A10 whilst Koller, Kopf and Miglbauer (forthcoming 2019) have been commissioned by Routledge to edit a collection on the discourses of Brexit before and after the referendum.

Strand 11: The discourse of social media

This emerging field in critical discourse studies has been addressed at length in a number of important texts. Dovey *et al.* (2009) and Barton and Lee (2013) provide overviews of language practices in 'new media'. Other significant works in the area have been produced by Seargeant and Tagg (2014), Page (2012) and Tagg (2015).

Several scholars have addressed specific areas of online landscapes. Myers (2010) analyses the discourse of blogs and wikis, Zappavigna (2012) deconstructs the language of Twitter in a book-length study and Georgalou (2017) examines identity on Facebook. Pihlaja (2014) presents a fascinating study on the antagonistic use of metaphors on YouTube. Ringrow and Neary (2018) address new media in their analysis of representation in Pihlaja, Seargeant and Hewings' extensive handbook on English Language studies.

Social media as a potential site for activism has been assessed by Fuchs (2014), and enthusiastically by Castells (2012). The collection edited by Mandiberg (2012) offers several perspectives on the potential power of social media.

Strand 12: The discourse of 'post-truth'

Popular books on the subject of post-truth include D'Ancona (2017) and Small (2017). Both books, written by journalists, position the emergence of post-truth against the international political climate from late 2015 onwards. Interestingly, both books offer helpful tips on how we might resist and oppose the advance of post-truth. The website of the Tow Center for Digital Journalism at Columbia University (director, Emily Bell) often has interesting posts and feeds on the subject.

A special issue of the journal *Language and Politics*, edited by Wodak and Krzyżanowski, appeared in late 2017. The issue comprises critical-linguistic explorations of the rise of right-wing populism in Europe and the USA, and there is sustained focus throughout the volume on the role of the media (including social media) in the creation of this discursive shift. While some of these individual studies (Montgomery and Lakoff) have featured more directly in this Strand, readers are encouraged strongly to consult the whole issue, not least because the focus extends beyond the UK and the USA to include developments in countries such as Hungary, Poland, Sweden, Turkey and Austria.

A detailed description of the Habermas model which features across this Strand can be found in Simpson (2003: 153–185). This description includes an account of the model's theoretical influences and its critical reception in the academe. It also charts the model's roots in the natural language philosophy of John Searle.

Fedler (1989) is an entertaining study of the history of fakery across three centuries of print media. The book contains many surprises – in addition to Mark Twain's hoax about the petrified man (A.12), other famous fake news, often designed to ridicule with a satirical intent, was peddled by Benjamin Franklin and Edgar Allan Poe.

REFERENCES

This section contains references to work cited in the printed form of the book, and/or in the additional resources and follow-up activities on the book's companion website.

Abousnnouga, G. and Machin, D. (2008) 'Defence discourse: the visual institutionalization of discourses in war monuments', in A. Mayr (ed.), *Language and Power: An Introduction to Institutional Discourse*, London: Continuum, pp. 115–138.

Agar, M. (1985) 'Institutional discourse', *Text 5* (3): 147–168.

Althusser, L. (1971) 'Ideology and ideological state apparatuses', in L. Althusser (ed.), *Lenin and Philosophy and Other Essays*, London: New Left Books, pp. 121–176.

Amnesty (2012a) 'Chased Away: Forced Evictions of Roma in Ille-de-France', *Amnesty International.*

Amnesty (2012b) 'France: Protect Against Forced Evictions', *Amnesty International.*

Andén-Papadopoulos K. and Pantti M. (2011) 'Introduction', in K. Andén-Papadopoulos and M. Pantti (eds), *Amateur Images and Global News*, Bristol: Intellect; Chicago, IL: The University of Chicago Press, pp. 9–20.

Apte, M.L. (1983) 'Humor research, methodology and theory in anthropology', in P.E. McGhee and J.H. Goldstein (eds), *Handbook of Humor Research, Vol. 1*, New York: Springer-Verlag, pp. 183–211.

Apte, M. (1985) *Humor and Laughter: An Anthropological Approach*, Ithaca, NY: Cornell University Press.

Attardo, S. (1994) *Linguistic Theories of Humor*, Berlin and New York: Mouton de Gruyter.

Attardo, S. (2001) *Humorous Texts: A Semantic and Pragmatic Analysis*, Berlin: Mouton de Gruyter.

Attardo, S. (2017) *The Routledge Handbook of Language and Humor*, London: Routledge.

Austin, J. (1962) *How to Do Things with Words*, Oxford: Clarendon Press.

Baker, P. (2006) *Using Corpora in Discourse Analysis*, London: Continuum.

Baker, P., Gabrielatos, C., KhosraviNik, M., Krżyzanowski, M., McEnery, T. and Wodak, R. (2008) 'A useful methodological synergy? Combining critical discourse analysis and corpus linguistics to examine discourses of refugees and asylum seekers in the UK press', *Discourse and Society 19* (3): 273–306.

Baker, P. and McEnery, T. (2005) 'A corpus-based approach to discourses of refugees and asylum seekers in UN and newspaper texts', *Journal of Language and Politics 4* (2): 197–226.

Bakhtin, M. ([1935] 1981) *The Dialogic Imagination*, Austin, TX: University of Texas.

Baldwin, J. and French, P. (1990) *Forensic Phonetics*, London: Pinter.

Barker, M. (1981) *The New Racism*, London: Junction.

Barker, M. (1984) 'Het nieuwe racisme' [The New Racism], in A. Bleich and P. Schumacher (eds), *Nederlands racisme* [Dutch Racism], Amsterdam: Van Gennep, pp. 62–85.

Barthes, R. (1977) *Image-Music-Text*, London: Fontana

Barthes, R. (1983) *The Fashion System*, Berkeley, CA: University of California Press.

Barton, B., and Lee, C. (2013) *Language Online: Investigating Digital Texts and Practices*, London: Routledge.

Baxter, J. (2003) *Positioning Gender in Discourse: Feminist Poststructuralist Discourse Analysis*, Basingstoke, UK: Palgrave.

Beaugrande, R. de (2001) 'Interpreting the discourse of H.G. Widdowson: a corpus-based Critical Discourse Analysis', *Applied Linguistics 22* (*1*): 104–121.

Beauvoir, Simone de (2004) 'Woman: myth and reality', in A. Prince and S.S. Wayne (eds), *Feminisms and Womanisms: A Women's Studies Reader*, Toronto: Women's Press, pp. 59–65.

Beck, U. (1999) *World Risk Society*, London: Blackwell.

Belfast City Council (2006) 'Kicking racism out of football', available at www.belfastcity.gov.uk/news/news.asp?id=682 (last accessed 26 January 2009).

Bell, A. (1991) *The Language of News Media*, Oxford: Blackwell.

Bennett, L.W. (2003) 'Lifestyle politics and citizen-consumers: identity, communication and political action in late modern society', in J. Corner and D. Pels (eds), *Media and the Restyling of Politics*, London: Sage, pp. 137–151.

Benwell, B. (2001) '"Have a go if you think you're hard enough!" Male gossip and language play in the letters pages of men's lifestyle magazines', *Journal of Popular Culture 35* (*1*): 19–33.

Benwell, B. (2002) 'Is there anything "new" about these lads? The textual and visual construction of masculinity in men's magazines', in L. Litosseliti and J. Sunderland (eds), *Gender Identity and Discourse Analysis*, Philadelphia, PA: John Benjamins, pp. 149–174.

Benwell, B. (ed.) (2003) *Masculinity and Men's Lifestyle Magazines*, Oxford: Blackwell.

Benwell, B. (2004) 'Ironic discourse and masculinity', *Men and Masculinities 7* (*1*): 3–21.

Benwell, B. (2005) '"Lucky this is anonymous!" Men's magazines and ethnographies of reading: a textual culture approach', *Discourse and Society 16* (*2*): 147–172.

Benwell, B. (2014) 'Language and masculinity', in Ehrlich, S., Meyerhoff, M. and Holmes, J. (eds) (2014) *Language, Gender and Sexuality*, London: Wiley Blackwell, pp. 240–259.

Bernstein, D. (1974) *Creative Advertising*, London: Longman.

Billig, M. (1988) 'The notion of "prejudice": some rhetorical and ideological aspects', *Text 8*: 91–110.

Billig, M. (2001) 'Humour and hatred: the racist jokes of the Ku Klux Klan', *Discourse and Society 12* (*3*): 267–289.

Billig, M. (2005) *Laughter and Ridicule: Towards a Social Critique of Humour*, London: Sage.

Bishop, H. and Jaworski, A. (2003) '"We beat 'em": nationalism and the hegemony of homogeneity in the British press reportage of Germany versus England during Euro 2000', *Discourse and Society 14* (*3*): 243–271.

Blakemore, D. (1992) *Understanding Utterances*, Blackwell, Oxford.

Blogs, *Guardian*, available at http://blogs.guardian.co.uk/tv/2008/03/last_nights_tv_phone_rage (last accessed 4 April 2008).

Blommaert, J. and Bulcaen, C. (eds) (2003) *Political Linguistics*, Amsterdam: John Benjamins.

Bloor, M. and Bloor, T. (2007) *The Practice of Critical Discourse Analysis*, London: Hodder Arnold.

Boers, F. (1999) 'When a bodily source domain becomes prominent', in R.W. Gibbs and G. Steen (eds), *Metaphor in Cognitive Linguistics*, Amsterdam: John Benjamins, pp. 47–56.

Bourdieu, P. and Wacquant, L. (2001) 'New liberal speak: notes on the new planetary vulgate', *Radical Philosophy 105*: 2–5.

Bouvier, G. (2017) 'How journalists source trending social media feeds: a critical discourse perspective on Twitter', *Journalism Studies,* https://doi.org/10.1080/1461670X.2017. 1365618.

Breazu, P. and Machin, A. (2018) 'A critical multimodal analysis of the Romanian press coverage of camp evictions and deportations of the Roma migrants from France', *Discourse and Communication,* https://doi.org/10.1177/1750481318757774.

Brennan, M. (1994) 'Cross-examining children in criminal courts: child welfare under attack', in J. Gibbons (ed.), *Language and the Law*, Harlow: Longman, pp. 199–216.

Brierley, S. (1995) *The Advertising Handbook*, London: Routledge.

Buckledee, S. (2018) *The Language of Brexit: How Britain Talked Its Way Out of the European Union*, London: Bloomsbury.

Butler, J. (1999) *Gender Trouble: Feminism and the Subversion of Identity*, 2nd edn, London: Routledge.

Caldas-Coulthard, C.-R. (1992) *News as Social Practice*, Florianópolis, Brazil: Universidade Federal de Santa Catarina.

Caldas-Coulthard, C.-R. (1994) 'On reporting reporting: the representation of speech in factual and factional narratives', in M. Coulthard (ed.), *Advances in Written Text Analysis*. London: Routledge.

Caldas-Coulthard, C.-R. (1996) '"Women who pay for sex. And enjoy it": transgression versus morality in women's magazines', in C.-R. Caldas-Coulthard and M. Coulthard (eds), *Texts and Practices: Readings in Critical Discourse Analysis*, London: Routledge, pp. 250–270.

Caldas-Coulthard, C.-R. (2003) 'Cross-cultural representation of "Otherness" in media discourse', in G. Weiss and R. Wodak (eds), *Critical Discourse Analysis: Theory and Interdisciplinarity*, London: Palgrave Macmillan, pp. 272–296.

Cameron, D. (1985) *Feminism and Linguistic Theory*, London: Macmillan.

Cameron, D. (1995) *Verbal Hygiene*, London: Routledge.

Cameron, D. (1997) 'Performing gender identity: young men's talk and the construction of heterosexual masculinity', in S. Johnson and U. Meinhof (eds), *Language and Masculinity*, Oxford: Blackwell, pp. 47–65.

Cameron, D. (1998) 'Is there any ketchup, Vera? Gender, power and pragmatics', *Discourse and Society 9* (4): 437–455.

Cameron, D. (1999) 'Better conversation: a morality play in twelve tapes', *Feminism and Psychology 9*: 315–333.

Cameron, D. (2000) *Good to Talk? Living and Working in a Communication Culture*, London: Sage.

Cameron, D. (2001) *Working with Spoken Discourse*, London: Sage.

Cameron, D. (2006a) 'Styling the worker: gender and the commodification of language in the global service economy', in D. Cameron, *On Language and Sexual Politics*, London: Routledge, pp. 112– 132.

Cameron, D. (2006b) *On Language and Sexual Politics*, London: Routledge.

Cameron, D. (2008) *The Myth of Mars and Venus*, Oxford: Oxford University Press.

Cameron, D. and Shaw, S., 2016. *Gender, Power and Political Speech: Women and Language in the 2015 UK General Election*. London: Palgrave Macmillan.

Cameron, D. and Frazer, E. (1987) *The Lust to Kill: A Feminist Investigation of Sexual Murder*, Cambridge, UK: Polity.

Cameron, D., McAlinden, F. and O'Leary, K. (1988) 'Lakoff in context: the social and linguistic function of tag questions', in J. Coates and D. Cameron (eds), *Women in Their Speech Communities: New Perspectives on Language and Sex*, New York: Longman, pp. 74–93.

Canning, P. (2017) '"No Ordinary Crowd": foregrounding a "hooligan schema" in the construction of witness narratives following the Hillsborough Football Stadium Disaster', *Discourse and Society 29* (3): 237–255.

Cap, P. (2017) *The Language of Fear: Communicating Threat in Public Discourse*, London: Palgrave Macmillan.

Caple, H. and Knox, J. (2012) 'Online news galleries, photojournalism and the photo essay', *Visual Communication 11* (2): 207–236.

Carter, R. (1990) 'The new grammar teaching', in R. Carter (ed.), *Knowledge about Language and the Curriculum: The LINC Reader*, London: Hodder & Stoughton, pp. 104–121.

Castells, M. (2012) *Networks of Outrage and Hope: Social Movements in the Internet Age*, London: Wiley.

Chaney, D. (1996) *Lifestyles*, London: Routledge.

Charteris-Black, J. (2004) *Corpus Approaches to Critical Metaphor Analysis*, London: Palgrave Macmillan.

Charteris-Black, J. (2014) *Analysing Political Speeches: Rhetoric, Discourse and Metaphor*, London: Palgrave Macmillan.

Chiapello, E. and Fairclough, N. (2002) 'Understanding the new management ideology: a transdisciplinary contribution from Critical Discourse Analysis and New Sociology of Capitalism', *Discourse and Society 13* (2): 185–208.

Chiaro, D. (1992) *The Language of Jokes: Analysing Verbal Play*, London: Routledge.

Chilton, M. (2016) 'The War of the Worlds panic was a myth' *Telegraph Online* 6 May 2016, available at www.telegraph.co.uk/radio/what-to-listen-to/the-war-of-the-worlds-panic-was-a-myth (last accessed 23 November 2017).

Chilton, P. (ed.) (1985) *Language and the Nuclear Arms Debate: Nukespeak Today*, London: Frances Pinter.

Chilton, P. (2004) *Analysing Political Discourse: Theory and Practice*, London: Routledge.

Chilton, P. (2005) Missing links in CDA: modules, blends and the critical instinct', in R. Wodak and P. Chilton (eds), *A New Agenda in (Critical) Discourse Analysis: Theory, Methodology, and Interdisciplinarity*, Amsterdam: John Benjamins, pp. 19–52.

Chilton, P. and Schäffner, C. (1997) 'Discourse and politics', in T.A. van Dijk (ed.), *Discourse as Social Interaction: Discourse Studies, Vol. 2: A Multidisciplinary Introduction*, Newbury, CA: Sage, pp. 206–230.

Chiluwa, I. and Ifukor, P. (2015) '"War Against Our Children": Stance and evaluation in #BringBackOurGirls campaign discourse on Twitter and Facebook', *Discourse and Society 26* (3): 267–296.

Chlopicki, W. and Brzozowska, D. (2017) *Humorous Discourse*, New York: De Gruyter.

Chomsky, N. (1999) *Profit over People: Neoliberalism and Global Order*, London: Seven Stories Press.

Chouliaraki, L. (2008) 'The symbolic power of transnational media: managing the visibility of suffering', *Global Media and Communication 4 (3)*, pp. 329–351.

Chouliaraki, L. and Fairclough, N. (1999) *Discourse in Late Modernity: Rethinking Critical Discourse Analysis*, Edinburgh: Edinburgh University Press.

Christensen, H.S. (2011) 'Political activities on the Internet: Slacktivism or political participation by other means', *First Monday 16 (3)*, available at http://firstmonday.org/ojs/index.php/fm/article/view/3336/2767 (last accessed 30 November 2017).

Clark, K. (1992) 'The linguistics of blame: representations of women in *The Sun's* reporting of crimes of sexual violence', in M. Toolan (ed.), *Language, Text and Context*, London: Routledge, pp. 208–224.

Clayman, S. and Heritage, J. (2002) *The News Interview: Journalists and Public Figures on the Air*, Cambridge, UK: Cambridge University Press.

Coates, J. (1986) *Women, Men and Language*, Harlow: Longman.

Coates, J. (1996) *Women Talk: Conversation between Women Friends*, Oxford: Blackwell.

Coldrey, J. (1987) 'Aboriginals and the criminal courts', in K.M. Hazlehurst (ed.), *Ivory Scales: Black Australia and the Law*, Sydney, NSW: University of New South Wales Press, pp. 81–92.

Coleman, L. (1990) 'The language of advertising', *Journal of Pragmatics 14*: 137–145.

Conboy, M. (2007) *The Language of the News*, London: Routledge.

Connell, R.W. (1995) *Masculinities*, Oxford: Polity.

Conrad, S. (2002) 'Corpus linguistic approaches for discourse analysis', *Annual Review of Applied Linguistics 22*: 75–95.

Cook, G. (1992) *The Discourse of Advertising*, London: Routledge.

Cook, G. (2001) *The Discourse of Advertising*, 2nd edn, London: Routledge.

Cotterill, J. (ed.) (2002) *Language in the Legal Process*, London: Palgrave Macmillan.

Cotterill, J. (2003) *Language and Power in Court: A Linguistic Analysis of the O.J. Simpson Trial*, London: Palgrave Macmillan.

Cotterill, J. (2007) *The Language of Sexual Crime*, London: Palgrave Macmillan.

Cottle, S. (ed.) (2000) *Ethnic Minorities and the Media*, Buckingham, UK: Open University Press.

Coulthard, M. (1992) 'Forensic discourse analysis', in M. Coulthard (ed.), *Advances in Spoken Discourse Analysis*, London: Routledge, pp. 243–258.

Coulthard, M. (1993) 'On beginning the study of forensic texts: corpus, concordance, collocation', in M. Hoey (ed.), *Data, Description, Discourse*, London: Harper Collins, pp. 86–114.

Coulthard, M. (2001) 'Whose text is it? On the linguistic investigation of authorship', in S. Sarangi and M. Coulthard (eds), *Discourse and Social Life*, London: Pearson, pp. 270–287.

Coulthard, M. (2002) 'Whose voice is it? Invented and concealed dialogue in written records of verbal evidence produced by the police', in J. Cotterill (ed.), *Language in the Legal Process*, London: Palgrave Macmillan, pp. 19–34.

Coulthard, M., Johnson, A. and Wright, D. (2016) *An Introduction to Forensic Linguistics: Language in Evidence*, 2nd edn, London: Routledge.

Crewe, B. (2001) 'Representing men: cultural production and producers in the men's magazine market', unpublished PhD thesis, Dept of Sociology, University of Essex.

Custódio, L. (2014) 'Off-line dimensions of online favela youth reactions to human rights violations before the 2016 Olympics in Rio de Janeiro', in N. Wood (ed.) *Brazil in Twenty-First Century Popular Media: Culture, Politics and Nationalism on the World Stage*, Lanham, MD: Lexington Books, pp. 139–156.

D'Ancona, M. (2017) *Post-Truth: The New War on Truth and how to Fight Back*. London: Ebury Press.

Davies, C. (1990) *Ethnic Humour around the World*, Bloomington, IN: Indiana University Press.

Davis, T. (1994) 'ESDA and the analysis of contested contemporaneous notes of police interviews', *Forensic Linguistics 1 (1)*: 71–89.

Deignan, A. (2005) *Metaphor and Corpus Linguistics*, Amsterdam and Philadelphia, PA: John Benjamins.

Delin, A. (2000) *The Language of Everyday Life*, London: Sage.

DES (1988) *Report of the Committee of the Inquiry into the Teaching of the English Language* (Kingman Report), London: HMSO.

Devlin, A. (1996) *Prison Patter: A Dictionary of Prison Words and Slang*, Winchester: Waterside.

Domke, D., Perlmutter, D. and Spratt, M. (2003) 'The primes of our times? An examination of the "power" of visual images', *Journalism 3*: 131–159.

Dougary, G. (1994) *The Executive Tart and Other Myths: Media Women Talk Back*, London: Virago.

Douglas, M. (1966) *Purity and Danger*, London: Routledge.

Dovey, J., Giddings, S., Kelly, K. and Lister, M. (2009) *New Media: a Critical Introduction*, London: Routledge.

Drew, P. and Heritage, J. (eds) (1992) *Talk at Work: Interaction in Institutional Settings*, Cambridge, UK: Cambridge University Press.

Drew, P. and Sorjonen, M.J. (1997) 'Institutional dialogue', in T. van Dijk (ed.), *Discourse as Social Interaction, Vol. 2*, London: Sage, pp. 92–118.

Du Gay, P. (1996) *Consumption and Identity at Work*, London: Sage.

Durant, A. and Leung J.H.C. (2016) *Language and Law*, London: Routledge.

Economou, D. (2006) 'The big picture: the role of the lead image in print feature stories', in I. Lassen, J. Strunck and T. Vestergaard (eds), *Mediating Ideology in Text and Image*, London: Continuum, pp. 211–233.

Economou, D. (2008) 'Pulling readers in: news photos in Greek and Australian broadsheets', in E.A. Thompson and P.R.R. White (eds), *Communicating Conflict: Multilingual Case Studies of the News Media*, London and New York: Continuum, pp. 253–280.

Edelman (2017) *The 2017 Edelman Trust Barometer Global Report*, available at www.edelman.com/trust2017/ (last accessed 3 January 2018).

Edginton, B. and Montgomery, M. (1996) *The Media*, Manchester: The British Council.

Edwards, T. (1997) *Men in the Mirror: Men's Fashion, Masculinity and Society*, London: Cassell.

Eggins, S. (2004) *An Introduction to Systemic Functional Linguistics*, 2nd edn, London: Pinter.

Eggins, S. and Slade, D. (1997) *Analyzing Casual Conversation*, London: Cassell.

Ellsworth, P.C. and Scherer, K.R. (2003) 'Appraisal processes in emotion', in R.J. Davidson, K.R. Scherer and H.H. Goldsmith (eds), *Handbook of Affective Sciences*, New York: Oxford University Press, pp. 572–595.

Erjaevec, K. (2001) 'Media representation of the discrimination against the Roma in Eastern Europe: the case of Slovenia', *Discourse and Society 12* (6): 699–727.

ERRC (2017) 'Will Macron turn the tide on Roma evictions?' European Roma Rights Centre, available at www.errc.org (last accessed 10 August 2017).

Fairclough, N. (1989) *Language and Power* (2nd edn 2001), London: Longman.

Fairclough, N. (1992) *Discourse and Social Change*, Cambridge, UK: Polity.

Fairclough, N. (1993) 'Critical discourse analysis and the marketization of public discourse: the universities', *Discourse and Society 4*: 133–168.

Fairclough, N. (1995a) *Critical Discourse Analysis: The Critical Study of Language*, London: Longman.

Fairclough, N. (1995b) *Media Discourse*, London: Arnold.

Fairclough, N. (2000) *New Labour, New Language?* London: Routledge.

Fairclough, N. (2001) 'Critical discourse analysis', in A. McHoul and M. Rapley (eds), *How to Analyse Talk in Institutional Settings*, London: Continuum, pp. 25–41.

Fairclough, N. (2003) *Analysing Discourse: Textual Analysis for Social Research*, London: Routledge.

Fairclough, N. (2004) 'Critical discourse analysis in researching language in the new capitalism: overdetermination, transdisciplinarity and textual analysis', in L. Young and C. Harrison (eds), *Systemic Functional Linguistics and Critical Discourse Analysis*, London: Continuum, pp. 103–122.

Fairclough, N. (2005) 'Global capitalism and critical awareness of language', available at www2.cddc.vt.edu/digitalfordism/fordism_materials/Fairclough.pdf (last accessed 7 August 2008).

Fairclough, N. (2010) *Critical Discourse Analysis: the Critical Study of Language*, 2nd edn, London: Routledge.

Fairclough, N. and Mauranen, A. (2003) 'The conversationalization of political discourse: a comparative view', in J. Blommaert and C. Bulcaen (eds), *Political Linguistics*, Amsterdam: Benjamins, pp. 89–121.

Fairclough, N. and Wodak, R. (1997) 'Critical Discourse Analysis', in T. van Dijk (ed.), *Discourse as Social Interaction*, London: Sage, pp. 258–285.

Fanon, F. ([1952] 1986) *Black Skin, White Masks*, London: Pluto Press.

Fedler, Fred. (1989) *Media Hoaxes*, Ames, IA: Iowa State University Press.

Filppula, M. (1999) *The Grammar of Irish English: Language in Hibernian Style*, London; Routledge.

Fishman, P. (1983) 'Interaction: the work women do', in B. Thorne, C. Kramarae and N. Henley (eds), *Language, Gender and Society*, Rowley, MA: Newbury House, pp. 89–101.

Forceville, C. (1995) *Pictorial Metaphor in Advertising*, London: Routledge.

Forceville, C. (2006) 'Non-verbal and multimodal metaphor in a cognitivist framework: agendas for research', in G. Kristiansen, M. Achard, R. Dirven and F. Ruiz de Mendoza Ibàñez (eds), *Cognitive Linguistics: Current Applications and Future Perspectives*, Berlin and New York: Mouton de Gruyter, pp. 379–402.

Forceville, C. (2013) 'The strategic use of the visual mode in advertising metaphors', in E. Djonov and S. Zhao (eds) *Critical Multimodal Studies of Popular Culture*, New York: Routledge, pp. 55–70.

Foucault, M. (1977) *Discipline and Punish: The Birth of the Prison*, London: Allan Lane.

Foucault, M. (1980) *Power/Knowledge: Selected Interviews and other Writings 1972–1977*, New York: Pantheon.

Fowler, R. (1991) *Language in the News: Discourse and Ideology in the Press*, London: Routledge.

Fowler, R. and Kress, G. (1979) 'Rules and regulations', in R. Fowler, R. Hodge, G. Kress and T. Trew (eds), *Language and Control*, London: Routledge & Kegan Paul, pp. 26–45.

Fowler, R. and Marshall, T. (1985) 'The war against peace-mongering: language and ideology', in P. Chilton (ed.), *Language and the Nuclear Arms Debate*, London: Frances Pinter, pp. 4–22.

Fowler, R., Hodge, R., Kress, G. and Trew, T. (1979) *Language and Control*, London: Routledge.

Frazer, E. (1987) 'Teenage girls reading *Jackie*', *Media, Culture and Society 9* (*4*): 407–425.

Freud, S. (1976 [1905]) *Jokes and their Manifestation in the Unconsciousness*, Harmondsworth, UK: Penguin Books.

Fuchs, C. (2014) *Social Media*, London: Sage.

Furedi, Frank (2006) 'Save us from the politics of behaviour', available at www.frankfuredi.com/articles/behaviour-20060911.htm (last accessed 12 December 2008).

Gabriel, J. (2000) 'Dreaming of a white …', in S. Cottle (ed.), *Ethnic Minorities and the Press*, Buckingham, UK: Open University Press, pp. 67–83.

Gabrielatos, C. and Baker, P. (2008) 'Fleeing, sneaking, flooding: a corpus analysis of discursive constructions of refugees and asylum seekers in the UK press, 1996–2005', *Journal of English Linguistics 36* (*1*): 5–38.

Galtung, J. and Ruge, M. (1973) 'Structuring and selecting news', in S. Cohen and J. Young (eds), *The Manufacture of News: Social Problems, Deviance and the Mass Media*, London: Constable, pp. 62–72.

Garzone, G. and Santulli, F. (2004) 'What can Corpus Linguistics do for Critical Discourse Analysis?' in A. Partington, J. Morley and L. Haarman (eds), *Corpora and Discourse*, Berlin: Peter Lang, pp. 351–368.

Gauntlett, D. (2008) *Media, Gender, Identity*, London: Routledge.

Gavins, J. and Simpson, P. (2015) '*Regina v John Terry*: the discursive construction of an alleged racist event', *Discourse and Society 26* (6): 712–732.

Gee, J.P. (1990) *Social Linguistics and Literacies: Ideology in Discourses*, London: Falmer.

Gee, J.P. (2001) 'Reading as situated language: a sociocognitive perspective', *Journal of Adolescent and Adult Literacy 44* (8): 714–725.

Gee, J.P., Hull G. and Lankshear, C. (1996) *The New Work Order: Behind the Language of the New Capitalism*, London: Allen & Unwin.

Geis, M.L. (1982) *The Language of Television Advertising*, New York: Academic Press.

Georgalou, M. (2017) *Discourse and Identity on Facebook*, London: Bloomsbury.

Gibbons, J. (ed.) (1994) *Language and the Law*, Harlow, UK: Longman.

Gibbons, J. (2003) *Forensic Linguistics: An Introduction to Language in the Justice System*, Oxford: Blackwell.

Giddens, A. (1976) *New Rules of Sociological Method*, London: Hutchinson.

Giddens, A. (1991) *Modernity and Self-Identity: Self and Society in the Late Modern Age*, Cambridge, UK: Polity Press.

Goatly, A. (2007) *Washing the Brain: Metaphor and Hidden Ideology*, Amsterdam: John Benjamins.

Goffman, E. (1959) *The Presentation of Self in Everyday Life*, New York: Anchor Books.

Goffman, E. (1963) *Behavior in Public Places: Notes on the Social Organization of Gatherings*, New York: Collier Macmillan.

Goffman, E. (1976) *Gender Advertisements*, Cambridge, MA: Harvard University Press.

Goffman, E. (1981) *Forms of Talk*, Oxford: Blackwell.

Gramsci, A. (1971) *Selections from the Prison Notebooks*, ed. and trans. Q. Hoare and G. Nowell-Smith, London: Lawrence & Wishart.

Gray, J. (1992) *Men are from Mars, Women are from Venus*, New York: Harper Collins.

Greatbatch, D. (1986) 'Aspects of topical organization in news interviews: the use of agenda-shifting procedures by interviewees', *Media, Culture and Society* 8 (4): 441–455.

Greatbatch, D. (1988) 'A turn-taking system for British news interviews', *Language in Society* 17 (3): 401–430.

Greatbatch, D. (1998) 'Conversation analysis: neutralism in British news interviews', in A. Bell and P. Garrett (eds), *Approaches to Media Discourse*, Oxford: Blackwell, pp. 163–186.

Grice, H.P. (1975) 'Logic and conversation', in P. Cole and J. Morgan (eds), *Syntax and Semantics 3: Speech Acts*, New York: Academic Press, pp. 41–58.

Habermas, J. (1979) 'What is universal pragmatics?', in T. McCarthy (ed.), *Communication and the Evolution of Society*, London: Heinemann, pp. 1–68.

Hall, K. (1995) 'Lipservice on the fantasy lines', in K. Hall and M. Bucholtz (eds), *Gender Articulated: Language and the Socially Constructed Self*, London: Routledge, pp. 183–216.

Hall, S. (1997) 'The spectacle of the "Other"', in S. Hall (ed.), *Representation: Cultural Representations and Signifying Practices*, London: Sage, pp. 223–297.

Halliday, M.A.K. (1978) *Language as Social Semiotic*, London: Arnold.

Halliday, M.A.K. (1994) *An Introduction to Functional Grammar*, 2nd edn, London: Edward Arnold.

Hammersley, M. (1997) 'On the foundations of Critical Discourse Analysis', *Language and Communication* 17 (3): 327–348.

Hansen, A. and Machin, D. (2008) 'Visually branding the environment: climate change as a marketing opportunity', *Discourse Studies* 10 (6): 777–794.

Harcup, T. and O'Neill, D. (2010) 'What is news? Galtung and Ruge revisited', *Journalism Studies* 2 (2): 261–280.

Harris, J. (1993) 'The grammar of Irish English', in J. Milroy and L. Milroy (eds), *Real English: The Grammar of English Dialects in the British Isles*, London: Routledge, pp. 139–186.

Harris, S. (1984) 'Questions as a mode of control in a Magistrate's Court', *International Journal of the Sociology of Language 49*: 5–27.

Harris, S. (1989) 'Defendant resistance to power and control in court', in H. Coleman (ed.), *Working with Language: A Multidisciplinary Consideration of Language Use in Work Contexts*, Berlin: Mouton de Gruyter, pp. 131–164.

Harris, S. (1991) 'Evasive action: how politicians respond to questions in political interviews', in P. Scannell (ed.), *Broadcast Talk*, London: Sage, pp. 76–99.

Harrison, A. (2016) 'Who Will Tell the Truth?' *The New Review. The Observer* 6–9.

Harrison, C. (2008) 'Real men do wear mascara: advertising discourse and masculine identity', *Critical Discourse Studies* 5 (1): 55–73.

Harrison, C. (2011) 'Studio5ive.com: selling cosmetics to men and reconstructing masculine identity', in K. Ross (ed.), *The Handbook of Gender, Sex and Media*, London: Wiley-Blackwell, pp. 189–204.

Hartmann, P. and Husband, C. (1974) *Racism and the Mass Media*, London: Davis-Poynter.

Harvey, D. (1990) *The Condition of Postmodernity*, Oxford: Blackwell.

Haworth, K. (2006) 'The dynamics of power and resistance in police interview discourse', *Discourse and Society* 17 (6): 739–759.

Heritage, J.C. (1985) 'Analyzing news interviews: aspects of the production of talk for an overhearing audience', in T.A. van Dijk (ed.), *Handbook of Discourse Analysis, Vol. 3: Discourse and Dialogue*, New York: Academic Press, pp. 95–119.

Herman, E. and Chomsky, N. (1988) *Manufacturing Consent: The Political Economy of the Mass Media*, New York: Pantheon.

Hermes, J. (1995) *Reading Women's Magazines: An Analysis of Everyday Media Use*, Cambridge, UK: Polity.

Hochschild, A. (1983) *The Managed Heart: The Commercialization of Human Feeling*, Berkeley, CA: University of California Press.

Hodge, R. and Kress, G. (1988) *Social Semiotics*, Cambridge, UK: Polity Press.

Hodge, R. and Kress, G. (1993) *Language and Ideology*, London: Routledge.

Hoey, M., Mahlberg, M., Stubbs, M. and Teubert, W. (2007) *Text, Discourse and Corpora: Theory and Analysis*, London: Continuum.

Holdaway, S. and O'Neill, M. (2006). 'Institutional racism after Macpherson: an analysis of police views', *Policing and Society* 16 (4): 349–369.

Holmes, J. (1995) *Women, Men and Politeness*, London: Longman.

Horton, D. and Wohl, R.R. (1956) 'Mass communication and para-social interaction: observations on intimacy at a distance', *Psychiatry* 19: 215–229.

Houghton, C. (1995) 'Managing the body of labour: the treatment of reproduction and sexuality in a therapeutic institution', in K. Hall and M. Bucholtz (eds), *Gender Articulated: Language and the Socially Constructed Self*, New York: Routledge, pp. 121–141.

Husband (2000) 'Media and the public sphere in multi-ethnic societies', in S. Cottle (ed.), *Ethnic Minorities and the Media*, Buckingham, UK: Open University Press, pp. 199–214.

Hutchby, I. (1996) 'Power in discourse: the case of arguments on a British talk radio show', *Discourse and Society* 7 (4): 481–498.

Jackson, P., Stevenson, N. and Brooks, K. (1999) 'Making sense of men's lifestyle magazines', *Environment and Planning: Society and Space* 17: 353–368.

Jackson, P., Stevenson, N. and Brooks, K. (2001) *Making Sense of Men's Lifestyle Maga-zines*, Cambridge, UK: Polity.

Jeffries, L. (2007) *Textual Constructions of the Female Body: A Critical Discourse Ap-proach*, Basingstoke, UK: Palgrave Macmillan.

Jeffries, L. and Walker, B. (2017) *Keywords in the Press: The New Labour Years*, London: Bloomsbury.

Jespersen, O. (1922) *Language: Its Nature, Development, and Origin*, New York: W.W. Norton.

Jessop, R. (2000) 'The crisis of the national spatio-temporal fix and the ecological dom-inance of globalising capitalism', *International Journal of Urban and Regional Re-search 24* (2): 273–310.

Jewkes, Y. (2011) *Media and Crime: A Critical Introduction*, London: Sage.

Johnson, S. and Meinhof, U. (eds) (1997) *Language and Masculinity*, Oxford: Black-well.

Keat, R. and Abercrombie, N. (eds) (1990) *Enterprise Culture*, London: Routledge.

Kelsey, D. and Bennett, L. (2014) 'Discipline and resistance on social media: discourse, power and context in the Paul Chambers "Twitter Joke Trial"', *Discourse, Context and Media 3*: 37–45.

Kennedy, G. (1998) *An Introduction to Corpus Linguistics*, Harlow, UK: Longman.

KhosraviNik, M. (2014) 'Critical discourse analysis, power and new media discourse', in Y. Kalyango and M. Kopytowska (eds), *Why Discourse Matters: Negotiating Identity in a Mediatized World*, London: Peter Lang, pp. 287–306.

Koester, A. (2013) *Investigating Workplace Discourse*, London: Routledge.

Koller V., Kopf, S. and Miglbauer, M. (forthcoming 2019) *Discourses of Brexit: Critical Approaches to Voices from Before and After the British EU Referendum*, London: Routledge.

Kress, G. (1985) 'Ideological structures in discourse', in T. van Dijk (ed.), *Handbook of Discourse Analysis, Vol. 4: Discourse Analysis in Society*, London: Academic Press, pp. 27–42.

Kress, G. (1987) 'Educating readers: language in advertising', in J. Hawthorn (ed.), *Propaganda, Persuasion and Polemic*, London: Edward Arnold, pp. 123–139.

Kress, G. (2000) 'Multimodality: challenges to thinking about language', *TESOL Quar-terly 34*: 337–340.

Kress, G. and Hodge, R. (1979) *Language as Ideology*, London: Routledge & Kegan Paul.

Kress, G. and van Leeuwen, T. (1996/2006) *Reading Images: The Grammar of Visual Design*, London: Routledge.

Kress, G. and van Leeuwen, T. (2001) *Multimodal Discourse: The Modes and Media of Contemporary Communication*, London: Hodder Arnold.

Lakoff, G. (1987) *Women, Fire and Dangerous Things: What Categories Reveal about the Mind*, Chicago, IL: University of Chicago Press.

Lakoff, G. (1991) 'The metaphor system used to justify war in the Gulf', *Journal of Urban and Cultural Studies 2* (1): 59–72.

Lakoff, G. (1993) 'The contemporary theory of metaphor', in A. Ortony (ed.), *Metaphor and Thought*, 2nd edn, Cambridge, UK: Cambridge University Press, pp. 202–251.

Lakoff, G. and Johnson, M. (1980) *Metaphors We Live By*, Chicago, IL: University of Chicago Press.

Lakoff, R. (1975) *Language and Women's Place*, New York: Harper & Row.

Lakoff, R. (2000) *The Language War*, Berkeley, CA: The University of California Press.

Lakoff, R. (2017) 'The hollow man: Donald Trump, populism, and post-truth politics', *Journal of Language and Politics* 16 (4): 595–606.

Lankshear, C. (1997) 'Language in the new capitalism', *The International Journal of Inclusive Education 1* (4): 309–321.

Lanzmann, C. (1985) *Shoah: An Oral History of the Holocaust: The Complete Text of the Film*, New York: Pantheon Books.

Lazar, M. (ed.) (2005) *Feminist Critical Discourse Analysis: Gender, Power and Ideology in Discourse*, Basingstoke, UK: Palgrave Macmillan.

Ledin, P. and Machin, D. (2017) *Doing Visual Analysis: From Theory to Practice*. London: Sage.

Lee, Y. and Hsieh, G. (2013) 'Does slacktivism hurt activism?: The effects of moral balancing and consistency in online activism', in *CHI Conference on Human Factors in Computing Systems,* CHI '13, Paris, 27 April–2 May 2013.

Leidner, R. (1993) *Fast Food, Fast Talk: Service Work and the Routinization of Everyday Life*, Berkeley, CA: University of California Press.

Lennon, N. (2008a) 'Just for laughs: the construction of non-verbal humour', in G. Watson (ed.), *The State of Stylistics*, Amsterdam: Rodopi, pp. 395–412.

Lennon, N. (2008b) '"War is over! If you want it": using intertemporal choice theory to monitor change in political discourse of Northern Ireland', Online Proceedings of the Annual Conference of the Poetics and Linguistics Association (PALA), available at www.pala.ac.uk/resources/proceedings/2008/lennon2008.pdf.

Litosseliti, L. (2006) *Gender and Language: Theory and Practice*, New York: Oxford University Press.

Litosseliti, L. and Sunderland, J. (eds) (2002) *Gender Identity and Discourse Analysis*, Amsterdam: John Benjamins.

Louw, B. (1993) 'Irony in the text or insincerity in the writer? The diagnostic potential of semantic prosodies', in M. Baker, G. Francis and E. Tognini-Bonelli (eds), *Text and Technology: In Honour of John Sinclair*, Amsterdam: John Benjamins, pp. 157–176.

Louw, E. (2005) *The Media and the Political Process*, London: Sage.

Lowndes, S. (2004) 'Barristers on trial: comprehension and misapprehension in courtroom discourse', unpublished PhD thesis, Queens University Belfast.

McCorkle, L.W. and Korn, R. (1954) 'Resocialization within walls', *The Annals of the Academy of Political and Social Science 293*: 88–98.

McEnery, T. and Wilson, A. (1996) *Corpus Linguistics*, Edinburgh: Edinburgh University Press.

McFarland, K. (2006) 'Strengthening Critical Discourse Analysis: the *Baby Book* revisited' (see accompanying web resources).

Machin, D. (2007a) *Introduction to Multimodal Analysis*, London: Arnold.

Machin, D. (2007b) 'Visual discourses of war: multimodal analysis of photographs of the Iraq occupation', in A. Hodges (ed.), *Discourses, War and Terrorism*, Amsterdam: John Benjamins, pp. 132–142.

Machin, D. (2016) 'The need for a social and affordance-driven multimodal critical discourse studies', *Discourse and Society 27* (3): 322–334.

Machin, D. and Mayr, A. (2007) 'Antiracism in the British Government's model regional newspaper: the "talking cure"', *Discourse and Society 18* (4): 453–477.

Machin, D. and Mayr, A. (2012) *How to do Critical Discourse Analysis: A Multimodal Approach,* London: Sage.

Machin, D. and Mayr, A. (2013) 'Personalising crime and crime fighting in factual television: analysis of social actors and transitivity in language and images', *Critical Discourse Studies 10* (4): 356–372.

Machin, D. and Niblock, S. (2008) 'Branding newspapers', *Journalism Studies 9* (2): 244–259.

Machin, D. and Polzer, L. (2015) *Visual Journalism,* London: Palgrave Macmillan.

Machin, D. and Thornborrow, J. (2003) 'Branding and discourse: the case of *Cosmopolitan*', *Discourse and Society 14* (4): 453–471.

Machin, D. and Thornborrow, J. (2006) 'Lifestyle and the depoliticisation of agency: sex as power in women's magazines', *Social Semiotics 16* (1): 173–188.

Machin, D. and van Leeuwen, T. (2003) 'Global schemas and local discourses in *Cosmopolitan*', *Journal of Sociolinguistics 7* (4): 493–512.

Machin, D. and van Leeuwen, T. (2004) 'Global media: generic homogeneity and discursive diversity', *Continuum Journal of Media and Cultural Studies 18* (1): 99–120.

Machin, D. and van Leeuwen, T. (2005a) 'Computer games as political discourse: the case of *Black Hawk Down*', *Journal of Language and Politics 4*: 119–141.

Machin, D. and van Leeuwen, T. (2005b) 'Language style and lifestyle: the case of a global magazine', *Media, Culture & Society 27* (4): 577–600.

Machin, D. and van Leeuwen, T. (2007) *Global Media Discourse,* London: Routledge.

McHoul, A.W. and Rapley, M. (2001) *How to Analyse Talk in Institutional Settings: A Casebook of Methods,* London: Continuum.

McKenna, B. (2004) 'Critical Discourse Studies: where to from here?', *Critical Discourse Studies 1* (1): 9–39.

McRobbie, A. (1991) *Feminism and Youth Culture: From Jackie to Just Seventeen,* London: Routledge.

McRobbie, A. (1999) *In the Culture Society: Art, Fashion and Popular Music,* London: Routledge.

Mahlberg, M. (2007) 'Lexical items in discourse: identifying local textual functions of sustainable development', in M. Hoey, M. Mahlberg., M. Stubbs and W. Teubert. (eds), *Text, Discourse and Corpora: Theory and Analysis,* London: Continuum, pp. 191–218.

Mandiberg, M. (ed.) (2012) *The Social Media Reader,* New York: New York University Press.

Martin, J.R. (1985) 'Process and text: two aspects of semiosis', in J.D. Benson and W.S. Greaves (eds), *Systemic Perspectives on Discourse, Vol. 1,* Norwood, NJ: Ablex, pp. 248–274.

Martin, J.R. (2000) 'Beyond exchange: appraisal systems in English', in S. Hunston and G. Thompson (eds), *Evaluation in Text,* Oxford: Oxford University Press, pp. 142–176.

Martin, J.R. and White P.R.R. (2005) *The Language of Evaluation: Appraisal in English*, London: Palgrave.

Martin, J.R., Matthiessen, C. and Painter, C. (1996) *Working with Functional Grammar*, Oxford: Hodder Arnold Publications.

Marx, K. [with Frederick Engels] ([1933] 1965) *The German Ideology*, ed. and trans. S. Ryazanskaya, London: Lawrence & Wishart.

Matoesian, G. (1993) *Reproducing Rape: Domination through Talk in the Courtroom*, Chicago, IL: University of Chicago Press.

Mateosian, G. (2001) *Law and Language of Identity: Discourse in the William Kennedy Smith Rape Trial*, Oxford: Oxford University Press.

Mautner, G. (2005) 'The entrepreneurial university: a discursive profile of a higher education buzzword', *Critical Discourse Studies 2* (2): 95–120.

Mayr, A. (2004) *Prison Discourse: Language as a Means of Control and Resistance*, Basingstoke, UK: Palgrave Macmillan.

Mayr, A. (2008) *Language and Power: An Introduction to Institutional Discourse*, London: Continuum.

Mayr, A. (2009) 'Representations of food on British television: Jamie Oliver's *School Dinners*', in E. Lavric and C. Konzett (eds), *Food and Language*, Frankfurt: Peter Lang.

Montgomery, M. (1999) 'Speaking sincerely: public reactions to the death of Diana', *Language and Literature 8* (1): 5–33.

Montgomery, M. (2005) 'The discourse of *war* after 9/11', *Language and Literature 14* (2): 149–181.

Montgomery, M. (2007) *The Discourse of Broadcast News: A Linguistic Approach*, London: Routledge.

Montgomery, M. (2017) 'Post-truth politics? Authenticity, populism and the electoral discourses of Donald Trump', *Journal of Language and Politics* Special Issue: Right-Wing Populism in Europe and USA, *16* (4): 619–639.

Mooney, A. and Evans, B. (2015) *Language, Society and Power*, 4th edn, London: Routledge.

Morozov, E. (2009) 'From slacktivism to activism', available at http://neteffect.foreignpolicy.com/posts/2009/09/05/from_slacktivism_to_activism (last accessed 28 November 2017).

Morse, F. (2014) 'The Bring Back Our Girls' campaign is working: Boko Haram should be scared of a hashtag. *The Independent*, 13 May, available at www.independent.co.uk/voices/comment/the-bring-back-our-girls-campaign-is-working-boko-haram-should-be-scared-of-a-hashtag-9360830.html.

Mortensen, M. (2011) 'When citizen photojournalism sets the news agenda: Neda Agha Soltan as a Web 2.0 icon of post-election unrest in Iran' *Global Media and Communication*, *7* (1): 4–16.

Moss, P. (1985) 'Rhetoric of defence in the United States: language, myth and ideology', in P. Chilton (ed.), *Language and the Nuclear Arms Debate: Nukespeak Today*, London: Frances Pinter, pp. 45–63.

Moubray, M. (2015) 'Alternative logics? Parsing the literature on alternative media', in C. Atton, (ed.) *The Routledge Companion to Alternative and Community Media*. London: Routledge, pp. 21-31.

Mulkay, G. (1988) *On Humour: Its Nature and its Place in Modern Society*, Cambridge, UK: Polity Press.

Mullany, L. (2011) *Gendered Discourse in the Professional Workplace*, London: Palgrave Macmillan.

Mumby, D. and Clair, R.P. (1997) 'Organizational discourse', in T. van Dijk (ed.), *Discourse as Social Interaction: Discourse Studies, Vol. 2: A Multidisciplinary Introduction*, Newbury, CA: Sage, pp. 181–205.

Murdock, G. (1984) 'Reporting the riots: images and impact', in J. Benyon (ed.), *Scarman and After*, Oxford: Pergamon Press, pp. 73–98.

Murray, S.O. (1987) 'Power and solidarity in "interruption": a critique of the Santa Barbara School of Conception and its application by Orcutt and Harvey (1985)', *Symbolic Interaction 10*: 101–110.

Myers, G. (1989) 'The pragmatics of politeness in scientific articles', *Applied Linguistics 10 (1)*: 1–35.

Myers, G. (1994) *Words in Ads* (2nd edn 2000), London: Arnold.

Myers, G. (2010) *The Discourse of Blogs and Wikis*, London: Continuum.

Nakano, Y. (2002) 'Who initiates a global flow? Japanese popular culture in Asia', *Visual Communication 1 (2)*: 229–253.

Nash, W. (1985) *The Language of Humour*, Harlow, UK: Longman.

Norrick, N. (1993) *Conversational Joking: Humor in Everyday Talk*, Bloomington, IN: Indiana University Press.

O'Barr, W. (1994) *Culture and the Ad: Exploring Otherness in the World of Advertising*, Boulder, CO: Westview Press.

O'Halloran, K. (2003) *Critical Discourse Analysis and Language Cognition*, Edinburgh: Edinburgh University Press.

O'Halloran, K. and Coffin, C. (2004) 'Checking overinterpretation and underinterpretation: help from corpora in critical linguistics', in C. Coffin, A. Hewings and K.A. O'Halloran (eds), *Applying English Grammar: Functional and Corpus Approaches*, London: Hodder Arnold, pp. 275–297.

O'Halloran, S. (2005) 'Symmetry in interaction in meetings of Alcoholics Anonymous: the management of conflict', *Discourse and Society 16 (4)*: 535–560.

O'Halloran, S. (2008) *Talking Oneself Sober: The Discourse of Alcoholics Anonymous*, New York: Cambria Press.

Ohmann, R. (1996) *Selling Culture: Magazines, Markets, and Class at the Turn of the Century*, London: Verso.

O'Keefe, A. (2006) *Investigating Media Discourse*, London: Routledge.

Olsson, J. (2004) *Forensic Linguistics*, New York: Continuum.

Olsson, J. and Luchjenbroers, J. (2014) *Forensic Linguistics*, London: Bloomsbury.

Ong, W.J. (1982) *Orality and Literacy – The Technologizing of the Word*, London: Methuen.

O'Reilly, T. (2005) 'What is Web 2.0? Design Patterns and Business Models for the Next Generation of Software', available at www.oreillynet.com/pub/a/oreilly/tim/news/2005/09/30/what-is-web-20.html (last accessed 5 September 2017).

Orelus, P. (2016) *Language, Race and Power in Schools*, London: Routledge.

Orpin, D. (2005) 'Corpus Linguistics and Critical Discourse Analysis: examining the ideology of sleaze', *International Journal of Corpus Linguistics 10 (1)*: 37–61.

Page, R. (2003) 'Cherie: lawyer, wife, mum: contradictory patterns of representation in media reports of Cherie Booth/Blair', *Discourse and Society 14* (5): 559–579.

Page, R. (2012) *Stories and Social Media: Identities and Interaction*, London: Routledge.

Page, R., Barton, D., Unger, J. and Zappavigna, M. (2014) *Researching Language and Social Media*, London: Routledge.

Palmer, G. (2004) 'The new you: class and transformation in lifestyle television', in D. Jermym and S. Holmes (eds), *Understanding Reality Television*, London: Routledge, pp. 173–191.

Partington, A. (2004) 'Corpora and discourse, a most congruous beast', in A. Partington, J. Morley and L. Haarman (eds), *Corpora and Discourse*, Berlin: Peter Lang, pp. 11–20.

Pelissier Kingfisher, C. (1996) *Women in the American Welfare Trap*, Philadelphia, PA: University of Pennsylvania Press.

Pennycook, A. (2001) *Critical Applied Linguistics: A Critical Introduction*, London: Lawrence Erlbaum.

Pihlaja, S. (2014) *Antagonism on YouTube: Metaphor in Online Discourse*, London: Bloomsbury.

Poole, B. (2010) 'Commitment and criticality: Fairclough's critical discourse analysis evaluated', *International Journal of Applied Linguistics 2* (1): 137–155.

Rayson, P. (2008) 'Wmatrix: a web-based corpus processing environment', Computing Department, Lancaster University, available at http://ucrel.lancs.ac.uk/wmatrix/

Reardon, G. (1996) *Dialling the Future? Phone Banking and Insurance*, London: Banking Insurance and Finance Union.

Redfern, W. (1982) 'Guano of the mind: puns in advertising', *Language and Communication 2*: 269–276.

Redfern, W. (2000) *Puns: More Senses than One*, 2nd edn, Harmondsworth, UK: Penguin.

Reich, R.B. (1994) 'The revolt of the anxious class', speech given to the Democratic Leadership Council, 22 November 1994, available at www.dol.gov/oasam/programs/history/reich/speeches/sp941122.htm (last accessed 2 August 2008).

Reid, J. (1995) 'A study of gender differences in minimal responses', *Journal of Pragmatics 24*: 489–512.

Reisigl, M. and Wodak, R. (1999) 'Austria First: a discourse-historical analysis of the "Austrian anti-foreigner petition" in 1992 and 1993', in M. Reisigl and R. Wodak (eds), *The Semiotics of Racism: Approaches in Critical Discourse Analysis*, Vienna: Passagen Verlag, pp. 269–303.

Reisigl, M. and Wodak, R. (2001) *Discourse and Discrimination: Rhetorics of Racism and Antisemitism*, London: Routledge.

Richardson, J. (2004) *(Mis)representing Islam: The Racism and Rhetoric of British Broadsheet Newspapers*, Amsterdam and Philadelphia, PA: Benjamins.

Richardson, J. (2007) *Analysing Newspapers: An Approach from Critical Discourse Analysis*, London: Palgrave Macmillan.

Richardson, J. (2008) '"Our England": discourses of "race" and class in party election leaflets', *Social Semiotics 18* (3): 321–333.

Richardson, J. (2014). Roma in the news: an examination of media and political discourse and what needs to change. *People, Place and Policy Online 8* (1): 51–64.

Richardson, J. and O'Neill, R. (2012) 'Stamp on the camps: the social construction of gypsies and travellers in media and political debate', in J. Richardon and A. Ryder (eds), *Gypsies and Travellers: Empowerment and Inclusion in British Society*, Bristol, UK: Policy Press, pp. 169–186.

Ringrow, H. (2016) *The Language of Cosmetics Advertising*, London: Palgrave Macmillan.

Ringrow, H. and Neary. C. (2018) 'Media, power and representation', in S. Pihlaja, P. Seargeant and A. Hewings (eds), *The Routledge Handbook of English Language Studies*, London: Routledge.

Ritzer, G. (1996) *The McDonaldization of Society* (2nd edn 2004), Thousand Oaks, CA: Pine Forge Press.

Rogers, R. (ed.) (2004) *An Introduction to Critical Discourse Analysis in Education*, London: Lawrence Erlbaum.

Rosen, J. (2012) 'The people formerly known as the audience', in M. Mandiberg (ed.), *The Social Media Reader*, New York: New York University Press, pp. 13–17.

Ross, A. (1998) *The Language of Humour*, London: Routledge.

Sacks, H., Schegloff, E. and Jefferson, G. (1974) 'A simplest systematics for the organization of turn-taking in conversation', *Language 50* (4): 696–735.

Sanz Sabido, R. and Price, S. (2016) 'The Ladders Revolution: material struggle, social media and news coverage', *Critical Discourse Studies 13* (3): 247–260.

Sarangi, S. and Roberts, C. (1999) *Talk, Work and Institutional Order: Discourse in Medical, Mediation and Management Settings*, Berlin: Mouton de Gruyter.

Sarangi, S. and Slembrouck, S. (2013) *Language, Bureaucracy and Social Control*, London and New York: Routledge.

Sassoon, R. (1999) *Handwriting of the Twentieth Century*, London: Routledge.

Saussure, F. de ([1916] 1960) *Course in General Linguistics*, London: Peter Owen.

Scannell, P. (1996) *Radio, Television and Modern Life*, Oxford: Blackwell.

Schane, S. (2006) *Language and the Law*, New York: Continuum.

Scollon, R. (1998) *Mediated Discourse as Social Interaction: A Study of News Discourse*, London: Longman.

Scollon, R. and Scollon, S. (1998) 'Literate design in the discourses of revolution reform and transition: Hong Kong and China', *Written Language and Literacy 1* (*1*): 1–3.

Scott, J.C. (1985) *Weapons of the Weak: Everyday Forms of Peasant Resistance*, New Haven, CT: Yale University Press.

Scott, J.C. (1990) *Domination and the Art of Resistance: Hidden Transcripts*, New Haven, CT: Yale University Press.

Scott, J. (2001) *Power*, Cambridge, UK: Polity Press.

Scott, M. (1996) *Wordsmith Tools 5.0*, Oxford: Oxford University Press.

Scraton, P. (2004) 'Death on the terraces: the contexts and injustices of the 1989 Hillsborough Disaster', *Soccer and Society 5* (2): 183–200.

Seargeant, P. and Tagg. C. (eds) (2014) *The Language of Social Media: Identity and Community on the Internet*, London: Palgrave Macmillan.

Sennet, R. (2006) *The Culture of the New Capitalism*, London: Yale University Press.

Sharrock, W. and Anderson, D. (1981) 'Language, thought and reality, again', *Sociology 15*: 287–293.

Short, M. and Hu, Wenzhong (1997) 'Analysing the changing character and sophistication of TV advertisements in the People's Republic of China', *Text 17* (4): 491–515.

Shuy, R. (1998) *The Language of Confession, Interrogation and Deception*, Thousand Oaks, CA: Sage.

Shuy, R. (2002) 'To testify or not to testify?', in J. Cotterill (ed.), *Language in the Legal Process*, London: Palgrave Macmillan, pp. 3–18.

Shuy, R. (2005) *Creating Language Crimes: How Law Enforcement Uses (and Misuses) Language*, New York: Oxford University Press.

Shuy, R. (2006) *Language and the Law*, New York: Continuum.

Shuy, R. (2010) *The Language of Defamation Cases*, Oxford: Oxford University Press.

Shuy, R. (2011) *The Language of Perjury Cases*, Oxford: Oxford University Press.

Shuy, R. (2012) *The Language of Sexual Misconduct Cases*, Oxford: Oxford University Press.

Shuy, R. (2013) *The Language of Bribery Cases*, Oxford: Oxford University Press.

Shuy, R. (2014) *The Language of Murder Cases*, Oxford: Oxford University Press.

Shuy, R. (2016) *The Language of Fraud Cases*, Oxford: Oxford University Press.

Simpson, M. (1994) *Male Impersonators: Men Performing Masculinity*, London: Cassell.

Simpson, P. (1993) *Language, Ideology and Point of View*, London: Routledge.

Simpson, P. (2001) '"Reason" and "Tickle" as pragmatic constructs in the discourse of advertising', *Journal of Pragmatics 33*: 589–607.

Simpson, P. (2003) *On the Discourse of Satire*, Amsterdam and Philadelphia, PA: John Benjamins.

Simpson, P. (2011) '"That's not ironic, that's just stupid": Towards an eclectic account of the discourse of irony', in M. Dynel (ed.), *The Pragmatics of Humour*, Amsterdam and Philadelphia, PA: John Benjamins.

Small, J. (2017) *Post-Truth: How Bullshit Conquered the World*. London: Biteback Publishing.

Solan, L.M. and Tiersma, P. (2005) *Speaking of Crime: The Language of Criminal Justice*, Chicago, IL: Chicago University Press.

Solan, L., Ainsworth, J. and Shuy, R. (eds) (2015) *Speaking of Language and Law: Conversations on the Work of Peter Tiersma*, Oxford: Oxford University Press.

De Sousa, R. (1987) 'When is it wrong to laugh?', in J. Morreall (ed.), *The Philosophy of Laughter and Humor*, Albany, NY: State University of New York Press, pp. 226–249.

Spender, D. (1980) *Man Made Language* (2nd edn 1990), London: Routledge.

Sperber, D. and Wilson, D. (1981) 'Irony and the use-mention distinction', in P. Cole (ed.), *Radical Pragmatics*, New York: Academic Press, pp. 295–318.

Statham, S. (2016) *Redefining Trial by Media: Towards a Critical-Forensic Linguistic Interface*, Amsterdam and Philadelphia, PA: John Benjamins.

Stringfellow, F. Jr. (1994) *The Meaning of Irony: A Psychoanalytic Investigation*, Albany, NY: State University of New York.

Stubbs, M. (1994) 'Grammar, text and ideology: computer-assisted methods in the linguistics of representation', *Applied Linguistics 15* (2): 201–223.

Stubbs, M. (1997) 'Whorf's children: critical comments on Critical Discourse Analysis (CDA)', in A. Rayan and A. Wray (eds), *Evolving Models of Language*, Clevedon: Multilingual Matters, pp. 100–116.

Stubbs, M. (2001) *Words and Phrases: Corpus Studies of Lexical Semantics*, Oxford: Blackwell.

Stygall, G. (1994) *Trial Language*, Amsterdam: John Benjamins.

Tagg, C. (2015) *Exploring Digital Communication*, London: Routledge.

Talbot, M. (1992) 'The construction of gender in a teenage magazine', in N. Fairclough (ed.), *Critical Language Awareness*, London: Longman, pp. 174–199.

Talbot, M. (1995) 'A synthetic sisterhood: false friends in a teenage magazine', in K. Hall and M. Bucholtz (eds), *Gender Articulated: Language and the Socially Constructed Self*, London: Routledge, pp. 143–165.

Talbot, M. (1997) '"Randy fish boss branded a stinker": coherence and the construction of masculinities in a British tabloid newspaper', in S. Johnson and U. Meinhof (eds), *Language and Masculinity*, Oxford: Blackwell, pp. 173–187.

Talbot, M. (2000) '"It's good to talk?" The undermining of feminism in a British Telecom advertisement', *Journal of Sociolinguistics* 4: 108–119.

Talbot, M. (2007) *Media Discourse: Representation and Interaction*, Edinburgh: Edinburgh University Press.

Talbot, M. (2014) *Language and Gender*, 2nd edn, London: Polity.

Tanaka, K. (1994) *Advertising Language*, London: Routledge.

Tannen, D. (1990) *You Just Don't Understand: Men and Women in Conversation*, New York: Morrow.

Tannen, D. (ed.) (1993) *Framing in Discourse*, Oxford: Oxford University Press.

Tannen, D. (1994) *Gender and Discourse*, Oxford: Oxford University Press.

Tannen, D. (1998) *The Argument Culture: Stopping America's War of Words*, New York: Ballantine.

Teo, P. (2000) 'Racism in the news: a critical discourse analysis of news reporting in two Australian newspapers', *Discourse and Society 11 (1)*: 7–49.

Teubert, W. (2007) 'Natural and human rights, work and property in the discourse of Catholic social doctrine', in M. Hoey, M. Mahlberg, M. Stubbs and W. Teubert (eds), *Text, Discourse and Corpora: Theory and Analysis*, London: Continuum, pp. 89–126.

Thomas, J. (1988) 'Discourse control in confrontational interaction', Lancaster paper in Linguistics, 50, University of Lancaster.

Thomas, L., Wareing, S., Singh, I., Peccei, J.S., Thornborrow, J. and Jones, J. (2004) *Language, Society and Power: An Introduction*, 2nd edn, London: Routledge.

Thompson, G. (1996) *Introducing Functional Grammar*, London: Arnold.

Thornborrow, J. (1994) 'The woman, the man and the filofax: gender positions in advertising', in S. Mills (ed.), *Gendering the Reader*, Hemel Hempstead, UK: Harvester Wheatsheaf, pp. 128–151.

Thornborrow, J. (2002) *Power Talk: Language and Interaction in Institutional Discourse*, London: Longman.

Thornborrow, J. (2003) 'Questions, control and the organization of talk in calls to a radio phone-in', *Discourse Studies 3*: 119–143.

Thornborrow, J. (2007) 'Narrative, opinion and situated argument in talk show discourse', *Journal of Pragmatics 39*: 1436–1453.

Tiersma, P. (1999) *Legal Language*, Chicago, IL: University of Chicago Press.

Toolan, M. (1988) 'The language of press advertising', in M. Ghadessy (ed.), *Registers of Written English*, London: Pinter, pp. 52–64.

Toolan, M. (1996) *Total Speech: An Integrational Approach to Language*, Durham, NC: Duke University Press.

Toolan, M. (1997) 'What is Critical Discourse Analysis and why are people saying such terrible things about it?', *Language and Literature* 6 (2): 83–103.

Tracy, S. (2000) 'Becoming a character for commerce: emotion labor, self-subordination, and discursive construction of identity in a total institution', *Management Communication Quarterly 14*: 90–128.

Trew, T. (1979) 'Theory and ideology at work', in R. Fowler, R. Hodge, G. Kress and T. Trew, *Language and Control*, London: Routledge, pp. 94–116.

Trilling, L. (1971) *Sincerity and Authenticity*, Oxford: Oxford University Press.

Trow, M.J. (1992) *'Let Him Have It, Chris': The Murder of Derek Bentley*, London: Grafton.

Trowler, P. (2001) 'Captured by the discourse? The socially constitutive power of new Higher Education discourse in the UK', *Organization 8* (2): 183–201.

Tsakona, V. and Popa, D.E. (2011) *Studies in Political Humour: In Between Political Critique and Public Entertainment*, Amsterdam and Philadelphia, PA: John Benjamins.

Van Dijk, T.A. (1990) 'Social cognition and discourse', in H. Giles and W. Robinson (eds), *Handbook of Language and Social Psychology*, New York: John Wiley & Sons, pp. 163–186.

Van Dijk, T. (1991) *Racism and the Press*, London: Routledge.

Van Dijk, T.A. (1992) 'Discourse and the denial of racism', *Discourse and Society 3* (1): 87–118.

Van Dijk, T.A. (1993a) *Elite Discourse and Racism*, Newbury Park, CA: Sage.

Van Dijk, T.A. (1993b) 'Elite discourse and the reproduction of racism', available at www.discourses.org/OldArticles/Elite%20discourse%20and%20the%20reproduction%20of%20racism.pdf (last accessed 7 December 2008).

Van Dijk, T. (1997) 'What is political discourse analysis?', in J. Blommaert and C. Bulcaen (eds), *Political Linguistics*, Amsterdam: John Benjamins, pp. 11–53.

Van Dijk, T.A. (2000) 'New(s) racism: a discourse-analytical approach', in S. Cottle (ed.), *Ethnic Minorities and the Media*, Buckingham, UK: Open University Press, pp. 33–49.

Van Dijk, T.A. (2005) 'Contextual knowledge management in discourse production: a CDA perspective', in R. Wodak and P. Chilton (eds), *A New Agenda in (Critical) Discourse Analysis: Theory, Methodology, and Interdisciplinarity*, Amsterdam: John Benjamins, pp. 71–100.

Van Dijk, T. (2008) *Discourse and Power*, Basingstoke, UK: Palgrave Macmillan.

Van Dijk, T.A., Ting-Toomey, S., Smitherman, G. and Troutman, D. (1997) 'Discourse, ethnicity, culture and racism', in T.A. Van Dijk (ed.), *Discourse as Social Interaction: Discourse Studies, Vol. 2: A Multidisciplinary Introduction*, Newbury, CA: Sage, pp. 144–181.

Van Leeuwen, T. (1996) 'The representation of social actors', in C.-R. Caldas-Coulthard and M. Coulthard (eds), *Texts and Practices: Readings in Critical Discourse Analysis*, London: Routledge, pp. 32–70.

Van Leeuwen, T. (2005) *Introducing Social Semiotics*, London: Routledge.

Van Leeuwen, T. (2008) 'The visual representation of social actors', in T. van Leeuwen, *Discourse and Practice: New Tools for Critical Discourse Analysis*, Oxford: Oxford University Press, pp. 136–149.

Van Leeuwen, T. and Wodak, R. (1999) 'Legitimizing immigration control: a discourse-historical analysis', *Discourse and Society 1 (1)*: 83–118.

Variety.com (2017) 'Donald Trump's Presidency Yields Boom in Satirical Comedy TV Series, Apps', available at http://variety.com/2017/tv/news/donald-trump-satire-comedy-tv-shows-apps-1202528613/ (last accessed 5 November 2017).

Vestergaard, T. and Shrøder, K. (1985) *The Language of Advertising*, Oxford: Blackwell.

Veum, A. and Undrum, L. (2017) 'The selfie as a global discourse', *Discourse and Society 29 (1)*: 86–103.

Wade, W.C. (1987) *The Fiery Cross: The Ku Klux Klan in America*, New York: Simon & Schuster.

Weaver, S. (2013) *The Rhetoric of Racist Humour*, Aldershot, UK: Ashgate.

Weaver, S, Mora, R.A. and Morgan, K. (2016) 'Gender and humour: examining discourses of hegemony and resistance', *Social Semiotics 26*: 227–233.

Weber, M. ([1914] 1978) *Economy and Society: An Outline of Interpretive Sociology*, G. Roth and C. Wittich (eds), E. Fischoff (trans.), Berkeley, CA: University of California Press.

Webster, G. (2003) 'Corporate discourse and the academy: a polemic', *Industry and Higher Education 17 (2)*: 85–90.

Weiss, G. and Wodak, R. (eds) (2003) *Critical Discourse Analysis: Theory and Interdisciplinarity*, London: Palgrave Macmillan.

West, C. and Zimmerman, D.H. (1983) 'Small insults: a study of interruptions in cross-sex conversations between unacquainted persons', in B. Thorne, C. Kramarae and N. Henley (eds), *Language, Gender and Society*, Rowley, MA: Newbury House, pp. 102–117.

Widdowson, H. (1995) 'Discourse analysis: a critical view', *Language and Literature 4 (3)*: 157–172.

Widdowson, H. (1996) 'Reply to Fairclough: discourse and interpretation: conjectures and refutations', *Language and Literature 5 (1)*: 57–70.

Widdowson, H. (1998) 'The theory and practice of Critical Discourse Analysis', *Applied Linguistics 19 (1)*: 136–151.

Widdowson, H. (2004) *Text, Context, Pretext*, Oxford: Oxford University Press.

Williamson, J. (1978) *Decoding Advertisements: Ideology and Meaning in Advertising*, London: Marion Boyars.

Willis, G., Muggah, R., Kosslyn, J. and Leusin, F. (2014) 'The changing face of technology use in pacified communities', Igarape Institute, Rio de Janeiro, Strategic note 13, February, 2014.

Wodak, R. (1996) *Disorders of Discourse*, London: Longman.

Wodak, R. (ed.) (1997) *Gender and Discourse*, London: Sage.

Wodak, R. (2000) 'The rise of racism – an Austrian or a European phenomenon?', *Discourse and Society 11 (1)*: 5–6.

Wodak, R. (2001) 'The discourse-historical approach', in R. Wodak and M. Meyer (eds), *Methods of Critical Discourse Analysis*, London: Sage, pp. 63–94.

Wodak, R. (2006) 'Critical Linguistics and Critical Discourse Analysis', in J. Verschueren and J.-O. Oestman (eds), *Handbook of Pragmatics*, Amsterdam: John Benjamins, pp. 1–25.

Wodak, R. and Chilton, P. (2005) *A New Agenda in (Critical) Discourse Analysis: Theory, Methodology, and Interdisciplinarity*, Amsterdam: John Benjamins.

Wodak, R. and Krzyżanowski, M. (2017) 'Right-wing populism in Europe and USA: contesting politics and discourse beyond "Orbanism" and "Trumpism"', *Journal of Language and Politics* Special Issue: Right-Wing Populism in Europe and USA, 16 (4): 471–484.

Wodak, R. and Meyer, M. (eds) (2001) *Methods of Critical Discourse Analysis*, London: Sage.

Wodak, R. and Meyer, M. (2015) *Methods of Critical Discourse Studies*, London: Sage.

Wodak, R. and Reisigl, M. (1999) 'Discourse and racism: European perspectives', *Annual Review of Anthropology 28*: 175–199.

Young, L. and Fitzgerald, B. (2006) *The Power of Language: How Discourse Influences Society*, London: Equinox.

Youth Justice and Criminal Evidence Act 1999, available at www.legislation.gov.uk/ukpga/1999/23/contents (last accessed 30 November 2017).

Zappavigna, M. (2012) *Discourse of Twitter and Social Media*, London: Continuum.

Zappavigna, M. (2015) 'Searchable talk: the linguistic functions of the hashtag', *Social Semiotics 25* (3): 274–291.

Zimmerman, D.H. and West, C. (1975) 'Sex roles, interruptions, and silences in conversation', in B. Thorne and N. Henley (eds), *Language and Sex: Difference and Dominance*, Rowley, MA: Newbury House, pp. 105–129.

Zito, S. (2016) 'Taking Trump Seriously, But Not Literally', *The Atlantic*, 23 September 2016, available at www.theatlantic.com/politics/archive/2016/09/trump-makes-his-case-in-pittsburgh/501335 (last accessed 1 March 2017).

NAME INDEX

Abercrombie, N. 106
Abousnnouga, G. 249
Agar, M. 9
Ainsworth, J. 252
Althusser, L. 4
Andén-Papadopoulos, K. 119
Apte, M.L. 203, 251
Aristotle 44
Arnold, M.B. 237
Attardo, S. 251
Austin, J. 114
Aziz, H. 28–9

Baker, P. 80, 133, 251
Bakhtin, M. 23
Baldwin, A. 29
Baldwin, J. 32
Bargiel, Rafal 128
Barker, M. 24–5
Barthes, R. 120, 191
Barton, B. 254
Barton, D. 49
Baxter, J. 21
Beck, U. 44
Bell, A. 128, 132
Bell, E. 255
Bennett, L. 44, 116
Bentley, D. 210–16
Benwell, B. 21, 87, 140–3, 189–90,
    194–5, 250
Berlusconi, S. 88, 149
Bernstein, D. 101, 156
Billig, M. 88, 197, 202–9, 252
Bin Laden, Osama 28
Bishop, H. 24
Blair, T. 39–40, 46–7, 71, 91, 124,
    165

Blakemore, D. 105
Blommaert, J. 254
Bloor, M. 249
Bloor, T. 249
Boers, F. 236
Bourdieu, P. 39
Bouvier, G. 51
Branson, R. 38
Breazu, P. 81–3
Brennan, M. 92
Brierley, S. 37–8
Brooks, K. 142–3, 191
Brown, G. 46–7, 106
Brown, M. 145
Brzozowska, D. 251
Buckledee, S. 47, 251, 254
Bulcaen, C. 254
Butler, J. 141, 191

Caldas-Coulthard, C.-R. 5, 21, 130, 132
Cameron, David 6, 18, 46, 68, 236–7
Cameron, Deborah 10–11, 18–21, 40–1,
    44, 79, 109–10, 223–9, 250
Canning, P. 120–1
Cap, P. 48
Caple, H. 115, 119
Castells, M. 53, 254
Chambers, P. 29
Chaney, D. 217–18
Charteris-Black, J. 44–5, 130, 229–36
Chiapello, E. 253
Chiaro, D. 251
Chilton, M. 54
Chilton, P. 44, 47–8, 67, 73, 111,
    113–15, 163, 253
Chiluwa, I. 236–41
Chlopicki, W. 251

Chomsky, N. 8, 44–5, 170
Chouliaraki, L. 120
Christensen, H.S. 238
Cicero 44
Clair, R.P. 7, 9
Clark, A. 47
Clark, K. 78–80
Clayman, S. 70–3
Clinton, H. 55, 88, 243–4, 247
Coates, J. 18–20
Colbert, S. 247
Coldrey, J. 154
Coleman, L. 253
Conboy, M. 77
Connell, R.W. 190
Conway, K. 55, 247
Cook, G. 35, 38, 100, 220, 253
Corbyn, J. 30, 160
Costello, E. 216
Cotterill, J. 252
Cottle, S. 80, 251
Coulthard, M. 32, 93–4, 154, 210–16, 252
Cowell, S. 87
Crewe, B. 191
Custódio, L. 116, 120

da Silva, D. R. P. 116
D'Ancona, M. 53, 55, 124, 254
Dandy, P. 94
Davies, C. 202, 252
Davies, D. 15
Davis, D. 128, 132
Davis, T. 93–4, 152
de Beauvoir, S. 16
De Sousa, R. 205
Delin, A. 99–100, 253
Destutt de Tracy, A. 4
Devlin, A. 138
Diana, Princess of Wales 124, 152, 165
Dobson, Gary 26
Domke, D. 118
Dormer, N. 143–5
Dougary, G. 194
Douglas, M. 23
Dovey, J. 254
Drew, P. 9–10, 249

Du Gay, P. 110
Durant, A. 32

Economou, D. 115, 118
Edginton, B. 122–3, 167
Edwards, T. 141
Eggins, S. 11, 65
Ehrlich, S., 250
Elizabeth II, Queen of England 124, 166
Ellsworth, P.C. 237
Erjaevec, K. 82
Evans, B. 249

Fairclough, N. 7, 12–13, 39–41, 44–5,
    59–63, 65, 100, 106–7, 109–10, 126,
    131–3, 135, 157, 179, 183, 195, 219,
    249, 253–4
Fanon, F. 24
Fedler, F. 255
Ferdinand, A. 85
Filppula, M. 92
Fishman, P. 227
Fitzgerald, B. 249
Forceville, C. 95, 253
Foster, A. 163–4
Foucault, M. 3, 21, 61, 136, 175
Fowler, R. 8, 24, 44, 58, 67, 129, 170,
    174–5, 249
Franklin, B. 255
Fransen, J. 164
Frazer, E. 79, 141
French, P. 32
Freud, S. 23, 207
Fuchs, C. 52–3, 254

Gabriel, J. 24
Gabrielatos, C. 80, 133, 251
Galloway, G. 45, 71–3
Galtung, J. 51, 87
Gauntlett, D. 142
Gavins, J. 85
Gee, J.P. 40–1, 59, 157, 223
Geis, M.L. 253
Georgalou, M. 50, 254
George, Prince of Cambridge 87
Gibbons, J. 34, 93, 152, 154, 252

Giddens, A. 41, 44, 110
Giddings, S. 254
Goatly, A. 253
Goffman, E. 69, 136, 253
Gramsci, A. 3, 63
Gray, J. 20, 228
Greatbatch, D. 70, 183–4, 187
Green, D. 128
Grice, H.P. 11, 104, 204
Grundy, K. 182, 186–7
Gusmão, F. 118

Habermas, J. 122, 124, 165–7, 255
Hall, K. 21
Hall, S. 23–4
Halliday, M.A.K. 49, 65, 74, 102, 138
Hansen, A. 253
Harcup, T. 51
Harington, K. 143–4
Harris, J. 92
Harris, S. 10, 44, 184, 187, 254
Harrison, A. 53, 56
Harrison, C. 98
Harry, Duke of Sussex 163–4
Hartmann, P. 22, 80
Harvey, D. 41
Haworth, K. 181–3
Heritage, J. 9–10, 15, 70–3
Herman, E. 45
Hermes, J. 141, 191
Hochschild, A. 110, 228
Hodge, R. 44, 58–9, 95, 97, 170, 249
Holdaway, S. 26
Holmes, J. 19–20, 250
Houghton, C. 136–7
Howard, M. 71
Hsieh, G. 238
Hu, W. 36
Hull, G. 40–1, 157, 223
Husband, C. 22, 80, 251
Hussein, S. 135

Ifukor, P. 236–41

Jackson, P. 142–3, 191
Jaworski, A. 24

Jefferson, G. 11, 69
Jeffries, L. 40, 141, 251, 254
Jespersen, O. 16
Jessop, R. 39
Jewkes, Y. 80, 145
Johnson, A. 32, 252
Johnson, M. 235
Johnson, S. 21
Jones, J. 47
Jong-Un, K. 248

Kaczynski, T. 152
Keat, R. 106
Kelly, K. 254
Kelsey, D. 116
Kennedy, J. F. 46–7
Kenny, E. 51
KhosraviNik, M. 116
King, O. 71, 73
Kinnock, N. 122
Know, J. 115, 119
Koester, A. 249
Koller, V. 254
Kopf, S. 254
Korn, R. 138
Kosslyn, J. 116
Kress, G. 11, 24, 42, 44, 58–9, 95–7, 99,
   116–19, 129, 170, 174–5, 192–3, 249,
   253
Krzyżanowski, M. 56, 255

Lakoff, G. 130, 232, 235–6, 254–5
Lakoff, R. 18, 20, 56, 124, 242–8
Lankshear, C. 40–1, 157, 223, 253
Lanzmann, C. 69
Lawrence, S. 25–6, 115
Lazar, M. 250
Le Pen, M. 134
Ledin, P. 83
Lee, C. 254
Lee, Y. 238
Leidner, R. 224
Lennon, N. 251, 254
Leslie, R. 144
Leung, J.H.C. 32
Leusin, F. 116

Lincoln, A. 246
Lister, M. 254
Litosseliti, L. 17, 19, 142, 189–90, 250
Louw, E. 3
Lowndes, S. 91
Luchjenbroers, J. 32

Machin, A. 81–3
Machin, D. 21, 42, 50, 61, 80, 83, 95, 97, 99, 101, 141, 143, 217–22, 249–50, 253–4
Macpherson, Lord 26
Macron, E. 134
Major, J. 123, 167
Mandiberg, M. 49, 254
Markle, M. 164
Marsh, K. 97
Marshall, T. 67
Martin, J.R. 65–6, 115–16, 118, 238
Martin, T. 145
Marx, K. 4
Matoesian, G. 252
Matthiessen, C. 65
Mauranen, A. 63, 254
Mautner, G. 106–8
May, T. 5–6, 26, 97, 165, 245–6
Mayr, A. 7, 13–14, 61, 80, 115–17, 249–50
McAlinden, F. 18
McCarthy, P. 148
McCorkle, L.W. 138
McHoul, A.W. 249
McRobbie, A. 141
McTell, R. 216
Medak, P. 216
Meinhof, U. 21
Meyer, M. 249
Meyerho, M. 250
Miglbauer, M. 254
Montgomery, J. 128, 132
Montgomery, M. 122–4, 165–7, 254–5
Mooney, A. 249
Mora, R.A. 251
Morgan, K. 251
Morozov, E. 238
Morse, F. 238

Mortensen, M. 119–20
Moss, P. 67
Moubray, M. 120
Muggah, R. 116
Mulkay, G. 205, 251
Mullany, L. 249
Mumby, D. 7, 9
Murdoch, R. 65
Murdock, G. 80
Murray, S.P. 148
Murray, S.O. 13
Myers, G. 38, 132, 253–4

Nakano, Y. 222
Nash, W. 86, 251
Neary, C. 254
Neil, A. 8
Nel, G. 89
Newsam, P. 199
Niblock, S. 42
Nolan, S. 137
Norrick, N. 252
Norris, D. 26

O'Leary, K. 18–19
Obama, B. 46, 52, 55, 88, 149, 247
Obama, M. 236–7
O'Barr, W. 253
O'Halloran, K. 250
Ohmann, R. 253
Olsson, J. 32, 252
O'Neill, D. 51
O'Neill, M. 26
O'Neill, R. 82
Ong, W.J. 221
O'Reilly, T. 49
Orelus, P. 251
Orwell, George 39, 44, 67

Page, R. 49, 78, 250, 254
Painter, C. 65
Pantti, M. 119
Par Par Lay 27–8
Paxman, J. 45, 71–3
Peccei, J.S. 47
Pelissier Kingfisher, C. 136

Perlmutter, D. 118
Pershing, J. 67
Pihlaja, S. 254
Pistorius, O. 89
Plato 44
Poe, E. A. 255
Polzer, L. 61
Poole, B. 61
Popa, D.E. 252
Powell, E. 111, 113–15, 163
Presley, E. 54
Price, S. 51–2

Rapley, M. 249
Rauff, W. 69
Reardon, G. 227
Redfern, W. 251, 253
Rees-Mogg, J. 97
Reich, R.B. 40
Reid, J. 227
Reisigl, M. 24, 131, 203, 251
Richardson, J. 59, 80, 82, 251
Ringrow, H. 38, 251, 254
Ritzer, G. 224
Roberts, C. 250
Rock, C. 209
Rogers, R. 59
Rosen, J. 50–1
Ross, A. 251
Ross, N. 14–15
Ruge, M. 51, 87

Sacks, H. 11, 69
Sanders, S. 165
Sanz Sabido, R. 51–2
Sarangi, S. 65, 175–6, 181, 250
Sartre, J.-P. 207
Sassoon, R. 217
Saussure, F. de 23
Scannell, P. 166
Schäffner, C. 47
Schane, S. 252
Schegloff, E. 11, 69
Scherer, K.R. 237
Schlesinger, J. 123
Scollon, R. 59, 222

Scollon, S. 222
Scott, J. 2, 8, 136
Scraton, P. 121
Seargeant, P. 49, 254
Sennet, R. 40
Shakespeare, W. 138
Sharapova, M. 18
Shipman, H. 182–3, 185
Short, M. 36
Shrøder, K. 253
Shuy, R. 91, 252
Silva, R. 116–19
Silverman, L. 87
Simpson, M. 192
Simpson, O.J. 152, 252
Simpson, P. 20, 29, 77, 85–6, 101, 251, 255
Singh, I. 47
Slade, D. 11
Slembrouck, S. 65, 175–6, 181
Small, J. 54–5, 254
Smith, J. 18
Smitherman, G. 24
Solan, L. 252
Sorjonen, M.J. 249
Spencer, C. (9th Earl Spencer) 124, 165
Spender, D. 19–20
Sperber, D. 85
Spicer, S. 55
Spratt, M. 118
Stanley, J. 14
Statham, S. 61, 252
Steenkamp, R. 89
Stevenson, N. 142–3, 191
Stringfellow, F. Jr. 190
Stubbs, M. 106
Stygall, G. 252
Sunderland, J. 189–90, 250

Tagg, C. 49, 254
Talbot, M. 141, 190, 228, 250
Tanaka, K. 253
Tannen, D. 19–20, 70, 226
Teo, P. 133, 251
Terry, J. 85
Thatcher, M. 8, 106, 124, 226

Thomas, J. 12–13
Thomas, L. 47
Thompson, G. 65
Thornborrow, J. 14–15, 21, 97, 141, 187, 250, 253
Tiersma, P. 33–5, 252
Ting-Toomey, S. 24
Tinney, A. 145
Toolan, M. 18, 38, 100, 253
Tracy, S. 40
Trew, T. 58–9, 170, 249
Troutman, D. 24
Trow, M.J. 212, 216
Trowler, P. 110
Trump, D. J. 29, 50, 52–3, 55, 88, 124, 160–1, 164–5, 242–8
Tsakona, V. 252
Twain, M. 54, 255
Tyldesley, C. 97

Undrum, L. 50
Unger, J. 49

van Dijk, T. 9, 21–2, 24–5, 43–4, 59, 61, 115, 130, 196–202, 249, 254
van Leeuwen, T. 21, 37, 42, 80–1, 95–7, 99, 116–19, 192–3, 217–22, 251, 253–4
Vestergaard, T. 253
Veum, A. 50
Virgil 111

Wacquant, L. 39
Wade, W.C. 203
Walker, B. 40, 254
Wareing, S. 47
Washington, G. 246
Weaver, S. 251–2
Weber, M. 2, 8
Webster, G. 106, 109
Welles, O. 54
Wells, H.G. 54
West, C. 13, 19
White, P.R.R. 116, 238
Whiteway, A. C. 213
Widdowson, H. 61
Wilders, G. 134
William, Duke of Cambridge 164
Williamson, J. 253
Willis, G. 116
Wilson, Darren 145–6
Wilson, Deirdre 85
Wodak, R. 7, 16–17, 24, 56, 59–61, 131, 203, 249, 251, 255
Wright, D. 32, 252

Young, L. 249
Yousafzai, M. 237

Zappavigna, M. 49–50, 254
Zimmerman, D.H. 13, 19
Zito, S. 242

SUBJECT INDEX

#BringBackOurGirls campaign 237–8
9/11 attacks 28, 254

abortion 51
accidental death 152
acculturation 227
acknowledgement tokens 70
adjectives: advertising discourse 100, 220; empty 18
adversarial system of law 33
advertising discourse: adjectives 100, 220; advertising body copy 156; advertising style 219–22; advertorials 37; analytical methods 95–101; analytical methods 155–6; anatomy of advertisements 37–8; beauty and cosmetics 251; body copy 37, 155; broadcast media 37; causal structures 103–5; checklist of features 155–6; conditional structures 102–3; definition 35; direct address 99–100; disjunctive syntax 100; gender positioning 253; hard sell vs soft sell 35–6; headline 37; jingles 38; language and 35–8; male grooming 98; multimodal discourse analysis 95–101; parallelism 100–1; pragmatics of 253; product vs non-product 35–6, 155; readings 253; reason and tickle 35–6, 101–5, 156; repetition 101; short copy vs long copy 35–7; signature 37–8; slogan 37–8, 155; slow drip vs sudden burst 35–6; social

semiotics 95–101; space-based 37; testimonial 37–8; time-based 37; transgressive nature of 221
affect 115–20
affective resonance 119
affirmative action 199
Afghanistan conflict 254
agent deletion 173, 175
aggregation 81
airports 29–30
Alcoholics Anonymous (AA) 250
All-England Law Reports database 151
alliteration 35, 155, 221
alternative facts 55, 247; see also post-truth politics
alternative questions 90–1; see also presupposition
Amnesty International 82
androcentrism 16
anecdotes 30
Anglo-Saxon writing 34–5
anthropology 251
antilanguages 8, 137–40
application forms 178–81
appraisal 115–20
appreciation 115–20
appropriateness 122–4, 150–1, 167; see also universal pragmatics
argument culture 70
asymmetrical talk: as institutional talk 11–15
asymmetrically gendered language items 17
attitude/emotional states 225–6
Australian Aborigines 93, 153–4
authenticity 124, 165; see also universal pragmatics

back-channelling 185, 226
background information 73
banking crisis 47
behavioural processes 75; *see also* transitivity
Belfast City Council 147
Bengali language 138
binomials 34–5
biological determinism 16–17
blogs 50–2, 254
Boko Haram 236–41
branding 42, 97; *see also* advertising discourse
Brexit 5–6, 46–7, 53, 55, 128–30, 133, 251–2, 254
Britain First 164–5
British Manifesto Corpus 229
Britishness 23
bureaucracy: bureaucratic events 176; citizens as clients 176–81; faceless 173–4; readings 175–81; social control and 175–81
burlesque 86: definition 31
Burma (Myanmar) dictatorship 27–9

calculability 224
Calcutta Underworld Language 138
call centre style 223–9: standardizing speech 224–5; women's language 225–7
capitalism 50; *see also* new capitalism
cartoons: satirical 26–7
categorical assertion 132
categorization 148, 175–6, 181
causal structures: advertising discourse 103–5
celebrities 87
censorship 48
Charlie Hebdo 26–7
chauvinism 20
children: cross-examination of 92; murder of 78–9
Chinese language 220
citizens: as clients 176–81
classification 181
classroom talk 12

cleft structures 90; *see also* presupposition
climate change 253
Cockney rhyming slang (CRS) 139–40
coercion: political discourse 48, 113–14
collateral damage 68
collectivization 147
collocations 155
colonization 107
command structures 171–2
commercialization: media 42–3
commodification of discourse 63, 223–9
commodities: healthy 156; luxury 156
Common Law 33
common sense 64–5
communication skills 42, 109
comparators 90; *see also* presupposition
computer games 254
computer-mediated communication (CMC) 49–50
conditional structures: advertising discourse 102–3
congruent discourse 135
conjunctive adjuncts 102–3, 156
connotations of language items 17–18
Conservative Party (UK) 71, 113: manifestos 229–36
consumerism 50, 101: consumer culture 4, 39
Conversation Analysis (CA) 69–70, 181–9
conversational style 100
conversationalization 63, 70
co-operative principle 11
corpus linguistics 254: political manifestos 229–36; social media 238–41
Cosmopolitan 144, 217–22, 253
Court TV Casefiles 151–2
courtroom interaction 10–11; *see also* law; legal discourse
criminality 133
critical discourse analysis (CDA) 59–65: CA and 181–3; definition 59–60; discursive power relations 60; Fairclough's three-tiered model 62–4;

gendered identities 189–95; humourous language 27, 31; ideological work 60; interpretative and explanatory 61; intertextual/historical 60–1; mediated discourse 61; multimodal 61, 81; power asymmetry 12; principles 60–1; sample analysis 126–34; social action/practice 61; social problems 60; society and culture 60; socio-political issues 43; *see also* multimodal discourse analysis
critical linguistics (CL) 58–9: humourous language 27; post-truth and 120–4; readings 170–5; socio-political issues 43
critical metaphor analysis 229–36; *see also* metaphor
cross-examination: forensic discourse analysis: 91–3, 153
culture 23: cultural difference in police interviews 153–4
customer care 228
Cyber-Creole Project 238

Daily Mail 25, 97, 123–8, 133, 145–7
Daily Mirror 22, 96–7, 150
Daily Star 150
Daily Telegraph 86, 198–200
death penalty 206, 210–16
declaratives 172–3
defamation 252
deficit: gender 18–21
definite referring expressions 90
dehumanization 207
delegitimation: political discourse 48
demand pictures 143–4, 148
democracy 69, 234; *see also* liberal democracy
democratization of discourse 63
dialect 92–3: definition 65
difference: gender 18–21
digital subcultures 119
direct address 219: advertising discourse 99–100
Direct Objects (DO) 6, 75
direct quotes 133
discourse: of allusion 86; community 190; definition 5; language as 5–6;

practice 62, 132–3; technologies 109
discrimination 199; *see also* racism
discursive authority 119
discursive shifts 56
disjunctive syntax: advertising discourse 100
dominance theory 18–21
double meaning 30
drug dealing 116–20

education 43, 157–9; *see also* new capitalism
edutainment 221
efficiency 224
Egyptian Revolution (2011) 53
elaborative probe 15
e-learning 158; *see also* new capitalism
election broadcasts 122, 167, 250
Electro-static Detection Apparatus (ESDA) 93–4, 152–3
eliteness 25, 87; *see also* racism: elite
Elizabethan Pelting Speech 138
empathy 226
enforcing explicitness 13–14
entailment 88–9; *see also* presupposition
Enterprise 54
enterprise culture 40, 106–11, 159; *see also* new capitalism
environmental politics 44
equivocation 247
essentialist notion of women 80
ethnic jokes 252
ethnicism 197; *see also* racism
ethnomethodology 70
euphemism 48–9, 201: political discourse 47
European Parliament 88, 149
evasive questioning 71–3
existential processes 77; *see also* transitivity
exnomination 24
experiential function 66
expertise 9, 32: expert systems 41–2; expert witnesses 32, 252

expressive intonation 225–6
Extra 118, 120

Facebook 49–50, 52, 116, 163, 237–41
factives 90; *see also* presupposition
factual television 61
fake news 54–5, 247, 255; *see also* post-
    truth politics
fashion magazines 141–5
favelas 116–20
female speech 248; *see also* women's
    language
feminism 16–17, 78: anti- 190; commod-
    ity 141; poststructuralist 21; Third
    Wave 21
feminized service style *see* women's
    language
Ferguson Unrest 145–7
fiend naming 79
figurative language 30, 133
flexibility: discourse of 40–1
football 137
forensic discourse analysis: cross-ex-
    amination 91–3, 153; developments
    88–94; interrogation 91–3, 153; lead-
    ing questions 88–91; presupposition
    88–91, 153; transcripts of evidence
    154; *see also* Electro-static Detection
    Apparatus (ESDA)
forensic linguistics 31–3, 252: duties and
    function 32; issues 216; judgement
    215–16; linguistic evidence 212–15;
    readings 210–16; verbal police evi-
    dence 210–12
form-filling 178–81
formulation 15: definition 15
fraud 252
freedom of movement 130
freedom of speech 26
French 139–40; *see also* Norman French
friendly fire 68
Front National party 134
functionalization 6, 81, 147; *see also*
    social actor analysis

Game of Thrones 143–5
Gaza Strip 6

gaze 147, 191, 195: undifferentiated 192
gender: analysis 140–5; commodifica-
    tion of language 223–9; construction
    in fashion magazines 141–5; deficit
    18–21; definition 16–17; dichot-
    omizing 195; difference 18–21;
    dominance 18–21; female speaking
    rights 13; identity 195; language and
    16–21; linguistic studies 18–21; me-
    dia representation 78–80; readings
    250–1; transitivity model 73–80; *see
    also* homosexuality; masculinity; sex;
    women's language
genitive constructions 90; *see also* pre-
    supposition
genocide 68–9
genre 66
German Ideology 4; *see also* ideology
global service economy: data 223–4;
    readings 223–9; themes and issues
    227–9
Global War on Terror *see* war on
    terror
globalization 42–3, 110, 223, 253
goal orientation 10
Gobbledygook 138
gossip 21
GQ magazine 194
grammar 126, 131, 155, 221: of visual
    design 95–9; *see also* multimodal
    discourse analysis
grassroots social movements 44
gratuitous concurrence 154
gratuitous modifiers 17
group cohesion 33
Guardian 6, 43, 228
Gulf War (1990–1991) 31, 254

half rhyme 221
harassment: aggravated 164; sexual 20
hard news 128
hashtags 27, 49–50, 117, 238
hatred: issues 207–9; jokes 204–7; ma-
    terials 203–4; politics of 202–9; *see
    also* racism
headlines 128–9
hedges 18

hegemony 63: concept of 3
Hillsborough disaster (1989) 120–1
homosexuality 21, 138, 192–4
human rights violations 116–20
humanitarianism 8–9
humour: analysis 149–51; appropriate-
    ness and 150; events 149; hatred and
    202–9; incongruity 30–1; irony in dis-
    course 84–8; jokes and hatred 204–7;
    language, power and 26–31; men's
    magazines 194–5; non-verbal 251–2;
    racist 87–8; readings 251–2; register
    mixing 149–50; as resistance 8; sexist
    87–8; tabloid 150–1; see also irony
hybridity 150

identification 81, 147; see also social actor
    analysis
identity 136
ideological state apparatuses (ISA) 4
ideology 4, 129–30, 134–5; see also criti-
    cal metaphor analysis
immigration 22–3, 80–3, 111–15,
    127–33, 177, 196, 199–201
imperatives 172–3
implicatures 104: political discourse 45
inaugural address 161–3
incongruity 208: as a humour mecha-
    nism 30–1
Independent 132
India: culture 86–7; language 220
individualization 147–8: de- 176
inferential frameworks 10–11
insider-ness 33
Instagram 49–50
institutions 7–9: concept of 9; discourse
    of 7–11; discourse and power 9–11;
    political 134–5; see also law
institutional dialogue 249
institutional discourse: readings
    249–50
institutional status 184, 186
institutional talk 9–10: as asymmetri-
    cal talk 11–15; goal orientations 10;
    inferential frameworks 10–11; special
    and particular constraints 10
intensifiers 18

interactional tasks 225
interdiscursivity 63, 133
interpersonal function 66
interrogation: forensic discourse analy-
    sis 91–3, 153
interruption 12–13, 185, 187
intertextuality 60–3: manifest 63, 150
interviews: appraisal 110; news 70–3;
    police 153–4, 181–9
intonation 18: expressive 225–6
Iraq War (2003) 8–9, 69, 73, 250, 254
Irish Gaelic 92–3
Irish Times 150–1
irony 27, 30, 48, 190: definitions 85;
    in discourse 84–7; echoic mention
    84–6; men's magazines 194–5; op-
    positional 84; racist humour 87–8;
    sexist humour 87–8; see also humour
Islam 251
Israeli Defence Force 6
iteratives 90; see also presupposition

Jackie magazine 141
jokes 18, 30, 195: ethnic 252; racism
    and extremism 202–9; see also hu-
    mour
journalistic discourse 198–200
Jurnalul National 81, 83

knowledge-driven economy 40–1; see
    also new capitalism
Ku Klux Klan 202–8

Labour Party (UK) 122–3: manifestos
    229–36; see also New Labour
Ladders Revolution (Spain, 2015) 51–2
language style: as lifestyle 218–19;
    issues 222; readings 217–23
Latin 34–5
law: forensic linguistics 31–3; as insti-
    tution 33–5; language 31–5; see also
    forensic discourse analysis; forensic
    linguistics; legal language
leading questions 88–91
leaflets 178
learning 158; see also education; new
    capitalism

legal agreements 155
Legal English 33–4
legal language: as register 152; everyday life 155; readings 252; *see also* forensic discourse analysis; forensic linguistics
legitimacy 3
legitimation: political discourse 48, 113
Leicester Mercury 81–2
lexical choice 24
lexical cohesion 129
lexical disparity 18
lexical gaps 17
liberal democracy 8–9; *see also* democracy
life politics 44
lifelong learning 40
lifestyle 218: language style as 218–19; politics 44; readings 217–23
Loaded magazine 142, 145, 190–3
lynching 206–7

machismo 242, 248
Macpherson report 26
magazines 21, 141–5, 189–96: global lifestyle 217–18; *see also* men's magazines
manifestos: political 229–36
manufacturing consent 45
marketization of discourse 63, 219; *see also* commodification of discourse; new capitalism
Mars and Venus genre 228, 250
Marxism 4, 70
masculinity 21, 250: hegemonic 142, 189–90; masculinist concepts 78; men's magazines 189–96; new lad 87, 142, 190; types of 194
material processes 75; *see also* transitivity
Maxim magazine 194
McDonaldization 224
media: commercialization of 42–3; gender representation 78–80
mediated/mediatized reactions 122
medical records 186
men's magazines 21, 141–3, 189–96: anxiety 192–3; discourse analysis 191;

gaze 192–3; humour and irony 194–5; identity of 191–2; image 192–3; issues 195–6; readings 189–96; textual and visual contruction 190–1
mental processes 75; *see also* transitivity
meta-discourse 202
metaphor 126: building 130, 231–2; common conceptual 45; conflict 231; disease 236; journey 232–3; metaphorical discourse 135; plant 233–4; political 45–6; political discourse 45–6, 160–1, 229–30; religious 234–5; source domain 45; target domain 45; themes and issues 235–6; *see also* critical metaphor analysis
metre 155
military humanism 8–9
Millennium Experience 64–5
minimal responses 136, 227
miscarriages of justice 210–16
misogyny 244
misrepresentation: political discourse 48–9
mnemonic devices 155
modality 97–9, 117, 126, 131–2, 156; *see also* multimodal discourse analysis
motherhood 77, 136
multiculturalism 80–1
multimodal discourse analysis 95–101, 115, 249
multimodality 253: social media 49
murder 78–9, 127, 129, 252
music 221

Nairaland Corpus 238
nationalism 43
natural language philosophy 255
naturalism: speech 154
naturalization 8, 24, 56, 59–60, 64–5,155: naturalizing difference 24
Nazism 68–9, 88, 200
nagative clauses 211, 214
negative evaluation 238–9
neo-capitalism 42

neo-liberalism 39–40
neologisms 221–2
neutralistic stance 70, 73
new capitalism 106, 223: developments 105–11; discourses in 40–1; knowledge-driven economy 40–1; language in 39–43; linguistic analysis 157–9; readings 253; socio-political context 106; *see also* enterprise culture
New Labour 39–40, 71, 233–5, 254: Third Way discourse 106; *see also* Labour Party (UK)
'new lad' *see* masculinity
new media *see* social media
news interviews 70–3
News of the World 77
Newsnight 71
Newspeak 39, 44, 67
newsworthiness 87
Nexis UK 61
'nigger' 204–9
nominalization 6, 69, 114, 126, 131
nomination 81, 148
non-congruent discourse 150
non-institutional talk 9; *see also* institutional talk
Norman French 34–5
nuclear weapons 67
Nukespeak 67–8

Occupy movement 53
office politics 44
officialese 134–5
Old English 34
Old Norse 34
online media activism 116–20; *see also* social media
opposition: political discourse 48
oppression 9
organizations: concept of 9; discourse of 7–11
Othering/Otherness 23–5
overexplicitness 154
overlapping speech 136
overlexicalization 129, 138

pacification 116
parallelism: advertising discourse 100–1; political 47, 163
parody 27, 30, 86
participant content 49
participatory media 116–20
passive construction 173, 175
performativity 21
perjury 252
Petty Sessions 34
phonological features 155
Plain English Campaign 152
plain language 32
plurifunctionality 13
podcasts 50
poetic devices 220–1
police interviews: cause of death 186–8; cultural difference 153–4; data 183; institutional status 184; integrated discourse analysis 183; interviews 188; issues 188–9; medical records 186; opening sequence 184–5; power and resistance in 181–9; question type 184; question-answer sequence 184; readings 181–9; topic 183–4; *see also* forensic linguistics
politeness 18
political consumerism 44
political correctness 150, 204
political discourse 43–9: analysis of 160–7; coercion 48, 113–14; 'Commander-in-Tweet' discussion 164–5; conversationalization of 254; definition 43–5; delegitimation 48; developments 111–15; euphemism 47; implicature 45; legitimation 48, 113; manifestos 229–30; metaphor 45–6; misrepresentation 48–9; Northern Irish 163–4, 254; opposition 48; parallelism 47; political institutions 134–5; political metaphor in the media 160–1; presupposition 45; pronouns 46–7; protest 48; readings 253–4; representation 48–9, 114–15; resistance 48; rhetoric 43; strategic

functions 47–9; tweeting politics 163–5

populism: definition 244–5; post-truth politics and 242–8; rise of 255

positive self-presentation 25, 198–200; *see also* racism

postmodernity 222

post-racial discourse 247

post-truth politics: critical linguistics and 120–4; death of truth 245–6; definition 54–6, 247; issues 248; discourse of 53–6; populism and 242–8; readings 242–8, 254–5; Trump and populism 244–5; Trump supporters 246–7; truth and consequences 247–8; universal pragmatics and 121–4

poverty 39–40, 47, 133, 136

power: definition 2–4; institutional discourse 9–11; language and 2–6, 249; mainstream 2–3; productive 3; second-stream 2–3; talk and 11–15

pragmatic devices 30

pragmatics 101, 156

predictability 225

presidential campaigns (US): Obama (2008) 52, 55; Trump (2016) 53, 55, 124, 161–4, 242–8

presupposition 201: forensic discourse analysis 88–91, 153; gender 18; political discourse 45, 163; televised interviews 71; triggers 89–90, 153

prevarication 247

prison discourse 8, 13–14, 19, 138, 249–50

Private Eye 86–7

pronouns 24, 126, 130–1: inclusive vs exclusive 46; political discourse 46–7

propaganda 44

prostitution 80

protest: political discourse 48

pseudo-biological culturalism 25

psychoanalysis 23–4

puns 30, 155, 251: advertising 38; definition 30; phonological sequencing 30

Question Time 91

questioning: alternative 90–1;

counter-questions 187; flexible 91; yes/no 91; *see also* interviews; tag questions

questionnaires 178–81

race: changing representations of 24–6; definition 21–2; discursive reproduction of 23–4; language and 21–6, 251; racial difference 24; racial tension 73

racialization: definition 22

racism 43, 60, 85, 249, 251: anti-racism campaigns 147–8, 197; cultural 197; defence 200–1; definition 22; denial of 25, 196–7; elite 25, 111–15, 163; institutional 25–6; issues 201–2; mitigation 200; offence 200–1; old vs new 24–5, 80; positive self-presentation 198–9; and the press 198; racist humour 87–8; readings 196–209; reproduction of 197; structural/systemic 25–6; subtle denial of 199–200; symbolic 25; *see also* discrimination; hatred; immigration; xenophobia

radio phone-ins 137, 250

Rafah incident 6, 74

rape 79–80, 127–9, 252

rapport talk 20, 109–10, 226

reason and tickle *see* advertising discourse

reasonable doubt 152

recipe language 175

reformulation 179

register 88, 134–5: field, tenor and mode 66; legal language as 152; mixing 31, 149–50; registers 65–9; registers of discourse 65–9

regulatory fictions 191

relational processes 76, 143; *see also* transitivity

relexicalization 138, 140, 173–4

Repeal the 8th movement (Ireland, 2017) 51

repetition: advertising discourse 101

report talk 20, 226

reported speech 133

representation: political discourse 48–9, 114–15

resistance 8: political discourse 48; spoken discourse 135–40
reverse discourse 48, 136–7
reverse discrimination 198
Rhodesia: civil disorder in pre-Independence 58–9
rhymes 155
Roma migrants 81–3
Roman Law 33
rule of law 33
rules and regulations 170–5: directive and constitutive rules 175

sarcasm: definition 247
satire 26–7, 30, 48, 255: cartoons 26–7; political 29, 251
Schengen zone 82
secret languages 48
selfies 50
self-reflexiveness 190, 194
semantic derogation 17
semantic extension 102
sex: definition 16–17; specification 17; *see also* gender
sexism 43: definition 17; sexist humour 87–8; sexist language 17–18
sexual assault 92
sexual harassment 20
sexual misconduct 252
sexual politics 44
sexual violence 79–80
sexuality 193; *see also* gender; homosexuality
Shari'ah Law 33
Shipman Inquiry 182–9
sincerity 122–4, 167, 228: validity claim of 150; *see also* universal pragmatics
slacktivism: definition 237–8
slang 48, 138; *see also* Cockney rhyming slang
slapstick 30
slavery 24
slogans: political 52
smiling 225
social actor analysis 80–3, 251, 254: application 81–3; categories 81; inclusion/ exclusion 81; representation of 145–8

social control: bureaucracy and 175–81; readings 175–81
social distance 24, 119
social exclusion 40
social media 8, 254: #BringBackOur-Girls campaign 237–8; crisis construction 238–9; discourse of 49–53; discursive structure of the campaign 239; issues 241; language of campaigns 115–20; methodology 238–41; online campaigns 236–41; readings 236–41, 254; representations 239–41; stance and evaluation 237–8; youth activism 116–19; *see also* Facebook; Instagram; Twitter
social practice 62–3, 133
social reality 7; *see also* institutions
social semiotics 95–101
sociology 69–70, 222, 224, 251
soft news 128
solidarity 26–7, 136
Spanish 220
speech naturalism 154
spoken discourse 69–73: news interviews 70–3; power and resistance 135–40; *see also* antilanguages; reverse discourse
spoof texts 29, 150, 205, 208
sports 50
Spycatcher trial (1986) 47
Standard English 92–3
standardized speech: call centres 224–5
Star Wars 67
state surveillance 175
stereotyping 18, 205
stigma 136
structural functionalism 70
structural linguistics 23
study skills 158; *see also* new capitalism
style: advertising 219–22; individual 217; social 217–18; *see also* language style; lifestyle
subpolitics 44
Suffolk Ripper case (2006) 79–80
Sun 64, 78, 198–9
Sunday Times 8
surveillance practices 175, 225

synthetic personalization 100
Syrian air strikes (2015) 68
Systemic Functional Linguistics 49, 65, 249

tabloid publications 5–6, 30, 54, 64, 77, 83, 96–7, 123–4, 251: headlines 151; humour and 150–1; opening text 151; straplines 151; tabloidese 150–1
taboo 150, 221
tag questions 18–19
talk: asymmetrical 11–15; institutional 11–15; power and 11–15, 250
teamwork 40–1
technological control 225
technologization of discourse 41–2
television talk shows 250
terrorism 26–8: Islamic 165; see also 9/11 attacks; #BringBackOurGirls campaign; war on terror
text 62, 128–32
textual function 66
Thatcherism 106
The Daily Sport 54–5
The People 22
The Times 8, 43, 132
therapy 136–7
tolerance 199
topic: control 14–15; grammatical 114–15
transcontexual techniques 42, 109
transitivity 6: agency 74; behavioural processes 75; definition 74–5; existential processes 77; gender and 73–80; gender representation in the media 78–80; material processes 75; mental processes 75; process types 74–7; relational processes 76; verbal processes 75
translation services 32
truth 122–4, 165–7, 198, 247–8; see also post-truth politics; universal pragmatics
turn-taking model 11, 62; see also Conversational Analysis (CA)
tweeting 241: politics 163–5
Twitter 27, 29, 49–52, 163–5, 237–41, 254

Unabomber case 152
under-lexicalization 17
unequal encounters 12, 19
Unique Selling Proposition (USP) 37, 101–2, 156
United States Presidents see presidential campaigns (US)
universal pragmatics 255: post-truth and 121–4
universalization 24
university education see new capitalism
unlawful killing 152

validity claim of sincerity 150, 165–7; see also sincerity
'verbal hygiene' 227–8, 250
verbal processes 75, 82; see also transitivity
verbs 126: change of state 90; continuous 131; non-factive 5
Verlan 139
vernacular folksiness 124
visual discourses 42
visual journalism 61
vocabulary (lexis) 126, 129, 221
voice 225

war: concept of 254; monuments 249–50
war on terror 24, 68; see also terrorism
Washington Post 55–6
'Web 2.0' 49
welfare systems 25, 39, 80, 136, 162, 181
Wh-type questions 90; see also presupposition
wikis 254
witticisms 30
women's language 223–7: attitude/emotional states 225–6; expressive intonation 225–6; minimal responses 227; rapport/empathy 226; smiling 225; see also female speech; gender
Wordsmith 238
workplace discourses 249

xenophobia 133; see also racism